"I can't believe this is real. Marc Vetri, the best pasta chef in America, is giving us all of his secrets on these pages. I've witnessed and tasted his magic for decades. Perfect pasta for everyone!"
—**BOBBY FLAY**

"Marc Vetri is one of the best chefs on the planet—not just because of his extraordinary skill, but because he never stops learning. Marc is also an exceptional teacher—ask anyone who's had the privilege to cook alongside him. This book beautifully captures Marc's innovative spirit and his profound respect for the pasta-making tradition. It's a testament to his boundless curiosity and dedication to sharing his remarkable knowledge."
—**DAVID CHANG**

"The semolina-blazed trail that legendary chef Marc Vetri has left for present and future generations of home cooks and professional chefs alike now spans countless days, nights, and decades. In his latest and greatest book thus far, *The Pasta Book*, his innovative methods of sharing time-honored traditions in new and deeper ways is the perfect remedy for insatiable students of the game from a true professor of pasta. . . Bravo, brother Vetri. Beautiful work and the pasta world and the world, period, are better for it."
—**CHRIS BIANCO**

"With a ball of pasta dough, Marc is an architect, a sculptor, and a painter—an artist in every sense of the word. This beautiful book will soon be wavy, cockled, and covered in bits of semolina from persistent use."
—**JIMMY KIMMEL**

"*The Pasta Book* is a lovingly dedicated, generous collection of straightforward fundamentals. At the core of every master is a student with a willingness to share and Marc is one of the best."
—**EVAN FUNKE**

"If you love pasta, which I think includes most breathing humans on the planet, this book is a must-have. It's noodles as art."
—**JIM GAFFIGAN**

"Marc Vetri was my earliest experience with pasta excellence in the States. As a Philadelphian myself who loves pasta fra diavolo, I was first exposed to the wonders of true Italian cooking by Marc, who at the same time always honored the place and flavors of where we were: Philly. The combo was transformative and I use all of his books as the ultimate resource when I wanna dive in deep."
—**ERIC WAREHEIM**

THE PASTA BOOK

THE PASTA BOOK

RECIPES, TECHNIQUES, INSPIRATION

Marc Vetri and David Joachim
Photographs by Ed Anderson

Clarkson Potter/Publishers
New York

To my father, Sal,
who taught me my love for pasta.
I miss you every day!
"You are the art, your life is your work of art . . .
make it a masterpiece, son."
I love you, Pop!

"Simply Sal," oil on canvas, 48 × 36 inches by Perry Milou

CONTENTS

10 Introduction: Logic, Rhythm, Pattern, Pasta

15 Getting Creative
Combining Ingredients 18
Pairing Pastas and Sauces 21

25 Pasta Wisdom
Get the Timing Right 27
Simplify It or Level Up 28
Cook the Pasta Properly 29
Saved Pasta Water 31
Marry the Pasta and Sauce 32
Buy Good Dried Pasta 34
Make It Nice 35
Our Cacio e Pepe 36

39 Pasta Doughs and Shapes
Flour 41
Mixing 42
Resting 45
Pasta Tools 46
Rolling and Shaping 47
Rolling Dough with a Machine 50
Pasta Thickness 52
Storing Finished Pasta 53
Hand-Rolled Dough 55
   Level Up: Culurgione Dough 54
Hand-Rolled Dough Shapes 56
   Orecchiette 57
   Troccoli 58
   Trofie 59
   Ferricelli 60
   Raschiatelli 61
   Gnocchi Sardi 62
   Lorighittas 63
   Andarinos di Usini 64
   Busiati 65
Chitarra Dough 67
   Level Up: Hay Dough 67
Chitarra Dough Shapes 68
   Chitarra Dough Tagliolini 68
   Straw and Hay Tagliolini or Chitarra 68
   Spaghetti alla Chitarra 69
Half-and-Half Egg Dough 70
   Level Up: Egg Yolk Dough 74
   Pimentón Dough 74
   Saffron Dough 74
   Mint Dough 74
   Chestnut Dough 74
   Buckwheat Dough 74
   Rye Dough 74
Egg Dough Shapes 75
   Mandilli 75
   Tagliolini 75
   Tagliatelle 76

Tajarin 76
Farfalle 77
Garganelli 78
Pimentón Sorpresine 79
Mint Fazzoletti 79
Chestnut Fettuccine 80
Pumpernickel Pappardelle 80
Buckwheat Maltagliati 81

Pici Dough 82
Pici 84

Corzetti Dough 87
Level Up: Saffron Corzetti Dough 87
Corzetti 88

Cialzons Dough 89
Grano Arso Dough 90
Masa Dough 91
Ricotta Cavatelli Dough 92
Level Up: Squash Cavatelli Dough 92
Ricotta Cavatelli 93

94 VEGETABLE PASTA

Strozzapreti with Radicchio, Walnuts, and Gorgonzola 99
Trofie with Pistachio, Artichokes, and Orange Zest 100
Mandilli with Perfect Basil Pesto 103
Pici Pomodoro 104
Raschiatelli Arrabbiata with Provolone 106
Garganelli with Corn and Scallions 108
Eggplant Lasagnetta 111
Mushroom Rotolo with Taleggio Fonduta 115
Zucchini-Stuffed Pappardelle with Squash Blossoms and Basil 119
Spinach Gnocchi with Brown Butter and Shaved Ricotta Salata 123
Ricotta Gnocchi with Brown Butter and Fried Leeks 126
Squash Cavatelli Pomodoro 129

Almond Tortellini with Truffle and Parmesan 131
Spring Pea Agnolotti with Mint and Butter 135

138 SEAFOOD PASTA

Paccheri with Clams and Charred Lemon Brodo 143
Mafaldine with Broccoli di Ciccio, Anchovy, and Spring Onion Pesto 145
Lorighittas with Calamari, Meyer Lemon, and Basil 148
Lobster Tagliolini with 'Nduja Bread Crumbs 150
Pimentón Sorpresine with Mussels 154
Spaghetti alla Chitarra Frutti di Mare with Bone Marrow Sofrito 158
Troccoli with Shrimp and Ginger Chili Crisp 161
Gnocchi Sardi with Monkfish Puttanesca 162
Pistachio Corzetti with Clams and Tarragon 164
Crab Cannelloni with Saffron 167
Scallop Raviolo with Champagne 171
Brandade Agnolotti with Chives 174

176 POULTRY AND GAME PASTA

Tagliolini with Chicken Liver Ragù 180
Straw and Hay Tagliolini with Chicken Liver Ragù 180
Pumpernickel Pappardelle with Duck Ragù 182
Buckwheat Maltagliati with Duck and Espresso Ragù 184
Tajarin with Rabbit Bolognese 187
Raschiatelli with Guinea Hen Bolognese 188
Andarinos di Usini with Capon Ragù, Pistachios, and Apricots 190

Chicken Liver Caramelle with Apples and Sage 193
Potato Ravioli with Escargots and Castelrosso Fonduta 197

202 PORK PASTA

Spaghetti alla Carbonara 206
Rigatoni with Fiorella Sausage Ragù 208
Chestnut Fettuccine with Wild Boar Ragù 211
Spaghetti alla Chitarra with Basil, Poppy Seed, and Prosciutto 215
Ziti with Fiorella Liver and Orange Sausage Ragù 216
Farfalle with Guanciale, Peas, and Tarragon 218
Fennel Sausage Ricotta Gnocchi with Zucchini Crema 220
Masa Ferricelli with Pork Shank Ragù 222

224 BEEF AND LAMB PASTA

Orecchiette with Lamb Merguez and Fiore Sardo 229
Mint Fazzoletti with Lamb al Latte Ragù 231
Ferricelli with Beef Heart Bolognese 234
Busiati Grano Arso with Beef Shank and Peaches 236
Lamb Tortellini in Brodo 239
Ricotta Cavatelli with Veal Shank Ragù 242
Cannelloni with Oxtail and Cipollini 244
Francobolli with Short Ribs and Celery Root 249

252 NEXT LEVEL PASTA

Fusilli with Clams, Cauliflower, and Speck Bread Crumbs 257
Gnocchi Sardi with Lobster, Corn, and Yuzu Kosho 259
Lobster Conchiglie with Sauce Américaine 261
Smoked Potato Culurgiones with Lemon Butter and Chicken Skin Gremolata 263
Scallop Corzetti with Clarified Pomodoro, Tomato Powder, and Basil Oil 269
Corn Anolini with Buttermilk Espuma and Caviar 271
Chestnut Triangoli with Fermented Honey, Ricotta, and Brown Butter 274
Sweet Potato Cappelletti with Granola and Foie Gras Torchon 276
Gnocchi di Susine with Cinnamon Bread Crumb Butter 279
Carrot and Brisket Doppio Ravioli with Brisket Jus and Red Pearl Onion Agrodolce 283
Casoncelli with Sage and Pancetta 289
Cialzons with Ricotta, Dried Fruit, and Foie Gras Sauce 292
Chicken Stock wtih Variations 294

296 ACKNOWLEDGMENTS

298 INDEX

INTRODUCTION

> A classic is a book that has never finished saying what it has to say.
>
> **—ITALO CALVINO,**
> ITALIAN NOVELIST AND JOURNALIST

gic,
ythm,
ttern,
sta

opened Fiorella pasta bar in Philadelphia in March 2020, right when the pandemic hit. Crazy timing! But the restaurant survived.

The original idea came from going to David Chang's first Momofuku Noodle Bar in New York City's East Village. Chefs were making cool, high-level food right there in front of you. It had such a great vibe. Over the years, I looked at the pasta stations at my restaurants and thought, "We could do that . . . the pasta station alone could be a restaurant. A pasta bar!"

Of course, Covid hit the month we opened. After three weeks of success, we closed and pivoted to become a market, selling things like sausage ragù and fresh noodles so people could make the dishes at home. We also made videos demonstrating how to do it. That taught us a valuable lesson: Anyone can enjoy the magic of pasta at home. You just need to get a handle on the process. Those pandemic videos and our streamlined pasta-making instructions were the inspiration for this book.

Vetri Cucina provided everything else. We've been turning out beautiful pasta dishes in that intimate restaurant for more than twenty-five years, honing our methods and exploring new flavor combinations. Vetri has only thirty-five seats. Fiorella opened with just fourteen seats. Both restaurants are tiny by today's standards. Both have proven you don't need a big restaurant with a fancy kitchen to make great pasta dishes. Italian cooks have been doing it in tiny home kitchens for centuries. You can do it in your kitchen any night of the week. Seriously!

The Pasta Book shares everything I've learned over the past thirty years, like how to simplify things so making pasta is fun and how to get creative with your own new flavor combinations. I cover getting organized, what kind of flour to use, how to pair pasta and sauces . . . everything you need to know to up your pasta game. I know a lot of home cooks just make dried pasta. That's cool. I show you how to buy good dried pasta and how to make recipes with dried noodles instead of fresh.

Along the way you'll hear about my philosophy of pasta and the underlying logic of everything from cacio e pepe to lasagna Bolognese. You see, the beautiful thing about pasta is that it's a repeating pattern, like petals on a flower. Each dish of pasta is built from the exact same blueprint, an infinitely repeatable process that's given birth to endless ribbons, strings, strands, sheets, tubes, and pockets with different sauces and condiments in various countries around the globe for millennia. It's amazing!

Once you see this pattern and start moving to the rhythm, every step gets easier. Then it's like dancing. Maybe you make a sauce on the weekend. You mix up some dough in the morning, then cook the noodles that night. Knowing the fundamental steps unlocks the door to endless creativity. That's when it gets fun! You can play around with different flavors, change up the shapes, and invent your own signature dishes.

It all comes together here in more than eighty recipes, including basic pasta doughs and shapes, plus my most-requested dishes. We show you how to make easy weeknight meals like Spaghetti alla Carbonara (page 206) and Eggplant Lasagnetta (page 111). When you want to go the extra mile, there's a whole chapter of Next Level Pasta (page 252), including things like Fusilli with Clams, Cauliflower, and Speck Bread Crumbs (page 257) and a couple sweet pastas like Gnocchi di Susine with Cinnamon Bread Crumb Butter (page 279). Even these "next-level" dishes are doable and satisfying to make at home; they just have more depth and layers of flavor.

The recipes are arranged, somewhat loosely, from easiest to more complex. They start with dried pasta dishes, then move to simple fresh pastas like tagliolini and on to stuffed pastas like half-moons and agnolotti. If you're new to making pasta, start at the beginning of each chapter. Start at the beginning of the book for that matter! The first couple of chapters are packed with things that recipes don't tell you, and the vegetable pastas (page 94) are the easiest ones in the book. Or spin the wheel and dip into whatever looks good to you. Soon you'll be experiencing my favorite thing in the whole world . . . that shudder going through me after biting into the perfect marriage of pasta and sauce, a singular bite that starts out chewy and flavorful, then goes creamy and ethereal as the noodle disappears on your tongue as if it were never there. Pure magic!

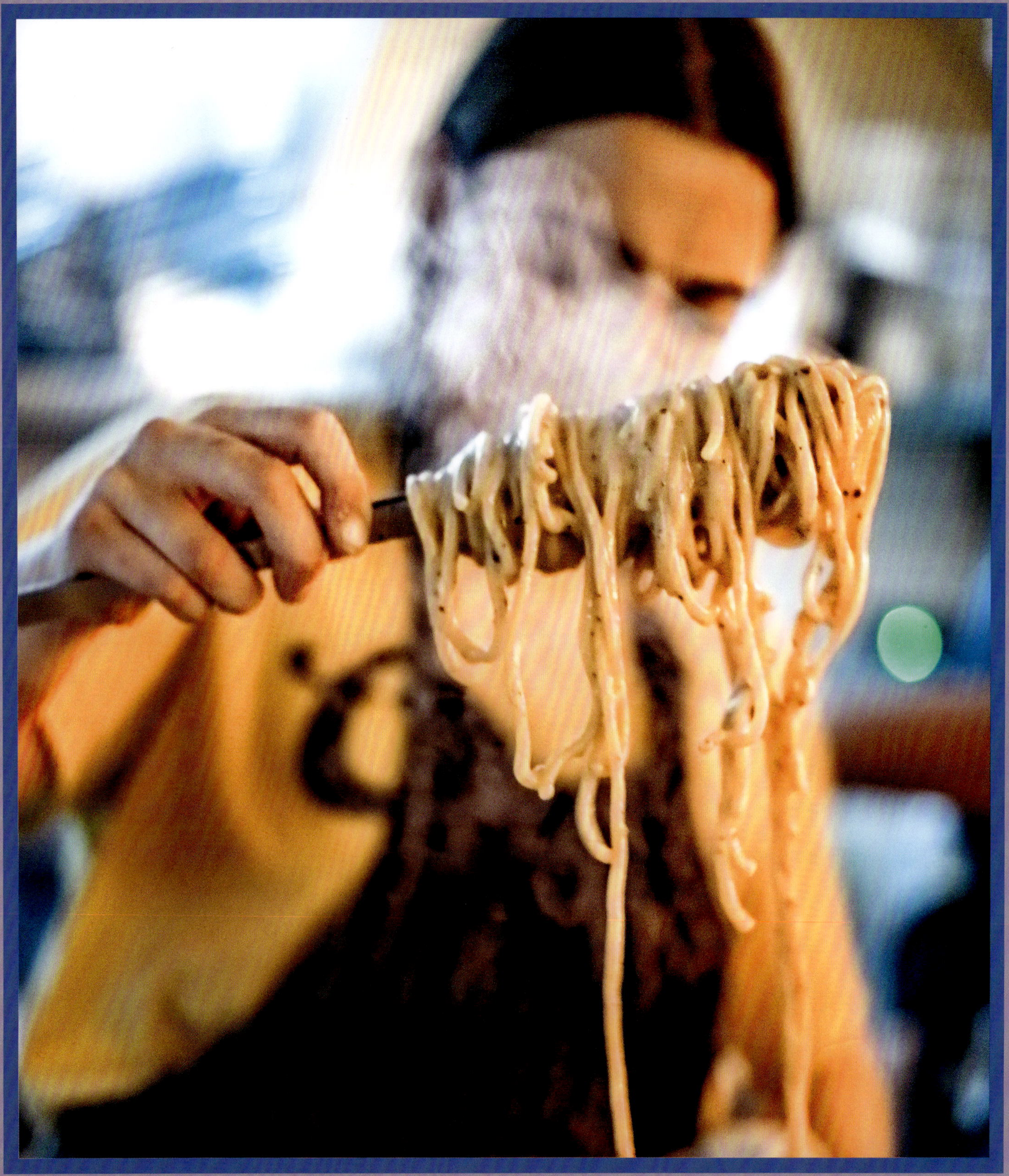

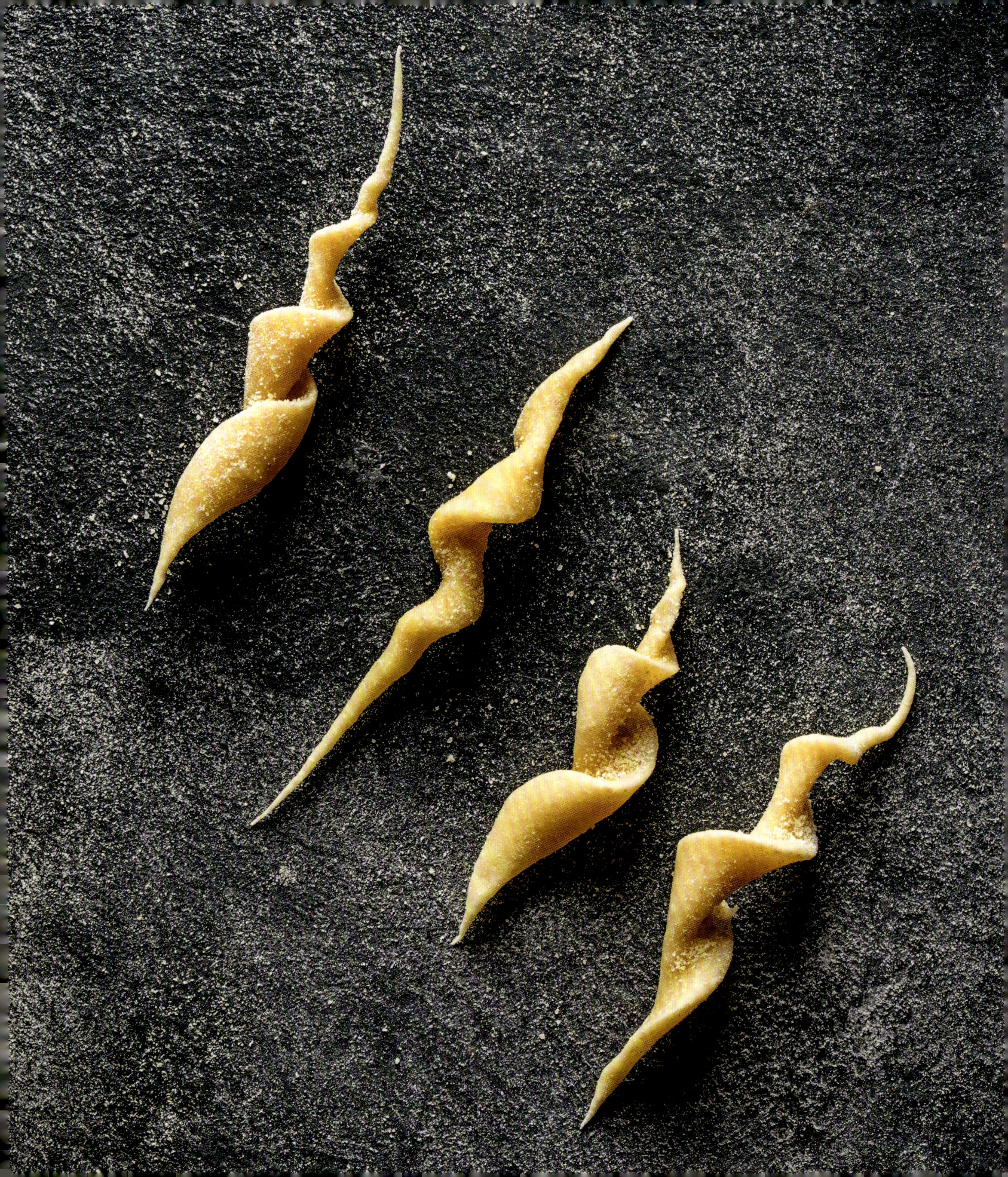

GETTING CREATIVE

> We must not forget that the kitchen is a combinatorial art of interpolation more than invention. The process which takes place is a sign of variation more than of true creation, and the history of cooking is fundamentally a history of the morphology of the dish, whose elements are differentiated by those variable of those constant.
>
> **—PIERO CAMPORESI,**
> ITALIAN HISTORIAN OF GASTRONOMY

In 1994, I'd been living and working in northern Italy for maybe a month when my friend Massimiliana said, "You should experience a meal at La Brughiera." It's a popular, Michelin-starred place now, but back then the restaurant had just opened a couple years before in the little town of Villa d'Alme outside Bergamo.

When we walked through the iron gate, a wide pebbled walkway took us to the front door of an old stone building that reminded me a of quaint home in Old City Philadelphia. In the foyer were these stunning modern paintings with vibrant colors. It was a cool juxtaposition with the old stone architecture. The meal began with us walking under a stone archway inside the restaurant to a small room that I can only describe as a cave. Italian wine lined the walls, which arched upward and led to another back room where prosciuttos and coppas were hanging from the ceiling, curing. The owner, Stefano Arrigoni, stood near a green marble table, smiling, pouring sparkling wine into glistening flutes, while his father, Walter, shaved tissue-thin tastings of prosciutto and coppa on an antique Berkel meat slicer. With the musty aromas of aging hams, the damp air, stone walls, and white wine made just down the road, it was like entering a time warp, going back one hundred years. Stefano and Walter handed us polenta crisps topped with lardo, blood-red 'nduja spread on crispy bruschetta, and exquisite bites of torta d'erbe made with local eggs and herbs. It was a such a beautiful start to the meal. This was the traditional food that I came to Italy to learn!

Over the years, I've returned to La Brughiera many times. I always get inspired, and after the restaurant evolved a bit, one of Stefano's pasta dishes really spoke to me: Zola Zucca Zenzero. Translation: Gorgonzola Squash Ginger. This is a very important dish. In Piedmont, there is a classic pasta called agnolotti del plin. Like a lot of old Italian raviolis, this local stuffed pasta was originally made to use up roasted meat leftovers. It's traditionally served on a napkin without any sauce, a nod to the local farmers who would often carry food wrapped in napkins to eat during the workday. Stick with me here. Another traditional dish in the Piedmont region is fonduta. It's typically made with Fontina cheese and used as a dipping sauce for vegetables or bread. In his pasta dish, Stefano took these two very traditional preparations from Piedmont—agnolotti del plin and fonduta—and without changing too much, created a Lombardia version with a modern twist.

He made a slightly different agnolotti shape and instead of just serving the ravioli on a napkin, he used the napkin like a pedestal to accentuate the beauty of the shape. He stuffed the noodle with squash instead of meat, and instead of Fontina, he made a Gorgonzola dolce fondue for the dip. To level it up and give it some kick, he topped the Gorgonzola fondue with a spoonful of fresh ginger steeped in melted butter. When you think of Italian food, ginger is not the first ingredient that comes to mind! The beauty here is that it's unexpected, and the ginger balanced all of the flavors perfectly. It's like the modern paintings on the restaurant's old stone walls—a beautiful juxtaposition.

This pasta is one of my favorite examples of taking something steeped in history and tradition and completely transforming it by taking a creative risk. Zola Zucca Zenzero fired up my passion for crafting pastas deeply rooted in Italian culture while embracing the potential for growth and transformation.

This is exactly the kind of creative process that we discuss in this chapter. You'll see it at work throughout the pastas in this book, many of which reflect both the diversity of Italy's regional cuisines and my own tastes and influences. A dish like Gnocchi Sardi with Lobster, Corn, and Yuzu Kosho (page 259) is rooted in the island cuisine of Sardinia yet also expresses my love for Pennsylvania's amazing produce (best sweet corn ever!) and Japan's incredible condiments (if you've never tried yuzu kosho, get some!). On the plate, this dish looks pretty straightforward and Italian: little pasta dumplings with seafood and corn. If no one told you it had Japanese ingredients, you might never know. All the flavors work together seamlessly.

Similar to Stefano at La Brughiera, my goal with pasta creativity is always the same . . . to take a nuanced approach that encourages experimentation and risk-taking while holding the traditions of classic Italian pastas in the highest regard. If you look closely at the pastas in this book, you'll see that the ingredients tell a story of Italy, my hometown of Philadelphia, and the places and foods that have influenced me throughout my entire life.

When I want to learn a new pasta shape, the first thing I do is find a video. If a picture is worth a thousand words, a video is worth a million! That's why I created dozens of videos for the pasta shaping and other techniques in this book. Just follow the QR (quick-response) codes below, and you can watch me demonstrate techniques like making orecchiette, marrying pasta and sauce, and twirling pasta so it looks good on the plate. As you follow along, stop and start the videos as much as you like.

If you've never used a QR code before, you need a smartphone. Just open the phone's camera and center it on one of the square QR barcodes below. The phone camera will scan the barcode automatically and take you to a web page for the video. From there, just select the video you want to watch, and hit play.

Scan this code for Pasta Doughs and Shapes Videos

Scan this code for Stuffed Pasta Videos

Scan this code for Classic Pasta Technique Videos

GETTING CREATIVE

COMBINING INGREDIENTS

It's actually not hard to make a new pasta dish. One slam-dunk method is to play with flavor combinations. There are a million possible permutations. Tomato and basil is not the only game in town! For instance, buckwheat and coffee go great together. That's part of what led to Buckwheat Maltagliati with Duck and Espresso Ragù (page 184), a dish that's firmly rooted in the Italian mountains of Lombardy. Sometimes, you can just pair ingredients in unexpected ways, as in the North African and Sardinian combo of Orecchiette with Lamb Merguez and Fiore Sardo (page 229). In any pasta dish, the flavor combination could be in the sauce alone, as in Trofie with Pistachio, Artichokes, and Orange Zest (page 100). Or you can add flavor directly to the pasta dough, as in Pimentón Sorpresine with Mussels (page 154). When juggling flavors, you've got a lot of room to play. Here's some basic advice.

Start with good ingredients.

This may seem simple and almost ridiculous to say, but if you start with crap, the result is gonna be crap! You can't cover up flavorless ingredients. Make it a point to buy good olive oil, good eggs with richly colored yolks, and local fresh produce that's in season. When we say "Parmesan" in this book, we mean Parmigiano-Reggiano, the king of cheeses. When we say "kosher salt," we mean Diamond Crystal kosher salt. Buy good ingredients and it will make a huge difference in the taste of your finished dish.

Follow the rule of three.

This very simple rule will change your game. Cooks often make dishes with four, five, or six different components in addition to the pasta. The best-tasting dishes have no more than three key flavors, and some have only two. Cacio e pepe is just cheese and pepper. Carbonara has three: bacon, egg, cheese. Eggplant lasagna has three: tomato, eggplant, cheese. When you put in too many flavors, they confuse the dish. I describe it like this:

- **3 or fewer is perfect**
- **4 can work, but you have to be careful and it has to be thoughtful**
- **5 rarely works—definitely consider eliminating an ingredient**

Here's a good example: Strozzapreti with Radicchio, Walnuts, and Gorgonzola (page 99). When we originally developed this dish, we charred wedges of radicchio in a cast-iron pan, added some red wine and some red grapes that had been charred in a basket over hot coals, and then braised the radicchio until tender, let it cool down, and chopped everything up into fork-friendly pieces. We added a little butter and starchy pasta water to marry this sauce to strozzapreti noodles, and then finished the dish with chopped walnuts and blue cheese. It tasted good. But it was too much. You don't really need the grapes, let alone grapes charred over coals. And you don't need the red wine. You don't really need to braise the radicchio, either. In the end, we just sautéed the radicchio with garlic. The final dish is even better because it's more focused. Now the three key flavors shine through bright as day: radicchio, walnuts, Gorgonzola. It's like Stefano Arrigoni's spin on agnolotti del plin: Gorgonzola, squash, ginger. That's it.

THE 10 COMMANDMENTS OF PASTA

I. THOU SHALT BEGIN WITH GOOD-QUALITY INGREDIENTS

II. THOU SHALT USE THY HANDS WHEN POSSIBLE

III. THOU SHALT MASTER AT LEAST ONE HAND-ROLLED SHAPE

IV. THOU SHALT USE ONLY FRESH OR SLOWLY DRIED PASTA

V. THOU SHALT VARY THY PASTA THICKNESS

VI. THOU SHALT MIND THE PASTA-TO-CONDIMENTO RATIO

VII. THOU SHALT USE A MAXIMUM OF THREE KEY INGREDIENTS IN A PASTA DISH

VIII. THOU SHALT SALT THY PASTA WATER GENEROUSLY

IX. THOU SHALT MARRY THY PASTA WITH THY SAUCE

X. THOU SHALT EAT MORE PASTA

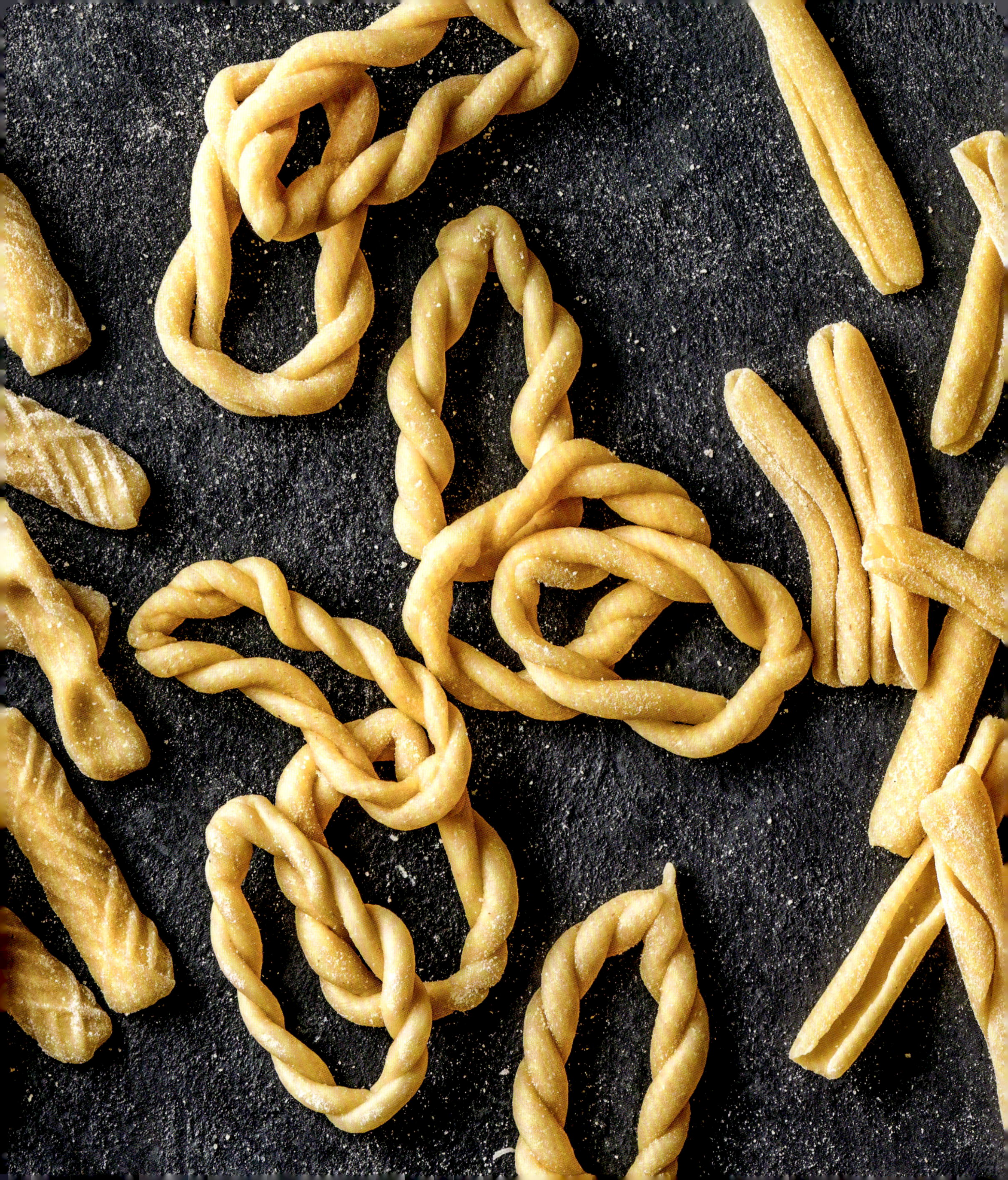

PAIRING PASTAS AND SAUCES

People always ask me this: What goes with what? What are the rules? On this point, I defer to Oretta Zanini de Vita, author of the incredible *Encyclopedia of Pasta*. "Foreigners who are intimidated by the strength and tenacity of Italian food habits, beliefs, and prohibitions," she writes, "will be surprised to learn that the pairing of shapes and sauces is mostly due to tradition." A-ha! There are no hard-and-fast rules! "Of course, there are a few guidelines," she continues, "for example, chunky sauces do better on short tubes than on long strings. But by and large, the sauces and condiments are dictated by what people have always done."

There you have it. Tagliatelle is the preferred shape for Bolognese sauce because that's the pairing that was made by the people of Bologna, where Bolognese originated. Corzetti is traditional with pesto because that's how it was done in Liguria, where basil pesto was born. Could you pair other sauces with tagliatelle or with corzetti? Absolutely! But you don't want to start throwing things together without respecting tradition. Make informed choices. For instance, Pistachio Corzetti with Clams and Tarragon (page 164) makes perfect sense because it combines all the classic elements of Ligurian pastas but a little differently. The corzetti are untouched, but the pesto is made with pistachios instead of basil. Clams are found all over the coast of Liguria, so they're a simple addition, and the herbs become a garnish of chives and tarragon. The truth is, a lot of pastas and sauces are interchangeable. But not all of them are. Here are some approaches to pairing that allow you to honor tradition while pushing innovation.

Match shapes.

You could match the pasta shape to the star ingredient in your dish. Picture calamari rings, for instance. They're nearly identical in size and shape to Lorighittas (page 63). That's part of the inspiration for Lorighittas with Calamari, Meyer Lemon, and Basil (page 148). A poultry ragù is more traditional with lorighittas, but calamari rings match the noodles perfectly. Or look at Mafaldine with Broccoli di Ciccio, Anchovy, and Spring Onion Pesto (page 145). We chose this ruffled ribbon pasta because it looks similar to broccoli di ciccio, an heirloom variety of broccoli that has long, slender stems and small florets. Mafaldine also complements the long slender sea beans we sometimes add to this dish to level it up. Like goes with like.

Choose a shape that traps the sauce.

This method always works because it helps complete the marriage of pasta and sauce. Take tortellini, for example. The empty round space in the middle of the noodle captures things like green peas and bits of ham, which is one reason you see cheese tortellini with ham and peas all over the place. Plus, the flavor combo is a natural! The same goes for *sorpresine,* which means "little surprises." This shape from Emilia-Romagna looks sort of like tortellini but with no filling. The empty space in the middle allows things to get caught up in it, creating a "little surprise." Small mussels are that surprise in Pimentón Sorpresine with Mussels (page 154). Or consider paccheri. I love the chewy taste of paccheri with seafood, and the big tubes make the perfect hideout for bits of it. In Paccheri with Clams and Charred Lemon Brodo (page 143), the clams get caught in the shape—the perfect marriage of pasta and sauce.

Mind the mouthfeel.

Sometimes, a flavor pairing may be on point, but you have to rethink the texture. It's important that pasta and sauce taste harmonious. Matt Rodrigue, who leads the kitchen at Fiorella in Philadelphia, was playing around with Troccoli with Shrimp and Ginger Chili Crisp (page 161). The flavor combo was awesome, but it just wasn't working when you ate it. The whole shrimp slid off the long noodles, and it felt awkward in the mouth. I suggested grinding the shrimp like sausage to better distribute them throughout the dish. Boom! The flavors *and* the textures all came together in one seamless bite. Sometimes just a little tweak can take a flavor pairing from good to great.

Consider the pasta thickness.

Different noodles chew differently and hold sauce differently. Some fresh pastas are rolled thin; others are rolled thicker (see Pasta Thickness, page 52). Thick noodles like pappardelle have a nice chew and can absorb a fair amount of sauce. If your sauce is juicy and wet, like a spicy sausage and tomato ragù, a thicker noodle like pappardelle will work nicely. A thinner fazzoletti or mandilli might be too delicate and get overwhelmed by the bold-tasting, wet ragù. It's all about finding the right relationship between the pasta and the *condimento,* which could be a sauce or seasoning. For me, a thin pesto sauce works best with a thinner handmade pasta like trofie. That doesn't mean pesto won't work with a thicker dried noodle like spaghetti;

it just might not be as good. Putting together pastas and sauces is like putting together a sentence. You can use a million different words to get your point across, and two people can make the exact same point, but one person might say it more eloquently.

Remember: The filling is part of the *condimento*.

In Italian, *condimento* refers to whatever brings flavor to a pasta dish. The condiment could be a seasoning, a sauce, or even a pasta filling. Your primary flavor pairing may be between the pasta and the filling, not the pasta and the sauce. The stuffing in Casoncelli with Sage and Pancetta (page 289) carries most of the flavor in that dish, so the sauce is little more than brown butter. On the other hand, the filling in Sweet Potato Cappelletti with Granola and Foie Gras Torchon (page 276) is just sweet potato puree, so we put more flavor into the sauce. When you're pairing pastas and sauces, consider all the flavors in the dish and how they all work together to best complement the pasta. And remember the rule of three!

Mind the pasta-to-sauce ratio.

You don't want your spaghetti swimming in a sea of ragù. Every bite should have an equal amount of ragù clinging to the noodle. You should actually taste more noodle than sauce. When you're done eating, that last noodle should leave an empty plate with little to no sauce left over. It's about balance. As a general guideline, we usually toss about 3 ounces (⅓ cup) of ragù with every 80- to 100-gram (3- to 4-ounce) portion of pasta. Of course, it varies, but that's a good starting point.

Same goes for the pasta-to-filling ratio.

In stuffed pasta, the filling is part of the *condimento*, the flavorful element clinging to the noodle. Some fillings like ricotta cheese taste mild, so the ravioli can handle a bit more of that filling. Other fillings with, say, braised duck or beef, taste strong, so you don't need to put as much with the pasta. That's why Lamb Tortellini in Brodo (page 239) doesn't have much filling—just one ½-inch ball of filling per 2-inch square of pasta. The braised lamb inside has tons of flavor! On the other hand, Potato Ravioli with Escargots and Castelrosso Fonduta (page 197) has twice as much filling—a 1-inch ball of filling per 2-inch square of pasta—because the potato filling tastes pretty mild. Size matters, too. If you make a bigger ravioli, you'll need more filling. Just don't drown out the pasta with too much filling. The pasta is always the star. Your goal is to balance the pasta and *condimento* in the perfect bite.

EAT MORE PASTA

These are just some of the approaches that have worked for me. I can't really tell you how to get creative. That has to come from you! I can tell you one thing that always inspires me: eating different pastas from different chefs all over the world. Taste unfamiliar noodle dishes at a variety of restaurants, preferably in Italy! Go as far outside your comfort zone as you can. When you get back to the kitchen, start experimenting and thinking outside the box. And try some of the crazier pastas in this book!

In my definition, the essence of pasta is creativity. We're talking about flour and water here! These are the cheapest, most basic ingredients in any kitchen. And yet with a little ingenuity, these two humble ingredients can be transformed into the most sublime noodles like Lorighittas with Calamari, Meyer Lemon, and Basil (page 148) and Andarinos di Usini with Capon Ragù, Pistachios, and Apricots (page 190). That's the magic of pasta. Its only real limitation is your imagination!

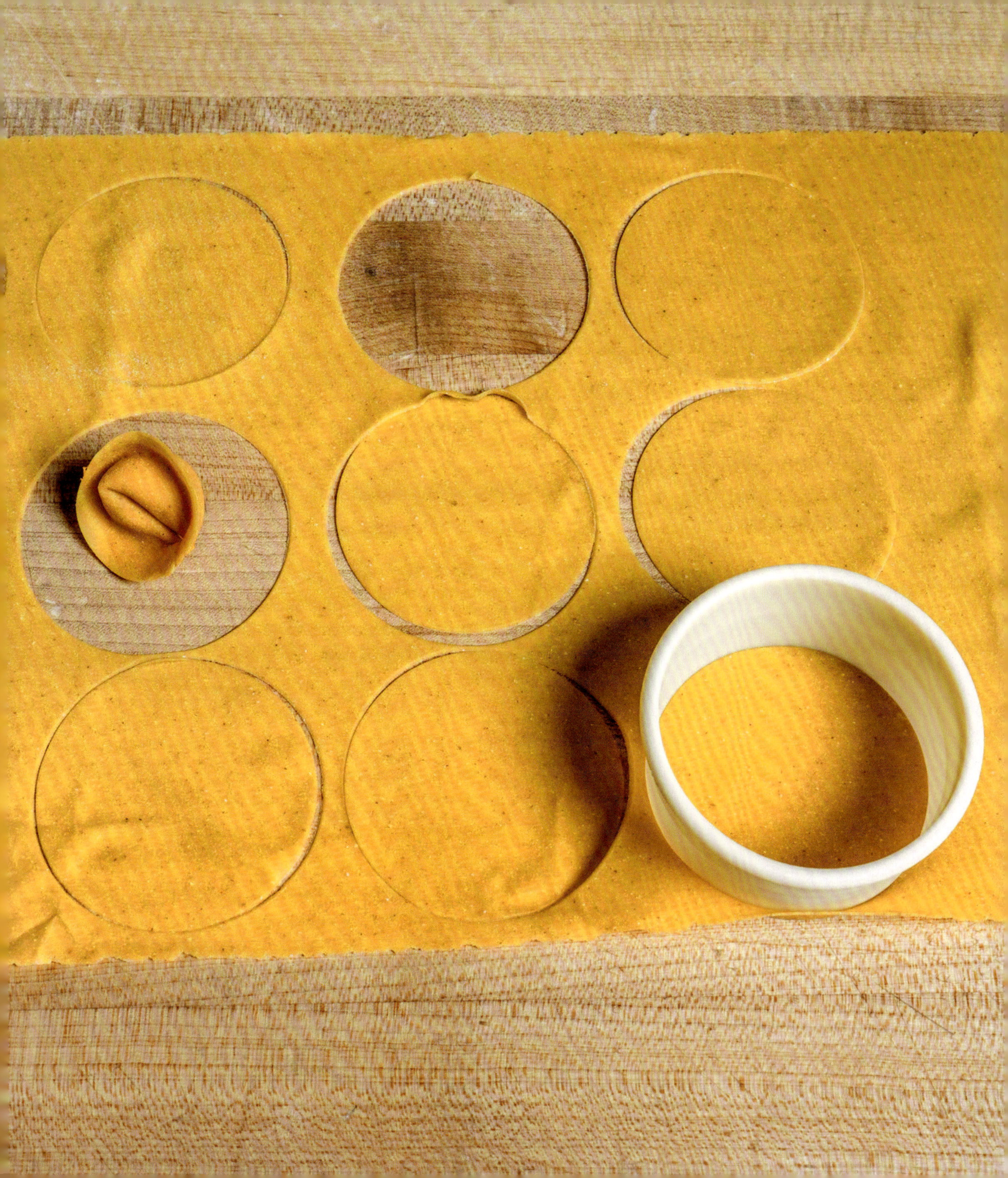

PASTA WISDOM

> Learning never exhausts the mind.
>
> **—LEONARDO DA VINCI,**
> ITALIAN ARTIST, SCIENTIST, ENGINEER, AND RENAISSANCE MAN

In September 2024, I hosted pasta maker Yum Hwa at Vetri Cucina in Philadelphia. Yum consults at a restaurant in Singapore called Ben Fatto and does pasta lessons and dinners in his home workshop. Five years before he came to Philly, he was an accountant. Then he took a left turn, devoted himself to pasta making, and bought a book called *Mastering Pasta*. My book! He started learning the ins and outs of making pasta, and then he traveled to Japan to work with Claudia Casu, a Sardinian woman who moved to Tokyo to teach ancient handmade pasta techniques that were in danger of dying out. Over the years, Yum continued to practice the craft of these Sardinian hand-formed pastas and got very good at making them.

In hopes of spreading the handmade pasta gospel, Yum contacted me as he built an American pasta-making tour. He was looking for places to teach Sardinian pasta classes and do dinners with the pasta that captivated his imagination and consumed his life. I jumped at the chance! I've been making pasta for the better part of my life, but I am relentless—almost crazy—in the pursuit of my craft. I will go to the ends of the earth to find a shape I've never seen, a variation in technique I've never tried, or anything I can add to my pasta game to make it just a little better. Yum and I set up a pasta-making day for me and my Philadelphia staff, as well as a dinner the next day for guests to enjoy the specialty pastas we made.

Yum and his assistant Denise arrived at Vetri Philly with little more than their smiling faces. As far as magical days go, this was one of the most intense and beautiful ones, sprinkled with a little feeling of . . . I wanna kill myself! I was in awe as I watched Yum and Denise effortlessly make Orecchiette (page 57), Andarinos di Usini (page 64) and su filindeu (an intricate threadlike pasta) with their hands, while my chefs and I (all accomplished professionals!) struggled to make any shape that felt worthy of the Varsity pile to be served to guests the next day, instead of ending up on the JV pile destined for the trash bin.

What we struggled with most was the hand motions. The finger work. How much pressure to use. How to hold your thumb for andarinos. How to angle the knife correctly for orecchiette. With nothing but a table knife and their own skill, Yum and Denise demonstrated how to drag the knife over a little nub of dough so it pops out the other side with the hollow dimple we all know and love as orecchiette. But it takes finesse. The more common method is to drag the nub of dough into a coin shape, then drape it over your fingertip to make the dimple. I watched. I listened. I practiced Yum's technique relentlessly. It's such a simple, elegant shaping method.

Filindeu is the same way. These crisscrossed, silk-thin threads of pasta are made with only your hands and a round board that you stretch the pasta over. *Filindeu* means "threads of God"—an apt name! This is one of the rarest and most difficult pastas to make, an embodiment of the craft of pasta making. The dough is just semolina flour and water, but you pull pieces of it by hand into strings, and then stretch the strings over a wooden board into long, silky, translucent filaments. Then you do it again and crisscross the filaments. Then you crisscross it all again! It's like Asian hand-pulled noodles taken to the nth degree.

When I think back to this day, it blows my mind. An accountant buys a book to learn pasta making, and five years later ends up teaching the guy who wrote the book a different way to make those pastas along with some new pastas. The student becomes the teacher. It's a beautiful thing. Days like these are what drive me to keep searching for a different shape, a different technique, a better way!

I hope this chapter inspires something similar in you. Cooking is a never-ending journey, and I think there is value in striving to make food as good as it can possibly be. We'll get into the details of rolling out pasta and shaping it in the next chapter. But first, I wanted to share some general insights that might up your pasta game, including tips on boiling pasta, salting the water, marrying the pasta and sauce, timing the meal, and all the little things that recipes don't usually tell you. These tips and approaches come from years of pasta making and working with various pasta chefs in both Italy and America.

GET THE TIMING RIGHT

It might seem overwhelming to make fresh pasta by hand along with a sauce at home. But, really, it's not. Little old Italian ladies have been doing it for centuries! It helps to cook in stages. Sure, some fresh pastas like Mandilli with Perfect Basil Pesto (page 103) come together start-to-finish in a single short cooking session. But with fresh pasta, more often than not you'll want to make at least one of the components ahead of time to get the timing right. Maybe you mix up an egg pasta dough in the morning, then shape and cook it that night. Or you might make your ragù the day before, then mix and shape the pasta the day you serve it. Many of the components can be held for at least a few hours, some even days, ahead of time. It all depends on the dish you are making.

Make fresh pasta ahead.

If you can make the pasta ahead of time, it usually helps speed things along come dinnertime. Fresh pasta ribbons and simple shapes can be dusted with flour, covered, and then left at room temperature for 1 hour, or up to 4 hours for pastas made with egg dough. You can also wrap fresh pasta tightly with plastic wrap and refrigerate it for a day or freeze it for a month. See Pasta Doughs and Shapes (page 17) for details on which types of pasta can be chilled or frozen for how long.

Use the rest period.

After you mix up a ball of fresh pasta dough, it needs to rest before you can roll it out and/or shape it, usually for about 30 minutes. That's the perfect time to make your sauce.

Make the sauce ahead.

Of course, some sauces take longer. Braised meat ragùs often cook for several hours. Mint Fazzoletti with Lamb al Latte Ragù (page 231) is a good example. For braises like that, it makes more sense to start the ragù first, then make the pasta while the meat is braising. Even after the ragù is done, it can be kept warm for an hour or two, and you can finish making and cooking your pasta then. If you want to get more of a jump on things, most ragùs can be refrigerated in an airtight container for a few days, and most ragùs taste better reheated after a day or two. That gives you plenty of time to make the pasta. You can even freeze some meat ragùs for a few weeks and then thaw them overnight in the fridge. In that case, get your pasta going, then reheat your ragù in the pan you'll use to combine the pasta and sauce. Simple.

Aim to have the pasta and sauce ready at the same time.

This is your ultimate goal. The exact timing depends on what you're making—and how fast you are as a cook! The recipes have lots of timing notes and indicate what to have ready ahead of time. Before you begin, read the whole recipe or think through the dish and map out a rough game plan that works for you.

SIMPLIFY IT OR LEVEL UP

> This book is designed to meet you where you're at with pasta. Whether you want to simplify things or take them to the next level, there are recipes and tips throughout to help you get there. Look for the Simplify It and Level Up notes throughout the book. Many of the Simplify It ways are similar, so if you're in a real time crunch, here are some tips on streamlining the recipes.

Use dried pasta instead of fresh. Many recipes here call for handmade shapes using our Hand-Rolled Dough (page 55). In a pinch, you can use store-bought dried versions of certain pastas, such as orecchiette, trofie, ferricelli, or lorighittas. Other recipes call for fresh tagliolini, tagliatelle, pappardelle, and other pastas made with Half-and-Half Egg Dough (page 70) or Egg Yolk Dough (page 74). You could also replace these fresh egg pastas with dried versions. You can even replace Ricotta Cavatelli (page 93) with frozen ricotta cavatelli. Of course, I encourage you to make the fresh pasta—it's so much more satisfying! Just keep in mind that dried pastas will be a bit chewier than fresh, and you'll need about 12 ounces of dried pasta to replace 1 pound fresh. Dried pastas also take longer to cook. Follow the manufacturer's cooking directions.

Buy fresh pasta instead of making it. Extruded shapes like paccheri and rigatoni are now sold fresh by local pasta makers in well-stocked markets and specialty stores. You can use fresh extruded pasta in place of the shapes called for in the recipes here. Some of our recipes, especially for stuffed pastas, call for Egg Yolk Dough (page 74) rolled into sheets and then stuffed to make ravioli, or cut into strands. In a pinch, you could use store-bought fresh pasta sheets. They may be rolled kind of thick, so lay the store-bought sheets on a lightly floured surface and roll them out to the thickness specified in the recipe. Again, follow the manufacturer's directions for cooking times.

Skip the flavored pasta and put the flavor in the sauce. I add flavors to some of my pastas, such as pimentón in sorpresine (page 79), fresh mint in fazzoletti (page 79), and chestnut flour in fettuccine (page 80). If you're pressed for time, you could buy fresh pasta sheets and put those flavors into your sauce instead.

Make the sauce in a pressure cooker or Instant Pot. Many of the ragùs in this book are made with bone-in cuts of beef, pork, or lamb that braise in a Dutch oven for hours. You can cut the cooking time by more than half with a manual or electric pressure cooker. Sear the meat and cook the vegetables as directed, but in the pressure cooker or Instant Pot. Return everything to the cooker, fasten the lid, and cook on high pressure for 45 minutes to 1 hour. Quick-release the pressure, check to make sure the meat is tender, and proceed with the recipe.

COOK THE PASTA PROPERLY

A recipe is awesome to start with, but please remember: It's just a guideline. If the recipe says to cook your dried pasta for 10 minutes, don't just set your timer and walk away. Proper doneness is the most important thing! If you live in the mountains, the actual cooking time for dried pasta might be 3 minutes longer than what it says on the box because you're at a higher altitude (with less air pressure at high elevations, water boils at a lower temperature, so the pasta takes longer to cook.) Or maybe you stuck a lot of pasta in a small amount of water. Then the water stops boiling and it takes a while to come back to a boil, extending the cooking time. There are so many variables. But they're not hard to get a handle on. Here's how to cook pasta perfectly every time.

Use plenty of water.

A good rule of thumb is to use 5 quarts of water per 1 pound of pasta (fresh or dried). That gives the noodles lots of room to move in the water. You want to see the pasta rolling around in the pot, which helps it cook evenly and prevents sticking.

Season the water.

Before you drop in the pasta, make sure your water is at a full boil and well seasoned. Some people say it should be "as salty as the sea." Have you ever been swimming in the ocean, gotten knocked over by a big wave, and come up with a big mouthful of seawater? It's pretty fucking salty! Your pasta water shouldn't be quite *that* salty. It should taste more like well-seasoned broth. The fact is, seawater is about 3.5% salinity by weight, which is a lot. Aim for about 1% salinity in your pasta water. That means adding about 1 tablespoon Diamond Crystal kosher salt or 2 teaspoons Morton kosher salt per 1 quart of water. For the average 5 quarts of water you'll use to boil 1 pound of pasta, that's 5 tablespoons Diamond Crystal or 3 tablespoons Morton kosher. Everyone's salt tolerance is different, though. Taste and adjust.

Stir to prevent sticking.

Right after you drop the pasta in the boiling water, give it a little stir to keep the noodles separate. It also helps to stir a couple times during cooking, especially for dried pasta, which takes longer to cook.

Use a lid.

Cover the pot to quickly return the pasta water to a boil. Watch it, though—it could boil over! Just keep an eye on it. And an ear. If you hear the lid rattling, the pot's about to boil over. As soon as the pasta water returns to a boil, use the lid to help maintain a gentle rolling boil. For some stoves, just keeping the heat on high will maintain a boil. For others, you may have it cranked to high but still need to partially cover the pot. Whatever happens, you don't want the pasta sitting in *un*-boiling water for long. That's when it starts to stick.

Have your tools ready.

I like to use a pasta fork to pull cooked strands and ribbons from the pasta water. You could also use tongs. For short shapes and ravioli, a spider strainer or big slotted spoon works best. Some pastas like lasagna noodles need to drain on kitchen towels. Others get scooped from the water and transferred straight to prewarmed plates. It all depends. Just get everything lined up so you're ready to go when the pasta is.

Taste for doneness.

Mouth texture is everything with pasta. You don't want the noodles too hard or you'll be biting into uncooked starch, which is like eating raw flour. You also don't want the noodles so soft that they feel like slippery eels in your mouth, which is equally unpleasant. The proper doneness depends on many factors. Is the pasta dried or fresh? Will you finish cooking it in the sauce, or should it be fully cooked when it comes out of the water? It depends on the dish, and our recipes have lots of guidance. If you think your pasta is done and you want to check, taste a piece. No, don't throw spaghetti against the wall! It will just fall to the floor and make a mess. If it sticks to the wall, it's overdone.

Look for the white line.

To test for doneness, cross-cut a piece of cooked pasta. You should be able to just make out a faint white line in the center of the noodle (see the photograph above). That is the undercooked part of the pasta. In a round strand like spaghetti, it will appear as a white dot in the center. If the white line or dot is too big and too white, you will taste that uncooked starch and it'll be chewy and hard on the teeth. The white line or dot should be faint and barely noticeable. Then it's perfect. But if you cross-cut the pasta and see nothing, it's probably overcooked.

THE PASTA BOOK

Check the thickest part.

Ravioli and handmade shapes are a little different because of their folds. Filled raviolis will have a double layer of pasta and that double layer takes longer to cook through. Shapes like Farfalle (page 77) will have pinched areas where the pasta is thicker than it is in other areas. When you're tasting for doneness, check the thickest part of the pasta.

Slightly undercook the pasta.

We often remove pasta from the boiling water when it's just shy of being perfectly done. Then we finish cooking the pasta in the sauce. This is a critical step and it's different from how most people make pasta at home. Think of it like parboiling the noodles. How long depends on the pasta and the sauce. A dried pasta like rigatoni might boil for 10 minutes, then we finish cooking it for 2 to 3 minutes in the sauce. Fresh pasta like Fazzoletti (page 79) might only boil for 1 to 2 minutes before putting it in the sauce. The goal is generally to parboil or "blanch" the pasta and then finish cooking it in the sauce so that the noodles have time to pick up the flavor of the sauce and vice versa. That cross-pollination is what allows the pasta and sauce to become one thing in the pan. You want both pasta and sauce to become perfectly cooked at the same time. When you serve the dish, that faint white line or dot in the center should be just disappearing from the pasta. That's when it's al dente ("to the tooth") but not so hard that it tastes super chewy. The timing can be tricky. Luckily, you have an ace in the hole here: your pasta water.

Save your pasta water.

A lot of people dump the cooked pasta and pasta water into a colander in the sink. Don't do it! Instead of draining the pasta in a colander, just lift the pasta from the water with tongs, a spider strainer, or a slotted spoon. This way, you still have the hot pasta water on the stove at the ready. In most cases, you'll need that pasta water to properly combine the pasta and sauce.

SAVED PASTA WATER

At our restaurants, we have pasta boilers going all night. By the end of the night, the pasta water looks super-cloudy from starch leaching out of the pasta and into the water. This stuff is liquid gold! Starchy pasta water helps thicken sauces, making them taste creamier, and it helps to marry the pasta and sauce when you toss them together in the pan.

At home, it's a different story. Most people aren't cooking pasta all night long. With a lot of pasta dishes, that's not an issue. But sometimes you want really starchy pasta water to emulsify the pasta with the sauce. You could possibly undercook your pasta and let it finish cooking in the sauce (see Cook the Pasta Properly, page 29).

Or try this: Save your leftover starchy pasta water! At the end of a pasta-cooking session, let the cooking water cool down, then pour it into quart, pint, or half-pint containers. Seal, label, and date the containers and then freeze them. You can even freeze pasta water in ice cube trays, so you have smaller portions ready to go. Boom! Starchy pasta water at the ready. The cloudier the pasta water, the starchier it is, and the more thickening power it has.

Another idea: If you're rolling out pasta dough and have leftover dough scraps after cutting and shaping, toss the scraps into a pot of salted water and boil them down to almost nothing to make starchy pasta water. Freeze it the same way.

Just be sure to thaw and reheat your saved pasta water before using it, so it's hot when you add it to the dish.

MARRY THE PASTA AND SAUCE

I admit it, not every pasta gets "married" to the sauce. For certain stuffed pastas, like Casoncelli with Sage and Pancetta (page 289), we just drain the pasta, put it on a plate, and pour brown butter over the top. Other pastas like Eggplant Lasagnetta (page 111) get baked, and still others get served in broth like Lamb Tortellini in Brodo (page 239).

But most of the time, we marry. First off, I gotta say, this isn't the Olive Garden! We're not dumping sauce on top of cooked noodles and calling it a day! The thing to understand is that a noodle is a noodle and a ragù is a ragù. When you make a long or short noodle with a sauce, you need to bring them together by briefly cooking them both in the same pan. Then you toss continuously until the pasta and sauce become one thing. In Italy, they call it *mantecare* (to cream). You know how risotto gets really creamy when you stir it constantly? As you stir, you're forcing starch out of the rice, and that's what makes it creamy. It's the same with pasta. When you shake, swirl, or toss the pasta in the sauce, the pasta loses some of its starch and mixes with water and fat in the sauce, and they all cook down a bit, thicken up, and create a creamy texture. The pasta absorbs some sauce. The sauce hugs the noodle. And the two become one. I like to call this marrying pasta and sauce. When the marriage is complete, each forkful of pasta is the perfect bite. Here's how to make it happen.

Choose a big enough pan.

When heating up your sauce, make sure the pan is deep and wide enough to hold both the sauce and the full amount of pasta. You also need some room in the pan to toss everything together, and sloping sides help with that. A 12-inch high-sided pan, like a large deep sauté or frying pan, usually works well for up to 1 pound of pasta tossed with sauce. You could even use a wok, especially one with a handle. And if you have a lot of people to serve, split the pasta and sauce between two pans.

Keep your sauce loose.

In most cases, before the pasta goes into the pan with the sauce, you want the sauce to be a little looser than you'd like the final product to be. It should look a little soupy. And the pasta should be just a hair undercooked. This way, as the sauce simmers and reduces in volume and the pasta finishes cooking in the sauce, they marry and become perfectly cooked together. It's especially important to keep the sauce loose if you'll be tossing in some Parmesan cheese off the heat, which we often do. The cheese will further thicken the sauce.

Use your saved pasta water.

Pasta water is your lever for regulating both the sauce looseness and pasta doneness in the pan. Let's say the sauce thickens up before the pasta is perfectly cooked in the pan. No problem. Just add pasta water. Keep things moving by shaking or swirling the pan, and the pasta will absorb the water and finish cooking, and the sauce will simmer down and begin to hug the pasta, completing the marriage. It's always a dance finding the right amount of water needed for the pasta dish you're cooking. But it's usually around 3 to 4 tablespoons pasta water for each portion of pasta that's in the pan. Adjust as you go. Bear in mind that the pasta water contains salt. If your sauce is already highly seasoned, you may want to use plain hot water instead of salted pasta water.

Keep the heat high.

When the pasta and sauce are in the pan, you generally want the heat under the pan high enough to simmer the pasta in the sauce. That helps the sauce and pasta emulsify or marry. Keep an eye on things and regulate the heat and pasta water to hit that sweet spot where everything's done at the same time.

Wait to toss.

Right after you transfer pasta from the boiling water to the pan, try to resist the impulse to toss. If the sauce is still pretty loose, tossing it now will just splash sauce all over the place—and over you. Shake and swirl the pan instead, letting the sauce simmer down until it begins to hug the pasta. That's when it's ready to toss. To toss, tilt the pan away from you so everything hits the far edge of the pan, then jerk it upward and back a little to throw the pasta and sauce back into the center of the pan. Repeat that motion until the pasta and sauce marry. To see how it's done, scan the QR code on page 17 for Classic Pasta Technique and watch the Cacio e Pepe video.

Give the marriage a moment in the pan.

After the pasta and sauce are hugging and married, remove the whole thing from the heat and let it settle. Before adding Parmesan or other final touches, let the pasta relax so everything can cool down a bit and emulsify. We're talking 10 to 15 seconds, tops. This is a good time to taste the pasta. Sometimes you may need to add salt, pepper, lemon juice, sherry vinegar, or another ingredient to balance all the flavors.

Add cheese off the heat.

If you boil cheese, it can separate. Then your beautiful marriage becomes a greasy mess! To perfectly emulsify cheese into your dish of pasta, use finely grated cheese, add it off the heat, sprinkle it evenly over the surface, and keep tossing until the cheese melts into the marriage. Generally, about 1 tablespoon grated Parmesan per portion of pasta is good. Aged cheeses like Parmesan and pecorino will add some saltiness to the dish. Keep that in mind when adjusting for seasoning in the previous step.

Maybe undercook dried pasta.

If your pasta doesn't release much starch when it cooks, you may not be able to consummate the marriage! That happens sometimes with less expensive boxed pasta that's extruded through Teflon dies (for details, see Buy Good Dried Pasta, page 34). In that case, you can undercook your pasta in the boiling water by several minutes. Boil it until the white line or dot in the middle is still pretty big and visible, then finish cooking the pasta in the sauce. As the pasta cooks in the pan, it'll release whatever starch it can into your sauce, helping to thicken it so the sauce hugs the noodle and the marriage happens. Add hot water as needed so both the pasta and sauce are done at the same time. Or you can use my new favorite ingredient: frozen pasta water! (See Saved Pasta Water, page 31.)

Buy Good Dried Pasta

I know a lot of you will just buy dried pasta instead of making it fresh. Please make it fresh if you can—it tastes so much better, and it's so much fun to make! Truth be told, though, I buy dried pasta, too. Look in my cupboards and you'll see Setaro, Benedetto Cavalieri, and other brands of dried pasta. Here's what to look for when you buy.

Look for a rough surface. Most dried pasta is made from a semolina-and-water dough extruded through different dies to make different shapes. Heavy bronze dies are traditional. They rough up the surface of the pasta and give it a sort of sandy appearance. But bronze dies are more expensive and they take a while to clean between batches. Nowadays, the big pasta manufacturers use Teflon-coated dies. That changes the surface texture of the noodle. It's slicker and more glassy looking. Why do you care? Because a rough-textured noodle is more porous, holds on to more sauce, and releases more starch, creating a better marriage between pasta and sauce. It tastes better, too. Before you buy dried pasta, look through the packaging window. Does the surface of the noodle look rough and sandy? Does the package say the pasta was extruded through bronze dies? If so, that's your best bet.

See if it's slow-dried. Some big brands, like De Cecco, say their pasta is "slow-dried." But how long, and at what temperature? De Cecco's short pasta shapes dry for 9 hours; their long pasta (like linguine) dries for 18 hours; and a few of their specialty noodles dry for 36 hours. The smaller artisanal *pastifici* (pasta makers) take longer. Setaro, an old-school pasta maker in Gragnano, Italy, dries their pasta for 3 to 5 days at a temperature of 104° to 113°F (40° to 45°C). The drying time and temperature matter. Slow-drying pasta at a low temperature keeps the protein in the semolina flour from heating up and firming up too quickly. That slower process results in a noodle texture that's supple and creamy when it's boiled. If you speed things up with higher heat and less time, the protein in the flour tightens up more, trapping the starch and preventing the starch from absorbing as much water and getting creamy when you boil the pasta. That leaves you with a cooked noodle texture that's rubbery and bouncy rather than supple and creamy. Barilla, one of the biggest pasta brands in the world, dries their pasta for just 7 to 10 hours, starting at around 131° to 149°F (55° to 65°C) and increasing the temperature to as much as 183°F (84°C), depending on the shape of the noodle. It speeds up production but sacrifices what I love most about pasta: that creamy mouthfeel of a noodle that just melts away on your tongue as you eat it. Look for slow-dried pasta. The packaging doesn't always say "slow-dried," but Setaro, Martelli, and Benedetto Cavalieri are some good artisanal brands.

MAKE IT NICE

You know how you get ready before you go out to a nice restaurant? You don't just wear a ratty shirt and sweatpants! You dress up a little. Do the same thing with your pasta. We eat with our eyes first. Before you serve a dish of pasta, take a moment to make it look as good as you can. That doesn't mean adding all sorts of elaborate garnishes. You just want to give the pasta some love.

Choose a nice plate.

Some pastas, like Rigatoni with Fiorella Sausage Ragù (page 208), look better in a wide, shallow bowl than on a flat plate. Other pastas will get lost in a big bowl. Have a look at Scallop Corzetti with Clarified Pomodoro, Tomato Powder, and Basil Oil (page 269). That pasta looks better on a flat plate. Visualize your finished pasta shape on the plate, and pick the plate that best complements the pasta.

Warm your plates.

Have you ever had perfectly cooked scrambled eggs served on a cold plate? They're gross! The cold plate cools down the eggs and ruins the whole dish. Don't ruin your perfectly cooked pasta. Warm your plates. If the oven's already on, put them in there for a minute or two before you plate your pasta. Or run them under hot water and then dry them with a kitchen towel. You could even stick a stack of plates in the microwave for a minute.

Serve a reasonable portion.

In restaurants in Italy, pasta is not really the main course, so pasta portion sizes are not huge. They're not small tasting portions, but they're not the "bottomless bowl of pasta" you might be used to getting from an American chain restaurant. We usually serve 3 to 4 ounces of fresh pasta per serving. I think that's reasonable. Most of the recipes in this book make 4 to 6 servings. Some make 6 to 8 servings. If you like a bigger portion on each plate, go by the low end of those ranges.

Give it some flair.

Please don't just dump your pasta on the plate. Take a second to make it look good! For ribbons and strands like tagliolini and pappardelle, twirl a whole portion of pasta around a pasta fork or tongs, then lay the pasta on the plate so it looks beautiful. The motion is like twisting a bite of pasta on your dinner fork, but you twist up the entire portion at once. You can lay down the twirled portion of pasta and leave it sort of loose like the Cacio e Pepe (page 36), or you can twist the mound a little tighter like the Spaghetti alla Chitarra with Basil, Poppy Seed, and Prosciutto (page 215). You could build up the mound, too. Check out the Paccheri with Clams and Charred Lemon Brodo (page 143) to see what I mean. Or, if you're serving fewer, larger ravioli, maybe put them in a circle or other pattern on the plate like I did for the Almond Tortellini with Truffle and Parmesan (page 131). You worked hard making this pasta. Now's the time to show it off!

Be sparing with garnishes.

I'm not a big fan of elaborate garnishes. Most pasta just needs a little shower of grated Parm or pecorino cheese—if that. When I do garnish with cheese, sometimes I like to sprinkle it over only half the plate (see the Buckwheat Maltagliati with Duck and Espresso Ragù on page 184). Maybe the pasta just needs a flick of chopped herbs or a dusting of spice. There's cocoa powder in my wild boar ragù, but it's blended into the sauce, so I like to dust the plate with a little cocoa powder (see Chestnut Fettuccine with Wild Boar Ragù on page 211). It all depends on the pasta and the sauce. For Casoncelli with Sage and Pancetta (page 289), bacon and herbs are crisped up in a pan with brown butter. All you need to do for that pasta is spoon the brown butter, crispy bacon, and sage over the ravioli. It's perfect as is. Just keep it simple.

OUR CACIO E PEPE

This dish demonstrates all the techniques discussed in this chapter. Like all the best dishes on earth, it is extremely simple, and relies mostly on your skills as a cook. The devil is in the details. Why do we crush the peppercorns instead of coarsely grinding them in a mill? Because the texture contrast of some fine, some coarse, and some cracked pepper makes it taste better. Why these amounts of pepper and cheese? If there isn't enough black pepper, or if the pecorino is off or even omitted in favor of Parmesan, the dish falls flat. Or if there's too much black pepper or pecorino, the dish tastes too sharp. The marriage of pasta and sauce is also paramount here (see Marry the Pasta and Sauce, page 32). Ultimately, if you skip over these details, the dish will become what most people erroneously refer to as "cacio e pepe"—buttered noodles garnished with black pepper. Executed properly, however, this pasta soars. Just follow the recipe. It's easy. To watch a video of making this pasta, scan the QR code for Classic Pasta Technique on page 17. **SERVES 4**

Kosher salt

1 pound store-bought dried spaghetti

2 teaspoons whole black peppercorns

8 tablespoons (4 ounces) unsalted butter, cut into pieces

2 cups finely grated Pecorino Romano cheese

¾ cup finely grated Parmesan cheese, plus more for garnish

Cook the spaghetti: Bring a large pot of water to a boil and add salt until it tastes like well-seasoned broth. Drop in the spaghetti, give it a stir, and cover the pot to quickly return the water to a boil. Uncover or partially cover to maintain the boil and boil the pasta, stirring occasionally, until it is tender but still a little chewy when bitten, 10 to 12 minutes.

Make the sauce: Right after dropping the pasta, crush the peppercorns on a cutting board by rocking a heavy pan such as cast-iron skillet over them. You want a variety of some tiny and some bigger bits of cracked pepper for texture contrast.

When the pasta is about halfway done, in a very large, deep sauté pan big enough to hold the pasta (a 12-inch high-sided pan works well), melt the butter over high heat. Add the cracked pepper and 2 cups of the hot pasta water or saved pasta water (see page 31). Bring to a boil and simmer until the mixture thickens slightly like a thin soup, 3 to 5 minutes. If the pasta isn't ready yet, remove the sauce from the heat.

When the pasta is ready, return the sauce to high heat and use tongs or a pasta fork to transfer the cooked spaghetti from the water straight to the pan. Shake and swirl the pan until the sauce begins to hug the pasta, 1 to 2 minutes (keep the pasta moving, adding a little more pasta water if necessary to create a loose, creamy sauce). Toss everything until the pasta and sauce begin to marry. For this pasta, you want the sauce a little runny because the cheese will thicken it up. Remove from the heat, add the pecorino and Parmesan, and keep tossing until the sauce thickens further and the pasta and sauce marry, leaving little to no sauce in the pan.

Using tongs or a pasta fork, dish out the pasta onto warmed plates, creating some volume by twirling it into a mound. Garnish with additional Parmesan and serve.

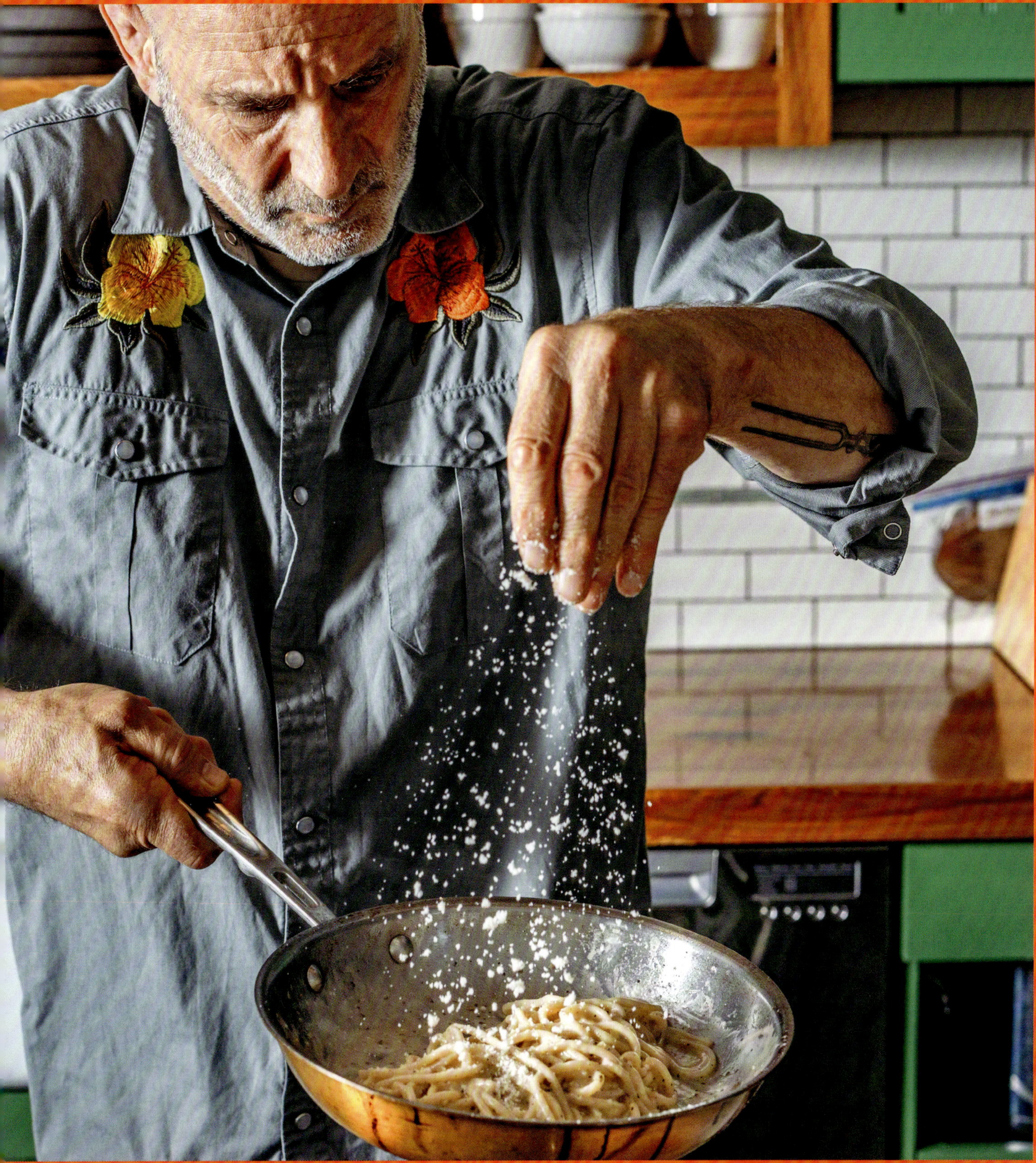

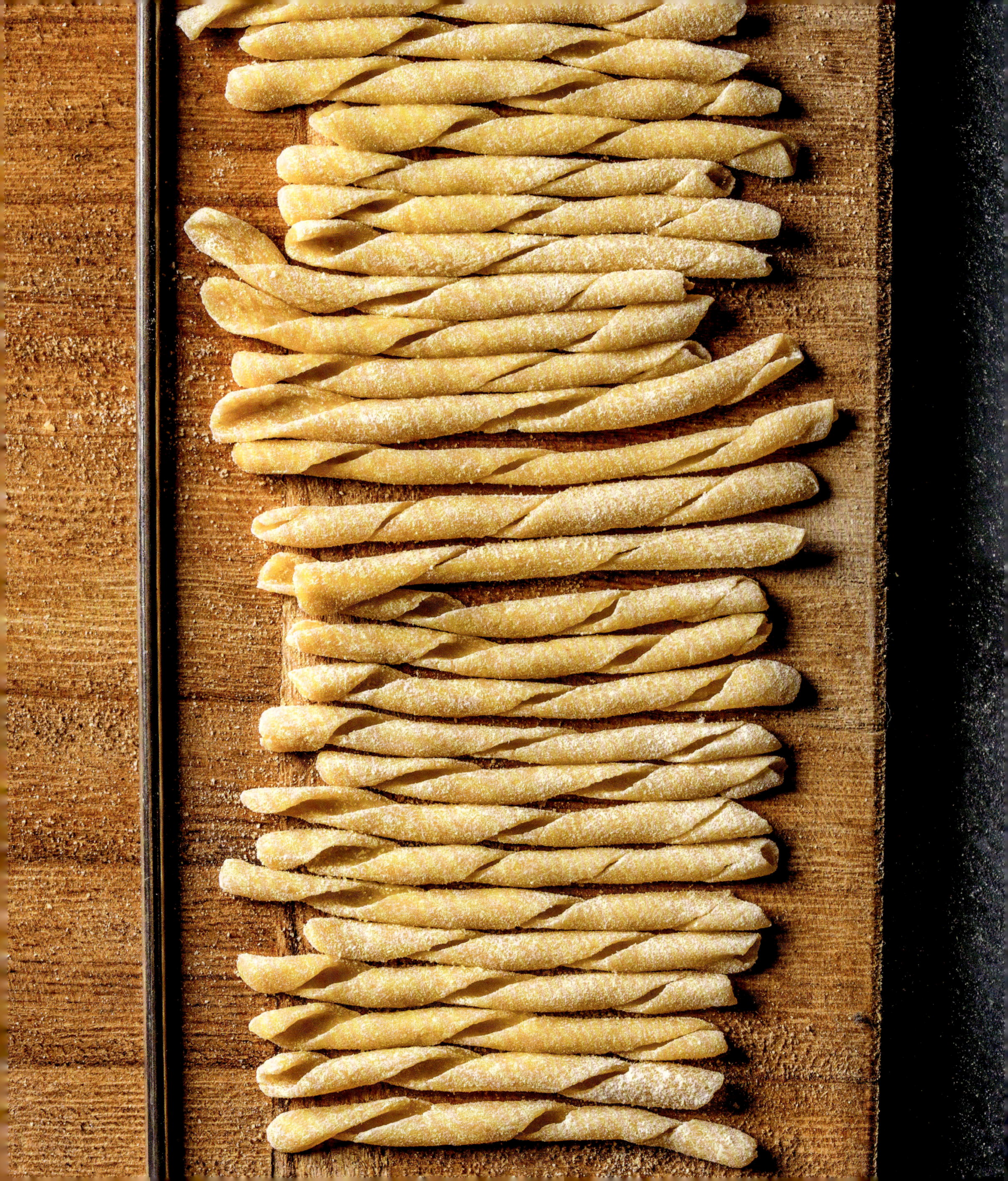

PASTA DOUGHS AND SHAPES

> Anyone who has never made a mistake has never tried anything new.
>
> **—ALBERT EINSTEIN,**
> NOBEL PRIZE-WINNING PHYSICIST

On a recent fall evening, I did a pasta class at Vetri Cucina in Philadelphia. It was dusk, the sun was setting, and the golden light was so beautiful on the wooden table upstairs where I do these classes. About ten people were seated across from me, and I said, "Let's make pasta!" There was no recipe. I didn't know what the sauces would be.

I poured some flour on the table, swished my fingers in it to make a volcano, and then started cracking eggs. I didn't know how many to add. I just kept cracking eggs until it looked right. Apparently, I added one egg too many because the eggs started running over the flour all over the table.

A few people sat up in their chairs, looking disturbed. A woman with a diamond bracelet folded her arms stiffly. One guy with a crisp button-down shirt had little beads of sweat on his forehead. I could see the nervousness in their eyes.

I don't know what it is about dough, but it really intimidates people! Admittedly, I did add too many eggs. But I did it for a reason. To teach a lesson: Rule #1 when making pasta dough is that it's easier to add flour than it is to add water. I gathered the runny egg, mixed the flour in from the edges of the volcano, and mashed it all together until it came together as a dough. It was sticky. "The dough is too wet," I said. Then I grabbed a handful of flour, kneading it into the dough until it was perfect . . . stiff, yet supple and smooth like a baby's bottom. Problem solved. Then I explained Rule #1: You always want to err on the side of too wet.

Everyone relaxed a bit. I could see their shoulders drop an inch or two. Some sat back in their chairs.

Then I started rolling out the dough. I usually use a KitchenAid stand mixer with a pasta roller attachment to show them that this is something you can easily do at home. After feeding the dough into the roller and going down a couple settings to make it thinner, the sheet of dough ripped. I looked up and the diamond bracelet lady raised her eyebrows, looking flabbergasted. Sweaty forehead man started sweating again.

I acted like it was it was no big deal. "The dough ripped," I said. "So what." I folded the sheet of pasta over itself and ran it through the rollers a few times, folding as I went to force more of the water in the dough into the flour. Then I explained hydration: "The point of resting pasta dough after you mix it is to allow the dough to fully hydrate." When the dough is resting, the flour is still absorbing all the water from the eggs, making the dough texture more homogeneous throughout. Resting also lets the gluten relax; it allows the protein structure you created during mixing to settle down so the dough rolls out more easily. "If I had rested the dough, it probably wouldn't have ripped," I added. Then I admitted that I had done something wrong, again, on purpose: I had failed to let the dough rest. Why? To reveal Rule #2 of pasta dough: Most mistakes are easily fixed.

I went on like this, intentionally doing things wrong, to show them that it's okay to mess up. I rolled a piece of dough super thin, cut it into tagliatelle, and the noodles fell apart in the boiling water. "That's because whole-egg doughs have less protein than all-egg-yolk doughs." That's important, because less protein in pasta dough means the dough may not have as much strength and may fall apart when rolled too thin. Now diamond bracelet lady unfolded her arms and looked happier. Sweaty man's forehead was dry. So I rolled out another piece, took my time, and the pasta started to dry out and crack. Then I grabbed a spray bottle and explained, "Sometimes as you work with pasta, you need to mist the dough with water to keep it from drying out."

I know that pasta dough strikes fear in the hearts of brilliant, competent people. The fear of failure. In my classes, I go ahead and fail on purpose to erase that fear. I mean, it's just flour and eggs! If the dough isn't doing what you want it to do, there's usually an easy fix. Pasta making is so much fun and shouldn't give you anxiety. Mixing up pasta dough is really not that different from making pancake batter. You just leave out a few ingredients and make it drier so it's dough. Yes, it's good to start off with a recipe, but once you have made pasta dough a few times, you'll get a feel for it, and you can just start cracking eggs into the flour. You'll know when to stop. When in doubt, add another egg!

By the end of that autumn class, the sun had set and everyone at the table was smiling and enjoying their Spaghetti alla Carbonara (page 206) and Eggplant Lasagnetta (page 111). They relaxed into their chairs and talked freely. The fear and anxiety had disappeared. Such is the power of pasta.

Please don't be afraid to mix up fresh pasta dough. It is so satisfying to eat and well worth the half hour or so it takes to mix it, rest it, and cut it. This chapter explains everything you need to know. We'll go through the entire process from raw flour to finished shaped pasta, and I'll share insights that my cooks and I have gleaned from decades of pasta making. I've included my favorite dough recipes, including whole-egg Chitarra Dough (page 67), my go-to Half-and-Half Egg Dough (page 70), a silky Egg Yolk Dough (page 74), and my new favorite, Hand-Rolled Dough (page 55). All these doughs have Level Up variations like adding Spanish smoked paprika to the Half-and-Half Egg Dough to make Pimentón Dough (page 74) and adding chestnut flour to the Egg Yolk Dough to make Chestnut Dough (page 74). I hope these little twists inspire you to make your own signature pasta dough. Once your dough is mixed, you can make hundreds of different shapes like Orecchiette (page 57), Tagliatelle (page 76), or Pumpernickel Pappardelle (page 80). Hopefully you'll get really into it and make something new that I never thought of!

FLOUR

You don't need special flours to make pasta. All-purpose flour works fine. In Italy, tipo "00" flour is very similar to American all-purpose flour and you can use the two interchangeably in this book. All-purpose flour is the only flour used to make Corzetti (page 88), a simple stamped-out pasta round from Liguria. Classic Pici Dough (page 82), a Tuscan shape that looks like long, thick spaghetti, is made with only bread flour. Of course, you can go the extra mile to make pasta dough more special—and I often do. My Egg Yolk Dough (page 74) and Half-and-Half Egg Dough (page 70) are made with all-purpose flour plus semolina flour for a more complex texture and taste. Grano Arso Dough (page 90) incorporates "burnt flour" for a toasted wheat flavor. I add spicy notes with a sour undercurrent by using rye flour in Rye Dough (page 74). Mexican masa harina gives noodles made with Masa Dough (page 91) a distinct corn flavor.

Just know that all you really need to start is some flour, some water, and your hands. My Hand-Rolled Dough (page 55) is simply that: flour and water. It makes a beautiful pasta similar to the dried pasta you're probably familiar with, but it's not dried. It's fresh. I recommend starting there. This dough comes together so easily, and you can roll it out into sheets and cut it into fettuccine, or shape it with your fingers into things like Orecchiette (page 57) and Trofie (page 59). Here's a quick rundown of the three key flours used in this book. If you want a deeper dive into different flours and their protein qualities, check out my book *Mastering Pasta*.

Tipo "00" flour.

Think of this as Italian all-purpose flour. The number refers to how finely the flour is ground. Tipo "00" (type 00) is ground extra-fine, like talcum power. Tipo 0, tipo 1, and tipo 2 get increasingly coarser. We tested the recipes in this book mostly with Spadoni Gran Mugnaio tipo "00" flour for pasta. We also tested with Caputo tipo "00" flours, including the Red, Blue, and Chef's versions they sell. They all worked well. A good common substitute is King Arthur all-purpose flour. We tested the doughs with this flour as well.

Bread flour.

American "bread flour" is higher in protein, which makes it better for the strong gluten network you need to make high-rising breads. You don't really need an elaborate gluten structure for pasta, but sometimes I add bread flour to get a little more chew and strength in a noodle. At my restaurants, I use a bread flour called Redeemer that's milled fresh at Castle Valley Mill in Doylestown,

Pennsylvania. It's ground from hard red winter wheat and is lightly sifted to remove some of the hard bran from the rest of the flour. If you're interested, pick up some bolted (sifted) Redeemer flour. We also tested the recipes here with the widely available King Arthur unbleached bread flour.

Semolina flour.

In Italian milling, semolina refers to grains ground slightly coarser than your average powdery flour. Think of cornmeal, polenta, and grits as types of corn semolina. Most often, though, semolina refers to flours that are coarsely milled from durum wheat. This kind of wheat is very hard (*durum* means "hard" in Latin), and it's high in protein, about 13%, which makes it perfect for creating structure in pastas and breads. Durum wheat semolina has a pale-yellow color because it's made with only the yellow endosperm of the grain (not the darker bran and the germ). The flour used to make your average dried penne or linguine is semolina. Things get confusing because different manufacturers may label that same type of flour as "semolina," "semolina flour," "durum wheat semolina," or "semola." *Semola* doesn't refer to any specific fineness or grade of flour; it's just Italian for "semolina," so don't let that throw you! You might also see references to just "durum flour," which is *finely* milled durum, so it's not called "semolina."

To simplify things, I call for just one product in this book: semolina flour. I like the semolina flour from the Italian miller Caputo, which is labeled "Semola Rimacinata di Grano Duro" ("remilled durum wheat semolina"). It's milled somewhat finer than other brands of semolina but not as fine as durum flour, so it makes fantastic silky fresh pastas, and it dries well, too. You could always use another brand of semolina flour; it'll probably work just as well, but you may have to adjust the water as you go. You could also mix durum flour and semolina, which we do at the restaurants sometimes to get different textures. Just know that whenever you switch flours, your mileage may vary, especially with the water . . . you may need to add more or less, so start wet and go slow!

If you really want to try something special, try Angelo Anedda's semolina flour. It's an organic, freshly milled semola from Sardinia that tastes incredible and holds shapes perfectly when you use it in my Hand-Rolled Dough (page 55).

MIXING

The point of mixing is to hydrate the flour with liquid and form a stiff paste or pasta. It goes from being a ragged pile of clumpy flour to a solid mass of dough. You can mix by hand or by machine. When mixing at home, there is literally no reason to use a machine. You're just making extra dirty dishes! Plus, mixing pasta dough on a countertop is therapeutic. I find that keeping my hands busy frees up my mind, allowing it to relax and destress. You just mix and knead until the flour absorbs enough liquid to stick to itself and all the separate particles clump into bigger and bigger bits and finally form one cohesive ball of dough. It's so easy. A small ball of dough, about a pound (the yield of most of the dough recipes in this book), can easily feed 4 to 6 people, or even 8, depending on what you're making.

People always ask, "Can you overmix?" It's not likely. Maybe if you mix in a machine and forget about it, you could overmix the dough. But when you use your hands, it's nearly impossible to overmix. Plus, with your hands, it's easier to know when you should stop kneading. You can feel the flour going from dry to wet as it absorbs the water and/or egg. As you knead everything together, you can also feel the dough getting stiffer, a sign that a gluten structure is forming and the dough will be able to hold a shape like Trofie (page 59). The more you mix and knead, the stronger the gluten becomes. The dough goes from a loose, raggy, soft mess to a cohesive mass that holds together, and finally to a ball of dough that has some strength but is still malleable. After a 30-minute rest, the liquid will have fully hydrated the flour and the gluten will have relaxed a bit, making the dough easier to roll out and shape. When the dough is ready, it will feel sort of like Play-Doh, or maybe slightly drier. Here are a few pointers on the whole mixing process:

Make a well. When mixing dough by hand on a countertop, create a well in your pile of flour with your hands so it looks like a shallow volcano, or press the bottom of a mixing bowl into the pile to make a well.

REDEEMER BREAD FLOUR

SEMOLINA FLOUR

TIPO "00" FLOUR

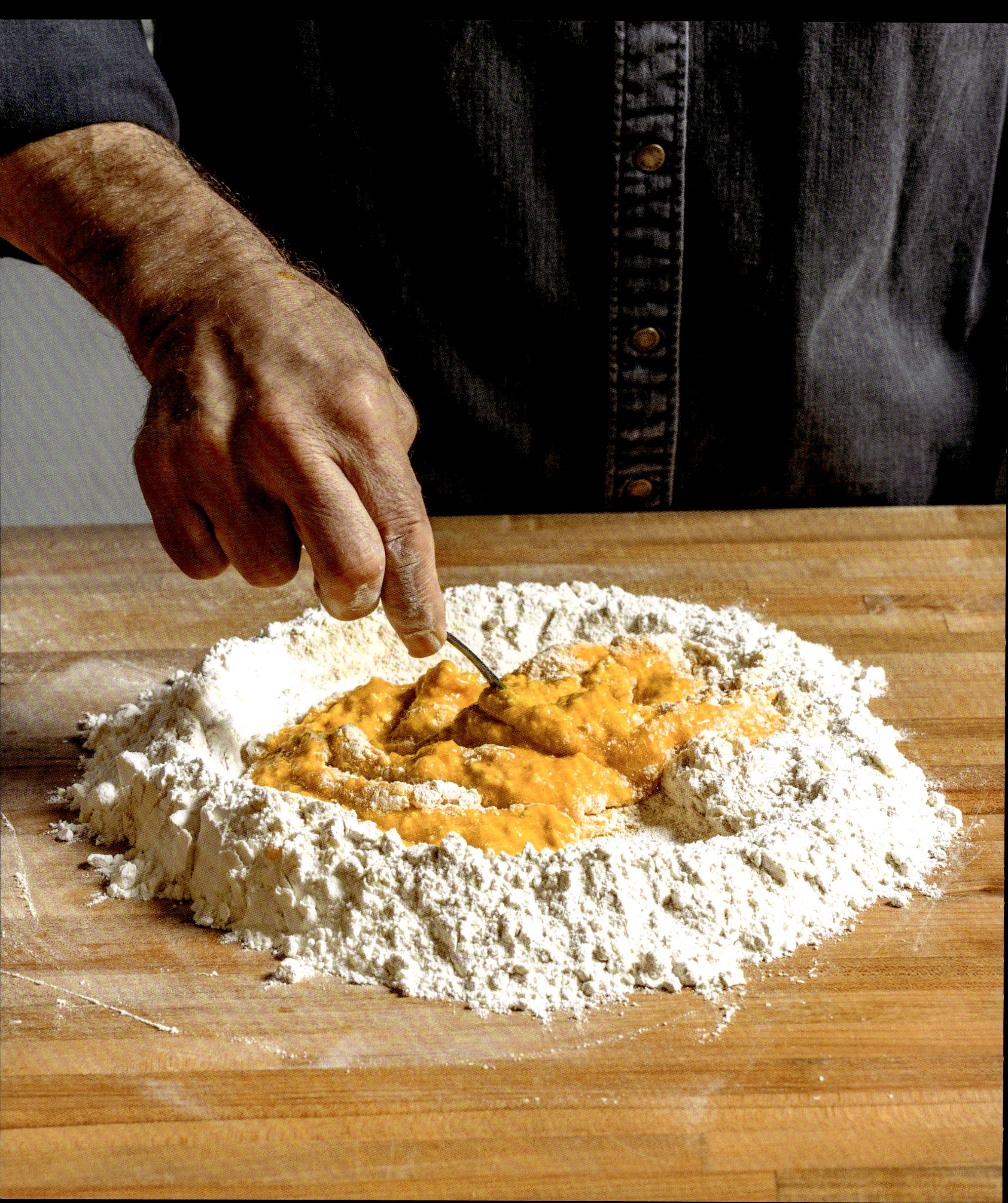

Start wet. For egg doughs, whisk the eggs (and oil, if using) with a fork in the center of the well until the eggs are blended, then whisk in a bit of water. Remember Rule #1: It's easier to start a little wet and correct with flour than to mix a dry dough and try to correct it later by adding water. This is why my dough recipes may seem a little wet at first.

Use a bench scraper. As you work in flour from the edges and the eggs become a paste in the well, switch from a fork to a bench scraper. Chop and scrape the paste together with the rest of the flour. The scraper will save a lot of mess from going on your hands.

Add flour when needed. If the dough feels sticky and very soft, add a handful of flour to the table and knead the dough until the flour gets incorporated.

Or mist with water. If the dough feels dry and crumbly, use a water-filled spray bottle to mist the dough and correct the hydration until the dough becomes a kneadable mass.

Feel the dough texture. When it's done, egg dough should feel smooth and firm, sort of like slightly dry Play-Doh. If it feels tacky, it's too wet. When you tug on the dough with your fingertips, it should gently pull back into place (a sign of strength). If you press a fingertip into the dough, the dough shouldn't crack and the indentation from your finger should stay in place. Other doughs will be similar, but some, such as Hand-Rolled Dough (page 55) and Chitarra Dough (page 67), may feel a little softer than this. Pici Dough (page 82) will feel very soft.

Mind added ingredients. If you add powders, such as cocoa powder, the dough will feel drier because the powder sucks up more moisture. If you add purees, such as spinach puree or squash puree, the dough will feel wetter and need less water because of the water in the puree.

Start wet in the mixer. If you mix your dough in a stand mixer instead of by hand, it helps to reverse the order of operations: Put the wet ingredients in the bowl first. This way you won't have to scrape the bowl as much to incorporate flour hidden under the liquids at the bottom of the bowl.

RESTING

You know that stiff gluten structure you created when mixing and kneading? It really needs a rest after all that forced hydration. After kneading, let the dough relax for about 30 minutes so the dough fully hydrates and is easier to shape. If your dough feels super stiff and it's not rolling or shaping easily, let it rest longer. The ideal scenario is a room-temp mix-and-rest, plus a same-day roll. Some tips:

Cover or wrap it. If you're using pasta dough within an hour or two, you can just cover it with a damp kitchen towel to keep it from drying out. Or you can wrap the dough in plastic wrap and let it rest at room temperature for up to 6 hours. If you're not using an egg dough right away, you can refrigerate the wrapped dough for up to 3 days. But a semolina-and-water dough is best used within a few hours for ideal results.

Better yet, vacuum-seal. When I store plastic-wrapped egg dough for more than a day or two (or freeze it for longer), the dough surface often oxidizes and gets a dull brownish color. That's totally fine, and the pasta is still good. However, vacuum-sealing helps preserve the bright yellow color and fresh flavor for longer, up to a week in the fridge. Plus, and this is even more important, the pressure exerted by vacuum-sealing forces more liquid into the flour, promoting more efficient and even hydration than you'll ever get by kneading alone. Basically, vacuum-sealing speeds hydration.

Maybe freeze it for later. If you're not rolling out or shaping an egg dough anytime soon, you could freeze the wrapped or vacuum-sealed dough for up to 1 month. Thaw frozen dough overnight in the refrigerator before using it. It can also be quickly thawed in a microwave oven on 50% power in 5-second increments just until cool to the touch. Be careful, though, you don't want to cook the dough!

PASTA TOOLS

Your hands are the most important pasta-making tool. They can mix and knead dough, feel when it's firm, and create pasta shapes that are totally unique to you. Depending on what you're making, you might also want a few other tools like a digital scale for weighing ingredients, a bench scraper and/or dough scraper (pastry card), mixing bowls in various sizes, a water mister for keeping your dough moist, a stand mixer with pasta rolling and cutting attachments (or a hand-crank model), a fluted cutting wheel, a corzetti stamp, round ravioli (or biscuit) cutters, and a grooved gnocchi, cavarola, or garganelli board. I also recommend a pasta fork, which looks sort of like a two-pronged tuning fork, but the prongs are sharp at the ends. You could always use tongs, but a pasta fork is ideal for gathering up long strands of pasta, twirling them into a mound, and laying the mound decoratively on the plate. I've had the same pasta fork for over thirty years. This tool is so special to me, I got it tattooed on my arm! Look for the pasta tools you need online and in specialty shops. Some of my favorites are Antica Aguzzeria del Cavallo and Artisanal Pasta Tools.

ROLLING AND SHAPING

There's one thing I urge you to do: Use your hands. They will tell you so much about the pasta . . . when it needs to rest longer . . . whether it wants more flour or water . . . and when it needs to be rolled thinner. Plus, your hands are the key to pasta shapes like Raschiatelli (page 61). Pick at least one handmade shape and try to master it. Follow the recipes here, watch the videos, and practice, and I promise, the satisfaction you'll feel at having successfully made and served your own beautiful pasta with your own hands is just indescribable! If you're the nervous type or need stress relief, forget about fidget spinners and stress balls. Make pasta! Think of it as pasta therapy. For centuries, handmade pasta has been one of the best stress relievers known to man. Here are some tips to help the rolling and shaping go smoothly. To watch videos of the rolling and shaping processes, scan the QR code for Pasta Doughs and Shapes on page 17.

Mise en place.

"Things in place" makes pasta making a lot easier. First, clean off your work surface or "bench." Any debris left on the bench will end up in the pasta! For rolling out long sheets of dough and making stuffed ravioli, you'll want a long countertop or table. You can also use a small table; it's just tighter. Either way, line up your tools and ingredients: tipo "00" or all-purpose flour for dusting the bench, semolina flour for dusting finished shapes, a spray bottle for misting dough with water and helping edges to stick together, a rolling pin (if needed), a ruler (if needed to measure pasta widths and lengths), any pasta cutters or stamps you'll need, and, of course, your rested dough and any fillings all ready to go. If the dough was chilled, let the pieces sit, covered, for 10 minutes to take the chill off.

Start small.

You don't need to roll out a whole pound of dough at once. The sheet will get super long and unwieldy! Start by rolling out 4 ounces of dough. When you make smaller roll-outs, the dough stays moist so you don't have to spray it over and over to keep it from drying out and cracking. Once you get comfortable sheeting pasta, try rolling out 8 ounces at once.

Cover it.

As you work with one piece of dough, keep the remaining dough covered so it doesn't dry out and develop a skin.

Make a disk.

Hand-press or roll the dough into a disk about ¼ inch thick and nearly as wide as your roller before sending it through the first time. It helps to use a rolling pin here to "preroll" the dough. You don't want the dough so thick that it stresses out the machine as you send it through the first few times.

Mind the hydration.

Use your fingers to test. If your fingertips stick to the dough when gently placed on top, the dough will most likely stick to the rollers and needs a dusting of flour. Aim to flour the dough early in the rolling process. As you roll thinner, extra flour will dry out the dough even faster. Generally try to keep the dough as wet as possible without sticking as you roll.

Wipe away excess flour.

After dusting dough with flour, make it a habit to wipe off the excess with your hands. Keep the bench clean of excess flour. Even a light dusting of flour will begin to dry out the bottom of your pasta sheet when it sits on the table.

Feed gradually.

Once the sheet of dough begins to thin out, feed the sheet into the roller gradually and hold it at the same height as the roller. If the sheet starts from too high or low, it can bunch up or stretch as the rollers pull it in.

Make your hands into paddles.

Avoid lifting the pasta sheets with your fingers. At best, they'll leave indentations in the pasta. At worst, they'll tear through the pasta—especially if your dough is weak. Instead, hold your hands flat and use the fronts and backs of your hands to feed the sheet through the roller and retrieve it on the other side.

Avoid stretching.

Try not to pull on the dough when feeding it into the roller and when retrieving it. Pulling can cause the dough to stretch and tear, especially when you're rolling it super thin. Just allow the dough to get sucked into the roller and then be there for it as it comes out the other side.

Prevent drying.

If your sheet of pasta begins to lift off the rolling surface, the dough is getting too dry. Mist the sheet with water.

Spray a fine mist.

Never point the spray bottle directly at the dough. Instead, point it straight ahead of you or up a little while hovering about a foot above the dough. That position allows a fine mist of atomized water to settle evenly on the dough without any pooling in one section.

Laminate.

When making noodles like pappardelle and fettuccine, do a few laminations or book folds on the dough to strengthen it. After going down a couple of roller settings, fold the sheet of dough in half crosswise over itself and cut about ¼ inch off the corners at the fold before feeding the folded sheet back into the roller. Folding laminates the dough, strengthening it, and cutting the corners helps to create an evenly wide sheet.

Mind the temperature.

If it's taking a long time to roll or shape the dough—especially if the room is warm—the dough may become sticky or too slack to hold a firm shape. If necessary, refrigerate unused dough briefly while you work.

Rolling Dough with a Machine

Using a rolling pin and your hands to roll pasta takes practice. I encourage you to try it! For most cooks, however, it's easier and faster to get an even thickness with a pasta rolling machine. Whether you use a hand-crank machine like a Marcato Atlas or an electric machine like a KitchenAid pasta roller attachment, here's a general guide on what to expect from 1 pound of any of the pasta doughs in this book. But please don't fixate on what number setting you roll the pasta on. The rollers move and stretch on these machines, and each machine is a little different. The important thing is the actual thickness of the pasta once it's rolled. For ravioli, you should be able to read a newspaper under the rolled-out dough. A longer noodle like fettuccine (page 80) should be a little thicker, but you should still be able to see the newspaper underneath, though you might not be able to read the news.

Pasta Dough	Sheet Length	Sheet Width	Sheet Thickness	Approximate Pasta Machine Setting	Possible Pastas
1 pound	2 to 3 feet	5 to 6 inches	1/8 inch (3mm)	4 or 5	Garganelli, Maltagliati, Pappardelle, Tagliatelle, Tagliolini, Tajarin
1 pound	3 to 4 feet	5 to 6 inches	1/16 inch (1.5mm)	6	Cannelloni, Farfalle, Fazzoletti, Fettuccine, Lasagna, Mandilli, Rotolo, Sorpresine
1 pound	4 to 5 feet	5 to 6 inches	1/32 inch (0.8mm)	7 or 8	Agnolotti, Anolini, Caramelle, Capelletti, Casoncelli, Francobolli, Ravioli, Tortellini, Triangoli

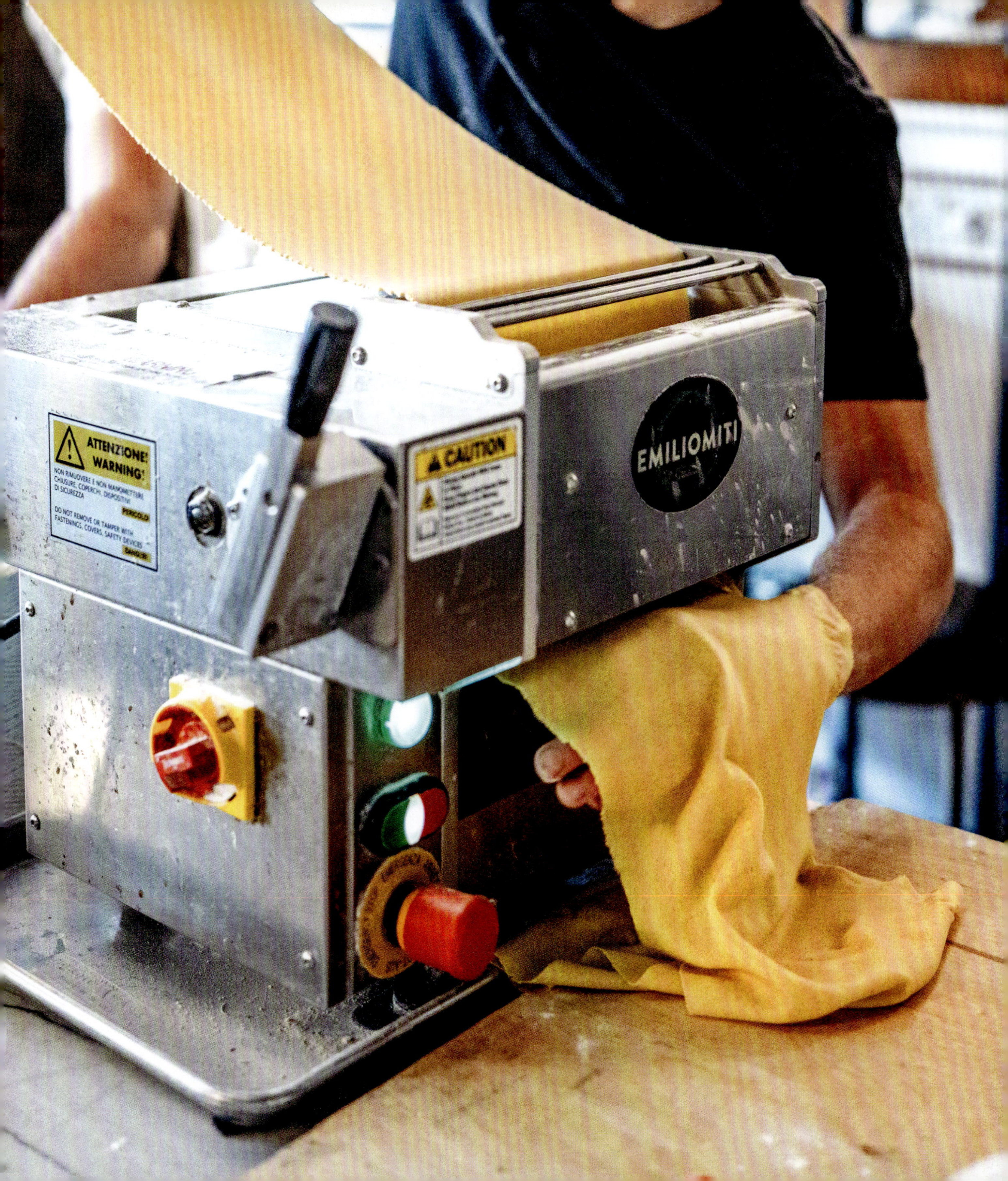
ATTENZIONE!
WARNING!
CAUTION
EMILIOMITI

PASTA THICKNESS

Thickness is key because it changes how the pasta eats. Thick or thin noodles feel different in the mouth, and some pasta doughs taste different when they are rolled thick as opposed to thin. Long noodles like pappardelle, fettuccine, and tagliatelle generally taste better when they're a little thicker, about ⅛ inch (3mm) thick. Stuffed pastas like agnolotti and ravioli are more delicate and taste better when the dough is rolled thinner. Of course, there are always exceptions! Here are some basic guidelines.

Roll whole-egg doughs thicker.

We use whole eggs in our Chitarra Dough (page 67) and it works great. You can roll the pasta somewhat thick, about ⅛ inch (3mm) thick, and then cut it ⅛ inch wide so the noodle looks like square spaghetti. That dough and that shape rolled to ⅛ inch thick leaves a nice pop in your mouth when cooked. But if you made noodles ⅛ inch thick or even thicker out of our Egg Yolk Dough (page 74), they would taste too tough. Stay with me, here.

Roll half-egg, half-yolk doughs a little thinner.

The rule of thumb is: The more egg yolks in your dough, the thinner the pasta needs to be rolled. Our Half-and-Half Egg Dough (page 70) is made with half whole eggs and half egg yolks by weight. The whole eggs add water from the whites and the egg yolks add protein. That extra protein from the yolks is the reason the dough should be rolled a bit thinner, closer to 1/16 inch (1.5mm) thick instead of ⅛ inch (3mm) thick.

Roll all-egg-yolk dough thinner still.

The fat in egg yolks gives all-egg-yolk dough a beautiful suppleness that feels so good in the mouth. But egg yolks add a fair amount of protein, too. It's a myth that egg whites have more protein than egg yolks. By weight, egg yolks have over 50 percent more protein than whites: Per 100 grams, egg yolks have 16.2 grams protein and whites have 10.7 grams. That extra protein in an all-egg-yolk dough adds strength, allowing you to roll the dough thinner, and the noodle still holds up when boiled. In fact, all-egg-yolk dough *must* be rolled thinner to taste good. You know how egg yolks in fried eggs get kind of chalky when they're overcooked? The same thing happens with an all-yolk dough if it's rolled too thick. To see my point, try making Egg Yolk Dough (page 74), rolling it a bit thicker (about ¼ inch), cut fettuccine, and then boil and taste it. The mouthfeel will be terrible.

Roll ravioli dough thinner still.

In ravioli, the dough on the edges overlaps, creating a double thickness of pasta. That's why I roll it super thin and why I prefer an all-yolk dough for stuffed pastas. But there are no hard-and-fast rules. Maybe you like your pasta chewier and prefer to make raviolis with whole-egg dough or Half-and-Half Egg Dough (page 70). You do you.

Manipulate the dough to match the intended thickness.

Pasta is all about the mouthfeel you're going for. You can manipulate any dough to match your intended thickness and change the mouthfeel. Let's say you love a whole-egg dough made with tipo "00" flour, but when you roll it thin, it falls apart when boiled. That's because the dough doesn't have enough protein in proportion to water. You could strengthen the dough by adding protein in the form of high-protein semolina flour. That's why our Chitarra Dough (page 67) works when rolled relatively thin. It's a whole-egg dough made with 100% semolina flour, plus a little olive oil for richness. Another option to get more strength from an all-purpose flour dough: Change the ratio of whole eggs to yolks. A higher proportion of yolks adds protein, strengthens the dough, and allows you to roll the dough thinner.

STORING FINISHED PASTA

Once your dough is rolled, it's time to shape it and store it until you cook it. Some of the shapes in this book take practice, but they're all fun to make. Get the kids involved. Make extra dough and let them play with it, shaping it however they want!

Keep it moist.

To prevent hand-rolled shapes from drying out as you work, cover the shapes with a damp kitchen towel or put them in a lightly floured lidded container.

Make the pasta ahead.

Most cut or shaped pasta can be dusted with flour, covered, and left at room temperature for about 1 hour. You can also refrigerate egg pasta, covered, on floured sheet pans for up to 4 hours.

Or freeze it for much later.

Nests of pasta ribbons and various handmade shapes can be frozen in a single layer, then transferred to zipper-lock bags or other firm lidded containers that can be stacked. Before freezing, I like to let shaped pasta sit at room temperature for a half hour or so. That way the surface dries a bit, helping to keep the pieces separate. Most unfilled strands, ribbons, and shaped pasta can be frozen for up to 1 month. More delicate stuffed pastas can be frozen for up to 3 days. You can take frozen pasta straight from the freezer to the pasta water, possibly adding a minute or so to the cooking time if it's, say, a stuffed pasta with a dense filling.

LEVEL UP **Culurgione Dough:** For Sardinia's classic stuffed pasta, I use slightly different proportions to make the dough easier to stuff and crimp. Use 355 grams (2 cups plus 2 tablespoons) semolina flour, 158 grams (⅔ cup) water, and 3 grams (1⅛ teaspoons) kosher salt. Knead in a little extra semolina if necessary to keep the dough from sticking. Makes 516 grams (a little over 1 pound). Try it in Smoked Potato Culurgiones with Lemon Butter and Chicken Skin Gremolata (page 263).

HAND-ROLLED DOUGH

This super-easy dough allows you to make something like extruded dried pasta shapes but fresh and by hand. It has only two ingredients—semolina flour and water. Semolina flour is high in protein (about 13%) with great plasticity, so this dough holds a shape well. We use 45% hydration, which is the amount of water in the dough relative to the flour by weight. If you live in a dry area at higher elevation, you may need to take the water up to, say, 49% hydration. For the best-looking shapes, mix up this dough and use it within an hour or two. **MAKES ABOUT 480 GRAMS (ABOUT 1 POUND); 4 TO 6 SERVINGS**

330 grams (2 cups) semolina flour, such as Caputo

150 grams (scant ⅔ cup) water

Make the dough: *To mix and knead by hand:* If you don't mind kneading (or even enjoy it like I do!), follow the same steps as for the machine, but pile the flour into a mountain on your countertop, make a well in the center, and then add the water. Mix the flour in from the edges until the flour and water combine into a cohesive mass. At that point, knead the dough until it feels stiff yet rollable like Play-Doh, about 5 minutes.

To mix and knead by machine: Pour the semolina into the bowl of a stand mixer fitted with the paddle attachment. Turn the machine to low speed and gradually add the water. Mix on low speed for about 5 minutes. The mixture will start out crumbly, then, as the flour hydrates, the clumps will get bigger. By the end of mixing, the dough should start clumping around the paddle and the mixer should struggle more because the dough is getting stiffer. You should also start to smell the semolina, a clean wheat aroma reminiscent of dried grass. If the dough is still in small crumbs by the end of mixing, drizzle in a little more water, 1 tablespoon at a time, just until the dough begins to come together.

Remove the paddle and use your hand to squeeze the dough together in the bowl, gathering the pieces into a single mass. The dough will be pretty stiff. Transfer it to your work surface and knead briefly yet forcefully with your hands to form a smoother dough. You'll know you're done kneading when you tug on the dough with your fingertips and it has enough strength to gently pull back into place. Shape the dough into a ball.

Let it rest: Cover and set aside for 30 minutes so the gluten can relax. You want the gluten relaxed so the dough can be shaped more easily by hand. At that point, if you cut the dough in half, it should have a consistently even pale-yellow color throughout, a sign of thorough hydration. It should also feel stiff yet rollable, almost like stiff Play-Doh. Use immediately or wrap the dough in plastic wrap and let it rest at room temperature for up to 6 hours.

Scan this code to watch a video of making this dough.

HAND-ROLLED DOUGH SHAPES

To keep things ultrasimple, you could just roll the dough into sheets with a pasta machine and cut it into strands of fettuccine or tagliolini. In that case, use the same rolling-and-cutting directions as for Chestnut Fettuccine (page 80) or Tagliolini (page 75). But the shapes that follow are so much more fun! Keep in mind: As this dough sits around, it will begin to dry out. Work quickly. To keep the dough shapeable as you work, have a spray bottle handy and mist the dough with water whenever it feels too dry to shape easily or, worse, starts cracking around the edges. After completing any of these shapes, cover the pasta loosely and use it within 1 hour. Or cover it tightly and refrigerate it for up to 1 day, or freeze it in a single layer, transfer it to an airtight container, and freeze it for up to 1 month. Take the pasta straight from the freezer to the pasta water. **To watch videos of making these shapes, scan the QR code for Pasta Doughs and Shapes on page 17.**

ORECCHIETTE

These "little ears" can be made into "big ears" (*orecchione*) by pinching off bigger pieces of dough. Either way, the rough side and the smoother dimple on the other side of the shape hold all kinds of ingredients, such as bits of lamb sausage in Orecchiette with Lamb Merguez and Fiore Sardo (page 229).

Cut the Hand-Rolled Dough (page 55) into 4 pieces and keep 3 pieces covered with a damp towel so they don't dry out. Roll the other piece on a lightly floured work surface into a rope about ½ inch in diameter. This shape is easier to make on a rough work surface than on a smooth surface. Use a table knife to cut off a ½-inch square piece of dough. This shape is all about finding and maintaining the right angle, pressure, and drag speed while pulling the knife blade over the dough. Place the knife parallel to your work surface and position the blade on the far side of the dough piece with your fingertips just touching the edge of the dough under the blade. Angle the blade against the dough at about 20 degrees to start, then drag the knife over the dough, gently holding the front edge of the dough down with your fingertips so the knife blade stretches the dough as you drag the knife toward you. As you drag, gradually widen the angle of the knife from 20 degrees to about 45 degrees. At the end of the drag, twist your fingers slightly to round off the shape. The pasta should have stretched and popped out the other end of the knife in a round shape about the size of a quarter (about 1 inch in diameter). The top side of the orecchiette should be rough. If necessary, put the smooth side over your thumb tip to deepen the dimple in the shape. Repeat with the remaining dough. Mist the ropes of dough with water as necessary to keep them moist enough to roll.

Scan this code to watch a video of making orecchiette.

TROCCOLI

Linguine-like ribbons from Puglia, troccoli are traditionally cut with a grooved rolling pin. Try them in Troccoli with Shrimp and Ginger Chili Crisp (page 161).

Divide the Culurgione Dough (page 54) into 4 pieces. Roll each piece into a sheet about 1/16 inch (1.5mm) thick and 14 inches long. You can do this with a rolling pin or a pasta machine. (As you work, keep the other dough pieces covered to prevent them from drying out.) Lay a pasta sheet on a lightly floured work surface and trim the edges square. Cut the sheet into troccoli using a troccoli cutter (grooved rolling pin) rolled over the length of the dough with firm pressure. You could also use a linguine cutter attachment on a pasta machine for a similar width of about 1/16 inch. Or use a sharp knife and a ruler, folding the dough over itself first to make it narrower, then cutting across the dough into 1/16-inch widths. The final shape should look somewhat like thick square spaghetti. Generously dust the noodles with semolina flour and coil them into 2 nests on a lightly floured sheet pan. Repeat with the remaining dough.

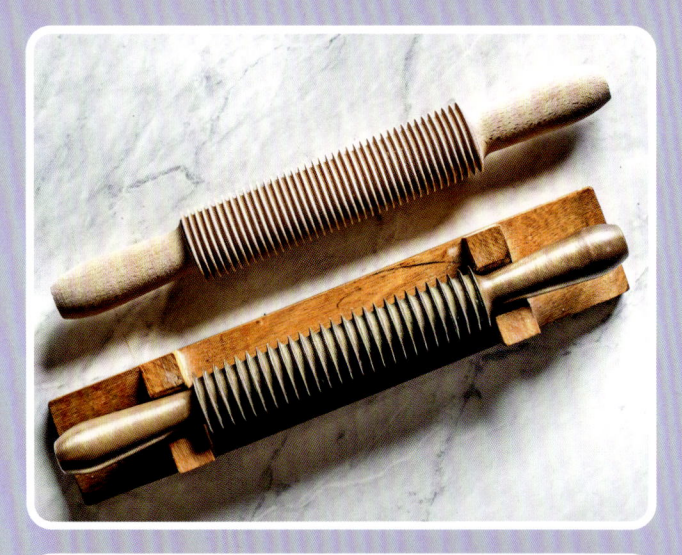

Scan this code to watch a video of making tagliolini. It's similar to making troccoli with a knife, but for troccoli you make the pasta a bit thinner and narrower.

58   THE PASTA BOOK

TROFIE

A classic Ligurian shape, these short pasta twists are made by rubbing your palm over a little piece of pasta. Try them in Trofie with Pistachio, Artichokes, and Orange Zest (page 100).

Pinch off about one-quarter of the Hand-Rolled Dough (page 55) and keep the remaining dough covered with a damp kitchen towel to prevent it from drying out. Moisten your work surface with a damp towel so the pasta has some stiction. Hold the pinched-off dough in one hand and with your other hand, pinch off about a nickel-size piece of dough and place it on the work surface. Roll the dough into a sort of slug shape with your palm. Hover the meaty outside part of your palm over it with the bottom of your palm near the top of the dough. Using heavy pressure, smoosh down and roll your palm over the dough toward your body diagonally, starting with the bottom of your palm and ending with the top. A corkscrew shape should twist out from under your hand. When you get the pressure even, each corkscrew should be 1 to 2 inches long and a little less than ¼ inch in diameter. Flick the trofie away onto a lightly semolina-floured area or transfer it to a lightly semolina-floured sheet pan. Repeat with the remaining dough.

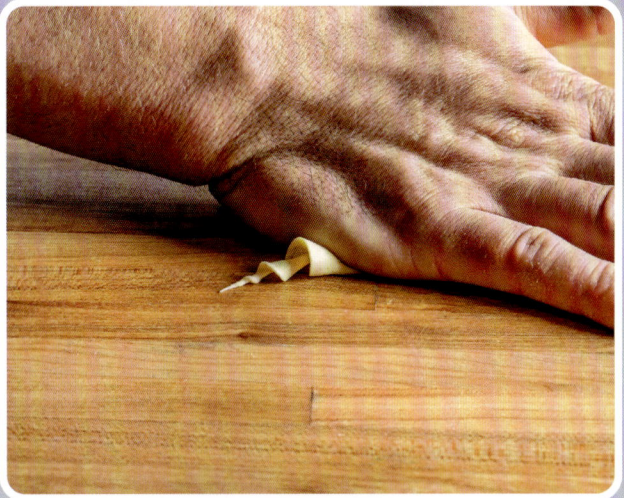

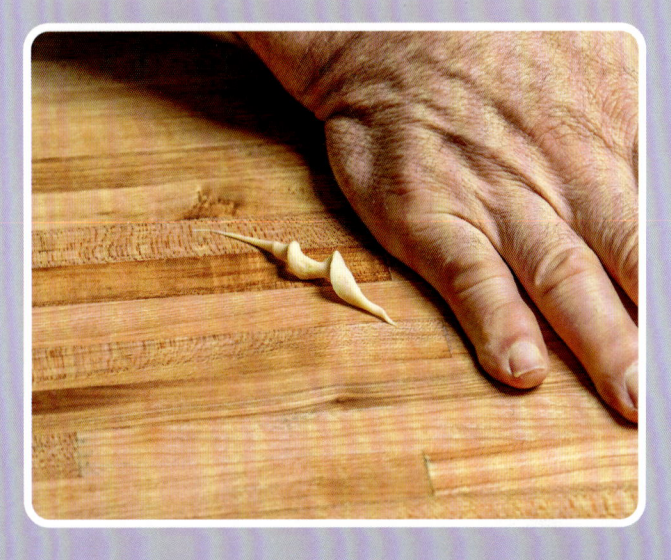

Scan this code to watch a video of making trofie.

FERRICELLI

From Basilicata in southern Italy, ferricelli is named for the metal rod that the pasta is rolled around. The hollowed-out center makes it great for thick sauces like Bolognese. Try it in Ferricelli with Beef Heart Bolognese (page 234). Or make masa ferricelli with the Masa Dough (page 91) and try it in Masa Ferricelli with Pork Shank Ragù (page 222).

Pinch off about one-eighth of the Hand-Rolled Dough (page 55) and roll it on your work surface into a rope about ¼ inch in diameter. Keep the remaining dough covered with a damp kitchen towel to prevent it from drying out. Cut the rope into pieces about 2 inches long. To shape the ferricelli, moisten the surface of a piece with a damp towel so the pasta has some stiction. Dip a thin metal rod, knitting needle, wooden skewer, or chopstick (about ⅛ inch in diameter) in flour, place it parallel on a dough piece, and then roll the dough and rod back and forth on the table to hollow out the center into an irregular twisted tube. The tube will get a thinner and longer as you roll. Place on a lightly semolina-floured sheet pan and repeat with the remaining dough.

Scan this code to watch a video of making ferricelli.

THE PASTA BOOK

RASCHIATELLI

Resembling cavatelli, this shape originates from Puglia. The groove in the center holds sauce like a hoagie roll holds fillings. Try it in Raschiatelli Arrabbiata with Provolone (page 106) and Raschiatelli with Guinea Hen Bolognese (page 188).

Pinch off about one-eighth of the Hand-Rolled Dough (page 55) and roll it into a rope about ¼ inch in diameter on a very lightly floured surface. Keep the remaining dough covered with a damp kitchen towel to prevent it from drying out. Cut the rope into pieces about 2 inches long. To shape the raschiatelli, use three fingers and medium pressure to roll each piece along the length of a cavarola board or gnocchi board so that the piece curls into an elongated C-shape and retains the design of the board on the outside. If you don't have a board, just roll each piece on your work surface to create the C-shape. The pasta should almost look like an empty peapod with indentations from your fingers where the peas would be (that's where the sauce will get caught). Place the raschiatelli on a lightly semolina-floured sheet pan and repeat with the remaining dough.

Scan this code to watch a video of making raschiatelli.

PASTA DOUGHS AND SHAPES

GNOCCHI SARDI

This is one of the most popular pastas in Sardinia, made a little differently in every home. It also goes by the name *malloreddus*, which could refer to "fat little calves" or "a little morsel," depending on who you ask. Like cavatelli, these little pastas are grooved on the outside, often bearing the imprint of whatever wicker basket is nearby to roll the pasta on. Try them in Gnocchi Sardi with Monkfish Puttanesca (page 162) and Gnocchi Sardi with Lobster, Corn, and Yuzu Kosho (page 259).

Cut the Hand-Rolled Dough (page 55) into 8 pieces and keep 6 of the pieces covered so the dough doesn't dry out. Roll the other pieces on a lightly floured work surface into ropes ¼ inch in diameter and then cut the ropes crosswise on a slight angle into ½-inch diamonds. Dust the pieces with semolina flour and roll each piece on a grooved gnocchi board, cavarola board, or the back of a fork on a slight angle from the short point to the short point with firm pressure to create a ridged oval shape similar to but a little shorter and fatter than cavatelli. Place on a lightly floured sheet pan and repeat with the remaining dough.

Scan this code to watch a video of making gnocchi sardi.

THE PASTA BOOK

LORIGHITTAS

Another Sardinian pasta, this one from the township of Morgongiori is so classic that the Italian government designated it as a traditional regional food product (Prodotto Agroalimentare Tradizionale, or PAT). It's made from spaghetti and looks like a loop of braided rope. Try it in Lorighittas with Calamari, Meyer Lemon, and Basil (page 148).

Divide the Hand-Rolled Dough (page 55) into 6 pieces and keep 4 of the pieces covered so the dough doesn't dry out. Roll the other pieces on a long floured work surface into narrow ropes about 1/16 inch in diameter. Cut the ropes into 9-inch lengths to make spaghetti. This may take a while, so keep your unused dough covered as you work. You could also roll the dough into sheets, cut the sheets into 9-inch lengths, and run each length through the spaghetti cutter on your pasta machine to make spaghetti. To form each lorighitta, flour your hands. Loosely wrap a piece of round spaghetti twice around two fingers (or three, if you have small hands). The ends of the spaghetti should meet and there should be two rounds of spaghetti around your fingers. Now pinch the two ends of the spaghetti strand together, wetting your fingers a little if necessary to get the ends to stick together. Remove your two fingers, and gently roll the double rounds of spaghetti together between your fingertips about five times to create a twisted rope shape 1½ to 2 inches in diameter. The finished pasta should look sort of like the loop of a lasso with no extra rope. Lay the lorighitta on a lightly semolina-floured sheet pan and repeat with the remaining dough.

Scan this code to watch a video of making lorighittas.

ANDARINOS DI USINI

Andarinos nearly became extinct! This shape is similar to trofie or fusilli but with a sharper edge and an imprinted design from ribbed glass or a grooved wooden board. The shape originated in Sardinia in the seventeenth century (and was often flavored with saffron), but it fell out of favor, except in the homes of a few women in Usini, a small town in the Sassari province. We can't thank them enough for keeping this traditional pasta alive. Try it in Andarinos di Usini with Capon Ragù, Pistachios, and Apricots (page 191).

Divide the Hand-Rolled Dough (page 55) into 6 pieces. Cover 5 pieces with a damp towel to keep them from drying out. From the other piece, pinch off a marble-size piece of dough. Roll it back and forth on a dry work surface into a slug about 3 inches long and ⅛ inch in diameter. Place the slug on a grooved gnocchi board or other grooved board, pointing the slug at 1 o'clock. It helps to use a board with shallow instead of deep grooves. Roll the long edge of your thumb over the slug toward 11 o'clock to make a sharp-ridged corkscrew shape. Use your other thumb at the same time to help make the shape. You could also hold a pastry card or bench scraper on a slight angle over the slug, then press and drag it over the slug with medium pressure to create the sharp-ridged corkscrew shape. Dust the piece lightly with semolina flour and repeat with the remaining dough.

Scan this code to watch a video of making andarinos di usini.

BUSIATI

These diagonal coils of pasta are named after busa, a thick, long-stemmed grass found in Sicily that was used to shape the pasta. You can also use a knitting needle or other long, narrow rod. Try it in Busiati Grano Arso with Beef Shank and Peaches (page 236).

Pinch off about one-eighth of the Hand-Rolled Dough (page 55) or Grano Arso Dough (page 90) and roll it on a work surface into a long rope about ¼ inch in diameter. Cut the rope into 3-inch pieces and lightly dust the pieces with flour. To shape each busiato, place a piece of dough so the ends point east and west as you look at them. Use a long, very narrow, round metal or wooden rod, such as a long, thin skewer, about as thick as an umbrella stretcher (¹⁄₁₆ to ⅛ inch in diameter). Position the tip of the rod at the left end of a 3-inch piece of dough at a 45-degree angle, and roll the rod away from you to gently flatten the pasta and wind it around the rod, creating a diagonal closed-coil shape. Gently remove the busiato from the rod and place on a lightly floured sheet pan. Repeat with the remaining dough. Cover the pasta loosely and use it within 1 hour. Or cover it tightly and refrigerate it for up to 1 day, or freeze it in a single layer, transfer it to an airtight container, and freeze it for up to 1 month. Take the pasta straight from the freezer to the pasta water.

Scan this code to watch a video of making busiati.

PASTA DOUGHS AND SHAPES

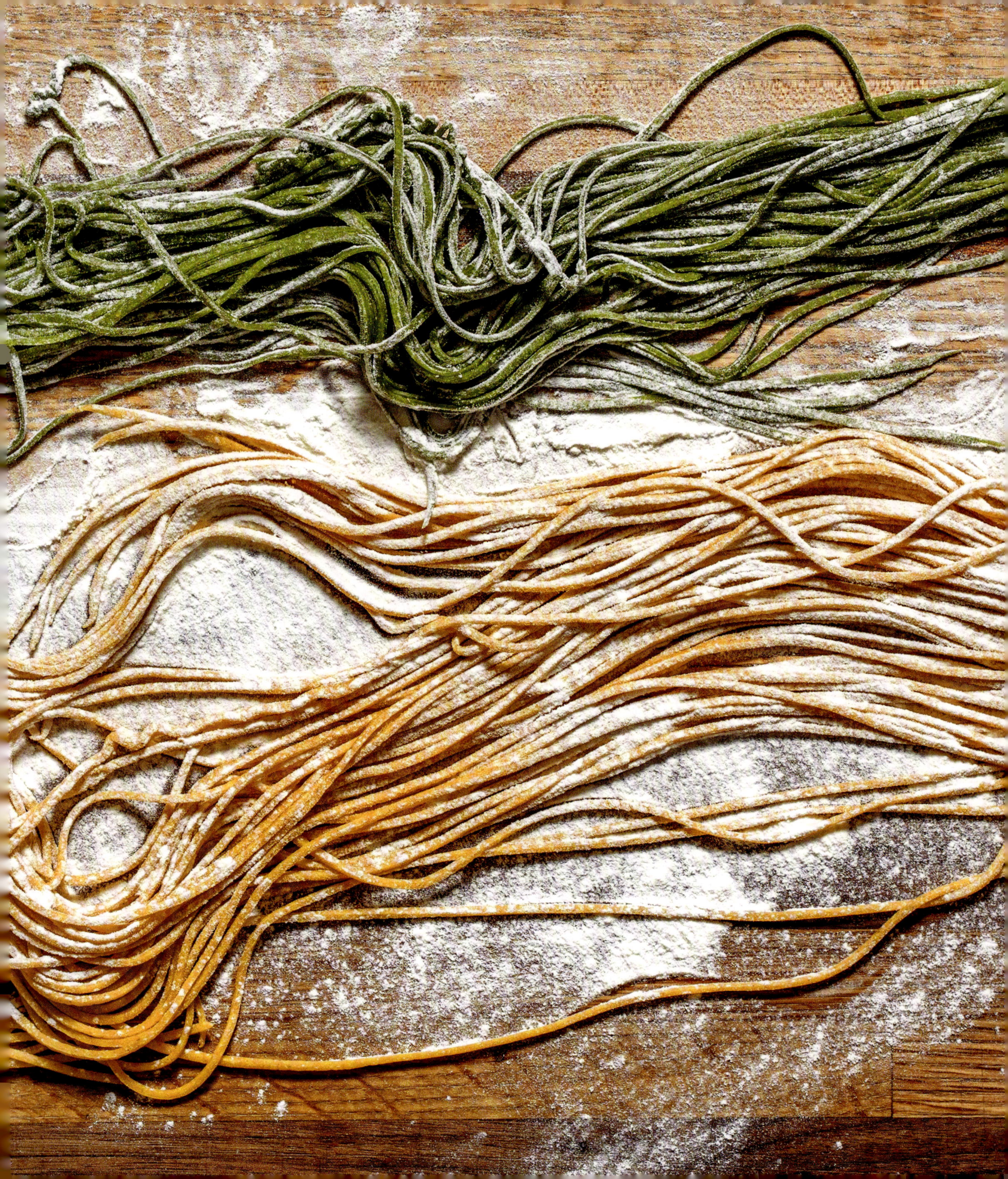

CHITARRA DOUGH

When I make semolina pasta, I often don't add eggs. But for long noodles, a little egg gives the dough more strength and a richer texture. This dough is perfect for a long spaghetti-like noodle that can be rolled thick and still melt away on your tongue. Try this dough with other long noodles, too, like pappardelle or fettuccine. In that case, just roll the dough a bit thinner. To watch a video of making chitarra pasta, scan the QR code on page 68. **MAKES 680 GRAMS (ABOUT 1½ POUNDS); 6 TO 8 SERVINGS**

- 415 grams (2½ cups) semolina flour, such as Caputo, plus more for dusting
- 240 grams eggs (4 large)
- 13.5 grams (1 tablespoon) extra-virgin olive oil
- Water, as needed

Make the dough: Pour the semolina flour onto a countertop or into a medium bowl. Make a well in the center and add the eggs and olive oil to the well. Using your hands or a fork, stir together the liquids until blended, then gradually stir in the flour from the edges. If needed, add water, a tablespoon at a time, until the dough comes together. Mix just until the dough can be formed into a rough ball, adding a little more water as necessary.

Turn the dough out onto a lightly floured work surface and knead it until it feels smooth, about 5 minutes, kneading in a little flour if necessary to keep the dough from sticking. You'll know the gluten is developed when you tug on the dough with your fingertips and it gently pulls back into place.

Let it rest: Shape the dough into a ball, cover, and let rest for 30 to 60 minutes. You can also wrap it in plastic and refrigerate it for up to 3 days, or freeze it for up to 1 month. Thaw frozen dough overnight in the refrigerator. Before using, take the chill off by letting the dough stand at room temperature for 15 minutes.

> **LEVEL UP**
>
> **Hay Dough:** Add spinach puree to create a different flavor and a green color (similar to hay). Dunk 8 ounces mature spinach leaves (tough stems removed) in salted boiling water and cook until bright green, 3 to 4 minutes. The spinach must be soft enough to puree until smooth or the pasta won't taste as silky and tender. Use tongs or a spider strainer to transfer the spinach to a bowl of ice water and let sit until cold, 1 to 2 minutes. Reserve the cooking water. Remove the spinach from the ice water, squeeze out all the moisture, and place in a small food processor. Process until very smooth, adding some of the reserved cooking water if necessary to make a smooth puree. Transfer the pureed spinach to a medium-mesh sieve set over a bowl, cover, and refrigerate for about 12 hours to drain off the excess moisture. Add ½ cup of the drained spinach puree along with the eggs when you mix the Chitarra Dough.

CHITARRA DOUGH SHAPES

CHITARRA DOUGH TAGLIOLINI

If you don't have a chitarra pasta cutter, you can cut the fresh pasta by hand. Technically, you'll be making tagliolini instead of chitarra, but it will still be good! Try this shape in Tagliolini with Chicken Liver Ragù (page 180).

Roll the Chitarra Dough (page 67) into sheets about ⅛ inch thick. Lay a pasta sheet on a lightly floured work surface and trim the edges square. Cut the sheets into 10-inch lengths. Fold each length in half crosswise over itself, then fold in half crosswise again. Using a sharp knife, cut each folded piece crosswise into thin strips about ⅛ inch wide. You should end up with long strands that resemble square spaghetti. Dust the strands with semolina flour and place them in nests on a floured sheet pan. Repeat with the remaining dough. Use the tagliolini within 1 hour or freeze the nests in a single layer, then transfer the pasta to an airtight container and freeze for up to 1 month. Take the pasta straight from the freezer to the pasta water.

STRAW AND HAY TAGLIOLINI OR CHITARRA

For the classic Tuscan combination of green spinach pasta and yellow egg pasta (*paglia e fieno*, or "straw and hay"), we use both chitarra dough and hay dough. Try this combo in Straw and Hay Tagliolini with Chicken Liver Ragù (page 180).

Make both the Chitarra Dough (page 67) and the Hay Dough (page 67), using 8 ounces of each. You can mix, roll, and cut the two doughs separately, then use both pastas in the same pasta dish. Or you can roll the two doughs together and cut them into a single pasta that's green on one side and yellow on the other. For the first way, flatten each dough ball into a disk and roll the disks separately into ⅛-inch-thick sheets. For the second way, place one disk on top of the other and roll the two doughs together into a ⅛-inch-thick sheet that is green on one side and yellow on the other. For tagliolini, follow the tagliolini cutting directions on page 75; for chitarra, use the chitarra cutting directions on the opposite page.

Scan this code to watch a video of making spaghetti alla chitarra.

SPAGHETTI ALLA CHITARRA

Similar to tonnarelli from the nearby Lazio region, this square spaghetti originated in Abruzzo. It's cut by laying a pasta sheet onto a chitarra, essentially taut guitar strings, and passing a rolling pin over the dough to cut it into thick, narrow strands. You can easily buy a chitarra pasta cutter online, or you can always use a knife. Try this shape in Spaghetti alla Chitarra with Basil, Poppy Seed, and Prosciutto (page 215).

Roll the Chitarra Dough (page 67) into sheets about ⅛ inch thick. Lay a pasta sheet on a lightly floured work surface. Cut the sheet into pieces just a little smaller than the width and length of your chitarra (the pasta will stretch as you roll it over the chitarra). Generously flour one of the pieces and lay it lengthwise on the chitarra strings. Roll a floured rolling pin back and forth over the pasta to press it into the strings, pressing harder if necessary to cut the pasta. To make the pasta fall beneath the strings, strum your fingers across the strings like playing a guitar. Generously dust the noodles with semolina flour and coil them into nests on a lightly floured sheet pan; you should get 8 nests from 1 pound of pasta. Cover and use within a few hours or refrigerate for up to 8 hours. You can also freeze the nests in an airtight container for up to 1 month. Take the pasta straight from the freezer to the pasta water. To watch a video of making Spaghetti alla Chitarra, scan the QR code for Pasta Doughs and Shapes on page 17.

PASTA DOUGHS AND SHAPES

HALF-AND-HALF EGG DOUGH

This is the first pasta dough I learned in Italy and it's still my go-to: versatile enough for everything from pappardelle to garganelli. It's made with half whole eggs and half egg yolks by weight. The whole eggs add water from the whites, making the dough a little easier to roll out than a straight Egg Yolk Dough (page 74). You can also roll it a bit thicker, which is perfect for noodles like tagliatelle and fettuccine where you want the pasta to hold more sauce. The mix of flours here—tipo "00" and semolina—gives the pasta a great balance of silkiness and chew. It's the perfect dough to start off your pasta-making journey. Once you're comfortable with this one, try the Egg Yolk Dough (page 74) and the other variations. To watch a video of making this dough and rolling it out, scan the QR code on page 72. **MAKES 475 GRAMS (ABOUT 1 POUND); 4 TO 6 SERVINGS**

187.5 grams (1⅓ cups) tipo "00" flour, such as Spadoni Gran Mugnaio, or King Arthur all-purpose flour, plus more for dusting

62.5 grams (½ cup) semolina flour, such as Caputo, plus more for dusting

120 grams whole eggs (2 large)

100 grams egg yolks (5 large)

7 grams (1½ teaspoons) extra-virgin olive oil

Water, as needed

Make the dough: *To mix and knead by hand:* Combine the tipo "00" flour and semolina flour on your countertop. Build the flour into a mountain, then make a well in the center so it looks like a volcano. Pour the whole eggs, egg yolks, and oil into the volcano and then mix the liquids together with your hands or a fork (you could also premix the liquids in a small bowl before adding them to the volcano). The egg whites and yolks should be well combined and well mixed with the oil. Start mixing the flour from the edges of the volcano into the liquid, and keep mixing in the flour until all or almost all the flour is combined with the liquid. To keep your bare hands from getting caked with dough, you could use a pastry card or bench scraper, gathering and "chopping" the flour and liquid together into a paste, and then using your hands to gather and press all the stray bits together into a cohesive dough. The mixture will be raggy at first and then come together into a cohesive dough, 2 to 3 minutes.

Eggs vary in water content so you may have enough water in the mix already. But if the dough is crumbly, add a little water, a tablespoon at a time. Or, if the dough is wet, add a little more tipo "00" flour, a tablespoon at a time, until the dough comes together. Generally, I like to start with a wetter dough because it's easier to add flour than it is to add water. When it comes together, the dough consistency should be somewhat soft, like Play-Doh.

Knead the dough it until it feels silky, smooth, and firm, about 5 minutes, kneading in a little flour if necessary to keep the dough from sticking. You'll know the dough is ready when it feels somewhat stiff and somewhat soft, just a bit stiffer than Play-Doh. When you tug on the dough with your fingertips, it should gently pull back into place.

RECIPE CONTINUES

PASTA DOUGHS AND SHAPES 71

To mix and knead by machine: Switch the order of operations, starting with the liquids, then adding the flour. Pour the whole eggs, egg yolks, and oil into the bowl of a stand mixer and mix with the paddle attachment on low speed until everything is well blended. Gradually add the tipo "00" flour and semolina flour, mixing just until the flour and liquids come together into a cohesive dough, 2 to 3 minutes. Add more flour or water if necessary for the dough to come together. It will be raggy at first and then reach a consistency similar to soft Play-Doh, sticking to the bowl and paddle.

To knead the dough in the machine, switch to medium-low speed and let it go until the dough becomes stiffer and you hear the mixer working harder, 2 to 3 minutes. (For larger quantities of dough, switch to the dough hook before kneading.) Use a dough scraper to scrape the dough from the bowl and paddle, then turn it out onto a lightly floured work surface. Gather the dough bits and knead them together into a ball, adding a little flour if necessary to prevent sticking. You'll know the dough is ready when it feels somewhat stiff and somewhat soft, just a bit stiffer than Play-Doh. When you tug on the dough with your fingertips, it should gently pull back into place.

Let it rest: Shape the dough into a smooth disk, cover, and set it aside for at least 30 minutes so the gluten can relax and the water can fully hydrate the flour. At that point, if you cut the dough in half, it should have a consistently even yellow color throughout, a sign of thorough hydration. If you're not using the dough right away, you can wrap it in plastic and refrigerate it for up to 3 days. Better yet, vacuum-seal the dough to help preserve the fresh flavor and yellow color for even longer, up to 1 week. You can also freeze the dough for up to 1 month. Thaw your frozen dough in the refrigerator overnight before using it. Or quickly thaw it in a microwave oven on 50% power in 5-second increments just until cool to the touch. Don't cook the dough!

Roll out the dough: Cut the rested dough into 4 equal pieces (or fewer if you're comfortable with bigger, longer sheets of pasta). If the dough was chilled, let the pieces sit, covered, at room temperature for 10 minutes to take the chill off. Gently flatten or preroll each piece with a rolling pin so it's wide enough to fit the width of your pasta roller and thin enough to fit in the roller on its widest setting.

Lightly flour your work surface and set the pasta roller to its widest setting. Lightly flour one disk of dough, pass it through the roller, and then lightly dust the rolled dough with flour, brushing off the excess with your hands. Set the roller to the next narrowest setting and pass the dough through, again dusting with flour and brushing off the excess. After going down two settings, fold the dough in half crosswise over itself and cut about ¼ inch off the corners at the fold. This folding and cutting laminates the dough, strengthening it and helping to create an evenly wide sheet of dough.

Scan this code to watch a video of making Half-and-Half Egg Dough and rolling it out.

Continue passing the dough once or twice through each progressively narrower setting, folding and laminating it once or twice more to strengthen it. As the sheet gets longer, drape it over the backs of your hands to easily feed it through the roller. Roll the pasta to your preferred thickness, using the chart on page 50.

Cut the dough: Lay a pasta sheet on a lightly floured work surface and use a cutting wheel or knife (or the cutting attachment on your pasta machine) to create the right pasta shape for the dish you are making. As you work, keep the remaining pasta sheets covered with a damp towel to keep them from drying out. After cutting or shaping the pasta, if you want to hold it for later, dust it with semolina flour, cover, and use within 1 hour. Or refrigerate it for a few hours. You can also freeze it in a single layer and then transfer the frozen pasta to a zipper-lock bag and freeze it for up to 1 month. Take the pasta right from the freezer to the pasta water.

PASTA DOUGHS AND SHAPES

LEVEL UP

For more flavor, replace half the tipo "00" flour in the Half-and-Half Egg Dough with bolted Redeemer flour, a hard red winter wheat flour that's been sifted to remove some of the bran. You can buy it online from Castle Valley Mill and other flour merchants.

Egg Yolk Dough: For a simple variation on the Half-and-Half Egg Dough, use all egg yolks. Follow the recipe as directed, but skip the whole eggs and use 200 grams egg yolks (10 large) instead, along with 2 tablespoons water. The extra yolks add more fat and protein for a super-tender, silky dough that's strong enough to roll super thin. Use this dough when you want something a little more special, like for delicate raviolis and extra-rich pasta dishes. To prevent it from drying out and cracking, work fast and keep a spray bottle handy to mist the dough with water as you work.

Pimentón Dough: You can use this variation with either the Half-and-Half Egg Dough or Egg Yolk Dough (page 70 and above). Mix a generous 18 grams (2½ tablespoons) pimentón (smoked paprika) into the flours. Increase the olive oil to 14 grams (1 tablespoon) and proceed with the recipe.

Saffron Dough: Use this variation with the Egg Yolk Dough (above). Steep 1 gram (1½ teaspoons) saffron threads in 2 tablespoons hot tap water in a medium bowl until the water cools to room temperature, about 30 minutes. When the water is at room temp, mix in the egg yolks. Mix the saffron-egg mixture into the flours and proceed with the recipe.

Mint Dough: Use this variation with either the Half-and-Half Egg Dough or Egg Yolk Dough (page 70 and above). Bring a large pot of water to a boil. Set up a bowl of ice water. Add 20 grams (¾ cup packed) fresh mint leaves to the boiling water and blanch them until bright green, about 15 seconds. Using a spider strainer or slotted spoon, immediately transfer the mint to the ice water to stop the cooking. When cooled, remove the mint from the ice water and shake off the excess water, pressing gently. You should have about 45 grams (¼ cup packed) blanched mint. Transfer the mint to a mini food processor or high-powered blender, add the egg yolks called for in the recipe, and puree until smooth. The finer you puree the mint, the fewer specks you'll have in the pasta. Add the puree to the bowl along with the oil and proceed with the recipe. For a deeper green color, cool the blanching water and use that as the water in the dough recipe.

Chestnut Dough: Use this variation with the Egg Yolk Dough (above left). For the flour, use 62.5 grams (½ cup) bread flour, such as King Arthur, 62.5 grams (½ cup) tipo "00" flour, 62.5 grams (½ cup) semolina flour, and 50 grams (⅓ cup) chestnut flour, such as Sanniti. Omit the oil. Proceed with the recipe.

Buckwheat Dough: Use this variation with the Egg Yolk Dough (above left). For the flour, use 70.25 grams (½ cup) bread flour, such as King Arthur, 70.25 grams (½ cup) tipo "00" flour, 62.5 grams (½ cup) semolina flour, and 47 grams (⅓ cup) buckwheat flour, such as Bob's Red Mill. Omit the oil. Proceed with the recipe.

Rye Dough: Use this variation with the Egg Yolk Dough (above left). For the flour, use 95 grams (1 cup) rye flour, such as Bob's Red Mill, 95 grams (⅔ cup) tipo "00" flour, 70 grams (½ cup) semolina flour, and 4.5 grams (2½ teaspoons) unsweetened cocoa powder, preferably Dutch-process. Omit the oil. Proceed with the recipe.

EGG DOUGH SHAPES

In general, you want to roll egg dough thicker for ribbon pastas like pappardelle, fettuccine, tagliatelle, and tagliolini. Roll a bit thinner for square shapes like mandilli and fazzoletti. Roll it as thin as you can for stuffed pastas like ravioli and agnolotti. For basic pasta rolling info, see Rolling and Shaping (page 47). After completing any of these shapes, cover the pasta loosely and use it within 4 hours, or freeze it in a single layer, transfer it to an airtight container, and freeze it for up to 1 month. Take the pasta straight from the freezer to the pasta water. To watch videos of making all these shapes, scan the QR code for Pasta Doughs and Shapes on page 17.

MANDILLI

This pasta is the simplest of all. Just cut the rolled dough into big squares. It's known in Liguria as *mandilli de saea* or "silk handkerchiefs" and served with the local specialty, pesto Genovese. Try them in Mandilli with Perfect Basil Pesto (page 103).

Roll 1 pound of Half-and-Half Egg Dough (page 70) or Egg Yolk Dough (page 74) into sheets about 1/16 inch (1.5mm) thick. Cover the remaining pasta with a damp towel to keep it from drying out. Lay a pasta sheet on a lightly floured work surface and trim the edges square. Cut the sheet into 7-inch squares, preferably with a fluted cutter. (If your pasta roller makes sheets less than 7 inches wide, just cut the sheet into 7-inch lengths to make rectangles instead of squares.) Dust the pieces with semolina flour and spread them on a lightly floured sheet pan. Repeat with the remaining dough.

TAGLIOLINI

In Italian, *taglio* means "cut," and these pasta ribbons are simply "cut small" or narrow, about 1/8 inch wide. When made with Egg Yolk Dough (page 74), the same cut is called Tajarin (page 76). Try these pasta ribbons in Lobster Tagliolini with 'Nduja Bread Crumbs (page 150).

Roll 1 pound of Half-and-Half Egg Dough (page 70) into sheets about 1/8 inch thick. Lay a pasta sheet on a lightly floured work surface and trim the edges square (keep the remaining pasta covered as you work). Cut the sheets into 14-inch lengths. Lightly flour the dough and then fold each length in half crosswise over itself, then fold in half crosswise again. Rotate the folded dough one-quarter turn and then use a sharp knife to cut each folded piece crosswise into thin strips about 1/8 inch wide. You should end up with 14-inch-long strands that resemble square spaghetti. Instead of cutting with a knife, if you have a pasta cutting machine, you could also pass the flat 14-inch-long sheets through the small spaghetti cutter. Either way, lightly dust the strands with semolina flour and place them in nests on a lightly floured sheet pan. Repeat with the remaining dough.

Scan this code to watch a video of making tagliolini.

PASTA DOUGHS AND SHAPES

TAGLIATELLE

Similar to tagliolini, these strands are just cut a bit wider, about ¼ inch wide. It's a very common pasta shape in the Emilia-Romagna region around Bologna and similar to the fettuccine of Rome. Try tagliatelle in place of fettuccine in Chestnut Fettuccine with Wild Boar Ragù (page 211).

Roll 1 pound of Half-and-Half Egg Dough (page 70) into sheets about ⅛ inch thick. Lay a pasta sheet on a lightly floured work surface and trim the edges square (keep the remaining pasta covered as you work). Cut the sheets into 14-inch lengths. Lightly flour the dough and then fold each length in half crosswise over itself, then fold in half crosswise again. Using a sharp knife, cut each folded piece crosswise into strips about ¼ inch wide. You should end up with 14-inch-long strands that resemble fettuccine or linguine. Instead of cutting with a knife, if you have a pasta cutting machine, you could also pass the flat 14-inch-long sheets through the tagliatelle or fettuccine cutter. Or if you have a rolling tagliatelle cutter, you can use that to cut the pasta. Either way, dust the cut strands of pasta with semolina flour and place them in nests on a lightly floured sheet pan. Repeat with the remaining dough.

TAJARIN

A Piemonte classic, famously made with 40 egg yolks per kilo of flour. Like tagliolini, tajarin is a narrow ribbon pasta, but it's made with a dough so rich in egg yolks that the pasta stays bright yellow even when cooked. Try it in Tajarin with Rabbit Bolognese (page 187).

Roll 1 pound of Egg Yolk Dough (page 74) into sheets a little less than ⅛ inch thick. Lay a pasta sheet on a lightly floured work surface and trim the edges square (keep the remaining pasta covered as you work). Cut the sheet into 10-inch lengths. Lightly flour the dough and then fold each length in half crosswise over itself, then fold in half crosswise again. Using a sharp knife, cut each folded piece crosswise into thin strips a little less than ⅛ inch wide. You should end up with 10-inch-long strands that resemble square spaghetti. Dust the strands with semolina flour and place them in nests on a floured sheet pan. Repeat with the remaining dough.

FARFALLE

These "butterflies" have been made in Lombardia for centuries. They're simply pasta rectangles cut with a fluted cutter and pinched to resemble butterflies or bow ties. Try them in Farfalle with Guanciale, Peas, and Tarragon (page 218).

Roll 1 pound of Half-and-Half Egg Dough (page 70) or Egg Yolk Dough (page 74) into sheets about 1/16 inch (1.5mm) thick. Lay a pasta sheet on a lightly floured work surface and trim the edges square (keep the remaining pasta covered as you work). Cut the sheet into 2½ × 1¼-inch rectangles, preferably with a fluted cutter to create a ruffled edge on the two short sides of each rectangle (these will be the "wings" of the "butterfly"). To form each farfalla, place your index finger in the center of a rectangle and place your thumb and middle finger on the straight edges of the rectangle on opposite sides of your index finger. Your fingers and thumb should be lined up in a row parallel with the ruffled edges of the rectangle. Pinch your thumb and middle finger toward your index finger in the center, keeping your index finger in place to help create the folds. As the pasta folds up, remove your index finger and firmly pinch the folds of pasta together in the center to hold the shape. Repeat with the remaining rectangles. Lightly dust the farfalle with semolina flour and place them on a lightly floured sheet pan. Repeat with the remaining dough.

Scan this code to watch a video of making farfalle.

PASTA DOUGHS AND SHAPES

GARGANELLI

Garganelli means "chicken gullets," and similar to penne, this pasta has a perfect hollow tube shape for sucking up creamy sauces. Try it in Garganelli with Corn and Scallions (page 108).

Roll 1 pound Half-and-Half Egg Dough (page 70) or Egg Yolk Dough (page 74) into sheets about ⅛ inch thick. Lay a pasta sheet on a lightly floured work surface and trim the edges square (keep the remaining pasta covered as you work). Cut the sheet into 2-inch squares. Place a garganelli comb or gnocchi board on your work surface, or securely tape a large, clean fine-toothed pocket comb to a clean part of the surface. (You can also use a more decorative cavarola board to create a unique look for the garganelli.) Flour it lightly. To form each garganello, place a square of pasta on the comb or gnocchi board so one corner is pointing in the same direction as the teeth of the comb. Lightly flour a wooden dowel or clean round pencil ¼ inch in diameter and lay it over the pasta perpendicular to the teeth of the comb. Fold the bottom corner of the pasta over the dowel, then roll the pasta loosely around the dowel. Roll back and forth on the comb or board a couple of times, pressing gently into the ridges of the comb to seal the edges of the pasta and create a ridged quill shape similar to penne. Slide the pasta off the dowel and set it on a lightly floured sheet pan. Repeat with the remaining sheets.

Scan this code to watch a video of making garganelli.

PIMENTÓN SORPRESINE

These "little surprises" look like tortellini but without any filling. Surprise! They're shaped from small pasta squares and are fun to make with kids. Try them in Pimentón Sorpresine with Mussels (page 154).

Roll 1 pound Pimentón Dough (page 74) into sheets about 1/16 inch (1.5mm) thick. Lay a pasta sheet on a lightly floured work surface and trim the edges square (keep the remaining pasta covered as you work). Cut the sheet into 2-inch squares. For each sorpresina, pick up a square and bring two opposite corners together, pinching them together at the point to make a triangle. Leave the other corners flared open. Hold the pasta by the newly conjoined corners and, using your other hand and thumb, make a dimple in the center and bend the pasta backward by the other two points, pinching those two points together. To help open up the hole in the middle, gently push the sides toward the center, creating a hole. The finished pasta should somewhat resemble a wonton or fortune cookie. Lightly dust the sorpresina with semolina flour and place it on a lightly floured sheet pan. Repeat with the remaining pasta dough.

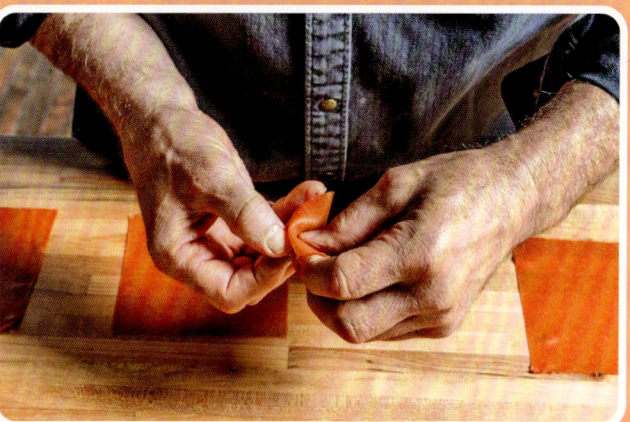

MINT FAZZOLETTI

Another name for "handkerchiefs," *fazzoletti* **are cut smaller than Mandilli (page 75) and are just as popular in Liguria. Try them in Mint Fazzoletti with Lamb al Latte Ragù (page 231).**

Roll 1 pound Mint Dough (page 74) into sheets about 1/16 inch (1.5mm) thick. Lay a pasta sheet on a lightly floured work surface and trim the edges square (keep the remaining pasta covered as you work). Cut the sheet into 2½- to 3-inch squares, using a fluted cutter if desired. Dust the squares with semolina flour and place on a lightly floured sheet pan. Repeat with the remaining dough.

Scan this code to watch a video of making pimentón sorpresine.

CHESTNUT FETTUCCINE

"Little ribbons," *fettuccine* are often paired with a thick, rich meat ragù. They're similar to tagliatelle but descended from the much more delicate *capelli d'angelo* or "angel hair" pasta popular during the Italian Renaissance. Try them in Chestnut Fettuccine with Wild Boar Ragù (page 211).

Roll 1 pound Chestnut Dough (page 74) into sheets about ⅛ inch thick. Lay a pasta sheet on a lightly floured work surface and trim the edges square (keep the remaining pasta covered as you work). Cut the sheet into 14-inch lengths. Fit your stand mixer or pasta machine with the fettuccine cutter (about ¼-inch widths) and set it to medium speed. Feed 1 length of dough at a time through the cutter and then dust the dough lightly with semolina flour as it comes out of the cutter. Form the fettuccine into round nests and set them on a floured sheet pan. Repeat with the remaining dough.

PUMPERNICKEL PAPPARDELLE

Originating in Tuscany, *pappardelle* get their name from the word *pappare*, which literally means "to gobble up," a reference to the thickness and width of these pasta ribbons. They're perfect for absorbing rich meat sauces. Try them in Pumpernickel Pappardelle with Duck Ragù (page 182).

Roll 1 pound Rye Dough (page 74) into sheets about ⅛ inch thick. Lay a pasta sheet on a lightly floured work surface and trim the edges square (keep the remaining pasta covered as you work). Cut the sheet into strips about 12 inches long and 1 inch wide, using a fluted cutter if you prefer. Dust the pappardelle with semolina flour and place on a lightly floured sheet pan. Repeat with the remaining dough.

BUCKWHEAT MALTAGLIATI

This pasta is traditionally made from scraps, so the pieces should not match. Just cut them any which way. *Maltagliati* **means "badly cut." Try it in Buckwheat Maltagliati with Duck and Espresso Ragù (page 184).**

Roll 1 pound Buckwheat Dough (page 74) into sheets about ⅛ inch thick. Lay a pasta sheet on a lightly floured work surface (keep the remaining pasta covered as you work). Cut the sheet into irregular shapes about 3 inches square. Lightly dust the pieces with semolina flour and place on a lightly floured sheet pan. Repeat with the remaining dough.

pici
DOUGH

Here's a classic Tuscan dough made with just one common flour: bread flour. It's perfect for thick, chewy, hand-rolled pasta strands, aka pici. I learned to make this shape with a long rolling pin (*mattarello*) more than thirty years ago at La Chiusa, a beautiful restaurant in the Tuscan hills, and they are still making this pasta tableside to this day. **MAKES 422 GRAMS (ABOUT 1 POUND); 4 TO 6 SERVINGS**

- 250 grams (1¾ cups) bread flour, such as King Arthur, plus more as needed and for dusting
- 100 grams (scant ½ cup) water, plus more as needed
- 60 grams egg (1 large)
- 10 grams (2¼ teaspoons) extra-virgin olive oil, plus more for rolling
- 2 grams (¾ teaspoon) kosher salt

Make the dough: Place the flour on a work surface or in a medium bowl and make a well in the center. In a small bowl, mix together the water, egg, oil, and salt with a fork, then pour them into the well. Gradually mix the flour into the liquid with the fork until the dough comes together. It will look raggy at first and you may need to add a little more flour or water for the dough to come together, depending on the humidity in the room.

When the dough holds together in a shaggy ball, turn it out onto a lightly floured work surface and knead it until it feels soft and smooth, 3 to 5 minutes.

Let it rest: Cover the dough and let it rest so the gluten can relax, at least 15 minutes or up to 1 hour. Or wrap the dough in plastic wrap and refrigerate it for up to 3 days. Before using, let the dough sit at room temperature for 15 minutes to take the chill off.

Scan this code to watch a video of making Pici Dough and shaping pici.

PICI

Rolling these long strands is still one of my favorite pasta-making techniques. It takes some practice, but it's well worth it. To watch a video of making pici, scan the QR code on page 83. Then enjoy the pici simply in dishes like Pici Pomodoro (page 104).

Using a rolling pin, roll out the Pici Dough (page 82) on a lightly floured work surface into an oval about ⅛ inch thick. Rub the surface of the dough with about 1 tablespoon of extra-virgin olive oil, coating it evenly. The oil enriches the dough and keeps it from drying out. Cover the oiled dough with plastic wrap to keep it from drying out. Pour a pile of semolina flour near one corner of your work surface, which could be the right or the left corner, depending on which hand you roll with. I keep the dough to my left and roll with my right hand toward the right, where the pile of semolina flour is waiting to collect the noodle as it coils up. Begin by lifting a bit of the plastic and cutting a strip ¾ to 1 inch wide from the dough; re-cover the rest. Starting at one end of the strip, use the fat part of your palm to roll the strip gently back and forth onto itself on the work surface, stretching it lengthwise until it forms a rope about ¼ inch in diameter. It's like rolling one long piece of thick spaghetti. If necessary, rub a little water on the work surface for more stiction. As you roll, coil the shaped portion of the rope into the pile of semolina to prevent it from sticking to itself. You should end up with a coiled rope 4 to 5 feet long in the pile of semolina. Pick up one end of the rope, drape it around a finger, and then continue to drape the entire rope around that finger and your other fingers. Place the rope in parallel lines on a sheet pan dusted with semolina. Repeat with the remaining dough. Cover the pasta loosely and use it within 2 hours. Or cover it tightly and refrigerate it for up to 1 day, or freeze it in a single layer, transfer it to an airtight container, and freeze it for up to 1 month. Take the pasta straight from the freezer to the pasta water.

PASTA DOUGHS AND SHAPES 85

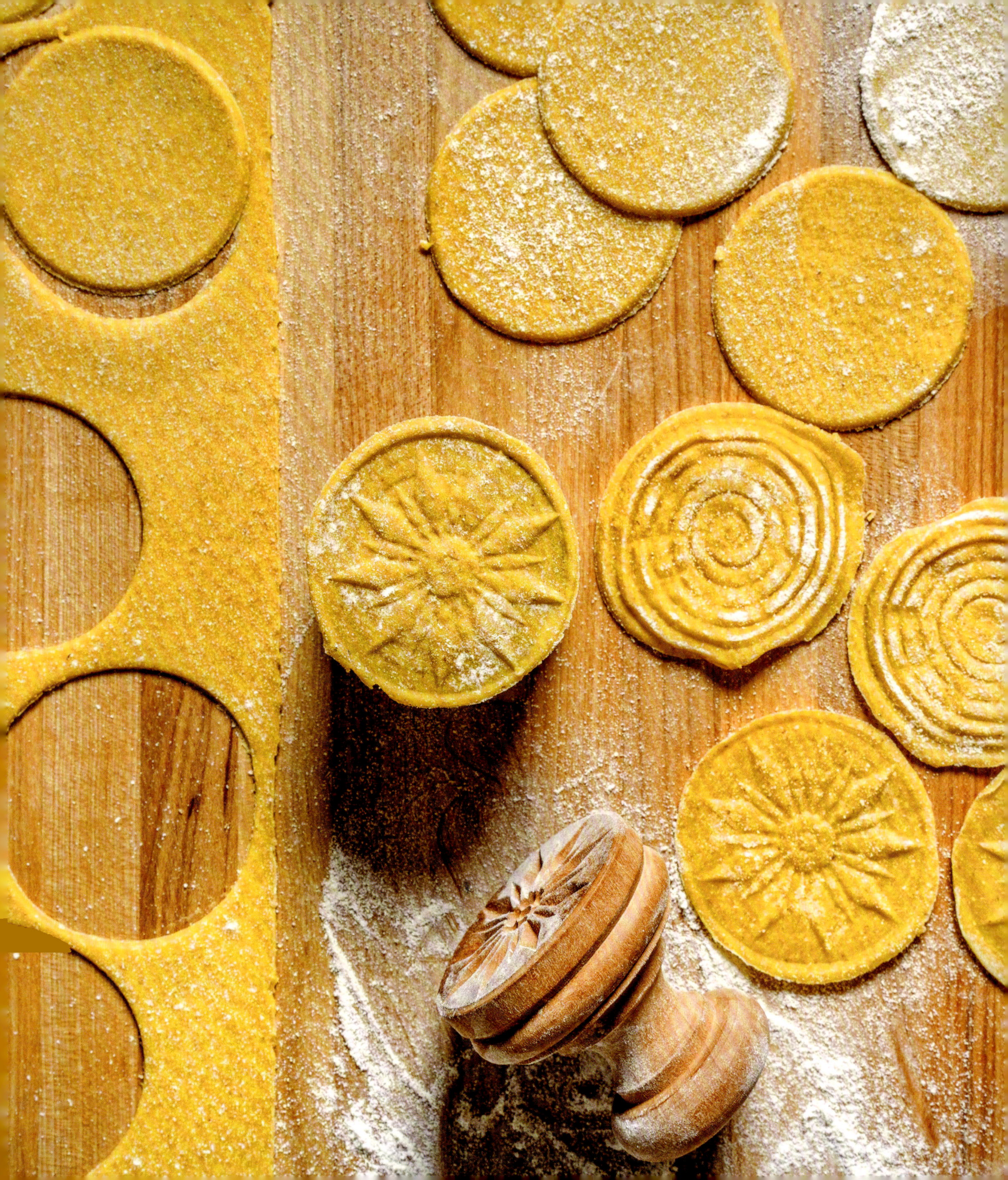

CORZETTI
DOUGH

You could use the Hand-Rolled Dough (page 55) for corzetti, but the finely milled tipo "00" flour here makes the dough softer and silkier. A little egg and oil also make it richer, which is a Piedmontese twist on classic Ligurian stamped pasta rounds of corzetti. **MAKES 505 GRAMS (ABOUT 1 POUND); 4 TO 6 SERVINGS**

300 grams (2 cups) tipo "00" flour, such as Spadoni Gran Mugnaio, or King Arthur all-purpose flour, plus more for dusting

118 grams (½ cup) water, plus more as necessary

60 grams egg (1 large)

27 grams (2 tablespoons) extra-virgin olive oil

Make the dough: Put the flour in a bowl or in the bowl of a stand mixer with the paddle attachment. In a small bowl, mix together the water, egg, and oil until the egg is incorporated but not foamy. Add the liquid to the flour and mix slowly with a spoon or on low speed just until the dough comes together, 2 to 3 minutes. If necessary, add a little more water, a tablespoon at a time, for the dough to come together in a shaggy ball. Turn the dough out onto a lightly floured work surface and knead it gently until it feels silky and smooth, 3 to 5 minutes, kneading in a little flour if necessary to keep the dough from sticking. The dough is ready when you tug on it and it gently pulls back into place.

Let it rest: Shape the dough into a disk, cover, and set it aside for at least 30 minutes so the gluten can relax. Or wrap it in plastic and refrigerate it for up to 3 days. You can also freeze the dough for up to 1 month. Thaw the dough overnight in the refrigerator before using it. It can also be quickly thawed in a microwave oven on 50% power in 5-second increments just until cool to the touch. (Don't cook the dough!)

LEVEL UP **Saffron Corzetti Dough:** Use the same amount of water, but use hot tap water, adding a generous 2 grams (2½ teaspoons) crushed saffron threads to the water. Let steep until the water cools to room temperature, 20 to 30 minutes, then use as directed.

CORZETTI

These flat pasta rounds are imprinted with a personal design carved into a wooden stamp. You can buy corzetti stamps pretty easily these days, but they used to be reserved for noble Ligurian families who would have their family crest carved into olive or walnut wood. Try this shape in Pistachio Corzetti with Clams and Tarragon (page 164) and Scallop Corzetti with Clarified Pomodoro, Tomato Powder, and Basil Oil (page 269).

To roll out the dough, cut it into 4 equal pieces. If the dough was chilled, let the pieces sit, covered, at room temperature for 10 minutes to take the chill off. You can roll this dough out with a rolling pin or in a pasta rolling machine, and if you have a very long work surface, you can cut the dough into fewer pieces for rolling. To use a machine, gently flatten each disk so it's wide enough to fit the width of your pasta roller. Lightly flour your work surface and set the pasta roller to its widest setting. Lightly flour one disk of dough, pass it through the roller, and then lightly dust the rolled dough with flour, brushing off the excess with your hands. Set the roller to the next narrowest setting and pass the dough through, again dusting with flour and brushing off the excess. Fold the dough in half crosswise over itself and cut about ¼ inch off the corners at the fold. Continue passing the dough once or twice through the roller. Roll the dough to about ⅛ inch thick, setting 4 or 5 on a KitchenAid attachment or manual pasta machine, or about as thick as a thick cotton bedsheet. If using a rolling pin, roll each disk from the center outward into a round that's ⅛ inch thick, flouring the pin and dough as needed.

To cut the corzetti, lay a pasta sheet on a lightly floured work surface and use the base of a corzetti stamp or a 2½-inch round cutter to cut out rounds of dough; you should have a total of 55 to 65 rounds. Stamp each round with the woodcut corzetti stamp to imprint its design. If you don't have a corzetti stamp, leave the rounds as they are or press the tines of a fork into them to imprint their shape. Repeat with the remaining sheets. Dust the corzetti with flour, cover them, and use them within 1 hour. Or refrigerate them for up to 4 hours. You can also freeze them in a single layer and then transfer them to a zipper-lock bag and freeze them for up to 1 month. Take the pasta right from the freezer to the pasta water.

Scan this code to watch a video of making corzetti.

CIALZONS DOUGH

In northern Italy, the cuisine of the Friuli region has distinct German influences. It's no surprise that Friulians often make their pasta dough with flour and potatoes instead of with eggs. Cooked and mashed potatoes make this dough especially soft and tender. Depending on how hydrated your cooked potato gets, the dough might need a little less or a little more flour than what's listed here. The finished dough should feel silky but have enough strength to be rolled into thin sheets. It makes beautiful Friulian ravioli, such as Cialzons with Ricotta, Dried Fruit, and Foie Gras Sauce, shown below (page 293). **MAKES 480 GRAMS (ABOUT 1 POUND); 4 TO 6 SERVINGS**

1 large russet potato (about 6 ounces/170 grams), unpeeled

Kosher salt

225 to 300 grams (1½ to 2 cups) tipo "00" flour, such as Spadoni Gran Mugnaio, or King Arthur all-purpose flour, as needed

Scan this code to watch a video of making cialzons.

In a small saucepan, combine the potato with water to cover by about ½ inch. Add a generous pinch of salt and bring to a boil over high heat. Boil until the potato is fork-tender, about 25 minutes, covering the pot partially or fully with a lid to maintain a boil. Drain and let cool enough to handle.

Make the dough: Pass the potato through the small holes of a food mill (or a ricer) into a medium bowl. Add about 40 grams (¼ cup) of the flour, season lightly with salt, and knead in as much of the remaining flour as needed to form a dough with a consistency similar to Play-Doh. Kneading in the flour may take up to 10 minutes. The kneaded dough should pull back gently when you tug on it and feel firm enough to be rolled into sheets.

Let it rest: Shape the dough into a disk and set it aside for at least 30 minutes so the gluten can relax. Or wrap it in plastic and refrigerate it for up to 3 days. You can also freeze the wrapped dough for up to 1 month. Thaw the dough overnight in the refrigerator before using it.

PASTA DOUGHS AND SHAPES

GRANO ARSO DOUGH

After the harvest in the Puglia region, farmers used to burn their wheat fields to help prepare the soil for the following season. The fire would burn the remaining wheat berries on the stalks, and workers would grab the burnt seeds, then grind them with whatever other wheat berries they had to stretch their flour supplies. Out of this thrifty practice came a nutty flavor in the flour that people now can't get enough of. Today, you can buy *grano arso* ("burnt flour") online. Or you can toast wheat berries before grinding them. Or you can simply toast your flour before using it. To make the "grano arso flour" called for here, just shake 75 grams (½ cup) tipo "00" flour in a thin layer on a sheet pan and toast in a 400°F oven until the flour smells nutty and looks golden brown, 40 to 50 minutes, shaking the pan every 10 minutes or so for even browning. Open a window—it might get smoky! Let the toasted flour cool, then make the dough. **MAKES 715 GRAMS (ABOUT 1½ POUNDS); 6 TO 8 SERVINGS**

300 grams (2 cups) tipo "00" flour, such as Spadoni Gran Mugnaio, or King Arthur all-purpose flour, plus more as needed

63 grams (½ cup) semolina flour, such as Caputo

63 grams (½ cup) grano arso flour (burnt flour)

177 grams (¾ cup) water, plus more as needed

60 grams whole egg (1 large)

20 grams egg yolk (1 large)

27 grams (2 tablespoons) extra-virgin olive oil

Make the dough: Stir together the tipo "00" flour, semolina flour, and grano arso flour on a countertop or in a medium bowl. Make a well in the center and add the water, whole egg, egg yolk, and olive oil to the well. Using your fingers or a fork, stir together the liquids until blended, then gradually stir in the flour from the edges. Stir just until the dough comes together, adding a little more water or flour if necessary to form a cohesive dough.

Turn the dough out onto a lightly floured work surface and knead it until it feels smooth, about 5 minutes, kneading in a little "00" flour if necessary to keep the dough from sticking. When you tug on the dough, it should gently pull back into place.

Let it rest: Shape the dough into a ball, cover, and let rest for 30 to 60 minutes. You can also wrap it in plastic and refrigerate it for up to 3 days, or freeze it for up to 1 month. Thaw frozen dough overnight in the refrigerator. Before using, take the chill off by letting the dough stand at room temperature for 15 minutes.

MASA DOUGH

Sometimes chefs add colored purees to pasta dough to make the noodles red or green. But it doesn't change the flavor much. Here, it's the opposite. Adding masa harina to pasta dough doesn't change the color much, but it gives the pasta a subtle toasted corn flavor. I love that! The texture doesn't change much either because the grind of most masa harina is similar to semolina. Noodles made with this dough can be paired with any ragù you might imagine eating in a taco.

MAKES 475 GRAMS (ABOUT 1 POUND); 4 TO 6 SERVINGS

250 grams (1½ cups) semolina flour, such as Caputo

65 grams (½ cup) masa harina, such as Masienda or Maseca

150 grams (⅔ cup) water, plus more as needed

10 grams (2¼ teaspoons) extra-virgin olive oil

Make the dough: Combine the semolina flour and masa harina on a work surface or in a medium bowl. Make a well in the center like a volcano, then slowly stir in the water and oil until combined, adding a little more water if necessary for the dough to come together.

Transfer the dough to your work surface and knead with your hands until it forms a rough-textured ball, about 5 minutes. It will be loose and raggy at first, and then form a ball.

As you knead and the flour absorbs the water, the dough will go from feeling somewhat coarse like damp sand to feeling smoother and softer. You'll know the gluten is developed when you tug on the dough with your fingertips and it gently pulls back into place. By the end of kneading, the dough should easily hold together and feel somewhat stiff yet be rollable.

Let it rest: Shape the dough into a disk and set it aside, covered, for 30 to 60 minutes so the gluten can relax. Or wrap it in plastic wrap and refrigerate it for up to 3 days. Before using, take the chill off by letting the dough stand at room temperature for 15 minutes.

RICOTTA CAVATELLI DOUGH

You can make cavatelli with Hand-Rolled Dough (page 55), but adding ricotta makes the dough so plush and soft, the pasta just melts in your mouth. Best cavatelli ever! At the restaurants, we make the dough with a housemade type of ricotta called ricotta impastata (see opposite). To roll the cavatelli with the signature ridges on the back, you can use your hands and a grooved wooden board or the back of a fork. Or use one of those tabletop hand-cranked gizmos available online. Whatever works for you! **MAKES 630 GRAMS (ABOUT 1¼ POUNDS); 4 TO 6 SERVINGS**

- 227 grams (1 cup) ricotta impastata
- 120 grams eggs (2 large)
- 7.5 grams (generous 2½ teaspoons) kosher salt
- 285 grams (2 cups) tipo "00" flour, such as Spadoni Gran Mugnaio, or King Arthur all-purpose flour, plus more as needed

Make the dough: Stir together the ricotta, eggs, and salt in a bowl with your hands or a fork, or mix in the bowl of a stand mixer on medium speed with the paddle attachment. Gradually add the flour until the dough comes together. If the dough is sticky, mix in more flour as needed until the dough is soft and supple on the surface but not tacky. Turn the dough out onto a lightly floured work surface and knead it until it feels silky and smooth, about 5 minutes, kneading in a little "00" flour if necessary to prevent sticking. The finished dough will feel soft and tender from the ricotta. The dough is ready when you tug on it with your fingertips and it gently pulls back into place.

Let it rest: Shape the dough into a disk, wrap it in plastic wrap, and refrigerate it for at least 30 minutes or up to 3 days.

> **LEVEL UP** For more flavor, use 28 grams (¼ cup) all-purpose einkorn flour and reduce the tipo "00" flour to 255 grams (1¾ cups plus 2 tablespoons).
>
> **Squash Cavatelli Dough:** Replace the ricotta with the same amount (1 cup/227 grams) of butternut squash puree. Peel a medium butternut squash (about 2 pounds) with a sharp vegetable peeler. To make the squash easier to peel, first soften it in the microwave: Prick the squash all over with a fork, then microwave for 2 minutes, turning once or twice. Remove and let cool a bit before peeling. Halve the squash lengthwise and scrape and discard the seeds and strings (a serrated grapefruit spoon or even a melon baller makes quick work of seeding). Cut the squash into 1-inch chunks. In a large sauté pan, melt 12 tablespoons (6 ounces) unsalted butter over medium-low heat. Add the squash, toss to coat, cover, and cook low and slow until the squash is so tender that it completely falls apart, about 1 hour, tossing frequently to prevent browning. Pass the cooked squash through a potato ricer or food mill to puree it, and then spread the squash puree on clean kitchen towels to cool and absorb excess moisture. When completely cool, about 1 hour, the puree should have the consistency and moisture level of ricotta. Add 1 cup of the puree to the dough in place of the ricotta. Reserve the remaining puree to make Squash Cavatelli Pomodoro (page 129) or for another purpose.

Scan this code to watch a video of making Ricotta Cavatelli.

RICOTTA CAVATELLI

Popular all over Italy, particularly in the south, this little shell-shaped pasta has a groove in the center and ridges on the back, both of which grab on to and hold sauce. Try it in Ricotta Cavatelli with Veal Shank Ragù (page 242) and Squash Cavatelli Pomodoro (page 129). To watch a video of making cavatelli, scan the QR code on page 92.

To shape cavatelli, we roll it by hand on a grooved wooden cavatelli board or gnocchi paddle. You could use the back of a fork, too. You can also make it in a tabletop cavatelli maker. Either way, make the Ricotta Cavatelli Dough (opposite) or Squash Cavatelli Dough (see Level Up, opposite), cut it into 4 equal pieces, and let them sit at room temperature for about 10 minutes to take the chill off. Lightly flour your work surface and roll a piece of dough into a long rope about ½ inch thick. Cut the dough on an angle into diamonds that measure about 1 inch from point to point. Dust all the diamonds with flour and dust a cavatelli board or the back of a long dinner fork as well. For each cavatelli, place the diamond lengthwise on the board or fork and then use your thumb to roll the diamond down the length of the board or fork to create a hollow football shape that's grooved on the outside. If using a tabletop cavatelli maker, roll out the dough according to the manufacturer's instructions. (Typically, you roll the dough into a rope about 16 inches long, flatten it slightly, flour it liberally, and then feed the rope into the cavatelli maker.) After shaping, dust the cavatelli with flour and use immediately. Or freeze in an airtight container for up to 1 month. Take the cavatelli straight from the freezer to the pasta water.

RICOTTA IMPASTATA
Ricotta impastata is a creamy ricotta that's low in water. If you can't find ricotta impastata (sometimes labeled "ricotta del pastaio"), drain your ricotta in a sieve overnight in the fridge to remove excess water and then whip it in a food processor.

PASTA DOUGHS AND SHAPES   93

VEGE

> A chef must think like a scientist, organize like an accountant, plate like an artist, and cook like a grandmother. But above all, he must know how to remove, to do without. Less is more.
>
> **—GUALTIERO MARCHESI,**
> FOUNDER OF MODERN ITALIAN CUISINE

TABLE
PASTA

When I got to Italy in 1993, the young chef Paolo Frosio had just put the province of Bergamo on the culinary map. He opened his eponymous restaurant a couple years earlier and earned a Michelin star at age twenty-three, the country's youngest chef to get the nod. Working with Paolo was awe-inspiring. I was a young chef fresh off the boat from America, and his ability to use everything—from root to fruit and nose to tail—taught me so much about the soul of Italian cuisine. He could look in the walk-in, almost bare from a week of cooking, see some fresh peas and mint, and create a beautiful dish of pasta from just those two ingredients. He was never tempted to "make it better" by adding another flavor.

Maybe that's because Italy is the land of beautiful produce! Some of the best dishes I've ever had there combine fresh seasonal vegetables and fruits with the most important ingredient of all: restraint. Great chefs like Paolo always let the ingredients speak for themselves. Porcini and blueberries. Peaches and prosciutto. Pumpkin and apple mostarda.

There's a reason simple pairings have stood the test of time and become enshrined as perfect flavor combinations: You don't need a third component when two is enough. Just look at pomodoro and basil. It's perfect.

Recently, at the start of spring cherry season, one of my sous-chefs at Vetri made a batch of beautiful half-moon burrata ravioli. He started messing around with flavors, including a combination of chanterelle mushrooms, pistachios, and cherries. I tasted the dish and it was fine. Mushrooms, pistachios, cherries, and burrata go great together. It's just that I'm going for something different. I want to take something good and make it great. In my opinion, the only way to do that is to make a star out of the main ingredient. There can only be one true star, so let's make it shine. In this pasta dish, cherry was the star. Pistachios and chanterelles were just noise, in the way. We ended up warming the cherries in brown butter, tossing them with the burrata ravioli, and finishing the dish with cracked black pepper. When well executed, restraint can take something from good to great.

As I've gotten older and more confident in my cooking skills, I've embraced the motto "less is more." And not just in the kitchen! Keeping life simple allows you to focus on the things that really matter . . . the things that are right in front of you on any given day and that excite you right now. Like much of life, food is fleeting. The fact is, a beautiful fruit or vegetable at the peak of ripeness will yield a flavor that you just cannot duplicate any other time of year. That's not a limitation. It's something to celebrate. When cooking with vegetables, follow the seasons and keep it simple. The more you mess with a vegetable-forward dish, adding layers and components, the worse the dish becomes.

The pastas in this chapter pretty much follow that philosophy. Pici with tomato (see page 104). Wild mushroom with Taleggio (see page 115). Spinach with brown butter (see page 123). These are simple pastas that let Mother Nature shine. Just keep in mind that quality matters a lot here. Seasonality matters. If you make the Spring Pea Agnolotti with Mint and Butter (page 135) in the middle of winter with frozen peas, you might not enjoy it as much. Save that dish for springtime when your local market is overflowing with fresh, plump peapods. In the summer, make Zucchini-Stuffed Pappardelle with Squash Blossoms and Basil (page 119) or Garganelli with Corn and Scallions (page 108). When summer becomes early fall, cook a crowd-pleaser like Eggplant Lasagnetta (page 111), or try Squash Cavatelli Pomodoro (page 129).

If you're new to making fresh pasta, this chapter is the perfect place to start. Even a dried pasta dish like Strozzapreti with Radicchio, Walnuts, and Gorgonzola (page 99) may be a revelation. Hopefully these pastas inspire you to go off script with your own favorite vegetables. Hit your local produce market and find a plump, seasonal vegetable that's just begging to be eaten. Choose a pasta that fits the sauce (see Pairing Pastas and Sauces, page 21), and do everything you can to make that vegetable sing, including not doing too much!

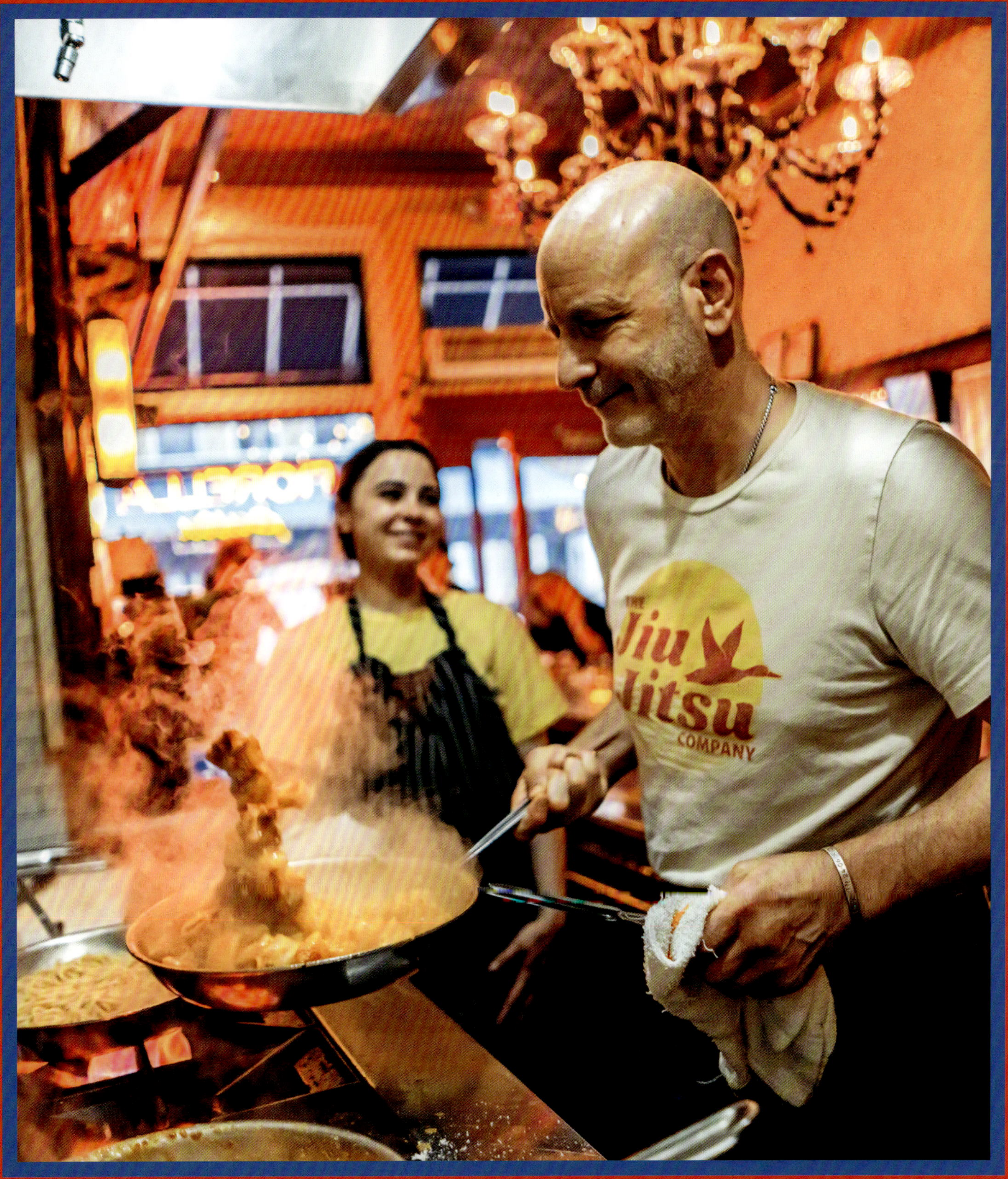
THE
Jiu
Jitsu
COMPANY

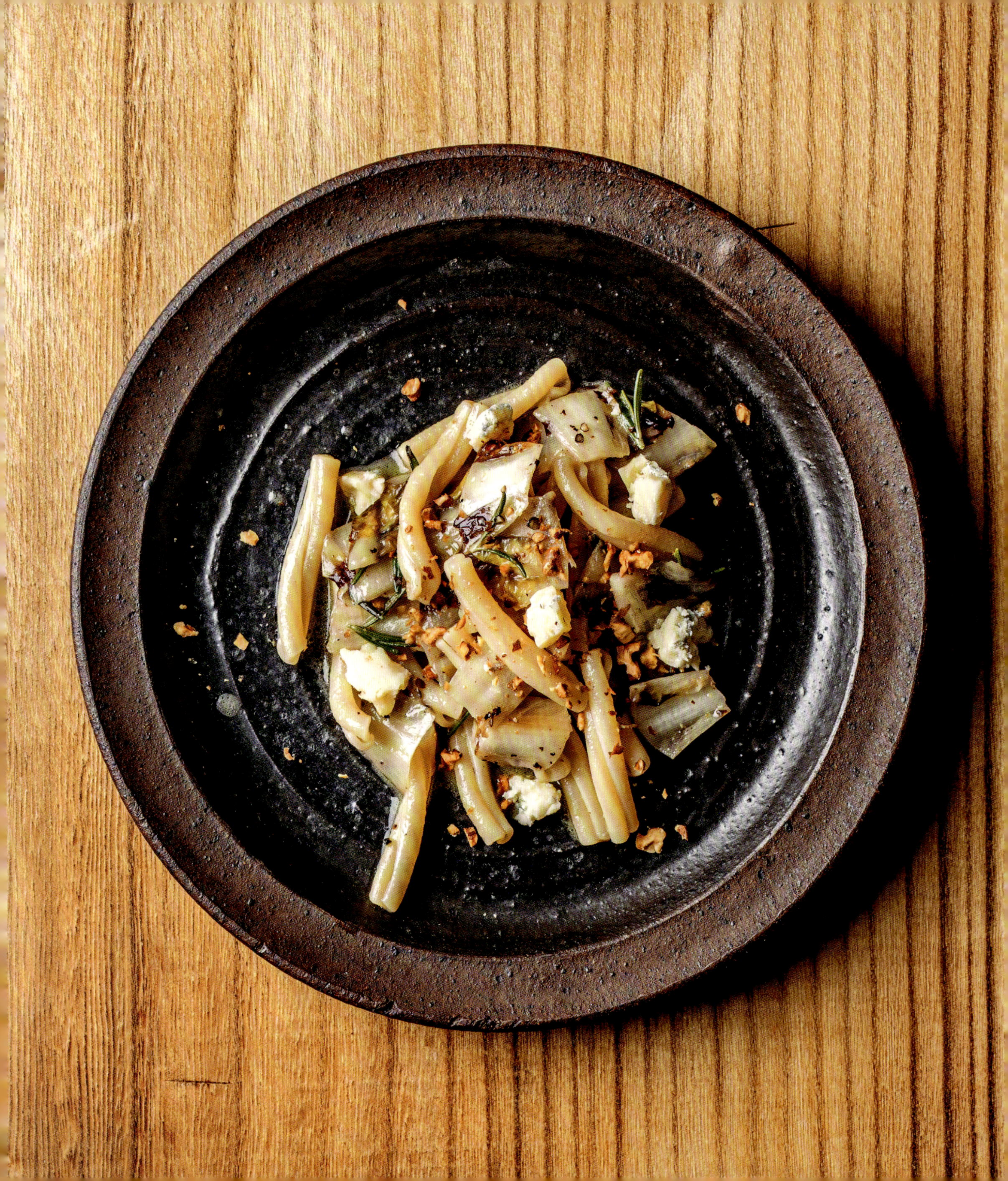

Strozzapreti with Radicchio, Walnuts, and Gorgonzola

In late September, we get fresh black walnuts from our Pennsylvania farmers. These are the best walnuts ever! Earthy, robust, with just a hint of bitterness. I love making this dish every fall because I can also get beautiful Treviso radicchio from local farmers and a creamy-crumbly local blue cheese from Birchrun Hills Farm that reminds me of some of the best Gorgonzola from Milan. If you can, use products that are local to you. To take this dish to the next level, drizzle some aged balsamic on top! **Serves 4 to 6**

Kosher salt

12 ounces store-bought dried strozzapreti ("priest stranglers")

10 tablespoons (5 ounces) unsalted butter, cut into pieces

⅓ cup extra-virgin olive oil

2 medium heads Treviso radicchio (or the more common round Chioggia radicchio), cut into ½-inch-wide ribbons

2 garlic cloves, peeled

Freshly ground black pepper

Leaves from 2 sprigs fresh rosemary, chopped if large

½ teaspoon red wine vinegar, plus more as needed

½ cup finely grated Parmesan cheese, plus more for garnish

6 tablespoons chopped toasted walnuts, preferably black walnuts, plus more for garnish

¾ cup crumbled Gorgonzola cheese

Cook the strozzapreti: Bring a large pot of water to a boil and add salt until it tastes like well-seasoned broth. Drop in the strozzapreti, give it a stir, and cover the pot to quickly return the water to a boil. Uncover or partially cover to maintain the boil and boil the pasta, stirring occasionally, until it is tender but still a little chewy when bitten, 10 to 12 minutes.

Meanwhile, start the sauce: In a deep 12-inch sauté pan, melt the butter and olive oil over medium heat. Add the radicchio and garlic and sauté, stirring now and then, until the radicchio is tender, about 5 minutes. Season with salt and pepper until it tastes good to you. If the pasta isn't ready yet, remove the pan from the heat.

When the pasta is ready, return the pan with the radicchio to high heat and add 1 cup of the hot pasta water or saved pasta water (see page 31) and the rosemary. Bring to a simmer and use a spider strainer or large slotted spoon to scoop the cooked strozzapreti from the water and transfer it straight to the pan. Shake and swirl the pan until the sauce reduces a bit more and begins to hug the pasta, 1 to 2 minutes (keep the pasta moving, adding a little more pasta water if necessary to create a loose, creamy sauce). Taste the sauce and season with the red wine vinegar, adding more, if you like, until it tastes good to you. Toss everything until the pasta and sauce begin to marry.

Remove from the heat, add the Parmesan and toasted walnuts, and keep tossing until the sauce thickens further and the pasta and sauce marry, leaving little to no sauce in the pan. Remove the garlic cloves before serving.

Dish out the pasta onto warmed plates, creating some volume by building it into a mound. Garnish with the Gorgonzola, some more toasted walnuts, and some Parmesan.

Trofie with Pistachio, Artichokes, and Orange Zest

We struggled for a long time to make a vegan pasta dish that tasted amazing. Pistachio and orange is such a classic combination in Italian desserts, and when we made it savory with pasta, it sang just as loud. Adding baby artichokes brought it all home by bringing in some earthy bittersweet flavors. But, honestly, you could make this dish without the artichokes and it'd be just as good! **Serves 4 to 6**

Pistachio Pesto

1⅓ cups shelled raw pistachios, preferably Sicilian

⅔ cup extra-virgin olive oil

Kosher salt

Artichokes

Juice of ½ lemon

6 baby artichokes

Trofie

Kosher salt

1 pound fresh Trofie (page 59)

2 tablespoons extra-virgin olive oil

Freshly ground black pepper

¼ cup finely grated Parmesan cheese, plus more for garnish (optional)

Finely grated or julienned zest of 1 orange

Make the pistachio pesto: In a blender, grind the pistachios and oil until the nuts are very finely chopped but not completely pureed, 1 to 2 minutes, adding a little water if necessary to get everything to blend. Taste the mixture and season with salt until it tastes good to you (maybe ¼ teaspoon or so). You should have about 1½ cups pesto. Measure out 1 cup for the pasta and save the rest to use in sandwiches or freeze it for up to 1 month.

Prep the artichokes: In a medium bowl, combine the lemon juice and 1½ cups cold water. Working with one artichoke at a time, snap off and discard all the fibrous outer leaves. Using a paring knife, peel the artichoke until you are left with only the very tender, pale-yellow leaves in a bullet shape about 1 inch by ½ inch in size. Slice the artichoke lengthwise into wedges about ¼ inch thick and drop them into the lemon water to keep them from browning. Repeat with the remaining artichokes.

Cook the trofie: Bring a large pot of water to a boil and add salt until it tastes like well-seasoned broth. Drop in the trofie, give it a stir, and cover the pot to quickly return the water to a boil. Uncover or partially cover to maintain the boil and boil the pasta, stirring occasionally, until it is tender but still a little chewy when bitten, 2 to 3 minutes.

Meanwhile, in a deep 12-inch sauté pan, heat the olive oil over medium heat. Drain the artichokes, add them to the pan, and cook, stirring once or twice, until they are mostly tender but still have a little bite to them, 3 to 5 minutes.

When the pasta is ready, use a spider strainer or large slotted spoon to scoop it from the water and transfer it straight to the pan with the artichokes. Add about 1 cup of the pistachio pesto and 1 cup of the hot pasta water or saved pasta water (see page 31). Shake and swirl the pan until the sauce thickens a bit and begins to hug the pasta, 1 to 2 minutes. Taste the sauce and add salt and pepper until it tastes good to you. Toss everything until the pasta and sauce begin to marry.

Remove from the heat, add the Parmesan (if using), and keep tossing until the sauce thickens further and the pasta and sauce marry, leaving little to no sauce in the pan.

Dish out the pasta onto warmed plates, creating some volume by building it into a mound. Garnish with the orange zest and serve with additional Parmesan, if you like.

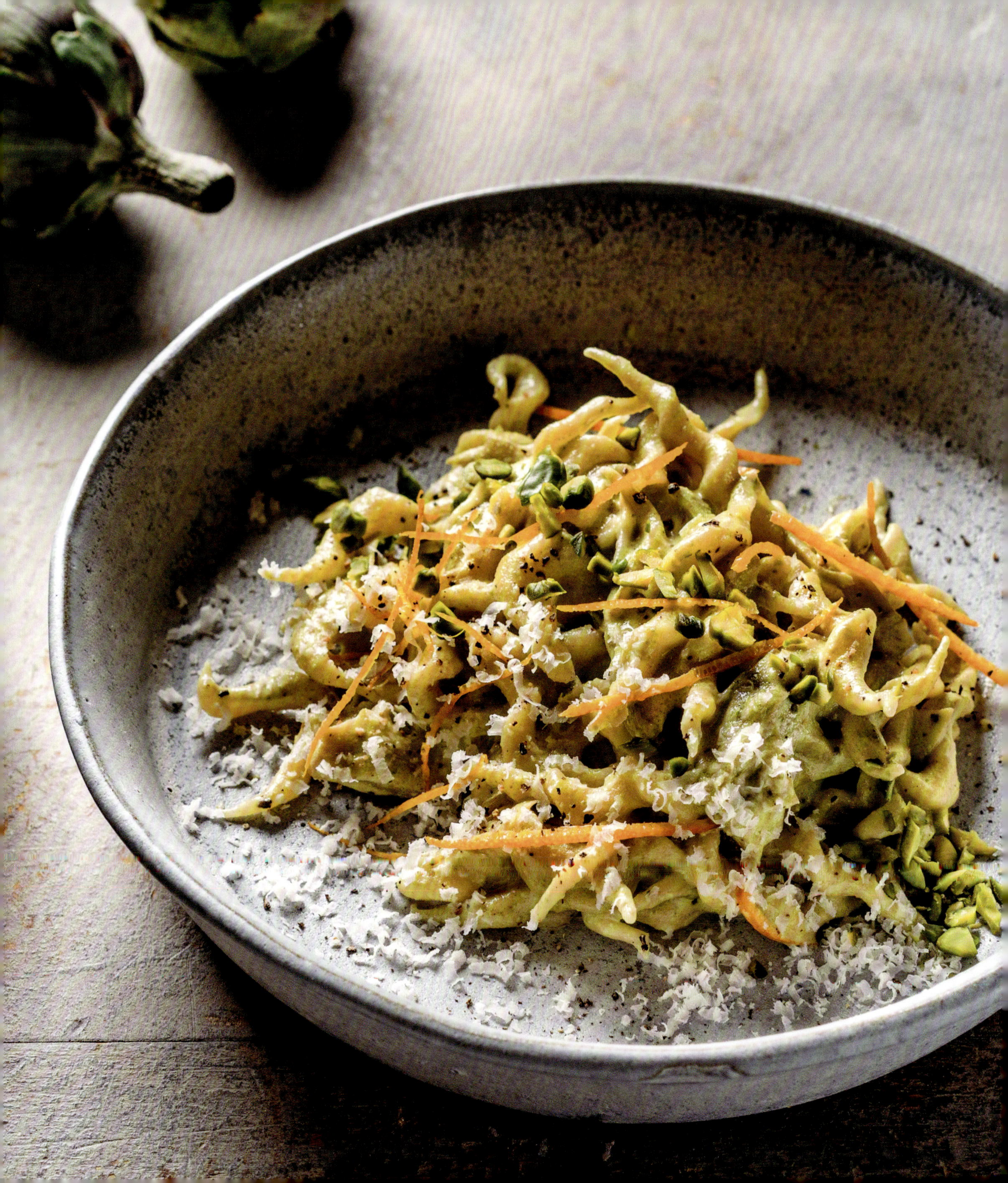

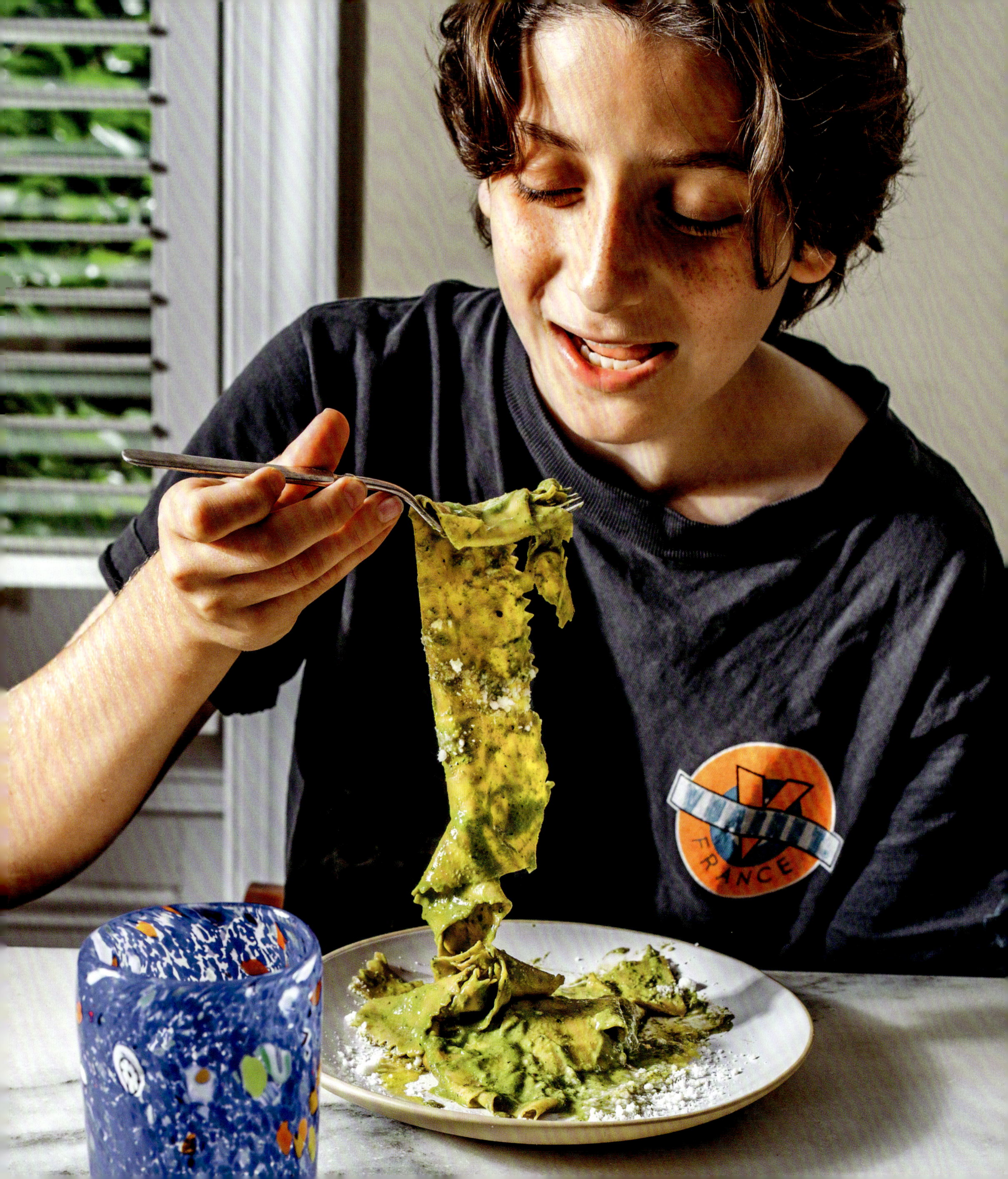
FRANCE

MANDILLI WITH PERFECT BASIL PESTO

We opened Fiorella restaurant in Philadelphia with this ultrasimple pasta on the menu. We use almonds in the pesto instead of pine nuts. Why? Because I love Marcona almonds! Let your tastes guide you. If you love cashews, use them instead of almonds. Or use walnuts, pistachios, or whatever nuts you like best. Where's the Parm in our pesto recipe? We leave that for the end. When you toss hot pasta in a pan with a delicate sauce like pesto, the heat can cause the Parm to clump up. To keep the sauce creamy, we add the Parm to the pesto only after the pan is off the heat. **SERVES 4 TO 6**

Basil Pesto

½ cup Marcona almonds

⅔ cup extra-virgin olive oil

8 cups lightly packed fresh basil leaves

Kosher salt

Mandilli

Kosher salt

1 pound fresh Mandilli (page 75)

5 tablespoons (2½ ounces) unsalted butter, cut into pieces

½ cup finely grated Parmesan cheese, plus more for garnish

Make the pesto: In a blender, combine the almonds with enough of the olive oil to cover them by about ½ inch (about ½ cup). Blend until the mixture becomes a smooth paste, about a minute. Let the blender cool down for a minute. Add the basil and the rest of the oil and blend in brief pulses until the mixture becomes a smooth sauce. Be careful not to blend continuously or your blender could overheat, causing the basil to turn an ugly shade of drab green. Taste the pesto and season with salt until it tastes good to you.

Cook the mandilli: Bring a large pot of water to a boil and add salt until it tastes like well-seasoned broth. Drop in the mandilli, give it a stir, and cover the pot to quickly return the water to a boil. Uncover or partially cover to maintain the boil and boil the pasta, stirring occasionally, until it is tender but still a little chewy when bitten, 1 to 2 minutes.

Meanwhile, in a deep 12-inch sauté pan, melt the butter over high heat. Add 2 cups of the hot pasta water or saved pasta water (see page 31) and boil the mixture until it thickens slightly, 3 to 4 minutes.

When the pasta is ready, use tongs or a spider strainer to scoop it from the water and transfer it straight to the pan with the butter mixture. Shake and swirl the pan until the sauce thickens a bit more and begins to hug the pasta, 1 to 2 minutes (keep the pasta moving, adding a little more pasta water if necessary to create a lightly thickened sauce).

Remove from the heat, add the pesto, and toss until the pasta and sauce begin to marry. Add the Parmesan and keep tossing until the cheese melts and the pasta and sauce marry, leaving little to no sauce in the pan.

Using tongs, dish out the pasta onto warmed plates, creating some volume by building it into a mound. Garnish with additional Parmesan.

PICI POMO

ODORO

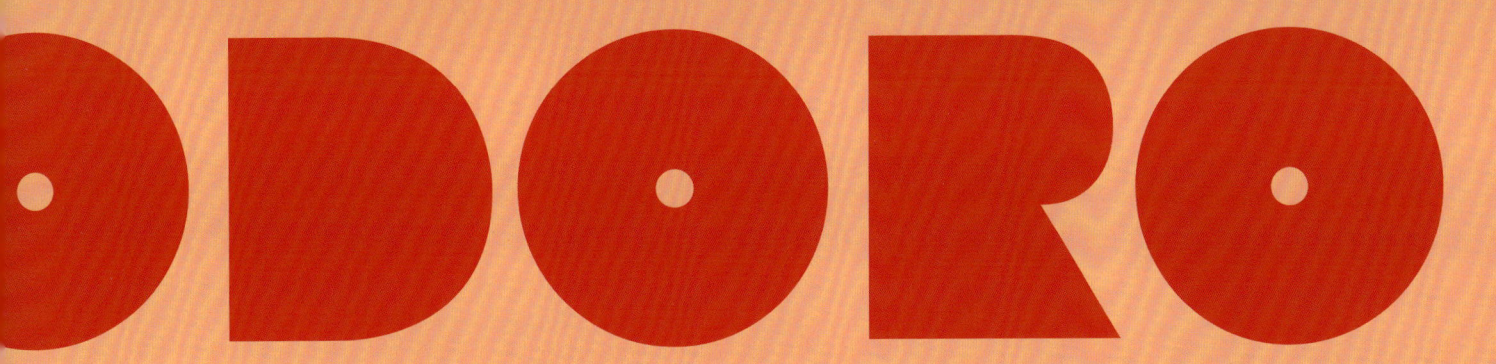

In the early 1990s, I worked at La Chiusa, a restaurant and hotel that sits on a stunning Tuscan hillside in the village of Montefollonico, near Montepulciano. That's where I learned to make pici with the head chef, Dania, and the other pasta cooks. Try your hand at this easy fresh pasta shape, and you'll begin to appreciate the beauty of handmade food. *SERVES 4 TO 6*

- 6 tablespoons extra-virgin olive oil
- 2 garlic cloves, peeled
- 4 to 6 anchovy fillets (optional)
- 1 (28-ounce) can peeled whole Italian plum tomatoes, preferably San Marzano, with their juice
- Kosher salt
- 1 pound fresh Pici (page 82)
- 12 to 15 fresh basil leaves, torn if large
- ¼ cup finely grated Parmesan cheese, for garnish (optional)

Make the sauce: In a deep 12-inch sauté pan, heat 4 tablespoons of the olive oil over medium heat. Add the garlic and anchovies (if using) and cook until aromatic but not browned, about 2 minutes, swirling the pan a few times. Using your hands, pinch and pull out the hard tomato cores, then crush the tomatoes into small pieces, letting the pieces drop into the pan. Add the tomato juice from the can to the pan. Increase the heat to bring the mixture to a simmer, then adjust the heat to maintain a simmer and cook the sauce gently until it thickens slightly, about 20 minutes. Taste the sauce and season with salt until it tastes good to you.

Meanwhile, cook the pici: Bring a large pot of water to a boil and add salt until it tastes like well-seasoned broth. Drop in the pici, give it a stir, and cover the pot to quickly return the water to a boil. Uncover or partially cover to maintain the boil and boil the pasta, stirring occasionally, until it is tender but still a little chewy when bitten, 2 to 3 minutes.

When the pasta is ready, use tongs to scoop it from the water and transfer it straight to the pan of sauce. Add 1 cup of the hot pasta water or saved pasta water (see page 31) and the remaining 2 tablespoons olive oil. Crank the heat to medium-high and shake and swirl the pan until the sauce reduces a bit more and begins to hug the pasta, 1 to 2 minutes (keep the pasta moving, adding a little more pasta water if necessary to create a lightly thickened sauce).

Remove from the heat, add the basil, and toss until the pasta and sauce marry, leaving little to no sauce in the pan. Remove the garlic before serving.

Using tongs or a pasta fork, dish out the pasta onto warmed plates, creating some volume by twirling it into a mound. Garnish with Parmesan if you like.

Raschiatelli Arrabbiata with Provolone

Arrabbiata is the Italian way of saying something is spicy. It literally means "angry" and refers to how hot chile peppers make your mouth feel. It's so poetic! This arrabbiata tomato sauce is one of many traditional Roman sauces that can be paired with any number of pastas. We went with raschiatelli here because the shape perfectly cradles the bits of chile peppers and vibrant, summery tomatoes. With some gooey provolone to tame the heat, it makes one banger of a dish! **SERVES 4 TO 6**

Arrabbiata Sauce

- 3 tablespoons extra-virgin olive oil
- 2 red bell peppers, small diced (about 2 cups)
- 4 or 5 Jimmy Nardello or other long red frying peppers, small diced (1 cup)
- ½ small red onion, small diced (about ½ cup)
- 6 shishito peppers, seeded and minced (about ⅓ cup)
- 6 fresh red Thai bird chiles, seeded and minced (about 2 tablespoons)
- 12 ounces beefsteak or cherry tomatoes (cored if large)
- 1½ teaspoons roasted garlic paste (from 4 to 6 cloves roasted garlic; see below)
- 3 sprigs fresh oregano
- Kosher salt
- Sherry vinegar

Raschiatelli

- Kosher salt
- 1 pound fresh Raschiatelli (page 61)
- 6 tablespoons (3 ounces) unsalted butter, cut into pieces
- ½ cup finely grated Parmesan cheese
- ¼ cup finely grated sharp provolone cheese, for garnish

Make the arrabbiata sauce: In a deep 12-inch sauté pan, heat the olive oil over medium heat. Add the bell peppers, Jimmy Nardellos, onion, shishitos, and Thai bird chiles and sweat until the onion is translucent and the bell peppers are just tender, 6 to 8 minutes.

Meanwhile, in a blender or food processor, buzz the tomatoes until reduced to a thick juice, about a minute. Buzz in the roasted garlic paste.

Pour the tomato liquid into the peppers. Bury the oregano sprigs in the sauce, adjust the heat so the mixture simmers gently, and simmer until the sauce thickens a bit and concentrates in flavor, about 30 minutes. Taste it and season with salt and sherry vinegar until it tastes good to you (about 1 teaspoon each should do it). Before using the sauce, remove and discard the oregano, squeezing it to extract any flavorful juices. You should have about 2 cups sauce.

Meanwhile, cook the raschiatelli: Bring a large pot of water to a boil and add salt until it tastes like well-seasoned broth. Drop in the raschiatelli, give it a stir, and cover the pot to quickly return the water to a boil. Uncover or partially cover to maintain the boil and boil the pasta, stirring occasionally, until it is tender but still a little chewy when bitten, 2 to 3 minutes.

Right after dropping the pasta, add the butter to the pan of sauce along with 1 cup of the hot pasta water or saved pasta water (see page 31). Boil the mixture over high heat until it reduces and thickens up again, about 5 minutes.

When the pasta is ready, use a spider strainer or large slotted spoon to scoop it from the water and transfer it straight to the pan. Shake and swirl the pan over high heat until the sauce begins to hug the pasta, 1 to 2 minutes (keep the pasta moving, adding a little more pasta water if necessary to create a loose, lightly thickened sauce).

Remove from the heat, add the Parmesan, and toss until the sauce thickens further and the pasta and sauce marry, leaving little to no sauce in the pan.

Dish out the pasta onto warmed plates, creating some volume by building it into a mound. Garnish with the provolone.

ROASTED GARLIC To roast a whole head of garlic, slice about ¼ inch off the top to expose some of the cloves. Drizzle on a little olive oil, wrap in foil, and roast in a 400°F oven until the cloves are very soft and browned, 40 to 50 minutes. Remove, let cool, and then unwrap and squeeze the whole head to pop out the roasted garlic cloves. Mash the garlic into a paste. Makes about 1 tablespoon roasted garlic paste.

VEGETABLE PASTA

GARGANELLI
with corn and scallions

Pennsylvania grows some amazing sweet corn like Silver Queen, a white corn, and Butter and Sugar, a yellow-and-white variety. I look forward to corn season every year and serve corn pasta throughout the summer. Use whatever variety you can get, preferably local and picked that morning! Keep it cold until the minute you use it and it will taste great here. To balance out the sweetness of the corn, I like the sharp taste of fresh scallions and the savory hit of saltiness in ricotta salata cheese. As for the garganelli, it's the ideal pasta shape for this sauce. The little corn kernels get stuck in the ends of the tubes! **SERVES 4 TO 6**

Corn Crema

- 4 medium ears sweet corn, shucked
- 5 tablespoons (2½ ounces) unsalted butter, cut in pieces
- 1 small leek, white and light green parts only, cleaned and thinly sliced crosswise
- Kosher salt

Garganelli

- Kosher salt
- 1 pound fresh Garganelli (page 78)
- 1 ear sweet corn, shucked
- 1 bunch scallions, trimmed
- 2 tablespoons (1 ounce) unsalted butter
- ½ teaspoon Espelette pepper or hot paprika
- Freshly ground black pepper
- ½ cup finely grated Parmesan cheese
- 1 chunk ricotta salata cheese, for shaving

Make the corn crema: Cut the kernels from the corncobs and scrape the cobs with the blunt side of your knife to extract as much juice as possible. You should have about 4 cups kernels.

In a large sauté pan, melt the butter over medium heat and add the corn and leeks. Sweat the corn and leeks, tossing now and then, until they are tender but not browned, 10 to 12 minutes. Transfer the mixture to a blender and puree until smooth. If necessary to get the puree going, add a little water, just a tablespoon at a time. Taste the crema and season with salt until it tastes good to you (maybe a teaspoon).

Cook the garganelli: Bring a large pot of water to a boil and add salt until it tastes like well-seasoned broth. Drop in the garganelli, give it a stir, and cover the pot to quickly return the water to a boil. Uncover or partially cover to maintain the boil and boil the pasta, stirring occasionally, until it is tender but still a little chewy when bitten, 2 to 3 minutes.

Meanwhile, cut the kernels from the ear of corn and scrape the cob to extract as much juice as possible. You should get about 1 cup. Finely chop the white and light green parts of the scallions and mince the darker green parts, setting them aside separately.

In a deep 12-inch sauté pan, melt the butter over medium heat. Add the corn kernels, corn juice, and white and light green parts of the scallions (reserve the green tops for garnish). Sauté the corn and scallions, stirring now and then, until they are tender but not browned, 3 to 4 minutes. Stir in the Espelette pepper and season with salt and black pepper until the mixture tastes good to you (maybe ½ teaspoon salt).

When the pasta is ready, use a spider strainer or large slotted spoon to scoop it from the water and transfer it straight to the pan with the corn and scallions. Add the corn crema and 1 cup of the hot pasta water or saved pasta water (see page 31). Shake and swirl the pan until the sauce begins to hug the pasta, 2 to 3 minutes (keep the pasta moving, adding a little more pasta water if necessary to create a loose, lightly thickened sauce).

Remove from the heat, add the Parmesan, and toss until the pasta and sauce marry, leaving little to no sauce in the pan.

Dish out the pasta onto warmed plates, creating some volume by building it into a mound. Garnish with the minced scallion greens and some shaved ricotta salata.

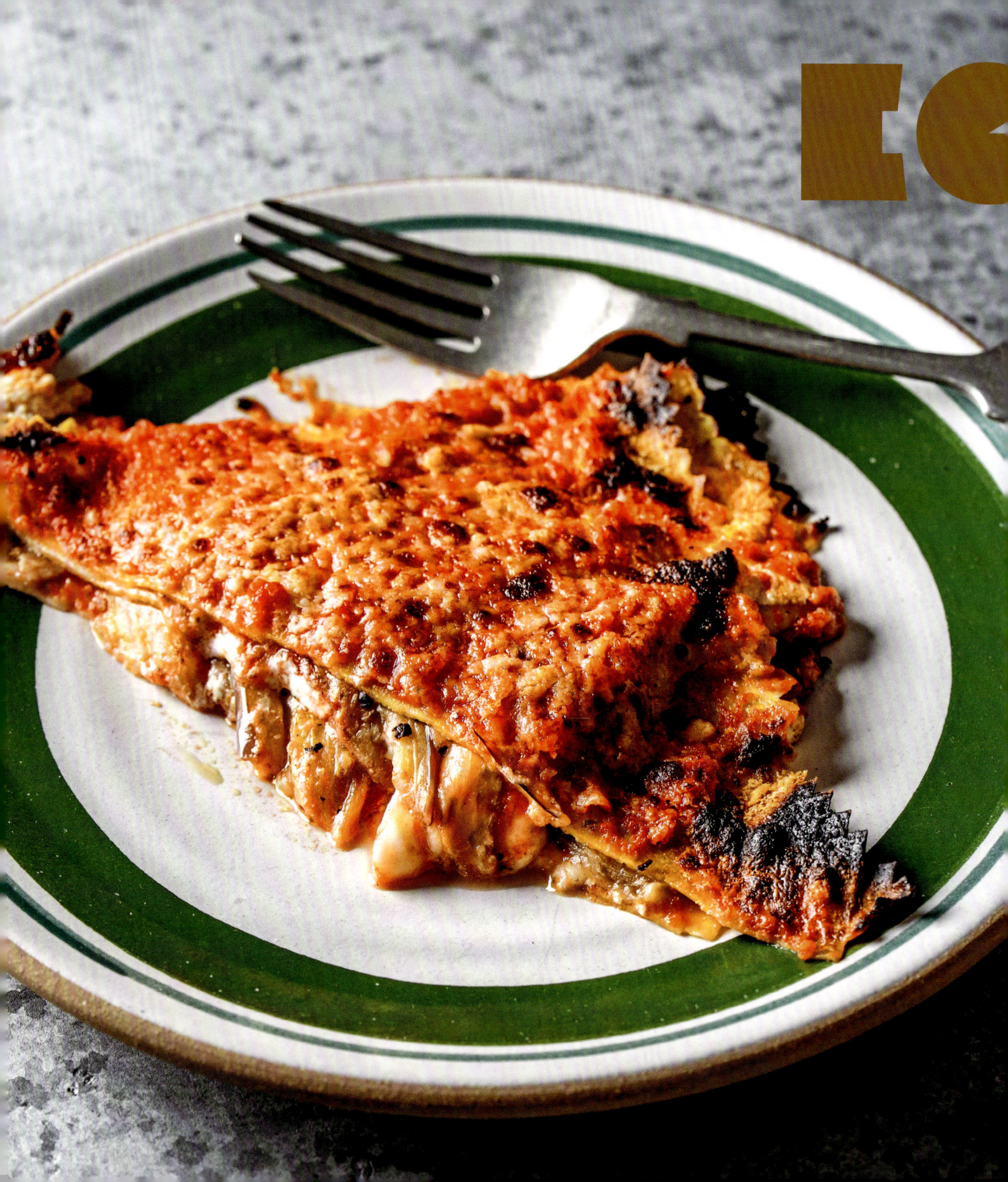

EGGPLANT LASAGNETTA

This is one of those sleeper dishes. People shy away from making it, but it's literally what everybody wants to eat. It's much easier than you think . . . just simple layers of good ingredients that go together in a timeless classic. The secret—if there is one? Cut the eggplant super thin, salt it for 20 minutes, dredge in flour, and fry lightly. With the fresh pasta, quick tomato sauce, and cheeses, it will just melt in your mouth. I like to make individual lasagnas on a sheet pan so everybody gets some crispy edges! To watch a video of making this pasta, scan the QR code on page 112. **SERVES 6**

Tomato Sauce
- ¼ cup extra-virgin olive oil
- 2 garlic cloves, peeled
- 1 medium yellow onion, small diced
- 1½ teaspoons crushed red pepper flakes
- 1½ teaspoons freshly ground black pepper
- 2 (28-ounce) cans peeled whole Italian plum tomatoes, preferably San Marzano, with their juice
- Large handful of fresh basil leaves
- Kosher salt

Make the tomato sauce: In a medium saucepan, heat the olive oil and garlic over medium heat until aromatic, 1 to 2 minutes, swirling the pan a few times. Add the onion and sauté until translucent, 4 to 5 minutes, stirring a few times. Add the pepper flakes and black pepper and cook until aromatic, about 1 minute. Using your hands, pull out and discard the cores from the tomatoes, then crush the tomatoes into the pan. Add the tomato juice from one of the cans to the pan (discard the other can's juice—or drink it!), along with the basil. Simmer over medium-low heat, stirring now and then, until the sauce thickens up a bit and is no longer runny, like jarred tomato sauce, 40 to 50 minutes. Taste and season with salt until it tastes good to you. Remove the garlic and basil leaves and use the sauce immediately, or keep it at room temperature for a few hours. Or transfer it to an airtight container and refrigerate for a few days or freeze for a couple months.

Meanwhile, shallow-fry the eggplant: Thinly slice the eggplant (about ⅛ inch thick) and season it with salt on both sides. Let stand for 20 minutes to draw out some moisture, and then sprinkle both sides with black pepper. Put the flour on a plate or in a shallow bowl and dredge the damp pieces of eggplant in the flour to coat all over, shaking off the excess.

Line a plate with paper towels and have it near the stove. In a large deep sauté pan, heat the olive oil over medium heat. Working in batches, add the eggplant pieces in a single layer and fry until lightly browned on both sides, 3 to 4 minutes per side. Transfer to the paper towels to drain. Repeat with the remaining eggplant.

RECIPE CONTINUES

VEGETABLE PASTA

Eggplant

1 medium Italian or 3 medium Japanese eggplants (about 1 pound total)

Kosher salt and freshly ground black pepper

1 cup tipo "00" or all-purpose flour, for dredging

1 cup extra-virgin olive oil, for frying

Lasagnetta

12 ounces Egg Yolk Dough (page 74), rolled into sheets a little less than ⅛ inch thick

Kosher salt

Extra-virgin olive oil, for the sheet pan

2 cups ricotta cheese

2 (8-ounce) balls fresh mozzarella cheese, sliced about ¼ inch thick

1½ to 2 cups finely grated Parmesan cheese

Cut the pasta squares: Keep a spray bottle of water near your work surface. Lay a pasta sheet on a lightly floured surface. Trim the edges square and then cut the sheet into 4½-inch squares, preferably with a fluted cutter. As you work, lightly mist the sheets with water to prevent them from drying out. Repeat with the remaining dough and then cover the squares with a damp towel to keep them from drying out.

Blanch the pasta: Bring a large pot of water to a boil and add salt until it tastes like well-seasoned broth. Set up a large bowl of ice water. Working in batches to prevent overcrowding, drop the pasta in the boiling water and blanch the squares for 30 seconds, stirring gently to prevent sticking. Using a spider strainer or slotted spoon, transfer the squares to the ice water. When cooled, transfer the squares to damp kitchen towels, laying them flat and mostly separate, and pat them relatively dry. The pieces will be delicate and some may stick, but you should have plenty.

Build the lasagnetta: Preheat the oven to 400°F. Lightly oil a sheet pan and lay out 6 blanched pasta squares on the pan (each square will become a personal lasagnetta with 3 layers of pasta; you can also build the lasagnetta in individual shallow baking dishes). For each lasagnetta, spoon 2 to 3 tablespoons ricotta over the pasta (or squirt the ricotta from a piping bag or zipper-lock bag with one corner cut off), spreading the cheese evenly across the surface. Distribute 1 or 2 mozzarella slices (about 1½ ounces) evenly over the ricotta and then sprinkle on 1 to 2 tablespoons of Parmesan. Spoon enough tomato sauce evenly over the cheese to reach the pasta's edges (3 to 4 tablespoons), covering the pasta edges. Then lay enough slices of fried eggplant over the sauce to cover it in a single layer. Repeat the layering one more time with a pasta square, ricotta, mozzarella, Parmesan, tomato sauce, and eggplant. Top with a third and final pasta square, and spoon a generous amount of tomato sauce over the pasta, covering it completely. Sprinkle on a generous amount of Parmesan.

Bake until the cheeses melt and brown around the edges, about 20 minutes. Remove and let cool for 5 to 10 minutes before serving to let the cheeses set up a bit.

Use a spatula to remove each lasagnetta and its crispy bits from the pan and transfer to a warmed plate (or serve in individual baking dishes).

Scan this code to watch a video of making Eggplant Lasagnetta.

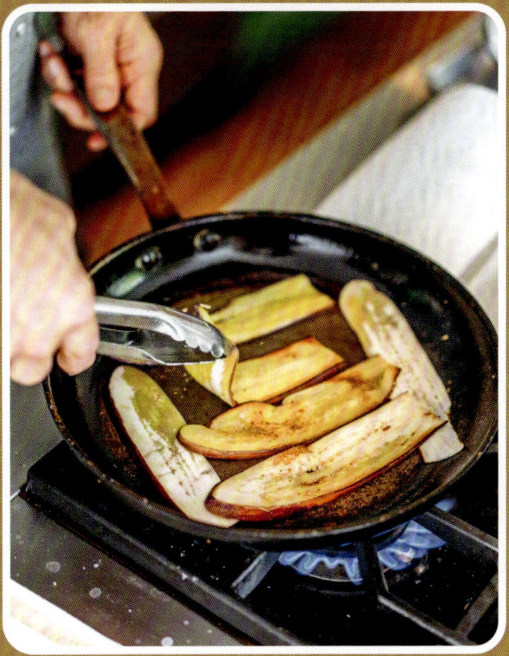

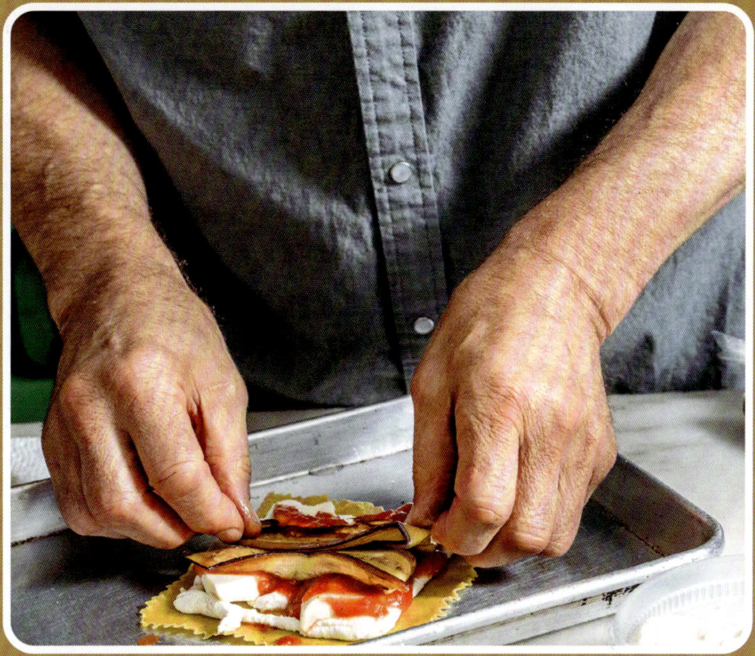

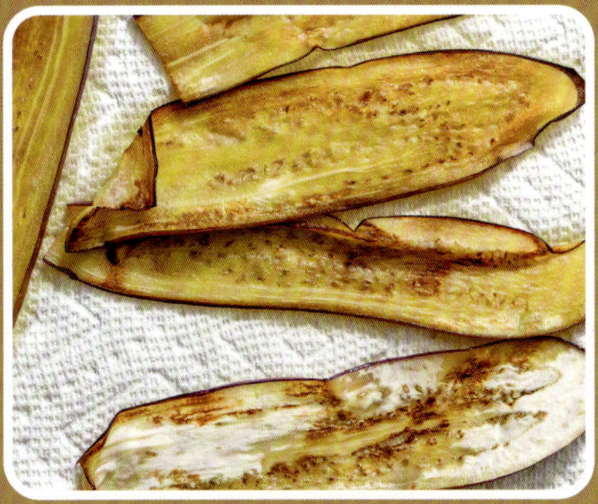

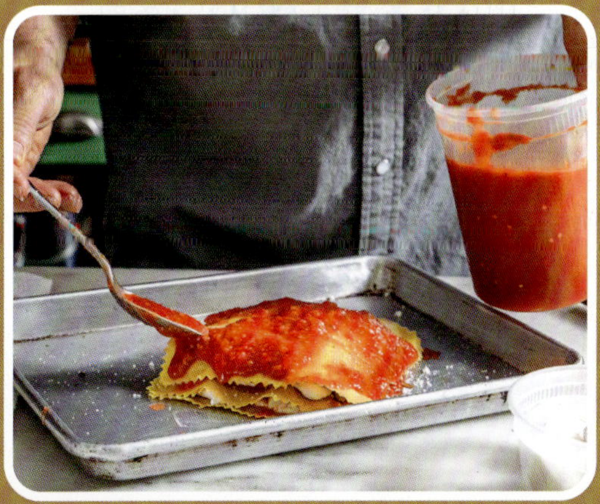

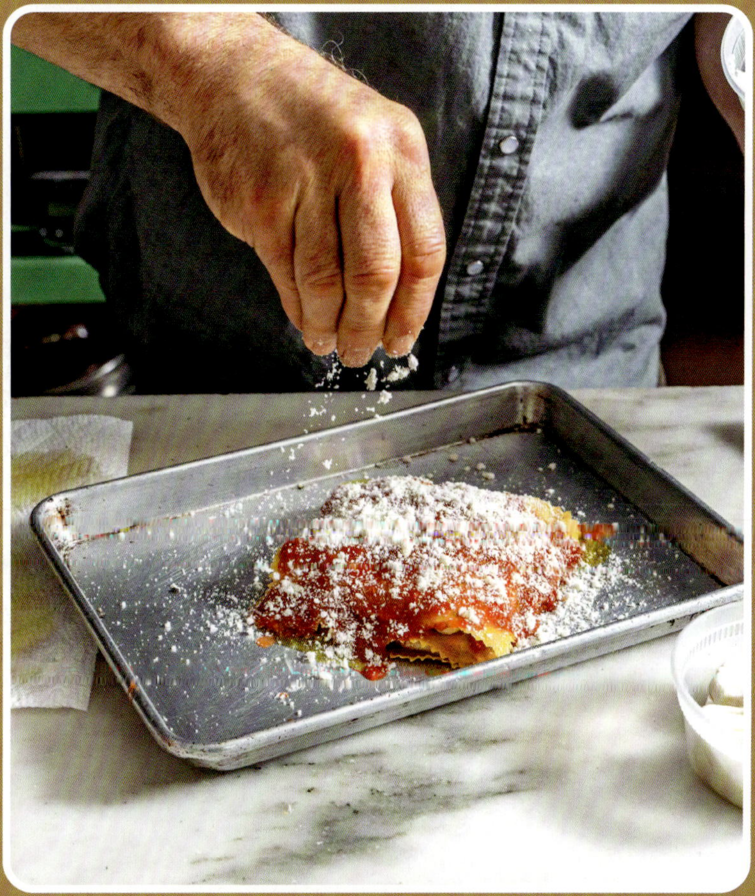

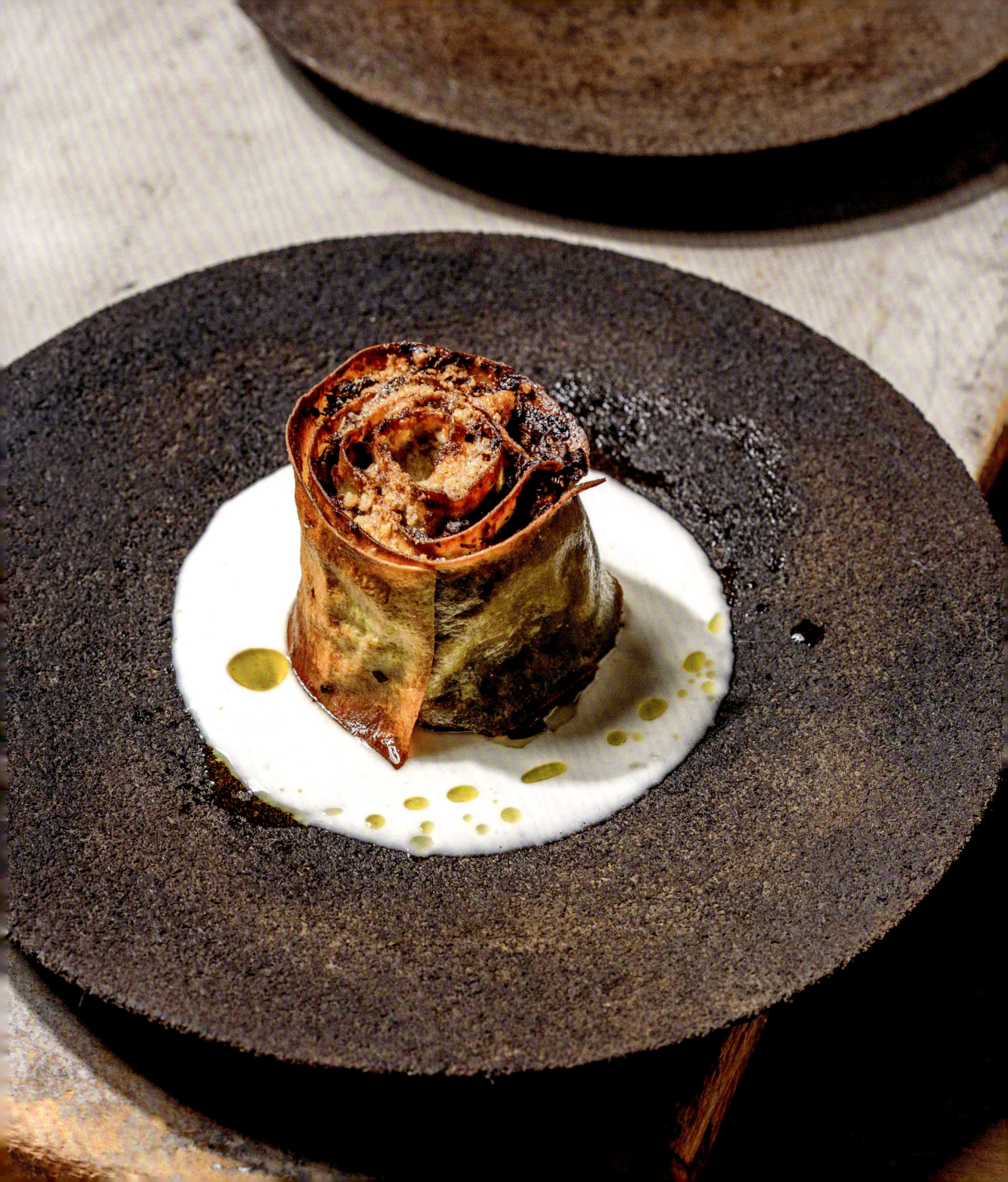

MUSHROOM ROTOLO WITH TALEGGIO FONDUTA

When I got to Bergamo in the fall of 1993, one of the first combinations I tasted was Taleggio cheese and local mushrooms. All of Lombardia makes Taleggio, and Bergamo makes some of the best. The region is overflowing with porcini mushrooms, too—they're everywhere! If you can find them, sub in fresh porcinis for the cremini mushrooms here. But, really, any mushroom mix will taste great. If you can't find black trumpets, use whatever wild mushrooms you can find. Just be sure all your shrooms are free of grit. Trimming the stems and soaking them briefly in water usually does the trick. **SERVES 6**

Mushroom Filling

2 pounds cremini (Baby Bella) mushrooms, cleaned and stems trimmed

1½ pounds mixed oyster, maitake, and/or black trumpet mushrooms, cleaned and stems trimmed

2 tablespoons grapeseed oil or canola oil

6 tablespoons (3 ounces) unsalted butter, cut into pieces

1 medium yellow onion, diced (about 1 cup)

⅛ medium fennel bulb, trimmed, cored, and diced (about ½ cup)

⅓ cup extra-dry vermouth

2 sprigs fresh rosemary and/or thyme

1 garlic clove, peeled

1 dried bay leaf

2-inch Parmesan rind

Kosher salt

Sherry vinegar

Make the mushroom filling: Finely chop all the mushrooms into small pieces. In a large deep sauté pan, heat the oil over medium-high heat. Add the cremini mushrooms and cook, tossing frequently, until they begin to brown, 5 to 6 minutes. Transfer to a bowl. Repeat with the remaining mushrooms, cooking in batches to avoid overcrowding and transferring all the mushrooms to the same bowl when browned.

Add 2 tablespoons of the butter to the pan, reduce the heat to medium, and add the onion and fennel. Sweat the onion and fennel, stirring a few times, until they are translucent but not browned, 4 to 5 minutes. Add the vermouth and cook until the pan goes dry, 3 to 4 minutes. Return all the mushrooms to the pan along with any accumulated juices in the bowl and add just enough water to cover the mushrooms, about 4 cups.

Tie the rosemary, garlic, bay leaf, and Parmesan rind in cheesecloth (or a coffee filter) with kitchen twine to make a sachet. Add the sachet to the pan and bring the mixture to a boil over high heat. Reduce the heat slightly and simmer rapidly, stirring frequently, until all the liquid has evaporated and the pan goes dry, 40 to 50 minutes.

Stir in the remaining 4 tablespoons butter until evenly incorporated. Taste the mixture and season with salt and sherry vinegar until it tastes good to you (maybe about 1½ teaspoons salt and 2 to 3 teaspoons vinegar). Use immediately, or cover and keep at room temperature for up to 2 hours, or refrigerate in an airtight container for up to 2 days.

RECIPE CONTINUES

Rotolo

Kosher salt

8 ounces Egg Yolk Dough (page 74), rolled into sheets about 1/16 inch (1.5mm) thick

Cooking spray

1 cup finely grated Parmesan cheese, plus some for each rotolo

1 teaspoon freshly ground black pepper

2 tablespoons (1 ounce) unsalted butter, cut into teaspoon-size pieces

Taleggio Fonduta

½ cup heavy cream

2 ounces Taleggio cheese without rind, cubed

Kosher salt

Extra-virgin olive oil, for drizzling

Assemble the rotolos: Bring a large pot of water to a boil and add salt until it tastes like well-seasoned broth. Working with one sheet at a time, drop in the pasta and blanch for 30 seconds, stirring and separating it with tongs to keep the sheet from sticking to itself. Carefully remove the pasta sheet, lay it out on a damp kitchen towel, and pat it dry. Repeat with the remaining sheet.

Lay a long sheet (or several smaller sheets) of parchment paper on your work surface to make a bed for the pasta sheets. Coat the parchment lightly with cooking spray and then lay the blanched pasta sheets over the parchment. Smear the mushroom filling over each sheet of pasta, covering it in a thin layer all the way to the edges. Sprinkle generously with the Parmesan and black pepper. Starting at one short end and using the parchment paper, roll each pasta sheet tightly over itself the full length of the sheet, like a fat jelly roll. It helps to put your hands on both sides of the rotolo to keep the mushroom filling from spilling out as you roll. Wrap the logs in the parchment and refrigerate until set, about 1 hour (this makes it much easier to slice).

Remove the rotolo logs from the fridge and set them on a cutting board. Remove and discard the parchment. Using a very sharp knife, carefully slice each log crosswise at 2-inch intervals to make large rotolos. You should have 6 rotolos total.

Preheat the oven to 500°F. Line a sheet pan with parchment paper.

Place the rotolos, cut-side up, on the prepared sheet pan. Top each with a pat (teaspoon) of butter. Sprinkle each rotolo with Parmesan and bake until golden brown and hot in the center, 10 to 15 minutes.

Meanwhile, make the fonduta: In a small saucepan, bring the cream to a brisk simmer over high heat. Reduce the heat to low and whisk in the Taleggio, a few cubes at a time, until the cheese is completely melted. Cook over low heat while whisking constantly until the fonduta thickens enough that you can draw lines through it with a spoon, 6 to 8 minutes. Taste it and add salt until it tastes good to you. For a super-silky texture, pass the fonduta through a fine-mesh sieve into a small heatproof bowl. Keep warm by setting the bowl over a medium saucepan of warm water.

Spoon a shallow pool of fonduta over each warmed plate and top with the rotolo. Drizzle with a little olive oil.

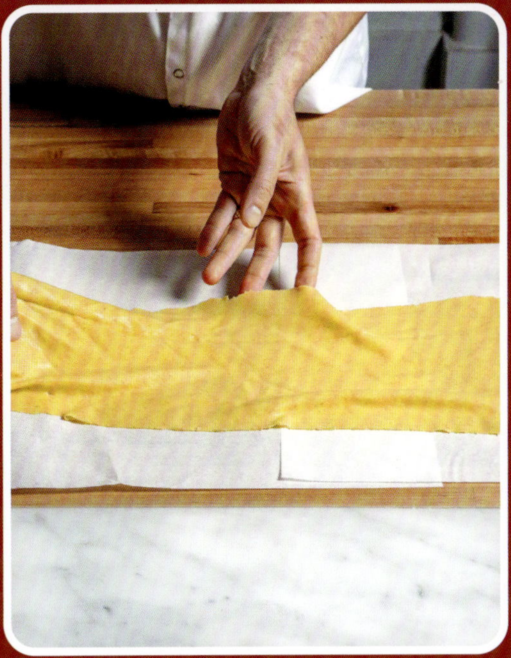
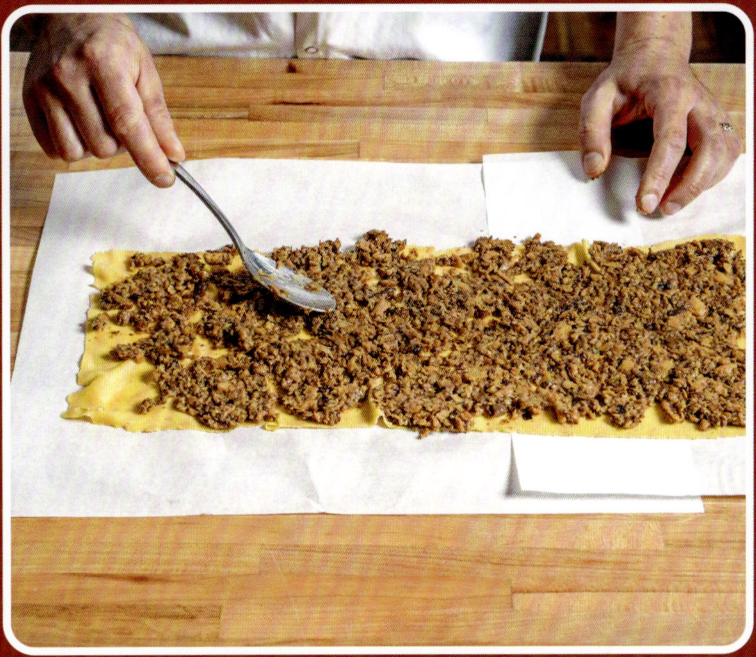
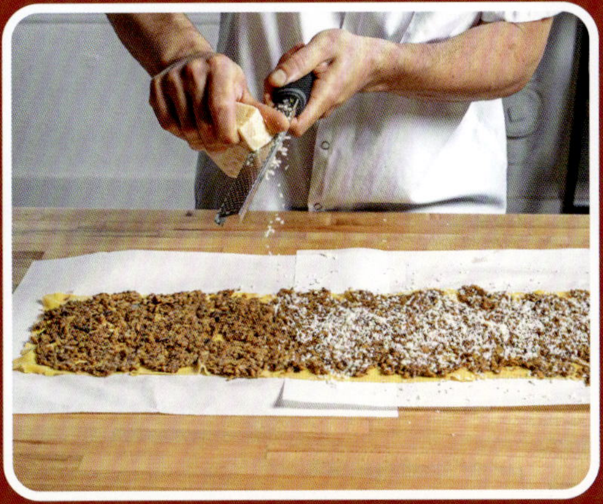
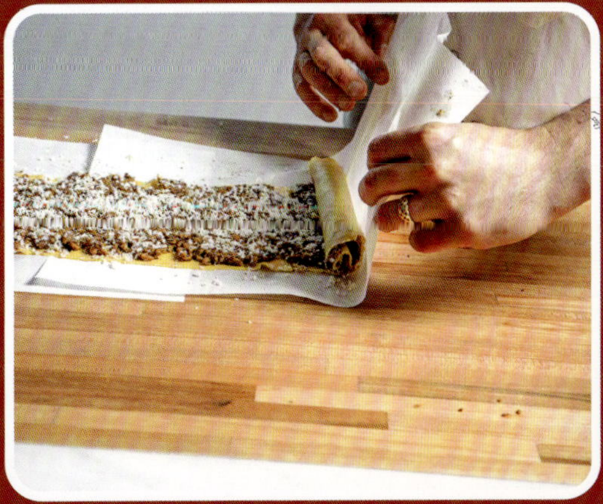
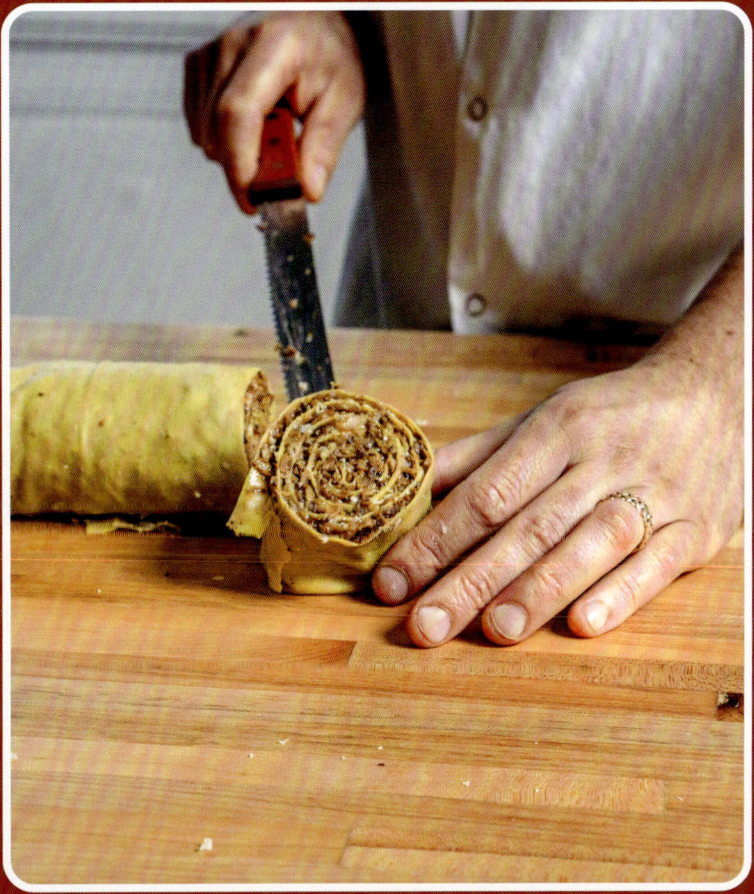

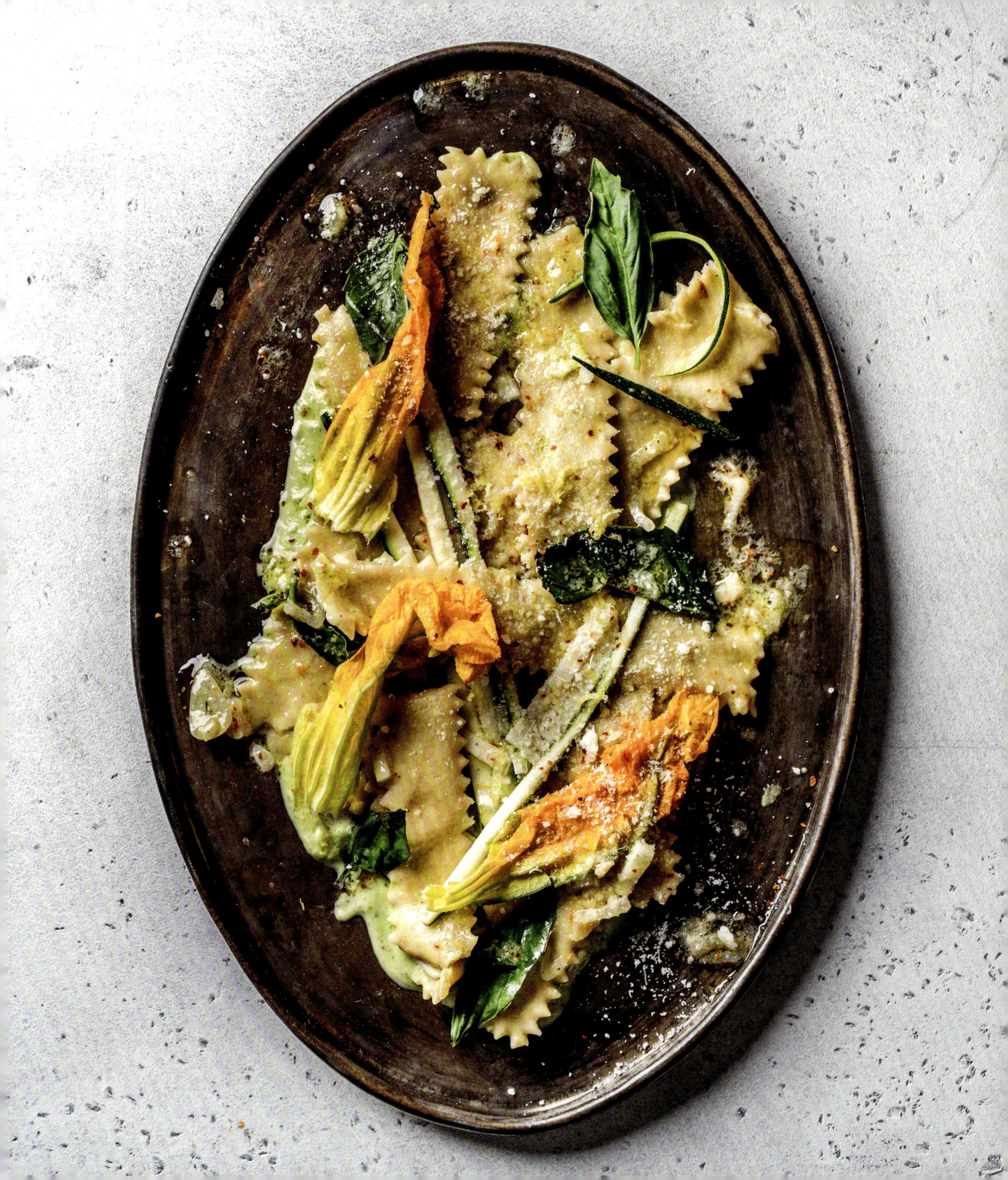

Zucchini-Stuffed Pappardelle with Squash Blossoms and Basil

Stuffed pappardelle? You read that right! This dish blurs the line between noodle and filled pasta. It looks like pappardelle but has a thin layer of creamy zucchini filling inside. The trick is to roll the pasta about twice as thin as you normally would for pappardelle. That's because each stuffed pappardelle has two layers of pasta! With a couple types of summer squash and some fresh basil, this is the perfect summer bite. Garnish the dish with a few squash blossoms to bring even more color and flavor to the plate. To watch a video of making this pasta, scan the QR code on page 120.

SERVES 4 TO 6

Zucchini Filling

- 6 tablespoons extra-virgin olive oil, plus more as needed
- 2 medium shallots, small diced
- 2 small garlic cloves, smashed
- 2 medium zucchini (about 12 ounces total), diced
- Kosher salt and freshly ground black pepper
- 1 cup finely grated Parmesan cheese
- 2 egg yolks

Pappardelle

- 8 ounces Chitarra Dough (page 67), rolled into 2 sheets, each about 1/16 inch (1.5mm) thick
- Semolina flour, for dusting
- Kosher salt and freshly ground black pepper

Make the zucchini filling: In a large sauté pan, heat the olive oil over medium heat. Add the shallot and garlic and sweat, stirring now and then, until the shallot is translucent, 3 to 4 minutes. Add the zucchini and sweat, stirring a few times, until it is tender but not browned, 5 to 7 minutes.

Transfer the pan contents to a blender or food processor and puree, adding a touch more olive oil only if needed to get the mixture to puree. Taste it and season with salt and pepper until it tastes good to you (maybe ¾ teaspoon salt). Scoop out and reserve about 1 cup of this puree for the plates. Add the Parmesan and egg yolks to the rest of the puree and blend to combine. Use immediately or refrigerate in an airtight container for up to 8 hours.

Fill the pappardelle: Lay both pasta sheets on a lightly floured work surface. As you work, lightly mist the sheets to prevent them from drying out. Spread the filling over one sheet of pasta, covering it entirely. Lay the second sheet of pasta evenly over the first, lining up the sheets from one end to the other. Gently pat the pasta to release any air bubbles. Using a heavy fluted pasta cutter, trim the edges square and then cut ribbons of stuffed pappardelle that are 7 inches long by 1 inch wide. If your sheet is 7 inches wide, just cut the pasta crosswise at 1-inch intervals. (Cutting will seal the edges, but as you cut, a small amount of filling may squish out the sides, which is fine.) Dust the pieces with flour and place on lightly floured sheet pans. Use immediately or cover and refrigerate for up to 4 hours.

RECIPE CONTINUES

- 2 tablespoons extra-virgin olive oil
- 3 medium shallots, minced
- 3 garlic cloves, minced to a paste (about 1½ teaspoons paste)
- 1 medium yellow summer squash (6 to 8 ounces), julienned
- 1 medium zucchini (6 to 8 ounces), julienned
- ½ lemon
- 12 to 18 fresh squash blossoms
- Leaves from 3 sprigs fresh basil

Scan this code to watch a video of making Zucchini-Stuffed Pappardelle.

Cook the pappardelle: Bring a large pot of water to a boil and add salt until it tastes like well-seasoned broth. Drop in the pappardelle, give it a stir, and cover the pot to quickly return the water to a boil. Uncover or partially cover to maintain the boil and boil the pasta, stirring occasionally, until it is tender but still a little chewy when bitten, 2 to 3 minutes.

Meanwhile, in a deep 12-inch sauté pan, heat the olive oil over medium heat. Add the shallots and garlic paste and sauté, stirring often, until the shallots are translucent, 2 to 3 minutes. Add the summer squash and zucchini along with ½ cup of the hot pasta water or saved pasta water (see page 31) and simmer over medium-high heat until the zucchini begins to soften, about a minute.

Using a spider strainer or a large slotted spoon, scoop the cooked pappardelle from the water and transfer it straight to the pan. Crank the heat to high and shake and swirl the pan until the sauce begins to hug the pasta, about a minute (keep the pasta moving, adding a little more pasta water if necessary to create a lightly thickened sauce, but keep in mind that the squashes will release water as they cook). Taste everything, adding a squeeze of lemon juice, salt, and pepper until it tastes good to you. Remove from the heat and add the squash blossoms and basil. Toss until the pasta and sauce marry, leaving almost no sauce in the pan.

Spread a swoosh of the reserved zucchini filling over the bottom of each warmed plate. Dish out the pappardelle and squash blossoms among the plates, distributing everything evenly.

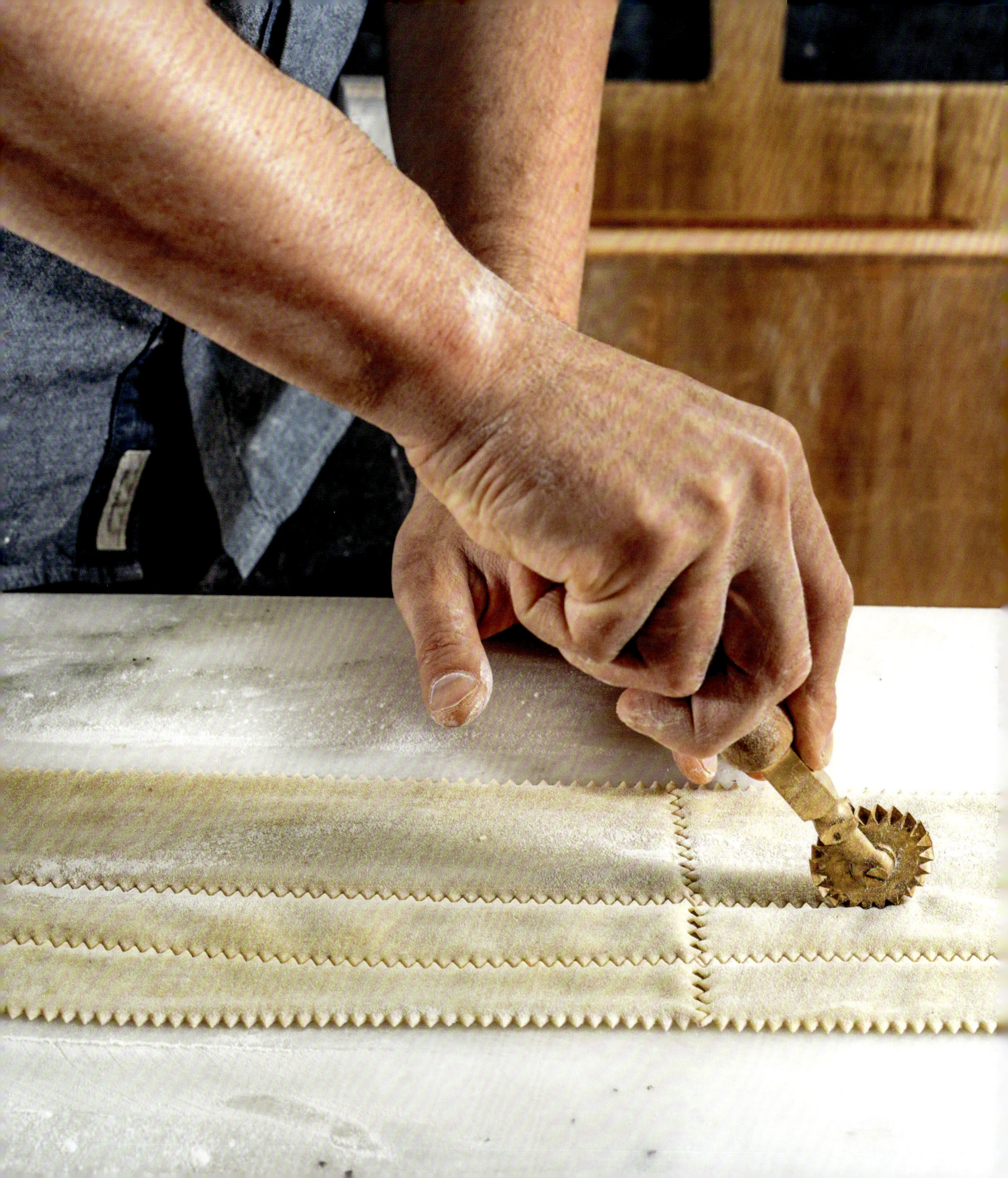

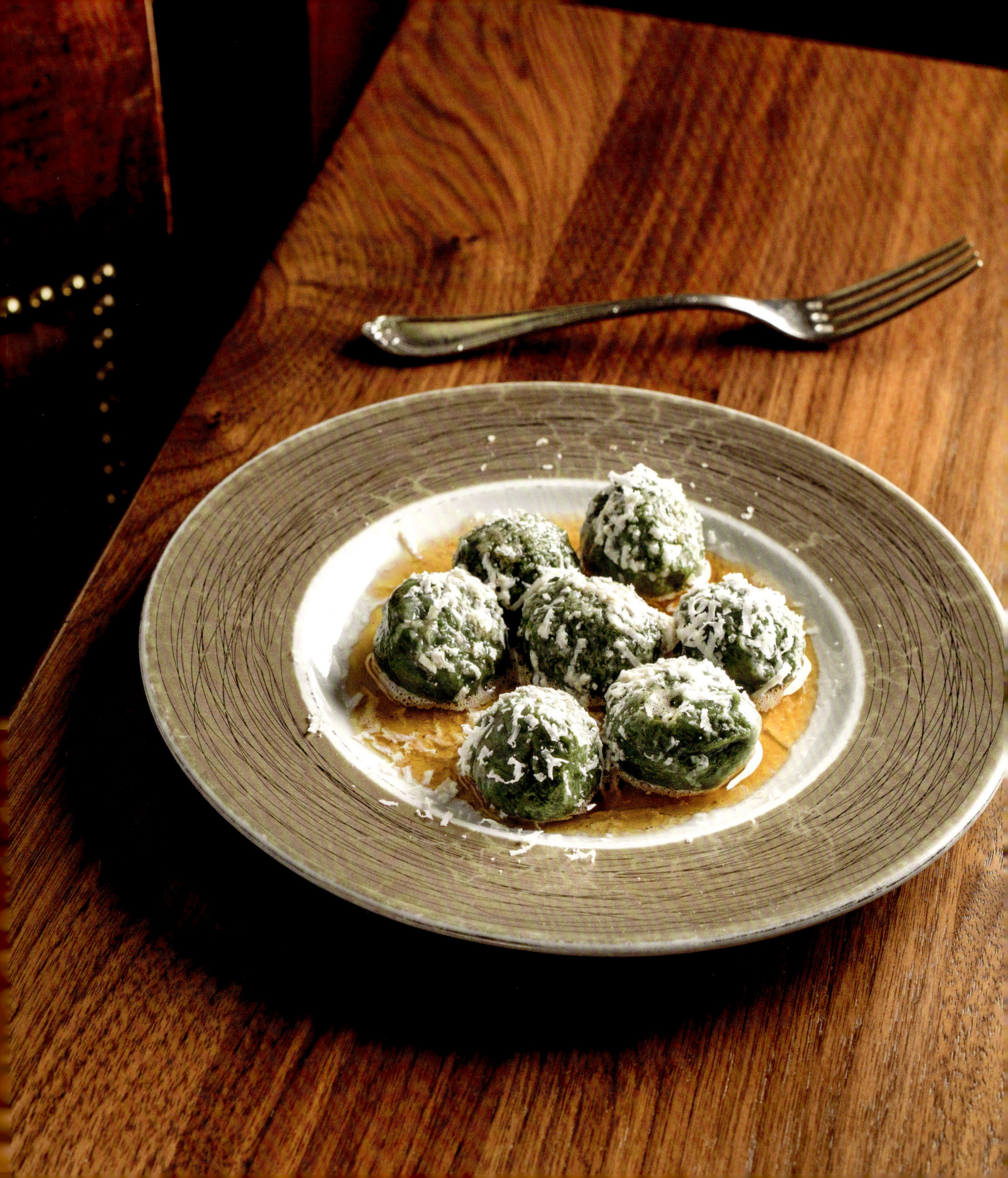

Spinach Gnocchi with Brown Butter and Shaved Ricotta Salata

About twenty years ago, I tried to remove this dish from the Vetri menu. I just wanted to switch things up. I literally received hate mail, so I put it back on. It will remain there forever! When you make this dish, keep in mind that the spinach needs to drain for a day to remove excess water, so start at least a day before you plan to serve it. The ethereal texture is worth the wait. To watch a video of making the gnocchi, scan the QR code on page 124. **SERVES 4 TO 6**

Kosher salt

2½ pounds fresh mature spinach, washed, large stems removed

⅔ cup finely grated Parmesan cheese

½ cup bread flour

⅓ cup plain dried bread crumbs

Pinch of freshly grated nutmeg

1 large egg

2 cups all-purpose flour

6 tablespoons (3 ounces) unsalted butter, cut into pieces

1 small chunk (about 3 × 3 inches) Parmesan cheese

1 small chunk (about 3 × 3 inches) ricotta salata cheese

SIMPLIFY IT

Use frozen spinach: You'll need 2½ boxes (10 ounces each) frozen spinach. Thaw the spinach, squeeze it with your hands to remove excess moisture, and then puree and hang it to drain as directed in the recipe.

Set up a large bowl of ice water. Bring a large pot of salted water to a boil. Add the spinach to the boiling water in a few batches and blanch until dark green and tender, 3 to 4 minutes per batch. Note that any remaining stems on the spinach must be soft enough to puree until smooth or the gnocchi will be stringy. Transfer the spinach to the ice water, swishing it around until cold. Reserve ½ cup of the spinach blanching liquid.

Remove the spinach from the ice water, squeeze it with your hands over a sink to remove any excess moisture, and place in a food processor. Process for a full 5 minutes, or until very smooth, adding up to ½ cup of the reserved blanching liquid if necessary to create a smooth mixture. The consistency of the spinach should be very mushy, like a wet batter. Transfer the pureed spinach to a medium-mesh sieve set over a bowl, cover, and refrigerate for 18 to 24 hours to drain off excess moisture. When fully drained, you should have about 1 pound of drained spinach puree.

Make the gnocchi batter: Place the drained spinach puree in a large bowl or in the bowl of a stand mixer fitted with the paddle attachment. Add the Parmesan, bread flour, bread crumbs, and nutmeg and mix with a rubber spatula or on medium-low speed until blended, 1 to 2 minutes. Taste the mixture and season with salt until it tastes good to you (about ½ teaspoon should do it). Add the egg and mix until it is evenly incorporated. Spoon the mixture into a piping bag or zipper-lock bag, seal, and use immediately. (Or seal and refrigerate for up to 1 day.)

RECIPE CONTINUES

Form the gnocchi: Dump the 2 cups all-purpose flour onto a sheet pan, shaking it to cover the pan bottom. This is your landing zone for the piped balls of gnocchi. Cut off the tip of the piping bag (or one corner if using a zipper-lock bag) to make ½-inch-diameter hole. To help form the gnocchi, quickly dip the index and middle fingers of your nondominant hand into the flour to coat. Use your dominant hand to pipe the gnocchi batter onto your floured fingers so that the batter begins to form a ball as it hits your fingers. Keep piping to create a ball about 1 inch in diameter and then drop the ball into the flour landing zone. Quickly reflour your fingers and continue piping and dropping 1-inch balls of gnocchi into the flour. Periodically shake the sheet pan to coat the gnocchi in flour to prevent sticking. When all the gnocchi are piped (you should have 40 to 50), pick up one ball with each hand and shake off the excess flour. Roll the gnocchi in your palms as if they are dice to help shape them into smooth spheres. Blow off or shake off the excess flour, letting the flour fall through your fingers. At this point, you can cook them immediately, or freeze them in a single layer on a parchment-lined sheet pan until solid and then transfer them to a zipper-lock bag and freeze them for up to 2 weeks. Take the gnocchi straight from the freezer to the boiling water, adding about 30 seconds to the cooking time.

Make the brown butter: In a medium sauté pan, melt the butter over medium heat. After a few minutes, it will stop bubbling and start to slowly brown. Swirl the pan for even browning and keep cooking until it turns a light golden color, 6 to 8 minutes. Remove from the heat (it will continue cooking off the heat) and continue swirling until the butter turns a deep amber brown like the color of hazelnuts, about 2 minutes. Season with about ¼ teaspoon salt and set aside. You might want to start this process after you get your pasta water boiling (next step).

Cook the gnocchi: Bring a large pot of water to a boil and add salt until it tastes like well-seasoned broth. Drop in the gnocchi, give them a gentle stir, and cover the pot to return the water quickly to a boil. Uncover or partially cover to maintain the boil and boil the gnocchi until they begin to float, 3 to 5 minutes. When they float, the gnocchi will be 20 to 30 seconds from being finished.

Using a spider strainer or slotted spoon, remove one gnoccho from the water and test its doneness by gently squeezing it. The outside "walls" of the sphere should feel firm and set, while the middle of the ball should feel "squishy." This is the desired doneness, as the gnocchi will be tender and somewhat oozy when split in half with a fork.

When the gnocchi are done, scoop them from the water with the spider or slotted spoon, let them drain over the pot, and divide them among warmed bowls, serving 6 to 8 gnocchi in each bowl. Grate the Parmesan and shave or shred the ricotta salata over each serving and pour on the brown butter.

Scan this code to watch a video of making Spinach Gnocchi.

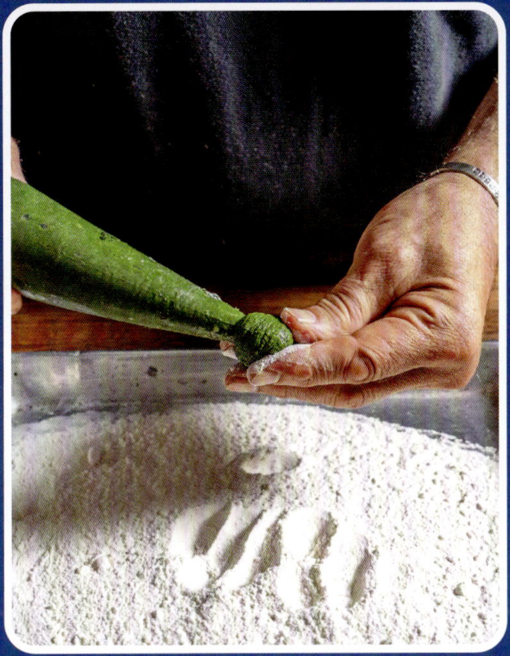
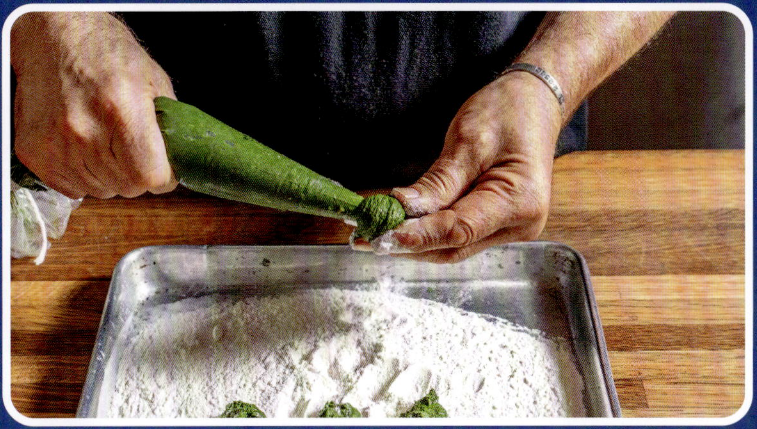
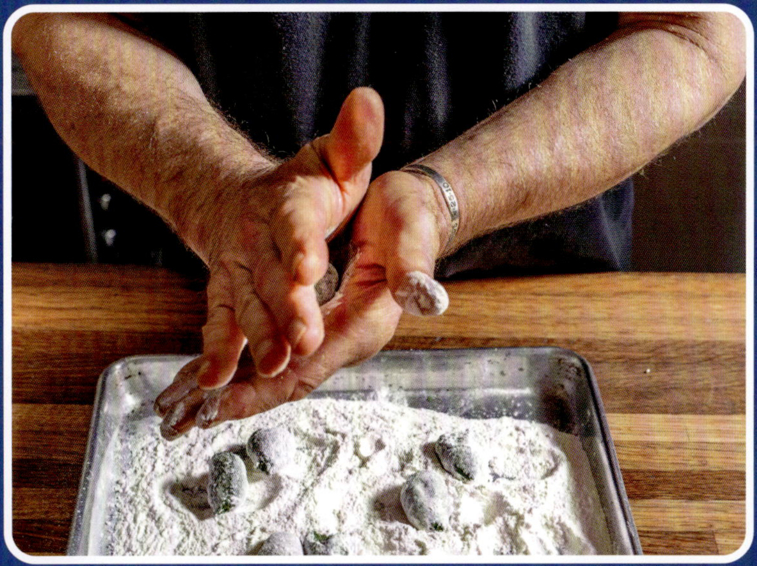
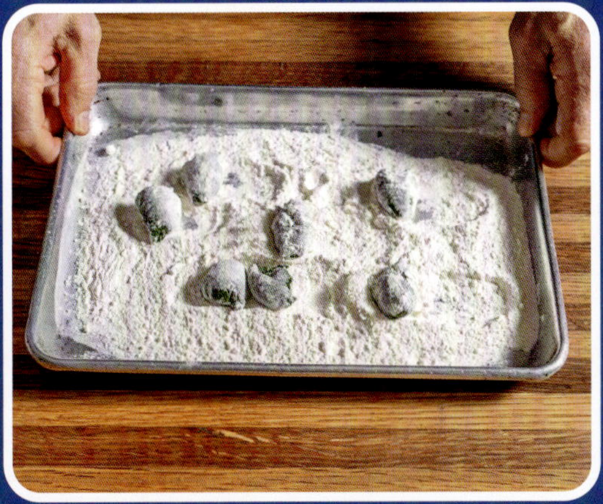
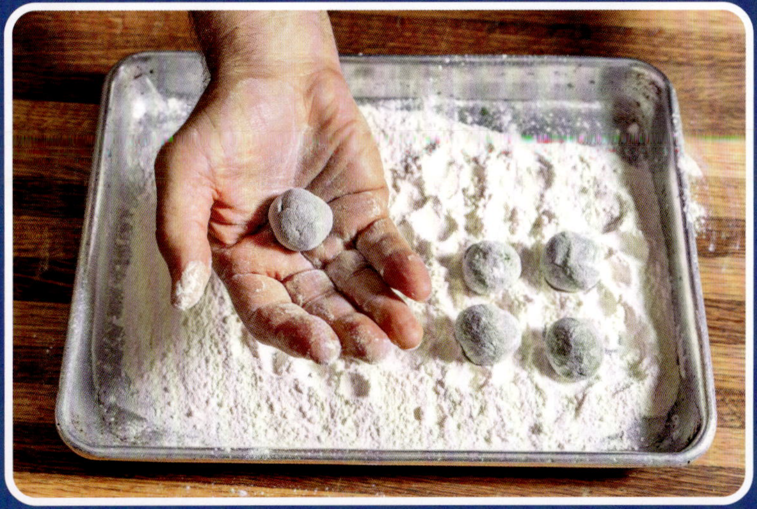
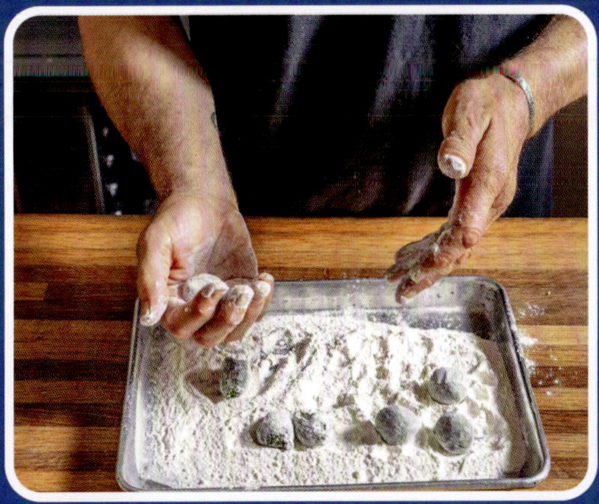

Ricotta Gnocchi with Brown Butter and Fried Leeks

Spinach Gnocchi (page 123) has been synonymous with Vetri Cucina since we opened in 1998. And now these ricotta gnocchi are synonymous with Fiorella, our sister restaurant focused on pasta. No matter the season, they are always on the menu with various accompaniments. Brown butter is the most basic and a legit sauce in its own right. With some fried leeks, this simple combo soars. Try it with fried sage in the fall or sautéed corn and blueberries in the summer, as shown in the photograph. Forget about the potato gnocchi gut bombs you may have tried in the past. These tender orbs just melt in your mouth. Plus, they're easy to make. **SERVES 4 TO 6**

Ricotta Gnocchi

- 1 cup ricotta impastata (see page 93)
- Scant ¾ cup all-purpose flour, plus 2 cups for shaping
- ⅔ cup finely grated Parmesan cheese, plus more for serving
- ⅛ teaspoon freshly grated nutmeg
- Kosher salt
- 2 large eggs

Fried Leeks and Brown Butter

- 2 medium leeks
- ½ cup grapeseed or canola oil
- Kosher salt
- 8 tablespoons (4 ounces) unsalted butter, cut into pieces

Mix the ricotta gnocchi batter: In the bowl of a stand mixer fitted with the paddle attachment, combine the ricotta, flour, Parmesan, and nutmeg and blend on medium-low speed until combined, 1 to 2 minutes. Taste the mixture, adding salt (about ¼ teaspoon) until it tastes good to you (when the salt level is perfect, it should bring the Parmesan alive!). Add the eggs and continue mixing until they are evenly blended throughout the batter. Spoon the mixture into a piping bag or zipper-lock bag, seal, and use immediately. (Or seal and refrigerate for up to 4 hours.)

Form the gnocchi: Form the gnocchi as directed on page 124. To watch a video of the process, scan the QR code on page 124.

Shallow-fry the leeks: Trim the ends of the leeks and then halve them lengthwise. Rinse under cool running water, separating the leaf layers near where the leek turns white to remove any grit (be vigilant—the grit hides in there!). Cut off and discard the dark green tops of the cleaned leeks and cut the white and light green parts crosswise into 2-inch lengths and then lengthwise into narrow strips (julienne). You should have about 1 cup julienned leeks.

Line a plate with paper towels and have it near the stove. Heat the oil in a medium sauté pan over medium heat (when the oil is hot enough, a julienned leek should immediately begin sizzling gently). Working in batches to prevent crowding, add the julienned leeks and fry until light golden brown, about 2 minutes. Use tongs to transfer the fried leeks to paper towels to drain. Spread them in a thin layer and immediately season with salt.

RECIPE CONTINUES

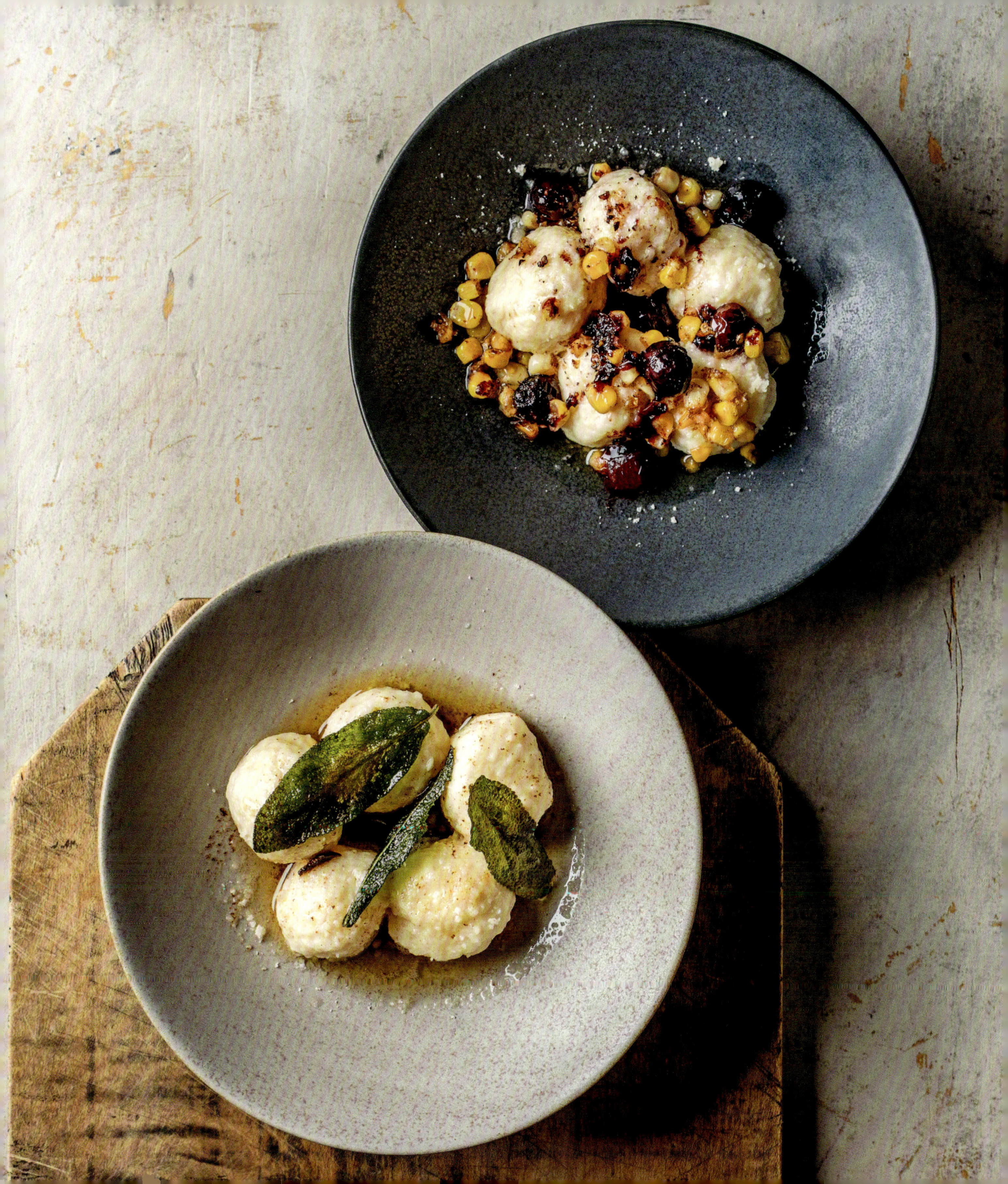

Make the brown butter: In a medium sauté pan, melt the butter over medium heat. After a few minutes, it will stop bubbling and start to slowly brown. Swirl the pan for even browning and keep cooking until it turns a light golden color, 5 to 6 minutes. Remove from the heat (it will continue cooking off the heat) and continue swirling until the butter turns a deep amber brown like the color of hazelnuts, about 2 minutes. Season with a big pinch of salt and set aside. If you're quick about it, you could start this process after you get your pasta water boiling (next step).

Cook the gnocchi: Bring a large pot of water to a boil and add salt until it tastes like well-seasoned broth. Drop in the gnocchi, give them a gentle stir, and cover the pot to return the water quickly to a boil. Uncover or partially cover to maintain the boil and boil the gnocchi until they begin to float, 3 to 5 minutes. When they float, the gnocchi will be 20 to 30 seconds from being finished.

Using a spider strainer or slotted spoon, remove one gnoccho from the water and test its doneness by gently squeezing it. The outside "walls" of the sphere should feel firm and set, while the middle of the ball should feel "squishy." This is the desired doneness, as the gnocchi will be tender and somewhat oozy when split in half with a fork.

When the gnocchi are done, scoop them from the water with the spider or slotted spoon, let them drain over the pot, and divide them among the bowls, serving 6 to 8 gnocchi in each bowl. Shower the gnocchi generously with Parmesan and then spoon on the hot brown butter. Garnish each serving with a little nest of fried leeks.

Squash Cavatelli Pomodoro

You often see squash paired with sage, apples, and other fall or winter flavors. We wanted to take a fresh approach and discovered a novel pairing in our pickle pantry: tomatoes. Moriah Greathouse, our pasta chef at Vetri in Philly, had put up a simple conserva with the summer's ripest cherry tomatoes. The conserva's bright acidity complemented a rich, creamy squash puree perfectly, especially with pillowy-soft squash cavatelli. This dish is ideal for the shoulder season between late summer and early fall. To make it extra special, drape each serving with a few super-thin slices of pancetta or lardo! **SERVES 4 TO 6**

Tomato Conserva
- 1 pound cherry tomatoes, halved
- 2 tablespoons extra-virgin olive oil
- Kosher salt and freshly ground black pepper
- 1 teaspoon sherry vinegar, plus more as needed

Cavatelli
- Kosher salt
- 1 pound fresh Squash Cavatelli (page 92)
- ¾ cup squash puree (see page 92)
- 4 tablespoons (2 ounces) unsalted butter, cut into pieces
- Sherry vinegar
- Freshly ground black pepper
- Leaves from 3 sprigs fresh thyme (about 1 tablespoon)
- Extra-virgin olive oil, for drizzling

Make the tomato conserva: Preheat the oven to 375°F.

Place the tomatoes on a sheet pan and drizzle on the olive oil. Season with salt and pepper until a tomato tastes good to you (about ½ teaspoon salt), shaking the pan to coat evenly. Turn the tomatoes cut-sides up.

Roast the tomatoes until they dry out slightly, brown some around the edges, and taste awesome, 20 to 25 minutes. Drizzle with the sherry vinegar, adding more if you like until they taste even better. Let the tomato conserva cool on the pan and use within a few hours or refrigerate in an airtight container for up to 2 days.

Meanwhile, cook the cavatelli: Bring a large pot of water to a boil and add salt until it tastes like well-seasoned broth. Drop in the cavatelli, give it a stir, and cover the pot to quickly return the water to a boil. Uncover or partially cover to maintain the boil and boil the pasta, stirring occasionally, until it is tender but still a little chewy when bitten, 2 to 3 minutes.

Right after dropping the pasta, in a deep 12-inch sauté pan, heat the squash puree and butter over medium-high heat. When the butter melts, add the tomato conserva and 1 cup of the hot pasta water or saved pasta water (see page 31). Crank the heat to high and simmer the mixture until it reduces slightly, 2 to 3 minutes.

Using a spider strainer or slotted spoon, scoop the cooked cavatelli from the water and transfer it straight to the pan. Shake and swirl the pan until the sauce begins to hug the pasta, about a minute (keep the pasta moving, adding a little more pasta water if necessary to create a lightly thickened sauce). Taste everything and season with sherry vinegar, salt, and pepper until it tastes good to you. Remove from the heat, add the thyme, and toss until the pasta and sauce marry, leaving almost no sauce in the pan.

Dish out the pasta onto warmed plates and drizzle with olive oil.

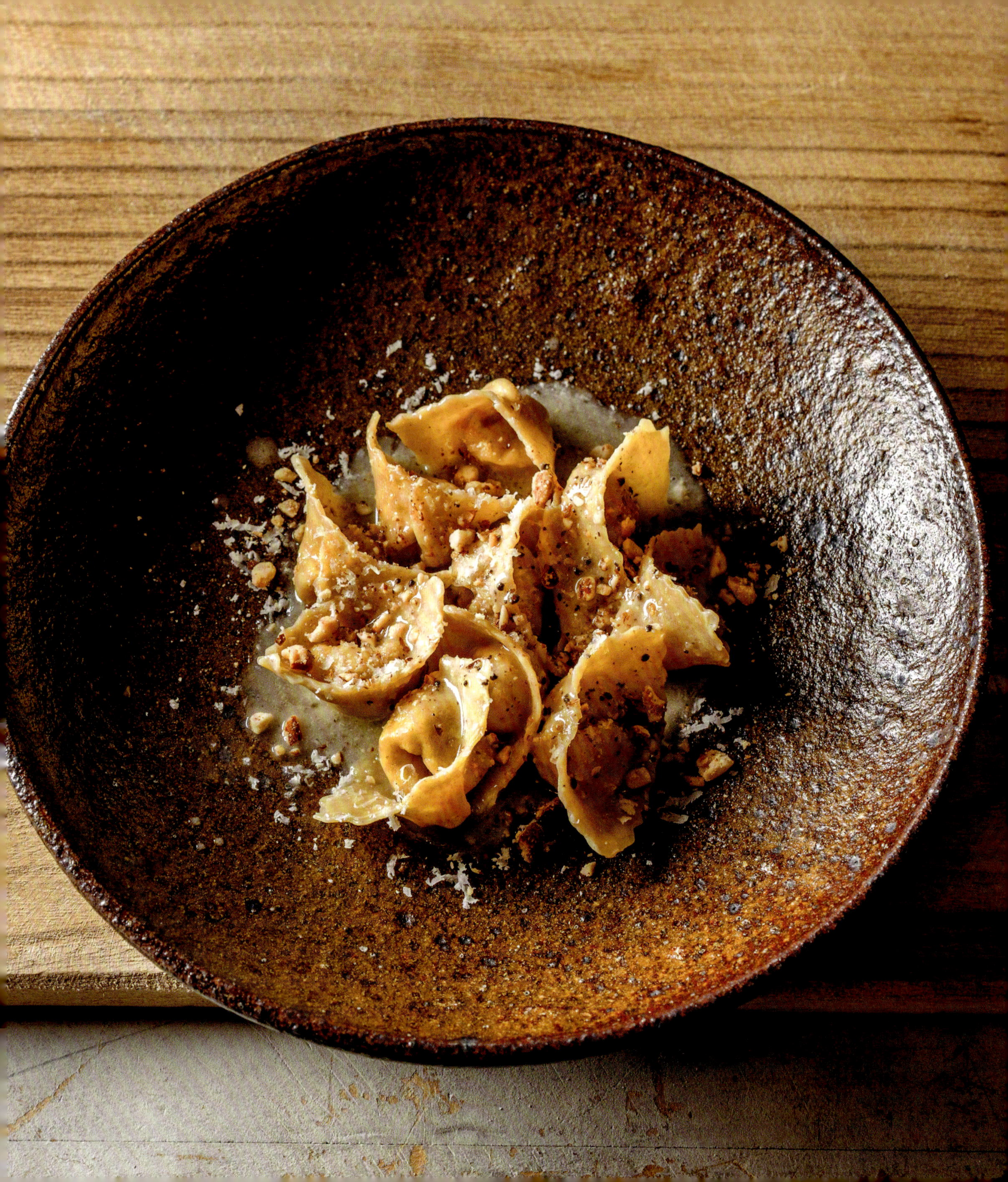

ALMOND TORTELLINI WITH TRUFFLE AND PARMESAN

One of the greatest bites of my life was—and still is—almond risotto tortellini with fresh shaved white truffles. My friend Luca Brasi served it at his restaurant La Lucanda near Bergamo. This pasta is such a head turner. No one expects to find risotto in a pasta stuffing, but it's so good and creamy when you puree it smooth. If you're lucky enough to get fresh white truffles during the fall season, this is the dish to shave them over. To watch a video of making this pasta, scan the QR code on page 132. **SERVES 6**

Almond Risotto Filling

¼ cup skin-on whole almonds

1 tablespoon extra-virgin olive oil

2 tablespoons small-diced yellow onion

½ cup Carnaroli or Arborio rice

2 tablespoons dry white wine, such as pinot grigio

2 cups boiling water, plus more as needed

¼ cup finely grated Parmesan cheese

Kosher salt and freshly ground black pepper

1 large egg

Make the almond risotto filling: In a dry medium saucepan, toast the almonds over medium heat until lightly browned and fragrant, 4 to 6 minutes, shaking the pan a few times for even toasting. Remove from the pan, let cool, and finely chop.

While the almonds are cooling, heat the olive oil in the same pan over medium heat. Add the onion and sauté until translucent, 2 to 3 minutes. Add the rice and cook until toasted and translucent around the edges, 3 to 4 minutes, swirling the pan to coat the rice evenly with oil. Before the onion and rice turn brown, pour in the wine, swirl to deglaze the pan, and cook until the pan goes dry, 2 to 3 minutes. Gradually add the boiling water, ¼ cup at a time, allowing the water to be absorbed completely before adding more, stirring occasionally (it's not necessary to stir constantly). Continue to add the water and cook the rice until it is very tender (not al dente), 20 to 25 minutes. The rice should be softer than when you are making risotto as its own dish.

Transfer the cooked rice to a food processor and process until a smooth, stiff paste forms. Transfer to a bowl and let cool slightly. Stir in the Parmesan and toasted almonds (use your hands if the filling is too stiff for a fork or spoon). Taste the filling and season with salt and pepper until it tastes good to you (maybe about ¼ teaspoon salt). Stir in the egg until evenly incorporated. Spoon the filling into a piping bag or zipper-lock bag, seal, and use immediately. (Or seal and refrigerate for up to 2 days.)

RECIPE CONTINUES

Tortellini

1 pound Egg Yolk Dough (page 74), rolled into sheets about 1⁄16 inch (1.5mm) thick

All-purpose flour, for dusting

Kosher salt

2 tablespoons skin-on whole almonds

7 tablespoons (3½ ounces) unsalted butter, cut into pieces

1½ teaspoons white truffle paste, or ¼ teaspoon white truffle oil

Freshly ground black pepper

6 tablespoons finely grated Parmesan cheese

Fresh white truffles, for shaving (optional)

Assemble the tortellini: Keep a spray bottle of water near your work surface. Lay a pasta sheet on a lightly floured surface and trim the edges square (cover the remaining pasta with a damp towel to keep it from drying out). Cut the sheet into 2½-inch squares and lightly mist the pieces with water. Cut off the tip of the piping bag (or one corner if using a zipper-lock bag) to make a ¾-inch-diameter hole. Pipe ¾-inch balls of filling in the center of each square.

To shape each tortellini, fold the bottom half of the pasta square over the filling in line with the top half to make a rectangle. Use your fingers to pat gently around the filling outward to the edges, pressing the edges closed. Pick up the tortellini and use your finger to make a dimple in the back of the pasta into the filling, and then bend the pasta points over the dimple overlapping them slightly and pinching them together to seal and make the tortellini shape. Transfer to a lightly floured baking sheet. Repeat with the remaining pasta and filling and dust the formed tortellini lightly with flour. You should have 70 to 80 tortellini. Use them within 1 hour. Or cover and refrigerate for up to 4 hours. You can also freeze them in a single layer, transfer them to a zipper-lock bag, and freeze them for up to 3 days. Take the pasta straight from the freezer to the boiling pasta water, adding about 30 seconds to the cooking time.

Cook the tortellini: Bring a large pot of water to a boil and add salt until it tastes like well-seasoned broth. Drop in the tortellini, give them a gentle stir, and cover the pot to quickly return the water to a boil. Uncover or partially cover to maintain the boil and boil the pasta, stirring occasionally, until it is tender but still a little chewy when bitten, about 2 minutes.

While the pasta water comes to a boil, in a deep 12-inch sauté pan, shake the almonds over medium heat until fragrant and evenly toasted, 4 to 6 minutes. Transfer to a cutting board and finely chop.

Crank the heat under the sauté pan to high and add the butter, the truffle paste (if using; otherwise, wait to add the truffle oil), and ¾ cup of the hot pasta water or saved pasta water (see page 31). Boil the mixture until it thickens lightly, about 2 minutes. If the pasta isn't ready, remove the sauce from the heat until it is.

When the pasta is ready, return the pan with the sauce to high heat. Using a spider strainer or slotted spoon, scoop the cooked tortellini from the water and transfer it straight to the pan with the sauce. Shake and swirl the pan until the sauce begins to hug the pasta, about a minute (keep the pasta moving, adding a little more pasta water if necessary to create a lightly thickened sauce). Taste everything and season with salt and pepper until it tastes good to you. Remove from the heat and toss until the pasta and sauce marry, leaving almost no sauce in the pan.

Dish out the tortellini onto warmed plates and top with the toasted almonds and Parmesan. If using truffle oil, drizzle a few drops over each serving. Or better yet, shave on some fresh white truffles.

Scan this code to watch a video of making Almond Tortellini.

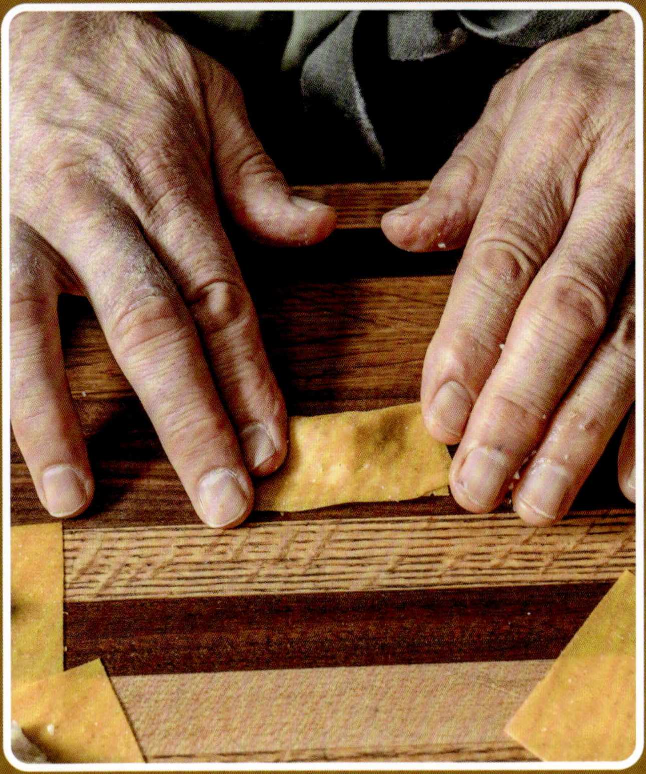
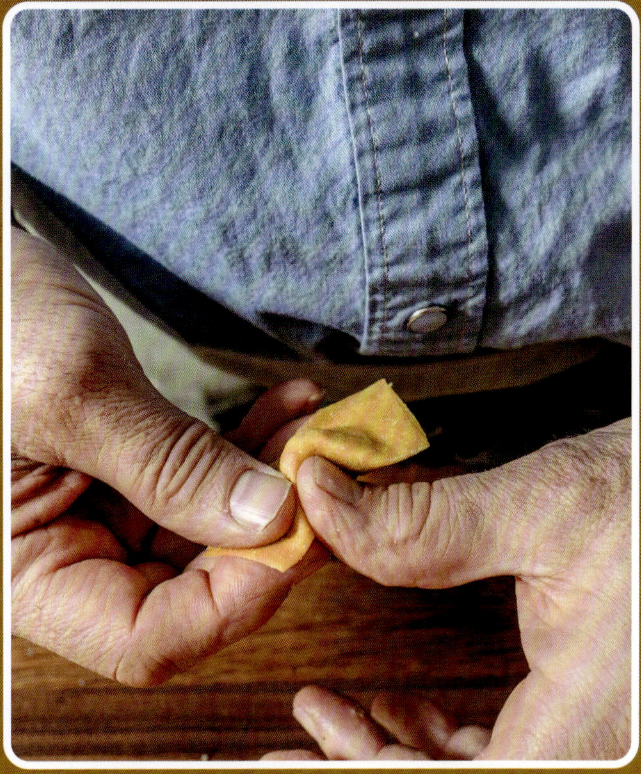
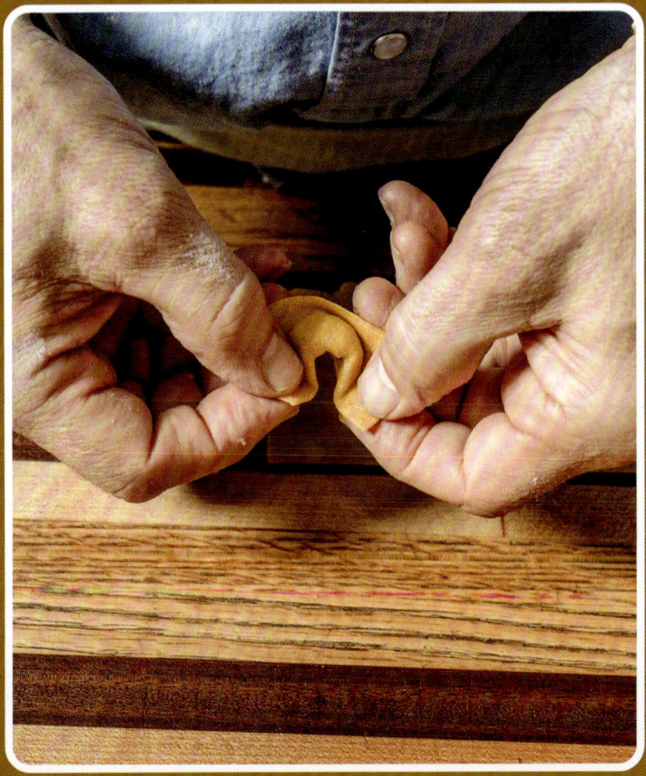
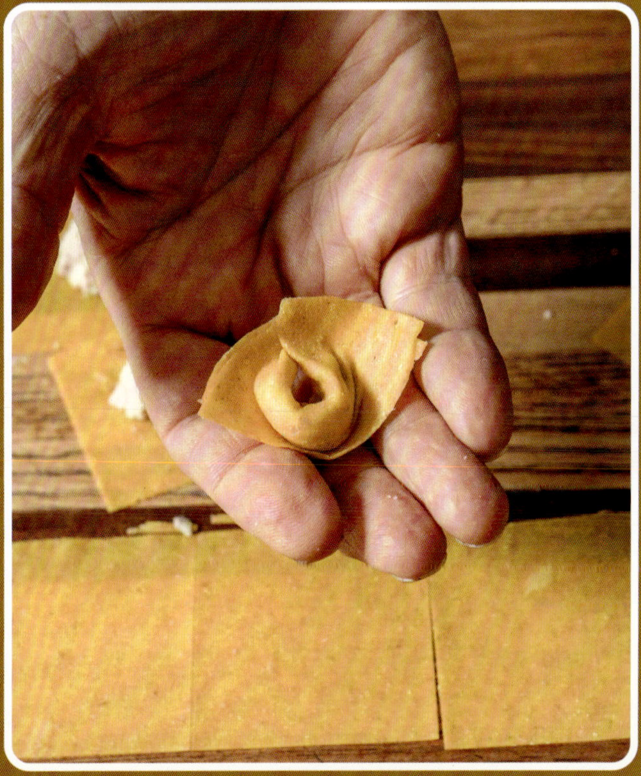

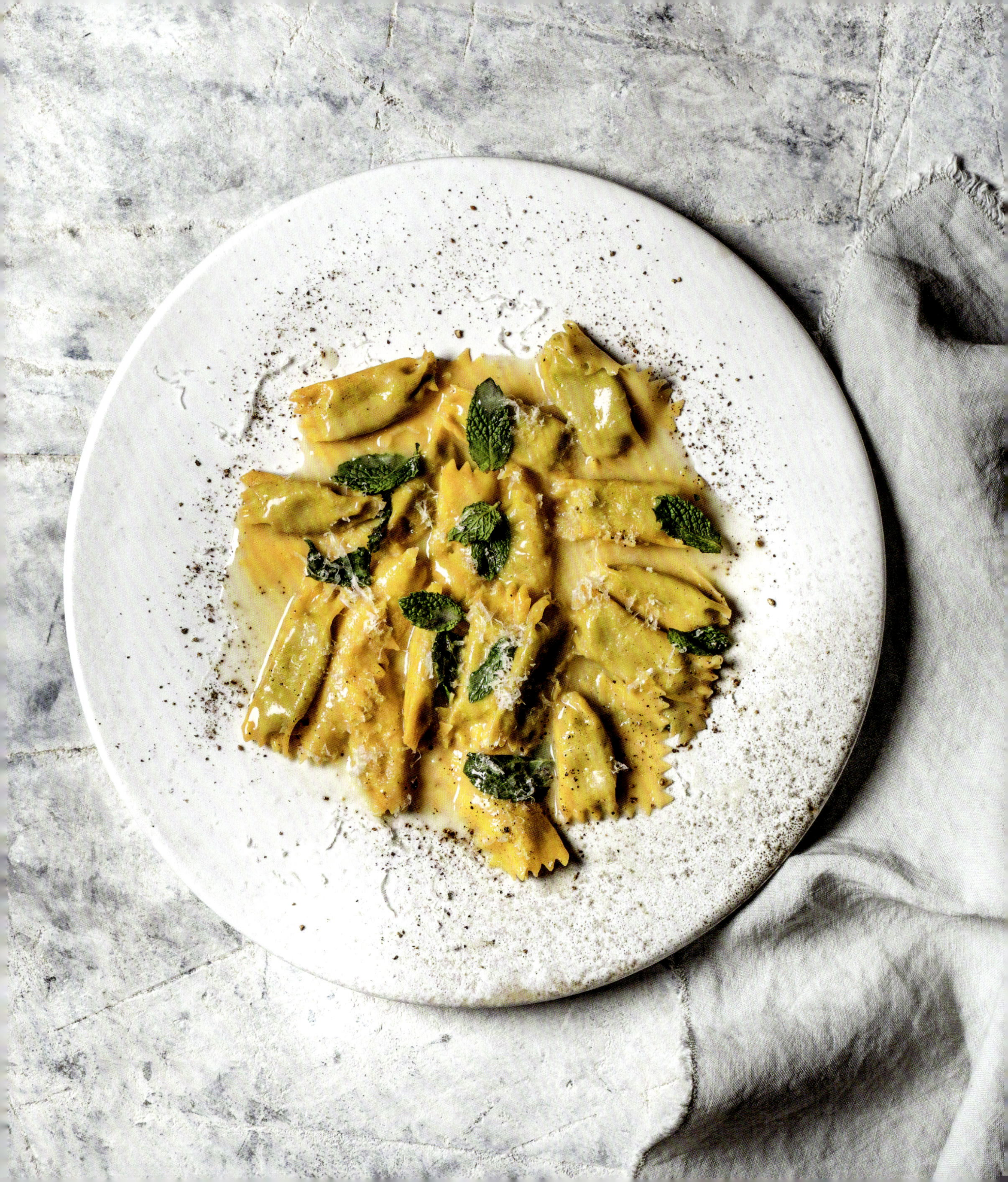

Spring Pea Agnolotti with Mint and Butter

I worked with a chef once who hated mint. I won't mention his name, but he knows who he is. It drove me batty. I love mint with fava beans, mint with peas . . . mint chocolate chip ice cream is my favorite flavor! But for almost six years, there was no mint at Vetri Cucina. When the chef left, the first thing I did was put this dish on the menu. The combination of peas and mint is so simple and beautiful. Look for fresh peas in the pod at farmers' markets. You'll need about 1½ pounds peas in the pod to get 1½ cups peas. To watch a video of making this pasta, scan the QR code on page 136.

Serves 4 to 6

Pea Filling

2 tablespoons extra-virgin olive oil

1 small garlic clove, smashed

1 medium shallot, minced

8 ounces shelled green peas (about 1½ cups), fresh or thawed frozen

Leaves from ¼ bunch fresh mint (about ½ cup packed)

4 ounces goat cheese

½ cup finely grated Parmesan cheese

Kosher salt and freshly ground black pepper

1 large egg yolk

Make the pea filling: Set up a large bowl of ice water wide enough to accommodate a medium saucepan and have it near the stove. In the saucepan, heat the olive oil and smashed garlic clove over medium heat, swirling the pan a few times, until the garlic is aromatic, about 2 minutes, then remove and discard the garlic. Add the shallot and sauté until translucent, 2 to 3 minutes, shaking the pan a few times. Stir in the peas and mint and cook until the peas are tender, 2 to 3 minutes. Dip the bottom of the pan in the ice water and stir the peas to quickly cool the mixture.

Once cool, transfer the mixture to a blender or food processor. Crumble in the goat cheese, sprinkle in the Parmesan, and puree until smooth. Scrape down the sides if necessary to get everything nice and smooth. Taste the filling and season with salt and pepper until it tastes good to you (about ½ teaspoon salt). Add the egg yolk and blend to incorporate. Spoon the filling into a piping bag or zipper-lock bag, seal, and use within 1 hour. (Or seal and refrigerate for up to 1 day.)

Make the agnolotti: Keep a spray bottle of water near your work surface. Lay a pasta sheet on a lightly floured surface and trim the edges square. Cut the sheet lengthwise to make narrower sheets, about 2½ inches wide. Mist the dough with water to keep it from drying out and help create a good seal on the pasta. Cut off the tip of the piping bag (or one corner if using a zipper-lock bag) to make a ½-inch-diameter hole. Pipe a ½-inch-wide line of filling along one long edge of each narrow sheet, leaving a ½-inch margin between the filling and the edge. Starting at one end and moving to the other, use your

RECIPE CONTINUES

Agnolotti

8 ounces Egg Yolk Dough (page 74), rolled into sheets about 1/32 inch (0.8mm) thick

All-purpose flour, for dusting

Kosher salt

6 tablespoons (3 ounces) unsalted butter, cut into pieces

1/3 cup chopped fresh mint leaves

Finely grated Pecorino Romano cheese, for garnish

fingers and/or a bench knife to lift up the long edge of the pasta and fold it all the way over the filling. Fold the dough over the filling again along the entire length of the sheet to completely enclose the filling. Leave a ½-inch "lip" of unfilled pasta on the other side. Use a fluted cutter to cut the sheet of filled pasta down its length on the very edge of the lip. Use your thumbs and forefingers to lift up the filled pasta and pinch to form mounds of filling at about 1½-inch intervals all down the length of the pasta. Once pinched, it should almost look like a big, long peapod.

Use the fluted cutter to cut between the mounds of fillings, cutting in the same direction you folded the pasta and rolling it forward slightly to create a sort of pillow shape with the fluted lip of pasta bisecting it on the other side. Transfer to a lightly floured sheet pan and dust lightly with flour. Repeat with the remaining dough and filling. You should have about 80 agnolotti. Use them within 1 hour. Or cover and refrigerate them in a single layer on a lightly floured tray for up to 4 hours. You can also freeze them in a single layer, transfer them to a zipper-lock bag, and freeze them for up to 3 days. Take the pasta straight from the freezer to the boiling pasta water, adding about 30 seconds to the cooking time.

Cook the agnolotti: Bring a large pot of water to a boil and add salt until it tastes like well-seasoned broth. Drop in the agnolotti, give them a stir, and cover the pot to return the water quickly to a boil. Uncover or partially cover to maintain the boil and boil the pasta until it is tender but still a little chewy when bitten, 3 to 4 minutes (about 30 seconds after they begin to float).

Right after dropping the pasta, in a deep 12-inch sauté pan, melt the butter over high heat. Add ¾ cup of the hot pasta water or saved pasta water (see page 31) and simmer the mixture until it reduces slightly, 2 to 3 minutes.

Using a spider strainer or slotted spoon, scoop the cooked agnolotti from the water and transfer them straight to the pan with the butter mixture. Add the mint and shake and swirl the pan until the sauce begins to hug the pasta, about a minute (keep the pasta moving, adding a little more pasta water if necessary to create a lightly thickened sauce). Taste the sauce and season with salt until it tastes good to you. Remove from the heat and toss until the pasta and sauce marry, leaving almost no sauce in the pan.

Dish out the pasta onto warmed plates and garnish with a generous shower of Pecorino Romano.

Scan this code to watch a video of making Spring Pea Agnolotti.

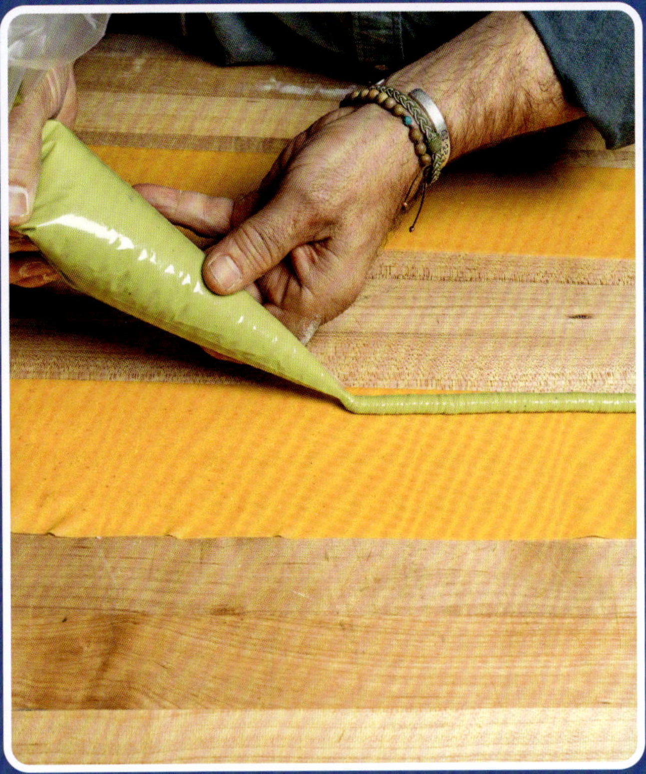
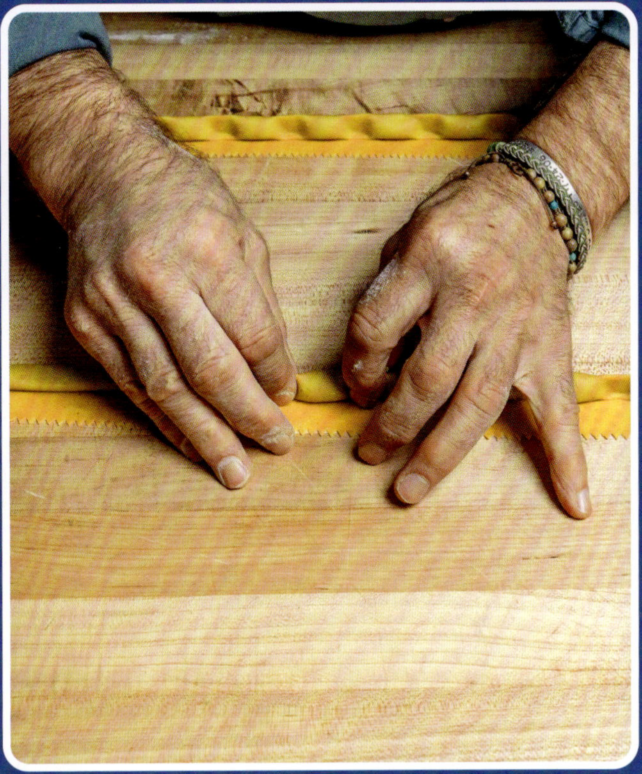
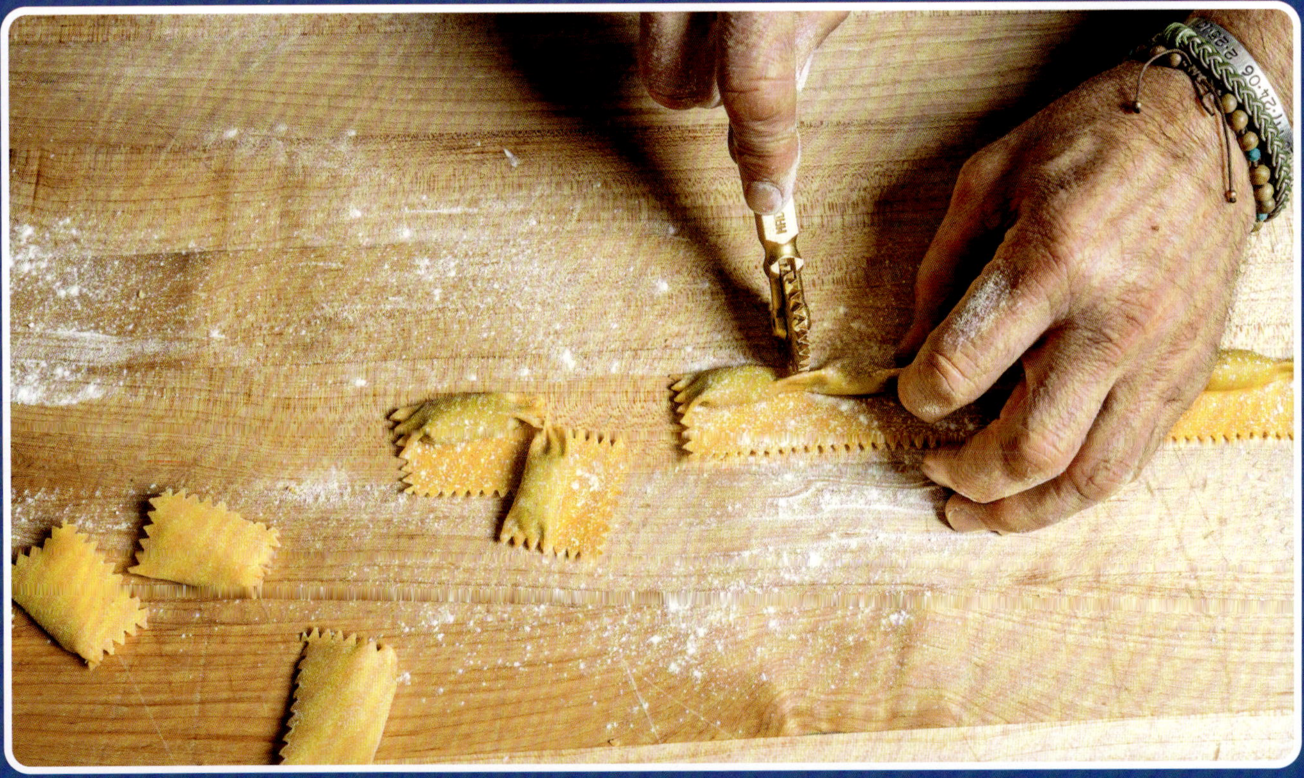

SEA

> The sea is a constant reminder of something far greater than us. It's mystery and beauty, endless and unknowable.
>
> **—FEDERICO FELLINI,**
> ITALIAN FILMMAKER

OOD

PASTA

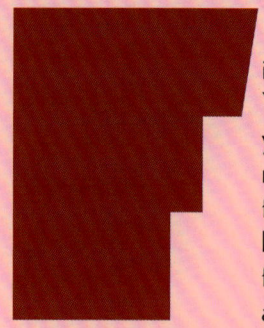

Fishing is completely mesmerizing. You almost have to surrender yourself to nature and allow it to make decisions for you. To catch a fish with dry flies, you start simply by observing the water, trying to find the ideal spot where the fish are biting. Then you choose a fly that you think will attract the fish. Finally, you wait, patiently, for that one fish to rise up from the deep and take the bait. It's a beautiful dance with nature.

I go fly-fishing in Colorado and Idaho often. A friend who I fish with told me once that there are four basic stages of learning to fish:

Stage 1: I want to go fishing.

Stage 2: I want to catch a fish.

Stage 3: I want to catch a big fish.

Stage 4: I want to go fishing.

Once you arrive at the fourth stage, you have many realizations, the most important being that it doesn't matter what you catch. To be out on the water, absorbing the beauty that it has bestowed upon us, appreciating the resource for what it gives to us, is in fact the complete lesson.

You could say the same thing about becoming a cook. There are four basic stages:

Stage 1: I want to cook.

Stage 2: I want to cook something delicious.

Stage 3: I want to cook something truly amazing that will blow people's minds.

Stage 4: I want to cook.

Like fishing, cooking isn't all about doing something big and creating some mind-blowing dish. The best cooks I know surrender themselves to nature and thoughtfully accentuate the best that it has to offer. It's more about observing and respecting the resource.

And like cooking, fishing can be frustrating. There is nothing more maddening than gathering all your fishing gear, hiking up twelve thousand feet to a mountain lake, seeing fish rise up through the water to load up on bugs for the day, and trying to figure out what they are eating. You have so many flies in your fly box to try, and nothing seems to work. Then you put on a big hopper you never thought they'd go for, and to your surprise, a fish comes up out of nowhere and chomps on it. You reel the fish in, and when it finally pops above the water and into your hands, the colors of these fish can be breathtaking: oranges, reds and yellows like nothing you have ever seen. You sit there in awe as you hold the beauty you have caught, release it back into the water, and watch it swim away like nothing ever happened.

Cooking is the same way. It can be infuriating to use all the tools in your toolbox when trying to make a great dish only to have it fall flat on the plate. Sometimes when a young cook gets a truly magnificent ingredient like a beautiful Maine lobster, they start by manipulating the product, trying to make it fit into some big idea they have in their head. But great cooking is more like figuring out what the fish want to eat. It's about letting nature call the shots. What is this ingredient telling me it wants? How can I highlight its natural beauty? A great cook crafts a dish by first observing and respecting the product, and only then judiciously enhancing it.

That's when magic happens. That's also why it's so important to start with good ingredients. Then you don't have to do much to make them sing on the plate. When buying seafood for the recipes in this chapter, get the best that you can. Yes, good seafood is expensive. My philosophy: Save it for a special occasion, buy the best that you can, and keep it simple. Respect the resource.

Dishes like Paccheri with Clams and Charred Lemon Brodo (page 143) are so simple that if your clams aren't very good, the dish will miss the mark. The same goes for Lorighittas with Calamari, Meyer Lemon, and Basil (page 148). The squid should be top quality, as should the lemons. Meyer lemon adds the ideal balance of sweetness and acid to wake up the calamari. If you make it with subpar calamari and regular lemons, the dish might be just ho-hum. That's why dishes like Scallop Raviolo with Champagne (page 171) have so few ingredients. The scallop is the star. Well, that and the egg pasta. And the Champagne. A little caviar never hurts either!

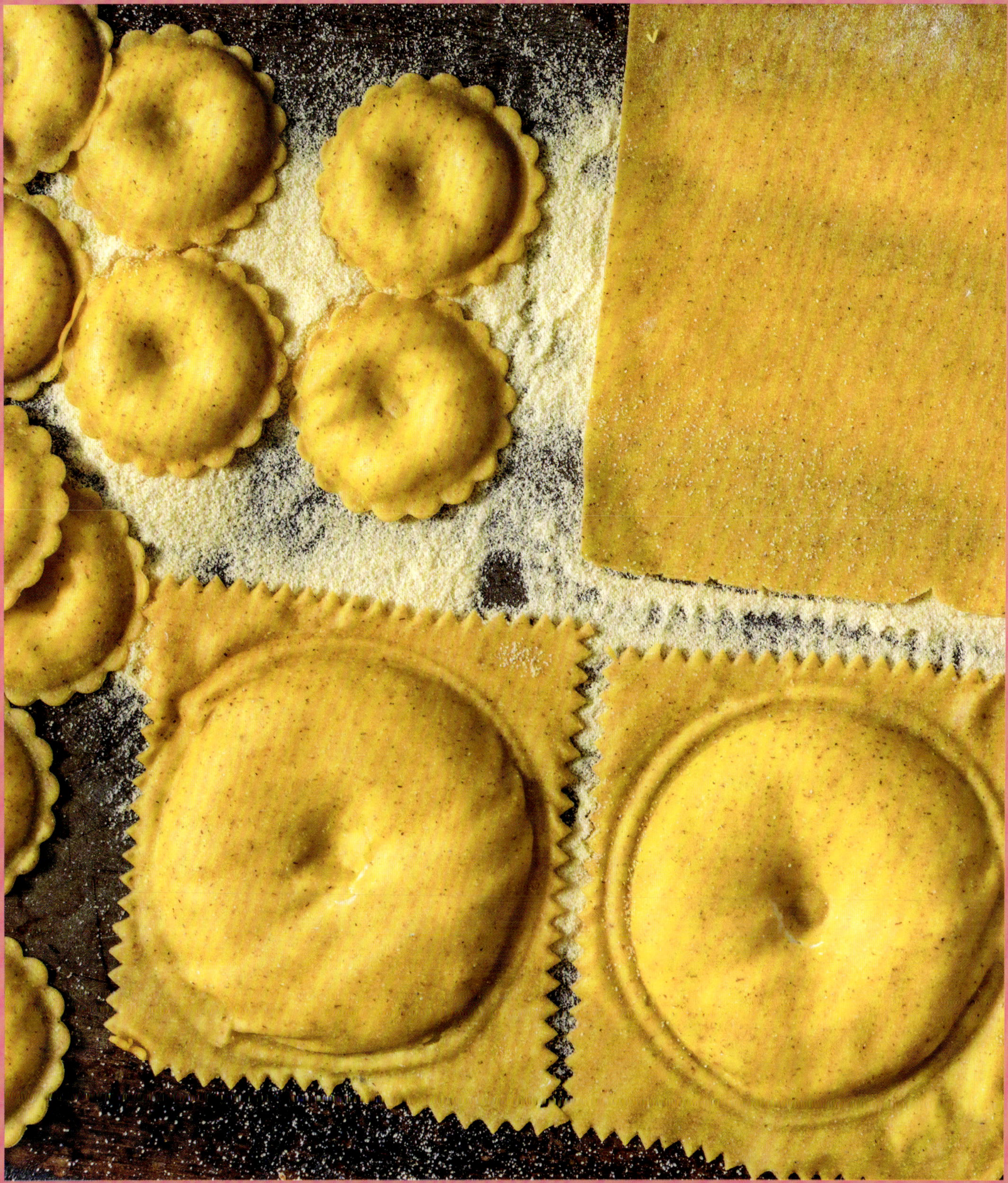

LEVEL UP **Add sea beans:** Blanch about 24 sea beans in plain, unsalted boiling water for 1 minute. (Sea beans are plenty salty on their own.) Immediately plunge into ice water to stop the cooking. Add the blanched and shocked sea beans to the pan along with the clams. After toasting the pepper flakes for the sauce, use plain hot tap water instead of hot pasta water to keep the salt level of the dish in check.

PACCHERI WITH CLAMS AND CHARRED LEMON BRODO

I love paccheri with clams because the clams end up nestled inside the tubes of pasta. Talk about marrying pasta and sauce for the perfect bite! We add a subtle smoky flavor to the clams by steaming them in Prosecco *brodo* (broth) made with lemons, leeks, and celery that have been charred in a hot pan. You'll need a half bottle of Prosecco for this one. Drink the rest with the meal—or while you cook! **SERVES 4**

Clams and Brodo

5 pounds small Manila or littleneck clams

Kosher salt

2 lemons, halved

½ medium leek, cleaned and halved lengthwise

2 celery stalks, cut crosswise in 2-inch pieces

½ (750ml) bottle Prosecco (1½ cups)

2 sprigs fresh flat-leaf parsley

1 dried bay leaf

¼ teaspoon whole black peppercorns

Purge the clams of sand: Put the clams in a large bowl and cover with salted water (dissolve about 2 tablespoons salt per quart of cold water). Soak in the fridge for at least 1½ hours or up to 3 hours. Remove with a slotted spoon and rinse.

Make the brodo (broth): When the clams are ready, heat a deep 12-inch sauté pan over medium-high heat. Place the lemon halves and leek cut-side down in the pan along with the celery. Cook in the dry pan until the lemons and leek are charred and blackened in spots, about 3 minutes, turning once or twice. Pour in the Prosecco and 1 cup water and add the parsley, bay leaf, and peppercorns. Squeeze in the juice of the remaining lemon and drop the spent halves into the pot. Bring the broth to a simmer over medium heat.

Add the purged clams to the broth. Cover and steam over medium heat until the clams open, 8 to 12 minutes, depending on their size. Remove the clams as they are done, and discard any that do not open after 12 minutes. Uncover, remove the clams, cool briefly, then pick the clam meat from the shells and place the meat in a medium bowl, discarding the shells.

Strain the broth through a fine-mesh sieve (lined with cheesecloth if you have it) into a large bowl. Rinse the pan and return the strained broth to the rinsed pan; keep warm over low heat. Return the clams to the broth, cover, and keep warm.

RECIPE CONTINUES

Paccheri

Kosher salt

12 ounces store-bought dried paccheri

¾ cup extra-virgin olive oil

2 garlic cloves, minced to a paste (about 1 teaspoon paste)

1 tablespoon chopped fresh flat-leaf parsley, plus more for garnish

1 teaspoon crushed pepperoncini flakes, or ¼ teaspoon crushed red pepper flakes

Cook the paccheri: Bring a large pot of water to a boil and add salt until it tastes like well-seasoned broth. Drop in the paccheri, give it a stir, and cover the pot to quickly return the water to a boil. Uncover or partially cover to maintain a gentle rolling boil and boil the pasta, stirring occasionally, until it is tender but still a little chewy when bitten, about 10 minutes.

Right after dropping the pasta, in a deep 12-inch sauté pan, heat ¼ cup of the olive oil over medium heat. Add the garlic and cook until the garlic flavor wakes up but before the garlic browns, about 1 minute, then add the parsley and pepper flakes. Toast for a couple seconds, shaking the pan, then add 1½ cups of the hot pasta water or saved pasta water (see page 31) and 1 cup of the broth from the clams (just the broth—save the clams for later). Simmer over medium heat until the sauce reduces by about one-third, 5 to 7 minutes.

Using a spider strainer or slotted spoon, scoop the cooked paccheri from the water and transfer it straight to the pan with the sauce. Add the remaining ½ cup olive oil and the clams (using a slotted spoon to remove them from the broth). Shake and swirl the pan until the sauce reduces more and begins to hug the pasta, 1 to 2 minutes (keep the pasta moving, adding a little more pasta water if necessary to create a lightly thickened, creamy sauce). Once thickened, remove from the heat and toss until the pasta and sauce marry, leaving just a little sauce in the pan.

Using the spider or spoon, dish out the pasta onto warmed plates, creating some volume by building it into a mound and dividing the clams equally among the plates. Spoon some of the sauce remaining in the pan over each serving and garnish with additional parsley.

MAFALDINE with BROCCOLI DI CICCIO, ANCHOVY, and SPRING ONION PESTO

Broccoli di ciccio is my favorite variety of broccoli. It's tender and sweet, sort of like broccolini. If you can't find it, broccolini works here. You could even use regular broccoli with the florets halved or quartered lengthwise. Either way, the savory-salty taste of anchovy and Parmesan balances out the sweet, char-grilled flavor in the broccoli. For vegetarians, you can always skip the anchovy and garnish the dish with a little more Parm. **SERVES 4 TO 6**

1 pound broccoli di ciccio or broccolini, halved lengthwise if heads are large

½ bunch spring onions or scallions, ends trimmed

½ cup extra-virgin olive oil

Grated zest and juice of ½ lemon

Kosher salt

1 pound store-bought dried mafaldine

1 anchovy fillet, finely chopped

1 small garlic clove, minced

Pinch of crushed red pepper flakes

½ cup finely grated Parmesan cheese, plus more for garnish

Blanch, shock, and grill the broccoli: Bring a large pot of unsalted water to a boil. Set up a large bowl of ice water, too. Drop the broccoli di ciccio or broccolini into the boiling water and cook it until bright green, just 30 seconds or so. Remove with tongs and immediately plunge the broccoli into the ice water to stop the cooking. Leave it there for a minute or two before transferring to a kitchen towel to drain.

Heat your oven broiler (or better yet, a grill) to high. Broil or grill the broccoli on a rack until lightly charred all over and fork-tender, about 5 minutes, turning for even charring. Transfer to a cutting board to cool. Leave the broiler or grill on but reduce the heat to low.

Make the spring onion pesto: Broil or grill the spring onions until tender and lightly charred all over, 3 to 5 minutes. Remove, cool slightly, and finely chop. Finely chop the cooled broccoli too. Transfer half the charred spring onions and broccoli to a blender or food processor with 2 tablespoons of the olive oil and pulse to a pesto consistency (minced to bits, but not totally smooth). Spoon the pesto into a medium bowl, add the remaining broccoli and spring onion, and fold in the lemon zest. Taste the pesto and season with salt until it tastes good to you (maybe about ½ teaspoon).

Cook the mafaldine: Bring a large pot of water to a boil and add salt until it tastes like well-seasoned broth. Drop in the mafaldine, give it a stir, and cover the pot to quickly return the water to a boil. Uncover or partially cover to maintain the boil and boil the pasta, stirring occasionally, until it is tender but still a little chewy when bitten, 10 to 12 minutes.

RECIPE CONTINUES

Right after dropping the pasta, in a deep 12-inch sauté pan, heat 1 tablespoon of the olive oil over medium heat. Add the anchovy and garlic and sauté until the anchovy melts and the garlic smells aromatic but isn't browned, 2 to 3 minutes, shaking the pan a few times. Add the pepper flakes and sauté until aromatic, about 1 minute. Add the pesto mixture along with ½ cup of the hot pasta water or saved pasta water (see page 31). Simmer until the sauce thickens slightly, 2 to 3 minutes.

When the pasta is ready, use tongs or a pasta fork to scoop it from the water and transfer it straight to the pan with the sauce. Add the remaining 5 tablespoons olive oil and shake and swirl the pan until the sauce reduces even more and begins to hug the pasta, 1 to 2 minutes (keep the pasta moving, adding a little more pasta water if necessary to create a lightly thickened, creamy sauce). Taste the sauce and add lemon juice until it tastes good to you. Once the sauce is lightly thickened, remove from the heat, add the Parmesan, and toss until the pasta and sauce marry, leaving little to no sauce in the pan.

Using tongs, dish out the pasta onto warmed plates, creating some volume by building it into a mound. Garnish with additional Parmesan.

LEVEL UP **Add bottarga:** Skip the Parmesan garnish and grate some bottarga over each serving instead. Go for Sardinian bottarga di muggine (cured and dried grey mullet roe), which has a beautiful reddish-orange color and a delicate, briny, umami taste.

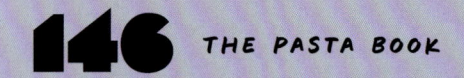

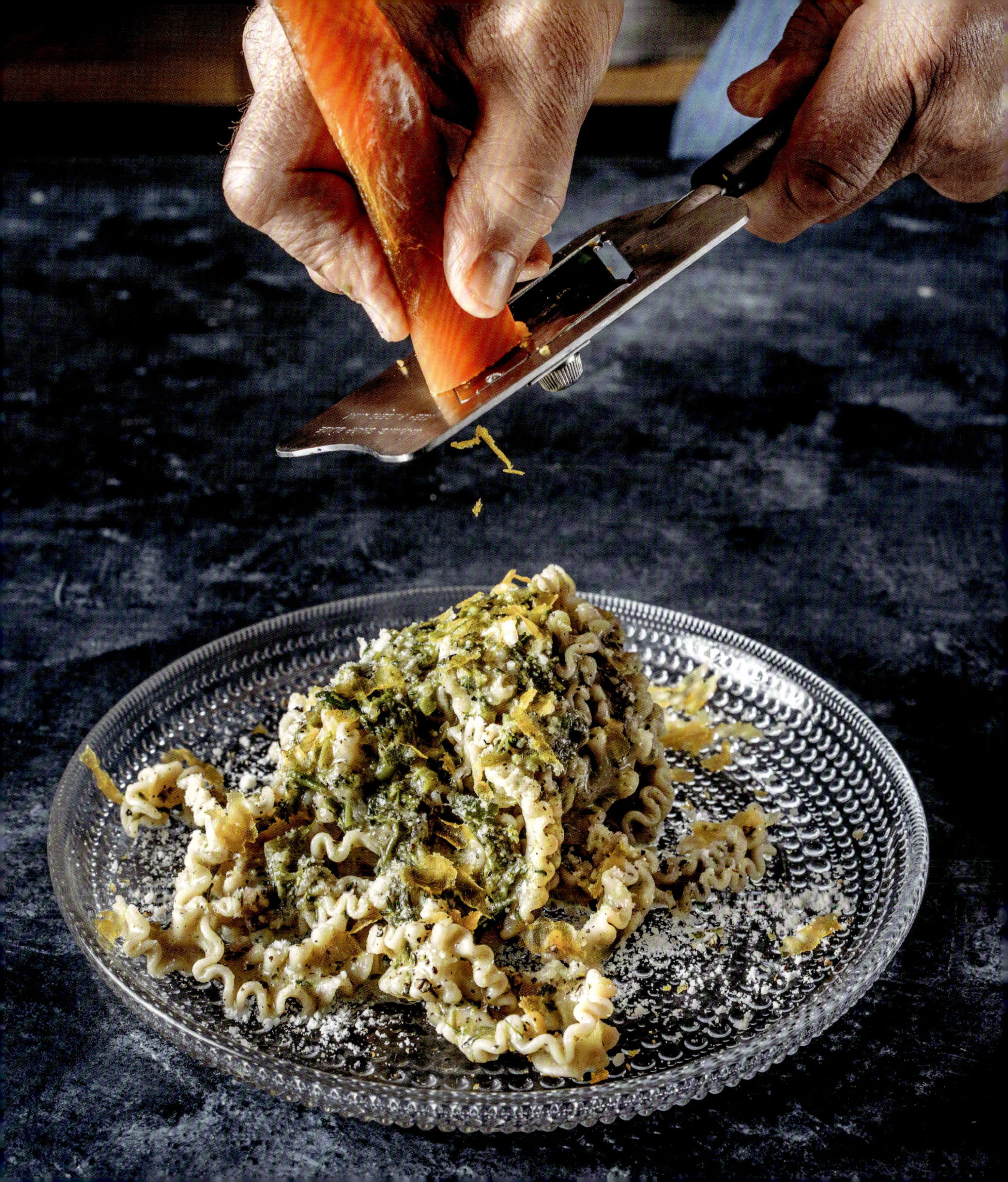

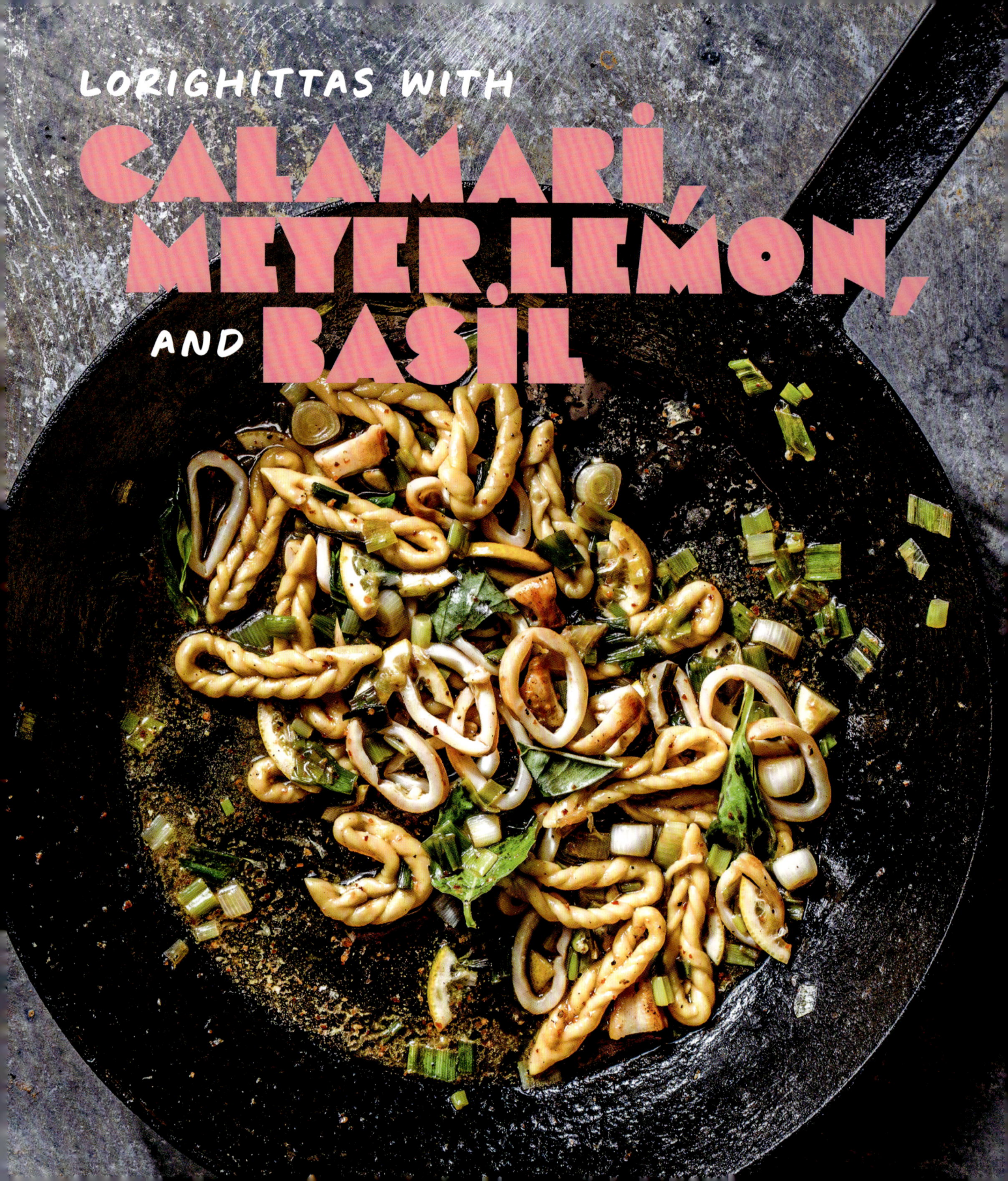

LORIGHITTAS WITH CALAMARI, MEYER LEMON, AND BASIL

The rule of thumb with calamari (squid) is to cook it super quick or super slow. Anything in between and it's like chewing on rubber bands. Here, we sear the calamari in a ripping-hot cast-iron pan. I've been known to add charred shishito peppers to the pan as well! When you slice the charred calamari into rings, it's obvious why lorighittas make the perfect complement. The size, shape, and even texture are so similar. I know Meyer lemons aren't in every market, but the sweet-tart juice and floral aromas are ideal here. If you can't find them, use half a large regular lemon cut the same way. Save this one for springtime, preferably when you're eating al fresco! **SERVES 4**

- 1 pound cleaned calamari tubes and tentacles (from about three 6-inch-long calamari/squid)
- ½ cup extra-virgin olive oil
- Kosher salt and freshly ground black pepper
- 1 Meyer lemon, quartered lengthwise and thinly sliced into triangles
- 12 ounces fresh Lorighittas (page 63)
- 1 bunch scallions, trimmed and finely chopped
- ½ cup Prosecco
- 1 cup loosely packed fresh basil leaves, coarsely chopped or torn

Char the calamari: Heat a large carbon-steel or cast-iron pan over high heat (no oil). When the pan is literally smoking, add the calamari tubes and tentacles, put a heavy weight on top to press them into the pan, and sear until charred all over, 1 to 3 minutes, turning once for even charring. You might want to turn on a fan and/or open a window. It's gonna smoke!

Remove the charred calamari to a medium bowl and add ¼ cup of the olive oil and about ½ teaspoon salt and ¼ teaspoon pepper, tossing to coat. Quickly and carefully lay the dressed calamari into the hot pan in a single layer and place a heavy weight such as another pan on top. Cook briefly, just until the calamari are evenly browned and still look moist, about 1 minute. Remove to a cutting board, let cool enough to handle, and then cut the tentacles into quarters and the tubes into thin rings. Return the cut calamari to the bowl of seasoned oil, add the Meyer lemon triangles, and toss to coat. Let marinate while you cook the pasta.

Cook the lorighittas: Bring a large pot of water to a boil and add salt until it tastes like well-seasoned broth. Drop in the lorighittas, give it a stir, and cover the pot to quickly return the water to a boil. Uncover or partially cover to maintain the boil and boil the pasta, stirring occasionally, until it is tender but still a little chewy when bitten, 2 to 3 minutes.

Right before you drop the pasta, in a deep 12-inch sauté pan, heat the remaining ¼ cup olive oil over medium-high heat. Add the scallions and sauté until they begin to get tender, about a minute.

Add the Prosecco and 1 cup of the hot pasta water or saved pasta water (see page 31). Crank the heat to heat to high, bring to a boil, and simmer until the mixture thickens slightly, about 2 minutes. Using a spider strainer or a slotted spoon, scoop the cooked lorighittas from the water and transfer the pasta straight to the pan. Add the entire squid mixture and shake and swirl the pan until the sauce reduces even more and begins to hug the pasta, 1 to 2 minutes (keep the pasta moving, adding a little more pasta water if necessary to create a lightly thickened, creamy sauce). Taste, adding salt and/or pepper until it tastes good to you.

Remove from the heat, add the basil, and toss until the pasta and sauce marry, leaving little to no sauce in the pan.

Using a large spoon, dish out the pasta onto warmed plates.

LOBSTER TAGLIOLINI with 'NDUJA BREAD CRUMBS

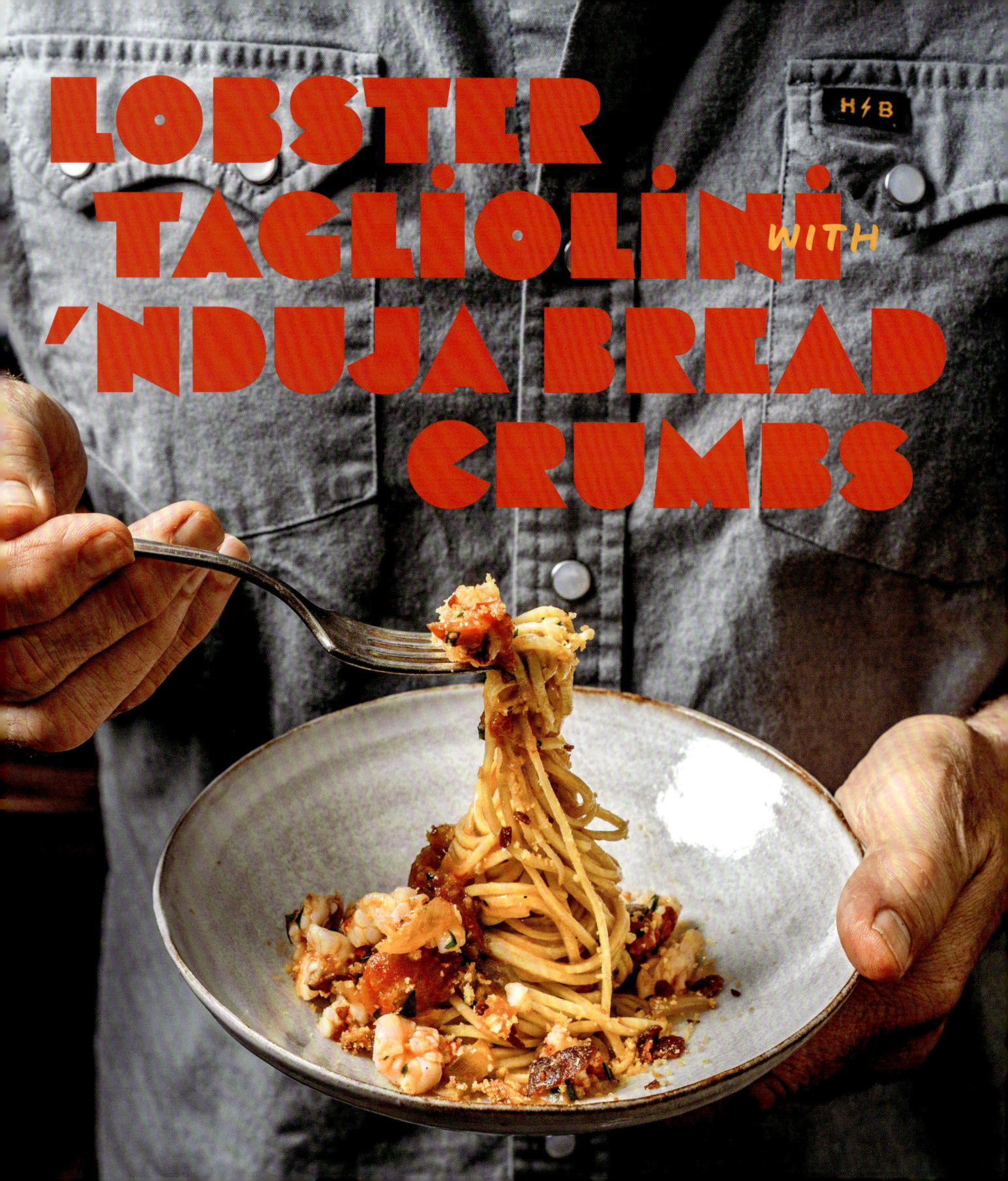

If you haven't tried 'nduja yet, it's high time you did. It's a briefly aged, spreadable sausage spiced with Calabrian chili peppers. Slather some on crostini for a snack! Save the rest for this dish, a magical combination of lobster, sausage, chili peppers, and lemon all tangled up with thin ribbons of tagliolini. There are a few steps to this pasta, but they're totally worth it. **SERVES 4**

Lobsters

3 pounds live Maine lobster (2 lobsters)

6 tablespoons extra-virgin olive oil

2 cups canned diced tomatoes, with their juice

2 cups dry white wine, such as pinot grigio

3 tablespoons chopped fresh flat-leaf parsley

Juice of 1 small lemon, plus more to taste

Kosher salt

'Nduja Bread Crumbs and Tagliolini

5 ounces 'nduja

¼ cup plain panko bread crumbs

⅓ cup extra-virgin olive oil

4 medium red Fresno or jalapeño peppers, seeded and minced

4 medium shallots, minced

4 garlic cloves, minced

Kosher salt

1 pound fresh Tagliolini (page 75)

Blanch the lobsters: Have ready a large bowl of ice water. Bring a large pot of water to a boil. To prepare the live lobsters for cooking as quickly and painlessly as possible, put 1 lobster belly down on a cutting board and uncurl the tail so the lobster is flat against the board. Position the tip of a chef's knife just behind the head (you'll be cutting through the head) and press the tip down firmly until the knife tip reaches the cutting board, then bring the blade down through the head between the eyes to cut the head in half. (The lobster will be dead but the claws may still twitch.) Twist the claws to remove them from the body. Twist the tail to remove it from the body. Rinse away any dark bits from the tail. Save the claws and tail and set aside the head and legs for the stock. Repeat with the remaining lobster(s).

Blanch the lobster tails in the boiling water for 1 to 2 minutes (the meat will still be raw in the center). Using tongs, remove them and plunge them into the ice water to stop the cooking. Blanch the lobster claws in the boiling water for 2 to 3 minutes and then plunge them into the ice water as well. When cool, remove to a medium bowl.

Make lobster stock: While the tail and claws are cooling, make lobster stock from the heads/bodies. Cut the lobster bodies in half lengthwise, starting at the previous cut made near the head. Remove and discard the dark and greenish gobs (tomalley and roe) from the bodies. Place the lobster bodies/heads in a medium saucepan slicked with 2 tablespoons of the olive oil, and cook over medium-high heat until the shells turn bright red, 4 to 6 minutes, turning a few times. Add the canned tomatoes and wine, shaking the pan to capture any browned bits from the pan bottom. Add enough water to barely cover the lobster and bring to a boil over high heat. Reduce the heat to medium and simmer for 15 minutes.

Discard the lobster bodies/heads and strain the liquid through a medium-mesh sieve. Rinse the saucepan, return the strained liquid to the clean pan, and simmer the liquid over medium heat until reduced by about half, 15 to 20 minutes. Set the lobster stock aside.

Remove the lobster meat: To remove the lobster meat from the tails, place it belly up on a cutting board and use scissors to cut lengthwise through the shell toward the tail (avoid cutting the meat). Flip over and cut through the top shell the same way. Spread apart the shell and remove the tail meat in one piece. Repeat with the other tail(s) and then chop the tail meat into fork-friendly pieces and place them in a medium bowl (see the photographs on page 153).

RECIPE CONTINUES

To remove the meat from the claws, first twist off the knuckles. For each knuckle, use scissors to cut the shell lengthwise from end to end. Repeat on the other side, spread apart the shell, and remove the knuckle meat. For the claws, use scissors to cut along both sides of the ridged shell (the thumb) and then spread the shell apart and carefully wiggle out the claw meat in one piece.

Remove and discard the digestive tract vein and then cut all of the meat into fork-friendly pieces, keeping the shape of the claw meat intact as much as possible (1 intact claw per serving). Toss the lobster meat with the remaining 4 tablespoons olive oil, the parsley, and lemon juice and season lightly with salt (about ¼ teaspoon). Set aside.

Make the 'nduja bread crumbs: In a small sauté pan, heat 1 ounce (about ¼ cup) of the 'nduja over medium heat. Stir in the panko and fry, tossing frequently, until it's crispy and toasted, 4 to 5 minutes. Transfer the 'nduja bread crumbs to paper towels to drain.

Make a sofrito: In a deep 12-inch sauté pan, heat the oil over medium heat. Add the Fresno peppers, shallots, and garlic and cook gently, stirring a few times, until translucent but not browned, about 5 minutes. Remove from the heat and set aside.

Cook the tagliolini: Bring a large pot of water to a boil and add salt until it tastes like well-seasoned broth. Drop in the tagliolini, give it a stir, and cover the pot to quickly return the water to a boil. Uncover or partially cover to maintain the boil and boil the pasta, stirring occasionally, until it is tender but still a little chewy when bitten, 2 to 3 minutes.

Right after dropping the pasta, add all of the lobster stock to the pan with the sofrito, along with 1 cup of the hot pasta water or saved pasta water (see page 31). Bring the mixture to a boil over high heat and simmer until slightly reduced in volume, about 3 minutes.

When the pasta is ready, use tongs or a spider strainer to scoop the cooked tagliolini from the water and transfer it straight to the pan. Shake and swirl the pan until the sauce thickens and begins to hug the pasta, 1 to 2 minutes (keep the pasta moving, adding a little more pasta water if necessary to create a sauce that hugs the pasta). Remove from the heat and add the remaining 4 ounces (1 cup) 'nduja broken in small pieces, the dressed lobster meat, and half of the 'nduja bread crumbs. Toss until the pasta and sauce marry, leaving little to no sauce in the pan. Taste a bite, adding more lemon juice and/or salt if you think it needs it (it should taste rich and spicy with a spark of lemon).

Using tongs or a pasta fork, dish out the pasta onto warmed plates, creating some volume by twirling it into a mound, and serving 1 intact lobster claw per portion. Garnish with the remaining 'nduja bread crumbs.

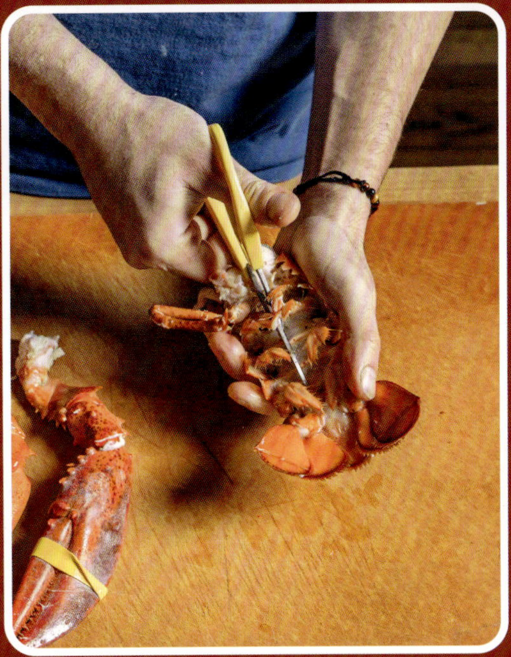

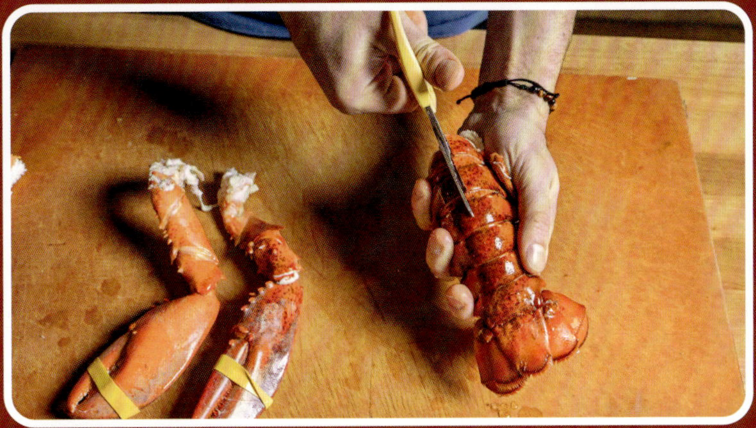

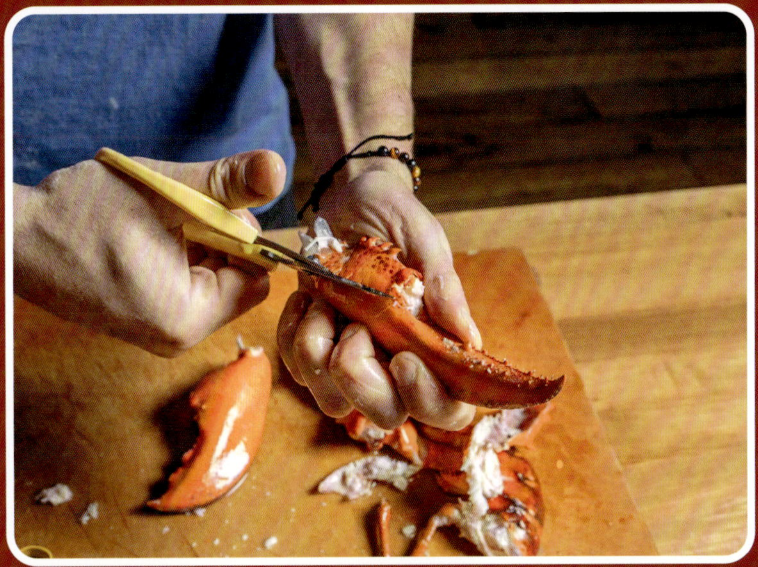

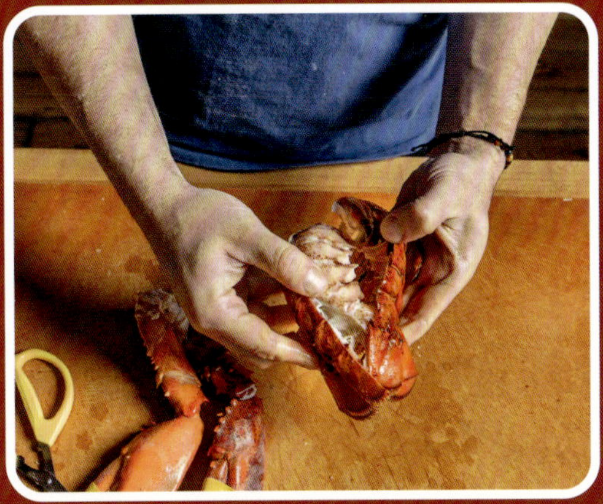

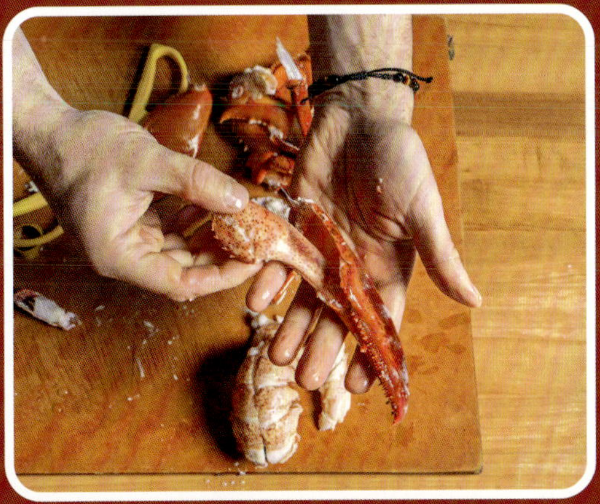

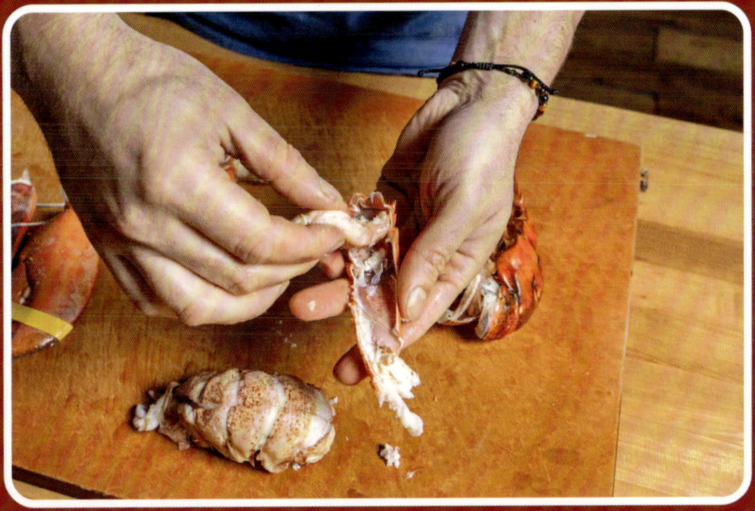

PIMENTÓN SORPRESINE with MUSSELS

This noodle is really fun to eat. It's sort of like a wonton or fortune cookie but with nothing inside. That empty space allows ingredients to get caught in the pasta, creating a little surprise, or *sorpresine* in Italian. Here, mussels are the surprise. Look for the smallest ones you can find. We added smoked pimentón to the dough to complement the mussels, a subtle but powerful flavor bump. **SERVES 6**

Mussels

⅓ cup extra-virgin olive oil

½ medium yellow onion, thinly sliced

½ medium fennel bulb, trimmed, cored, and thinly sliced lengthwise

Small pinch of crushed red pepper flakes

1 cup dry white wine, such as pinot grigio

2 pounds small mussels, scrubbed clean and debearded

Steam the mussels: In a deep 12-inch sauté pan, heat the oil over medium heat. Add the onion, fennel, and pepper flakes and sweat, stirring often, until the veg is soft but not browned, 5 to 6 minutes. Pour in the wine and bring to a boil over high heat. Add the mussels, shaking them into an even layer in the pan. Cut the heat to medium, cover, and steam until the mussels open, 5 to 7 minutes. Uncover and discard any mussels that haven't opened after 7 minutes. Pull the mussels from their shells and reserve the meat in a medium bowl (discard the shells). Strain the steaming liquid through a medium-mesh sieve and reserve the strained steaming liquid in a small bowl.

Cook the sorpresine: Bring a large pot of water to a boil and add salt until it tastes like well-seasoned broth. Drop in the sorpresine, give it a stir, and cover the pot to quickly return the water to a boil. Uncover or partially cover to maintain the boil and boil the pasta, stirring occasionally, until it is tender but still a little chewy when bitten, 3 to 4 minutes.

RECIPE CONTINUES

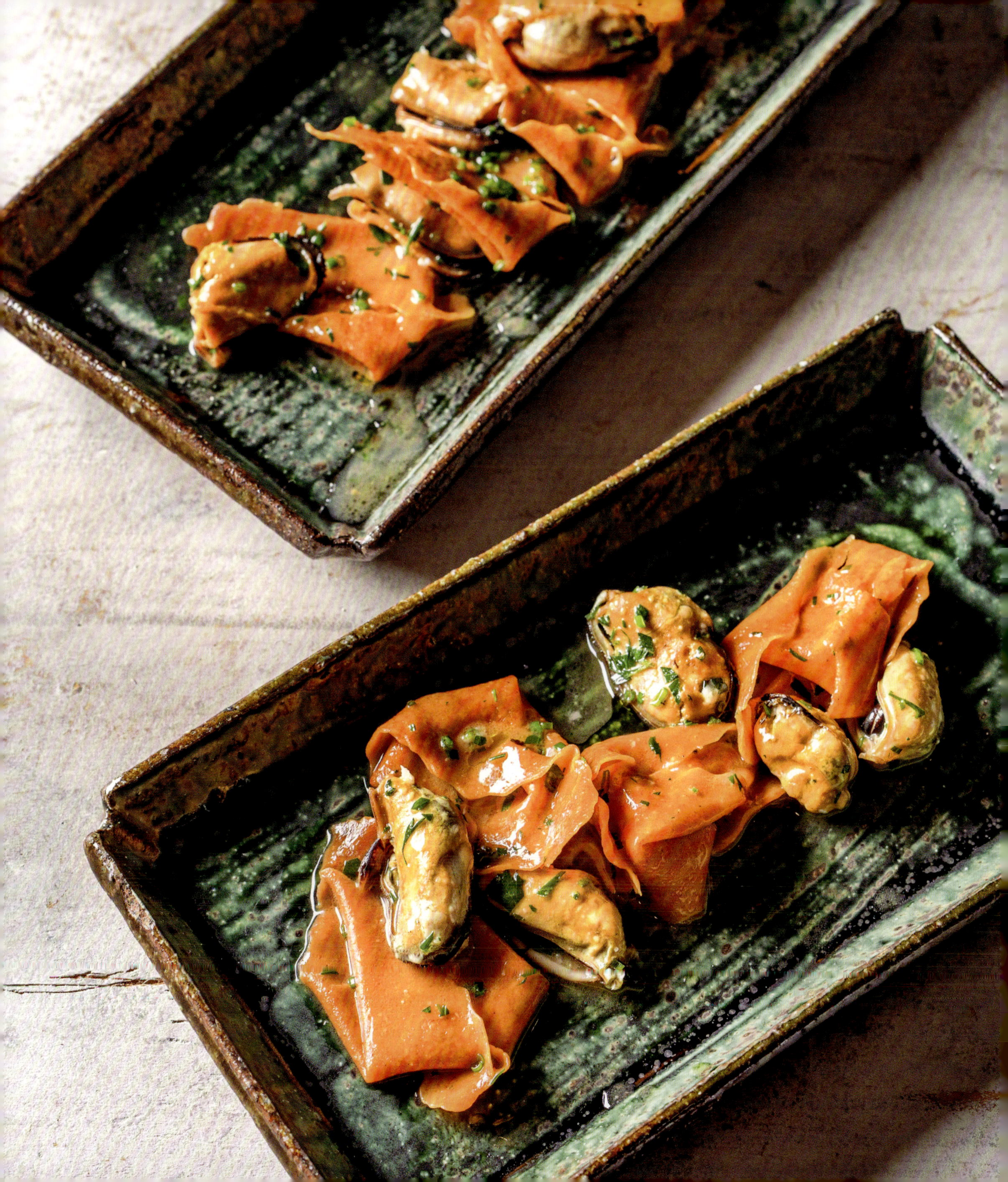

Sorpresine

Kosher salt

1 pound fresh Pimentón Sorpresine (page 79)

⅔ cup extra-virgin olive oil

1 cup chopped fresh flat-leaf parsley

1 cup chopped fresh chives

Juice of 3 lemons (about ½ cup)

While the pasta water is coming to a boil, rinse the same pan used to steam the mussels. Set over high heat and heat the oil, 1 cup of the reserved steaming liquid, and 1 cup of the hot pasta water or saved pasta water (see page 31). Boil the mixture until it thickens slightly to a thin saucy consistency, 5 to 7 minutes. Keep warm over low heat until the pasta is ready.

Using a spider strainer or a slotted spoon, scoop the cooked sorpresine from the water and transfer it straight to the pan. Crank the heat to high and shake and swirl the pan until the sauce begins to get creamy and hug the pasta, 1 to 2 minutes (keep the pasta moving, adding a little more pasta water if necessary to create a lightly thickened, creamy sauce). Toss in the mussels, parsley, chives, and about ⅓ cup of the lemon juice. Taste the pasta, adding salt and/or more lemon juice until it tastes good to you. Keep tossing until the pasta and sauce marry, leaving little to no sauce in the pan.

Using a large spoon, dish out the pasta onto warmed plates in an artful arrangement.

> **LEVEL UP** **Garnish with toasted garlic bread crumbs:** Buzz ½ garlic clove, a pinch of salt, ¼ cup olive oil, and 1 cup plain panko bread crumbs in a small food processor or mini-chopper. The crumbs should look a little coarser than damp sand. Spread the mixture in an even layer on a sheet pan and bake at 350°F until golden brown and crispy, 15 to 20 minutes, stirring occasionally for even browning.

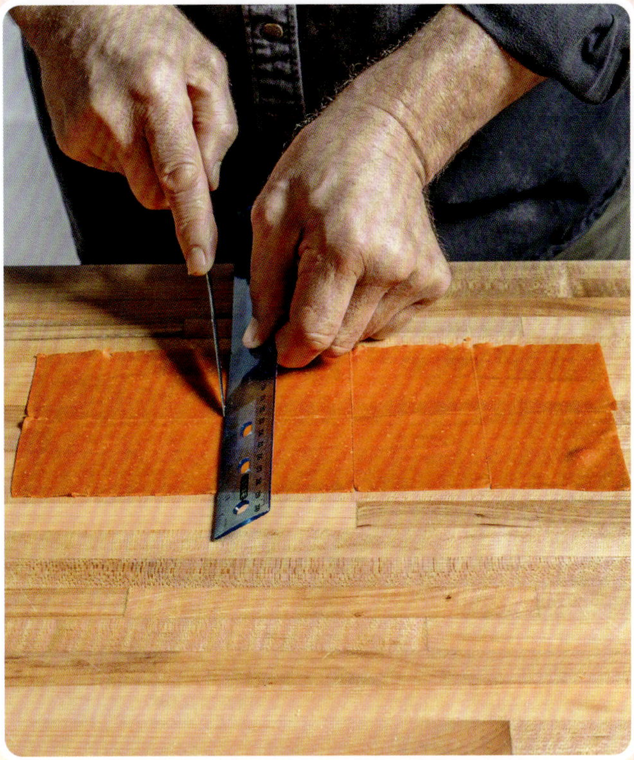
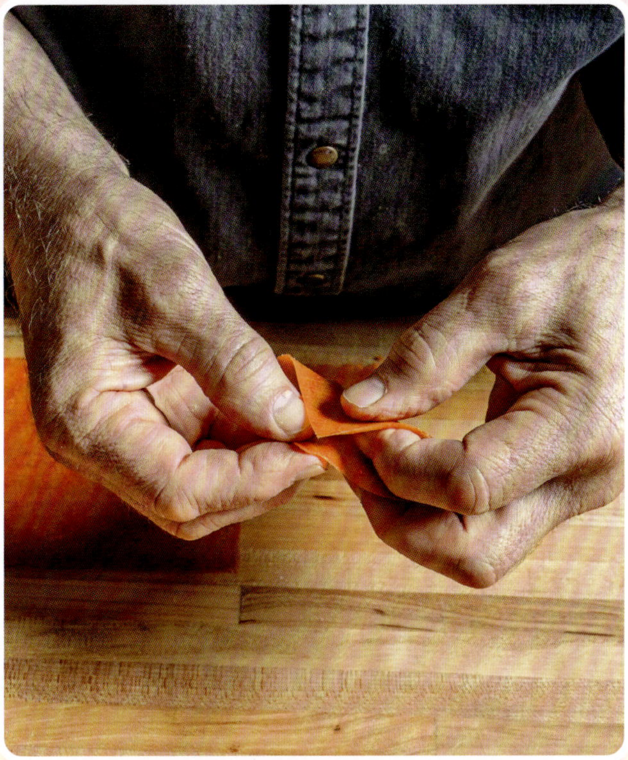
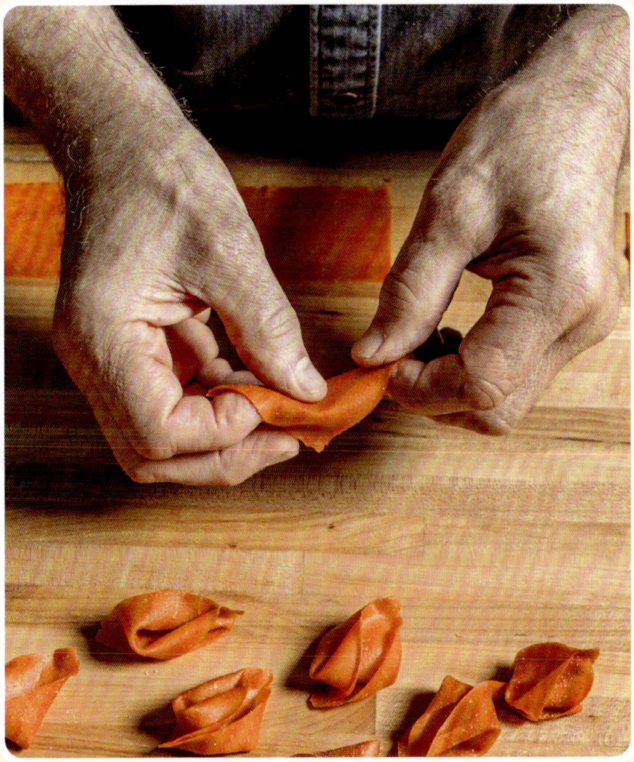
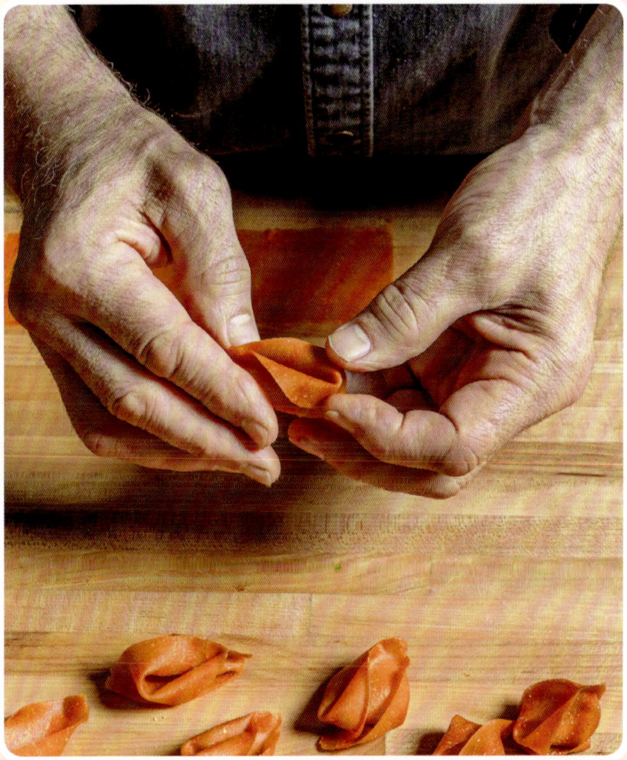

SPAGHETTI ALLA CHITARRA FRUTTI DI MARE with BONE MARROW SOFRITO

This dish started in that sweet spot at the end of a restaurant dinner shift when the whole staff was hungry, but we still had cleanup ahead of us. The pasta water was still boiling. We had some bone marrow on hand, and we thought, Why not have it with pasta? Who says olive oil or butter has to be the fat in your pasta dish? We melted the bone marrow and made sofrito with it for the sauce, and the marrow lent the pasta a ridiculously rich mouthfeel. Adding a mix of different seafood took the whole combination to another level entirely. **SERVES 4 TO 6**

Frutti di Mare

1 live Maine lobster (1 to 1½ pounds)

½ cup plus 2 tablespoons extra-virgin olive oil

1 cup canned diced tomatoes, with their juice

1 cup dry white wine, such as pinot grigio

1 cup Prosecco or Champagne

3 sprigs fresh flat-leaf parsley

½ medium shallot, thinly sliced

1 pound mussels, scrubbed and debearded

12 ounces cleaned calamari tubes and tentacles (from two to three 6-inch-long calamari/squid), tubes cut into thin rings and tentacles halved lengthwise

4 large sea scallops (about 4 ounces), cleaned and cut into ¾-inch cubes

½ cup chopped fresh flat-leaf parsley

Juice of 2 lemons (about ⅓ cup), plus more to taste

Cook the lobster and make the stock: Cook and cut up the lobster as described in Lobster Tagliolini (page 150). Make a stock as described, using the lobster head and body, 2 tablespoons of the olive oil, the canned tomatoes, and white wine. Transfer the reduced stock to a bowl.

Cook the mussels: In a deep 12-inch sauté pan, combine 1 cup water, the Prosecco, parsley, and sliced shallot and bring to a boil over high heat. Add the mussels in an even layer and after the liquid returns to a simmer, cut the heat to medium. Cover and steam until the mussels open, 5 to 7 minutes. Uncover and discard any mussels that haven't opened after 7 minutes. Pull the mussels from their shells and add the meat to the bowl with the lobster (discard the mussel shells). Strain the steaming liquid through a medium-mesh sieve into the bowl with the reduced lobster stock. Set the seafood stock aside.

Assemble the remaining seafood: Add the calamari rings, tentacles, and cubed scallops to the bowl with the mussels and lobster. Add the remaining ½ cup olive oil, the parsley, and lemon juice and stir until the seafood is evenly coated. Let marinate at room temperature while you make the sofrito (it can sit for up to 1½ hours).

Make the bone marrow sofrito: Soak the marrow bones in hot tap water for 10 minutes to soften the marrow. When it's soft, push the marrow out of the bones, being careful with any sharp edges on the bones (you should have 3 to 4 ounces marrow). Push the marrow through a fine-mesh sieve and into a large sauté pan so it can be melted more easily. (Save the bones to make Beef Stock, page 295, or discard them.)

Melt the bone marrow in the sauté pan over medium heat, 2 to 3 minutes. Add the leek, onion, carrot, and fennel and sweat the vegetables, stirring often, until they are soft and aromatic but not browned, 8 to 10 minutes. Season the sofrito with salt and black pepper until it tastes good to you. You should have about 1 cup total.

Cook the spaghetti: Bring a large pot of water to a boil and add salt until it tastes like well-seasoned broth. Drop in the spaghetti, give it a stir, and cover the pot to quickly return the water to a boil. Uncover or partially cover to maintain the boil and boil the pasta, stirring occasionally, until it is tender but still a little chewy when bitten, 2 to 3 minutes.

RECIPE CONTINUES

Bone Marrow Sofrito

2 pieces split marrow bones (each 4 to 6 inches long)

½ medium leek, white and light green parts only, cleaned and diced

½ large yellow onion, small diced

½ medium carrot, small diced

½ medium fennel bulb, trimmed, cored, and small diced

Kosher salt and freshly ground black pepper

Spaghetti

Kosher salt

1 pound fresh Spaghetti alla Chitarra (page 69)

¼ cup extra-virgin olive oil

Big pinch of crushed red pepper flakes (optional)

While the pasta water is coming to a boil, in a deep 12-inch sauté pan (just rinse out the pan used for the mussels), combine the bone marrow sofrito, about 1½ cups of the reserved seafood stock, and 1 cup of the hot pasta water or saved pasta water (see page 31). Bring the mixture to a boil over high heat and then reduce the heat and simmer until the liquid reduces slightly in volume, 4 to 5 minutes.

When the pasta is ready, use tongs or a spider strainer to scoop the cooked spaghetti from the water and transfer it straight to the pan. Add the olive oil, reserved seafood mixture, and pepper flakes (if using) and shake and swirl the pan until the raw seafood cooks through and the sauce begins to thicken and hug the pasta, 2 to 3 minutes (keep the pasta moving, adding a little more pasta water if necessary to create a loose, lightly thickened sauce). Taste the sauce, adding more lemon juice and salt if you think it needs it. Remove from the heat and toss until the pasta and sauce marry, leaving just a little sauce in the pan.

Using tongs or a pasta fork, dish out the pasta onto warmed plates, creating some volume by twirling it into a mound and evenly distributing the seafood among the plates.

Troccoli with Shrimp and Ginger Chili Crisp

This was one of those trial-and-error dishes. Chili crisp tastes bangin' on seafood, but when we ate this pasta, the long noodle strands with the short shrimp didn't eat right. The flavors worked perfectly, but the textures didn't. So we ground the shrimp in our sausage grinder. Who'da thunk shrimp sausage would be the answer?! (You can also pulse the shrimp in a food processor or fine-chop it with a knife.) Top this pasta with paper-thin slices of lardo and it really soars. **SERVES 4**

Ginger Chili Crisp
- ¼ cup canola oil
- ½ small shallot, minced (1½ tablespoons)
- 1 × 1-inch piece fresh ginger, peeled and minced (1 tablespoon)
- ½ teaspoon Aleppo pepper flakes
- ½ teaspoon crushed red pepper flakes
- ¼ teaspoon kosher salt

Shrimp
- 8 ounces peeled and deveined medium or large shrimp
- 1¼ teaspoons kosher salt
- ½ small garlic clove, minced
- ¼ × ¼-inch piece fresh ginger, minced (¾ teaspoon)

Troccoli
- Kosher salt
- 1 pound fresh Troccoli (page 58)
- 5 tablespoons (2½ ounces) unsalted butter, cut into pieces
- ¼ cup extra-virgin olive oil
- 1 to 2 tablespoons fresh lemon juice

Make the ginger-chili crisp: In a medium sauté pan, combine the oil, shallot, ginger, Aleppo pepper, red pepper flakes, and salt. Cook over medium heat until the shallots are crispy and bubbles stop forming in the oil, 6 to 8 minutes, swirling the pan a few times. Remove from the heat and let cool.

Grind the shrimp: In a small food processor, combine the shrimp, ginger, garlic, and salt. Drizzle in 1½ teaspoons oil from the chili crisp and pulse until the mixture is coarsely ground like sausage (don't puree the shrimp to a mousse). Set aside.

Cook the troccoli: Bring a large pot of water to a boil and add salt until it tastes like well-seasoned broth. Drop in the troccoli, give it a stir, and cover the pot to quickly return the water to a boil. Uncover or partially cover to maintain the boil and boil the pasta, stirring occasionally, until it is tender but still a little chewy when bitten, 2 to 3 minutes.

Right after dropping the pasta, in a deep 12-inch sauté pan, heat the butter, olive oil, and 1 cup of the hot pasta water or saved pasta water (see page 31). Bring to a boil over high heat and simmer until the mixture thickens slightly, 2 to 3 minutes.

When the pasta is ready, use tongs or a slotted spoon to scoop the cooked troccoli from the water and transfer it straight to the pan. Shake and swirl the pan until the sauce reduces even more and begins to hug the pasta, 1 to 2 minutes (keep the pasta moving, adding a little more pasta water if necessary to create a thickened, creamy sauce). Stir in the shrimp and 1 tablespoon of the lemon juice, tossing until the shrimp cooks through, about 1 minute. Taste the sauce, adding more lemon juice until it tastes good to you. Once the sauce is lightly thickened, remove from the heat and toss until the pasta and sauce marry, leaving little to no sauce in the pan.

Using tongs, dish out the pasta onto warmed plates, creating some volume by building it into a mound. Evenly spoon the chili crisp onto each portion.

Gnocchi Sardi with Monkfish Puttanesca

I never loved monkfish just seared, which results in a very stiff texture. Monkfish benefits from a braise instead. Cooked this way, it is one of the only fish that flakes apart in big pieces like a meat. Poaching it in a ragù like puttanesca also brings out its best qualities. Tomato, garlic, red pepper flakes, and olives add tons of flavor. If you're not a fan of olives, use about ¼ cup small capers instead. **SERVES 4 TO 6**

Monkfish Ragù

- 1 pound cleaned monkfish fillets
- Kosher salt
- 3 tablespoons extra-virgin olive oil
- 1 medium red onion, small diced (about 1½ cups)
- 3 garlic cloves, smashed
- ¼ teaspoon crushed red pepper flakes
- ⅓ cup dry white wine, such as pinot grigio
- 1 (14.5-ounce) can peeled whole Italian plum tomatoes, preferably San Marzano, with their juice

Make the monkfish ragù: Season the monkfish all over with salt (a generous 1½ teaspoons or so) and let rest for 30 to 40 minutes.

Meanwhile, in a medium saucepan, heat the oil over medium heat. Add the onion, smashed garlic, pepper flakes, and a fat pinch of salt (maybe ½ teaspoon) and sweat, stirring a few times, until the onion is translucent but not browned, 4 to 5 minutes. Pour in the wine, bring to a simmer, and cook until the liquid reduces in volume by about half, 2 to 3 minutes. Using your hands, pull out and discard the cores from the tomatoes, and then crush the tomatoes straight into the pan. Bring to a boil over high heat. Cut the heat to low and simmer for 10 minutes.

Buzz the sauce smooth with a stick blender (or in an upright blender and then return to the pan). Bring the pureed sauce to a gentle simmer over medium-low heat and then add the monkfish. Poach the fish in the barely simmering sauce (it may not cover the fish completely) until the fish looks opaque on the surface but is still slightly translucent and moist in the center (about 140°F internal temperature), 10 to 15 minutes, depending on the thickness of your fish. Remove from the heat and transfer the monkfish to a cutting board. When cool enough to handle, use a fork to gently flake the fish into fork-friendly pieces. Return the flaked fish to the sauce, cover, and set aside.

Gnocchi Sardi

Kosher salt

1¼ pounds fresh Gnocchi Sardi (page 62)

½ cup extra-virgin olive oil

5 garlic cloves, Microplaned or grated

¼ teaspoon crushed red pepper flakes

¾ cup chopped pitted Castelvetrano olives (about 15 olives)

⅓ cup chopped fresh flat-leaf parsley

2 to 3 tablespoons sherry vinegar

Meanwhile, cook the gnocchi sardi: Bring a large pot of water to a boil and add salt until it tastes like well-seasoned broth. Drop in the gnocchi sardi, give them a stir, and cover the pot to quickly return the water to a boil. Uncover or partially cover to maintain the boil and boil the pasta, stirring occasionally, until it is tender but still a little chewy when bitten, 3 to 4 minutes.

While the pasta water is coming to a boil, in a deep 12-inch sauté pan, heat the olive oil over medium heat. Add the garlic and pepper flakes and cook until the garlic is fragrant but not browned, about 30 seconds. Add the monkfish ragù along with about 1 cup of the hot pasta water or saved pasta water (see page 31). Bring the mixture to a boil over high heat and simmer until thickened slightly, 3 to 4 minutes.

Using a spider strainer or slotted spoon, scoop the cooked gnocchi sardi from the water and transfer it straight to the pan. Add the olives, parsley, and 2 tablespoons of the sherry vinegar and shake and swirl the pan until the sauce begins to thicken and hug the pasta, 2 to 3 minutes (keep the pasta moving, adding a little more pasta water if necessary to create a lightly thickened sauce). Taste the sauce, adding more salt and/or sherry vinegar if you think it needs it. Remove from the heat and toss until the pasta and sauce marry, leaving little to no sauce in the pan.

Using a large spoon, dish out the pasta onto warmed plates, creating some volume by building it into a mound and evenly distributing the monkfish among the plates.

> **LEVEL UP** **Garnish with fried capers:** Drain about 1 cup pickled capers, pat dry with paper towels, and then fry the capers in 3 tablespoons olive oil in a small saucepan over medium heat until they are crispy, 4 to 5 minutes. Spoon the fried capers straight from the pan evenly over each serving.

PISTACH

On the Ligurian coast, a classic sauce for corzetti pasta is pesto. One summer, our line cook, Moriah Greathouse, prepped a pistachio pesto for me to serve with corzetti at one of my upstairs pasta classes at Vetri in Philadelphia. At the end of the class, I shared the leftovers with our staff and, at the time, another of our chefs, Jesse Grossman, was working on a clam conserva dish. Jacob Rozenberg, the chef de cuisine, had just tasted the clam conserva. Then he tasted the pistachio corzetti. The flavors clicked, and—boom!—a new dish was born. Some of the best dishes are collaborations like this that seem to pop up out of nowhere. **SERVES 4 TO 6**

Pistachio Pesto

1½ cups raw pistachios, preferably Sicilian

½ cup extra-virgin olive oil, plus more as needed

Clams

2 tablespoons extra-virgin olive oil

1 medium yellow onion, sliced into half-moons

4 sprigs fresh flat-leaf parsley

Freshly ground black pepper

½ (750ml) bottle Prosecco or Champagne (about 1½ cups)

5 pounds Manila or littleneck clams (about 50), scrubbed and purged of sand (see page 143)

½ cup white wine vinegar

Generous 1½ tablespoons sugar

Kosher salt

Make the pistachio pesto: In a blender or food processor, buzz the pistachios with the olive oil until completely smooth, 2 to 3 minutes. If necessary, add a little extra oil to get the mixture to blend. Set aside until needed. (You'll have a little pesto left over after making this dish. Drizzle it on focaccia or use it wherever you'd use basil pesto.)

Steam the purged clams: In a deep 12-inch sauté pan, heat the oil over medium heat. Add the onion, parsley, and a generous grinding of black pepper and sweat, stirring now and then, until the onion is translucent but not browned, 4 to 6 minutes. Pour in the Prosecco and bring to a simmer. Add the purged clams, cover, and steam until the clams open, 8 to 12 minutes, depending on their size. Remove the clams as they are done and discard any clams that do not open after 12 minutes. Uncover, cool briefly, and then pick the clams from their shells and place the meat in a medium bowl, discarding the shells. Strain the steaming liquid through a fine-mesh sieve (lined with cheesecloth if you have it) into a large measuring cup, leaving behind any grit and discarding the solids. You should have about 2½ cups steaming liquid.

Make a quick pickling liquid: In a medium saucepan, combine the vinegar, sugar, ¾ teaspoon salt, the garlic, ginger, and chile. Bring to a simmer over medium heat and simmer until the sugar and salt dissolve, 1 to 2 minutes. Remove from the heat and add ¾ cup of the reserved clam liquid to the pickling liquid. Strain out the solids and then return the liquid to the pan. Add the clam meat to the liquid and keep warm over very low heat.

10 Corzetti with Clams and Tarragon

5 garlic cloves, thinly sliced

1 × 1-inch square fresh ginger, unpeeled, thinly sliced

1 dried chile de árbol or dried cayenne-type chile pepper

Corzetti

Kosher salt

1 pound fresh Saffron Corzetti (page 87)

Freshly ground black pepper

Extra-virgin olive oil, for drizzling

1 tablespoon chopped fresh tarragon

1 tablespoon chopped fresh chives

Cook the corzetti: Bring a large pot of water to a boil and add salt until it tastes like well-seasoned broth. Drop in the corzetti, give it a stir, and cover the pot to quickly return the water to a boil. Uncover or partially cover to maintain the boil and boil the pasta, stirring occasionally, until it is tender but still a little chewy when bitten, 2 to 3 minutes.

While the pasta water is coming to a boil, in a deep 12-inch sauté pan (just rinse the pan you used to steam the clams), combine 1½ cups of the hot pasta water or saved pasta water (see page 31), ¾ cup of the remaining clam steaming liquid, and about ½ cup of the pistachio pesto. Bring to a simmer over medium-high heat and simmer until the mixture thickens slightly, 2 to 3 minutes.

Using a spider strainer or a slotted spoon, scoop the cooked corzetti from the water and transfer the pasta straight to the pan. Shake and swirl the pan until the sauce reduces more and begins to hug the pasta, 1 to 2 minutes (keep the pasta moving, adding a little more pasta water if necessary to create a lightly thickened sauce). Taste the pasta, adding salt and/or pepper until it tastes good to you. Remove from the heat and toss until the pasta and sauce marry, leaving little to no sauce in the pan.

Using a large spoon, dish out the pasta onto warmed plates. We like to shingle the corzetti in a circular pattern on the plates. Divide the hot clams and a spoonful of pickling liquid among the plates and garnish with a drizzle of olive oil, the tarragon, and chives.

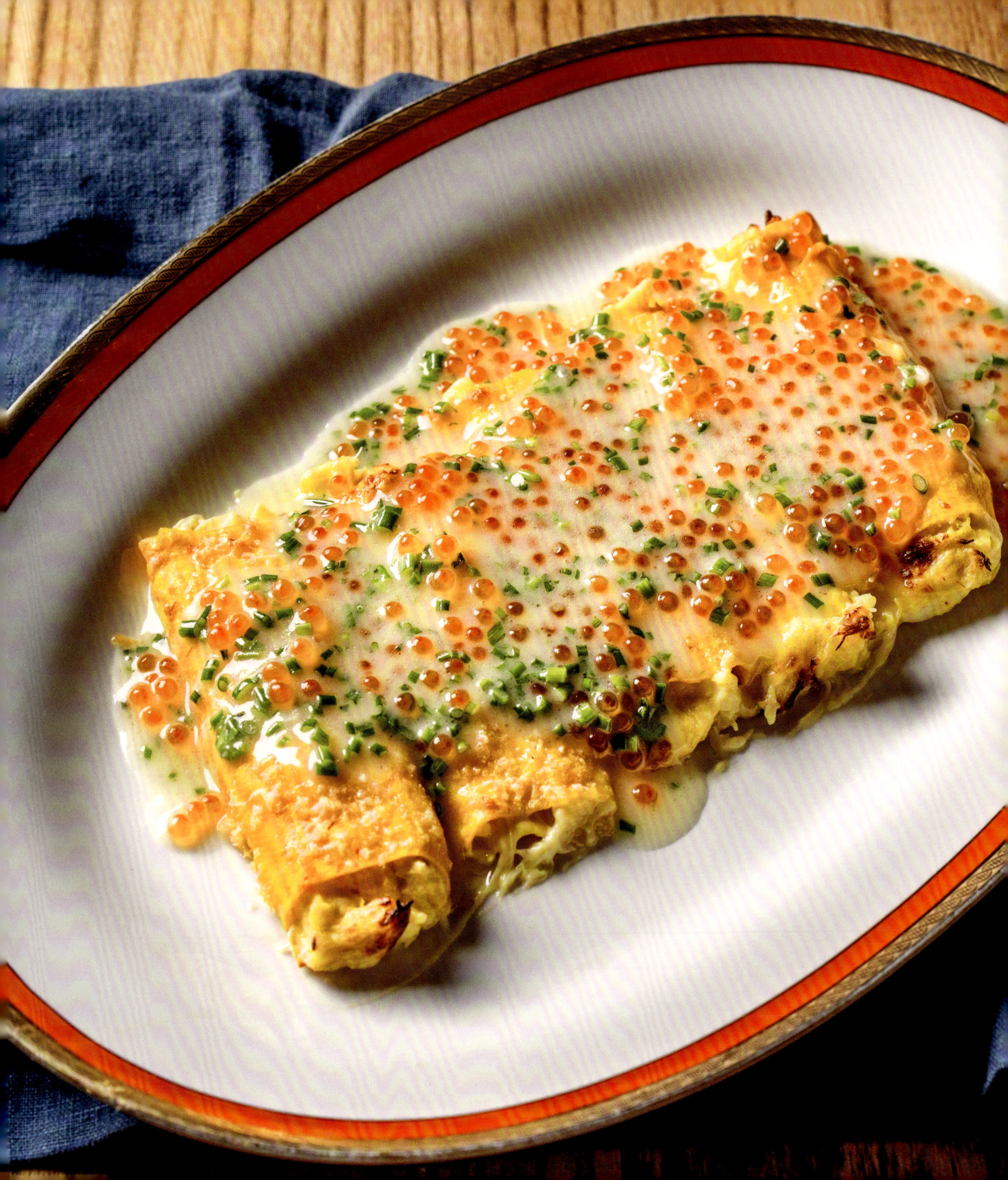

CRAB CANNELLONI WITH SAFFRON

Like lobster, crab has a subtle sweetness that doesn't need much to make it sing. A little butter and salt does the trick. To up the ante, we made a creamy béchamel sauce infused with the floral aromas of saffron. With the rich crab béchamel, delicate sheets of saffron cannelloni, and a simple butter chive sauce, this dish hits all the flavor buttons. To add a wisp of smoke, mix about 3 ounces smoked trout roe into the sauce. The orange roe and green chives make a beautiful plate! To watch a video of making this pasta, scan the QR code on page 168. **SERVES 6**

Crab Béchamel

3 tablespoons (1½ ounces) unsalted butter, cut into pieces

¾ teaspoon crushed saffron threads

6 tablespoons tipo "00" flour or all-purpose flour

3¼ cups whole milk, warmed

Kosher salt

12 ounces jumbo lump crabmeat

½ lemon

Cannelloni and Chive Sauce

1 pound Saffron Dough (page 74), rolled into sheets between ⅛ and 1/16 inch thick

All-purpose flour, for dusting

Kosher salt

Cooking spray

½ cup grated Parmesan cheese

10 tablespoons (5 ounces) unsalted butter, cut into pieces

¼ cup minced fresh chives

Make the crab béchamel: In a large saucepan, melt the butter over medium heat until bubbling. Add the saffron and let bloom until fragrant, 30 seconds or so. Stir in the flour until it absorbs the butter (to make a roux) and then shake it flat in the pan and cook out the raw flour taste for another 30 seconds or so, stirring and shaking flat to prevent toasting the flour. Gradually whisk in the warm milk, whisking constantly to evenly incorporate the milk into the roux until it is smooth. Bring to a simmer over medium-high heat, stirring constantly to prevent any browning on the pan bottom. Cut the heat to medium-low and simmer gently until the béchamel thickens to a medium-thick consistency and tastes sweet instead of like raw flour, 15 to 20 minutes, stirring often. For the silkiest texture, remove from the heat and strain the béchamel through a fine-mesh sieve and into a medium bowl. Season it with salt until it tastes good to you (a generous teaspoon or so).

Put the crab in a medium bowl and break up most of it until it is finely flaked, but break up about one-quarter of it in several pieces about small dice in size. That contrast gives the cannelloni a more interesting texture. Season the crab with salt (about ⅛ teaspoon) and lemon juice (about 1 tablespoon) until it tastes good to you. Then fold all of the crab into the béchamel. Spoon into a piping bag or gallon-size zipper-lock bag, seal, and use within 1 hour. (Or seal and refrigerate for up to 8 hours.)

Cut the pasta: Preheat the oven to 450°F.

Keep a spray bottle of water next to your work surface. Lay a pasta sheet on a lightly floured work surface and cut it into 4-inch squares. As you work, lightly mist the sheets to prevent them from drying out. Repeat with the remaining dough. You should have a total of 20 to 24 squares. Cover them with a damp towel to prevent them from drying out.

RECIPE CONTINUES

Blanch the pasta: Set up a large bowl of ice water. Bring a large pot of water to a boil and add salt until it tastes like well-seasoned broth. Working in batches to prevent overcrowding, drop the pasta into the boiling water and blanch the squares for about 30 seconds, stirring gently to prevent sticking. Using a spider strainer or slotted spoon, transfer the squares to the ice water. When cooled, transfer the squares to damp kitchen towels, laying them flat and mostly separate, and patting them relatively dry. The pieces will be delicate and some may stick, but you should have plenty.

Assemble the cannelloni: Snip off one of the bottom corners of the béchamel bag to make a 1-inch-diameter hole. Line a baking sheet with parchment paper and coat the paper with cooking spray. To fill each cannelloni, pipe a line of béchamel about 1 inch in diameter (about 2 tablespoons of filling) along the bottom of the square that is closest to you, leaving about ½ inch on the left and right sides of the square. Sprinkle about ½ teaspoon of the Parmesan over the béchamel, and then roll the square onto itself, rolling away from you, so that the pasta resembles a thick cigar. Place the cannelloni, seam-side down, onto the sheet pan as they are done and cover to prevent them from drying out. Repeat until all the cannelloni are filled. Mist the top of the cannelloni with cooking spray and sprinkle with the remaining Parmesan.

Bake until the filling is heated through and the top is golden brown, 8 to 10 minutes, rotating the pan front to back halfway through for even browning.

Make the chive sauce: While the cannelloni are baking, in a medium saucepan, combine ¾ cup water and the butter. Bring to a simmer over high heat and let simmer, stirring frequently, until the mixture thickens to a saucy consistency, 5 to 7 minutes. When it coats the back of a spoon, gently stir in the chives and remove from the heat. Season with salt until it tastes good to you and keep warm over the lowest heat.

Divide the cannelloni among warmed plates or serve on a warm platter. Spoon on the chive sauce.

Scan this code to watch a video of making Crab Cannelloni.

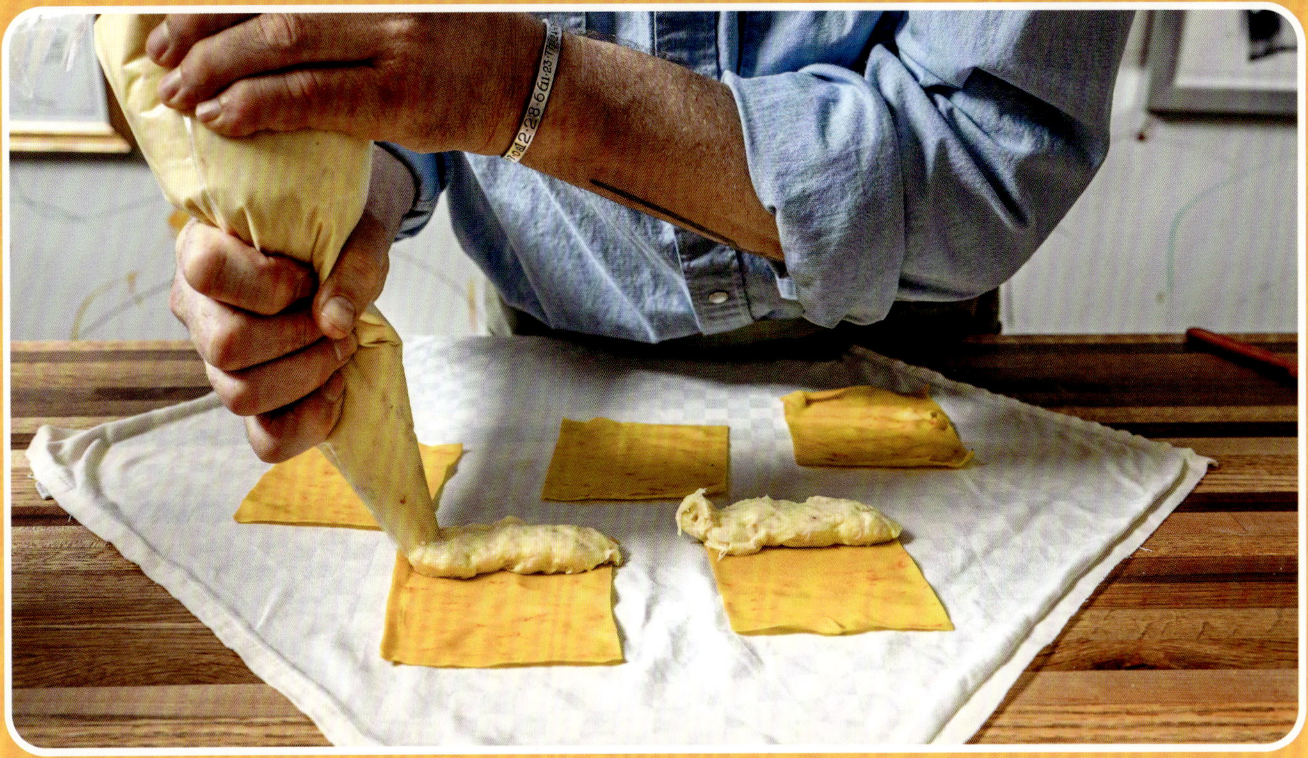

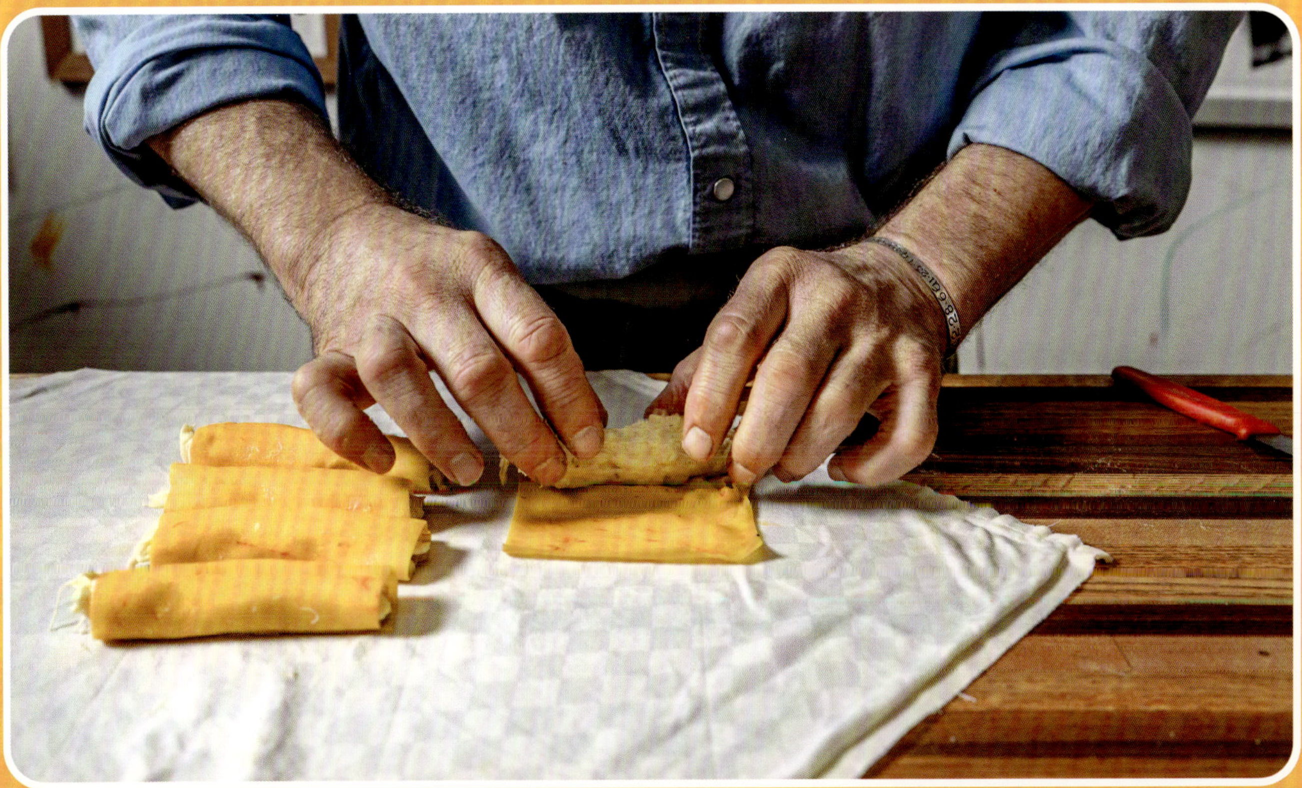

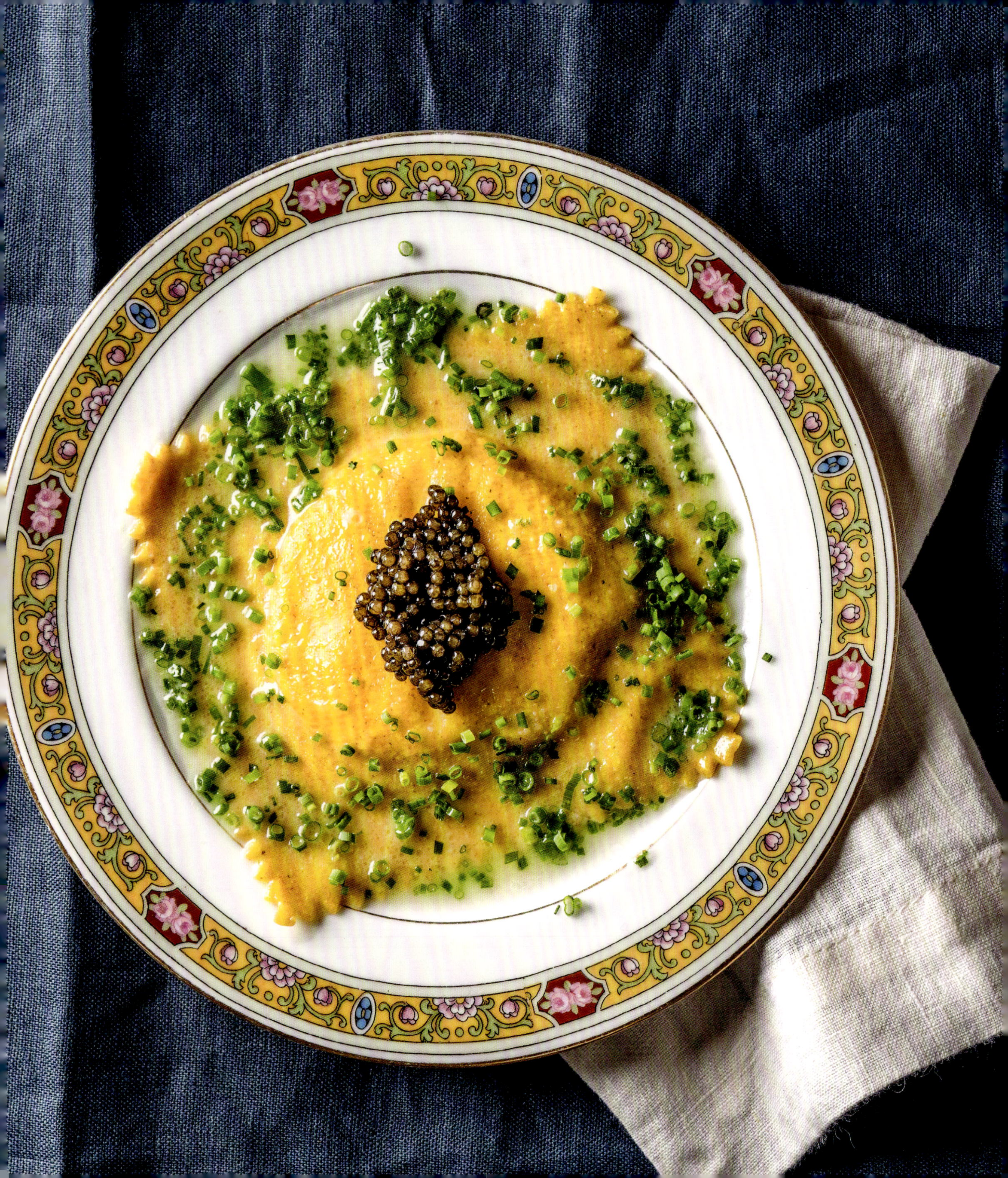

SCALLOP RAVIOLO WITH CHAMPAGNE

Save this one for a special occasion like New Year's Eve when you might have Champagne anyway. I love making the sauce with Franciacorta, the "champagne" of Brescia, a province in northern Italy. When buying the scallops, look for "dry scallops" at your market. The cheaper "wet scallops" are treated with sodium tripolyphosphate (STPP), a preservative that plumps them up with water weight, bumps up the price per pound, and makes them taste soapy. Dry scallops are not treated this way. They taste fresh and sweet, the way a scallop should. **SERVES 8**

Scallop Mousse Filling

6 ounces sea scallops, cleaned

1 large egg white

1½ teaspoons kosher salt

Finely grated zest of ½ large lemon

⅔ cup heavy cream

Ravioli

6 ounces Egg Yolk Dough (page 74), rolled into 2 sheets each about 1/32 inch (0.8mm) thick

All-purpose flour, for dusting

Kosher salt

8 tablespoons (4 ounces) unsalted butter, cut into pieces

⅓ cup Champagne, Franciacorta, or Prosecco

⅓ cup chopped fresh chives

Make the scallop mousse filling: In a blender, puree the scallops, egg white, salt, lemon zest, and cream until velvety smooth, about 2 minutes, scraping down the sides as needed. Spoon the filling into a piping bag or gallon-size zipper-lock bag, seal, and use within 1 hour. (Or seal and refrigerate for up to 8 hours.)

Fill the ravioli: Keep a spray bottle of water next to your work surface. Lay both pasta sheets on a lightly floured work surface. As you work, lightly mist the sheets to prevent them from drying out. Cut off a corner of the piping bag to make a 1-inch-diameter hole. On the sheet of pasta closest to you, pipe 8 rounds of scallop mousse, using about 3 tablespoons filling for each and making them about 3 inches in diameter with 1½ to 2 inches between the rounds (the finished ravioli are square and should have a ½- to 1-inch border of pasta around the filling). As you pipe, rotate the piping bag in the center of each round to make a slight depression in the center about 1 inch wide.

Lightly mist the dough with water to create a good seal and then lay the second sheet of pasta evenly over the first. Gently press the blunt side of a 3-inch ring mold (or a 3-inch-diameter drinking glass) over the rounds of filling to seal the filling. Gently press your thumb into the center of each round so the filling look more like a donut. And then gently press the flat sides of your fingers or outside of your palm around the filling on all surfaces of the pasta to seal the pasta. Using a fluted ravioli cutter (or a knife), cut evenly between the fillings and trim the edges to make 4-inch square ravioli. You should have 8 large ravioli. Lightly dust them with flour and use them within 1 hour. (Or cover and refrigerate them in a single layer on a lightly floured tray for up to 4 hours. You can also freeze them in a single layer, transfer them to a zipper-lock bag, and freeze them for up to 3 days. Take the pasta straight from the freezer to the boiling pasta water, adding about 30 seconds to the cooking time.)

Scan this code to watch a video of making Scallop Raviolo.

RECIPE CONTINUES

Cook the ravioli: Bring a large pot of water to a boil and add salt until it tastes like well-seasoned broth. Drop in all the ravioli, give them a stir, and cover the pot to quickly return the water to a gentle boil. Uncover or partially cover to maintain the boil and boil the pasta, stirring occasionally, until it is tender but still a little chewy when bitten, 2 to 3 minutes.

Right after dropping the pasta, in a deep 12-inch sauté pan, melt the butter over high heat. Add about 1 cup of the hot pasta water or saved pasta water (see page 31) and boil the mixture until it thickens slightly into a thin velvety sauce, 2 to 3 minutes. Add the Champagne and chives and simmer for 1 minute.

Using a spider strainer or a large slotted spoon, scoop the cooked ravioli from the water and transfer them straight to the pan. Shake and swirl the pan until the sauce begins to get creamy and hug the pasta, about 1 minute (keep the pasta moving, adding a little more pasta water if necessary to create a lightly thickened, creamy sauce). Taste the sauce, adding salt until it tastes good to you. Toss gently until the pasta and sauce marry, leaving just a few spoonfuls of sauce in the pan.

Using a spider strainer or large spoon, dish out one raviolo on each warmed plate. Spoon some of the remaining sauce over each raviolo.

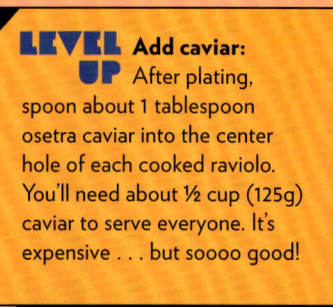

LEVEL UP **Add caviar:** After plating, spoon about 1 tablespoon osetra caviar into the center hole of each cooked raviolo. You'll need about ½ cup (125g) caviar to serve everyone. It's expensive . . . but soooo good!

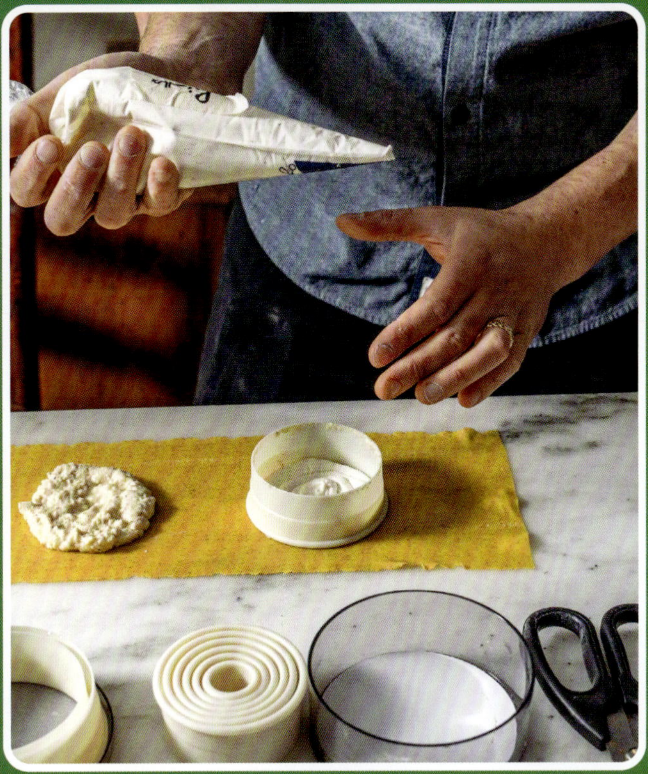

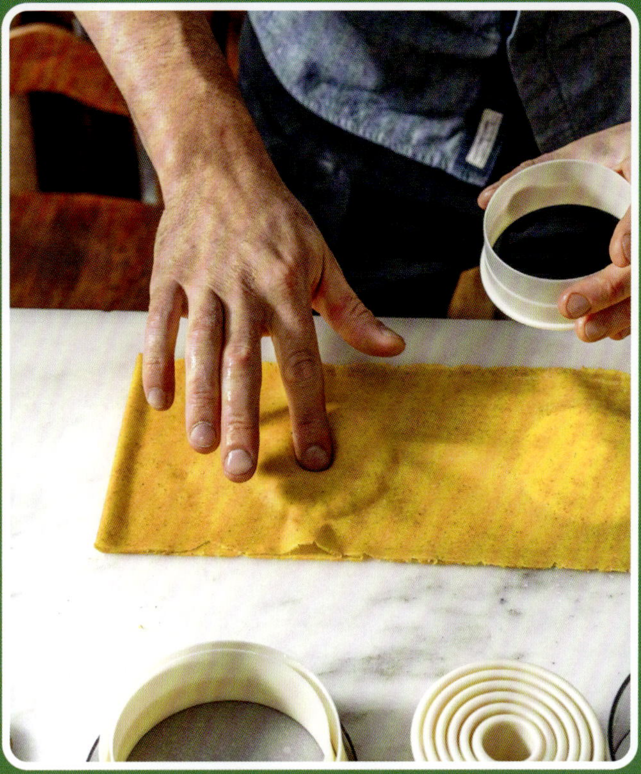

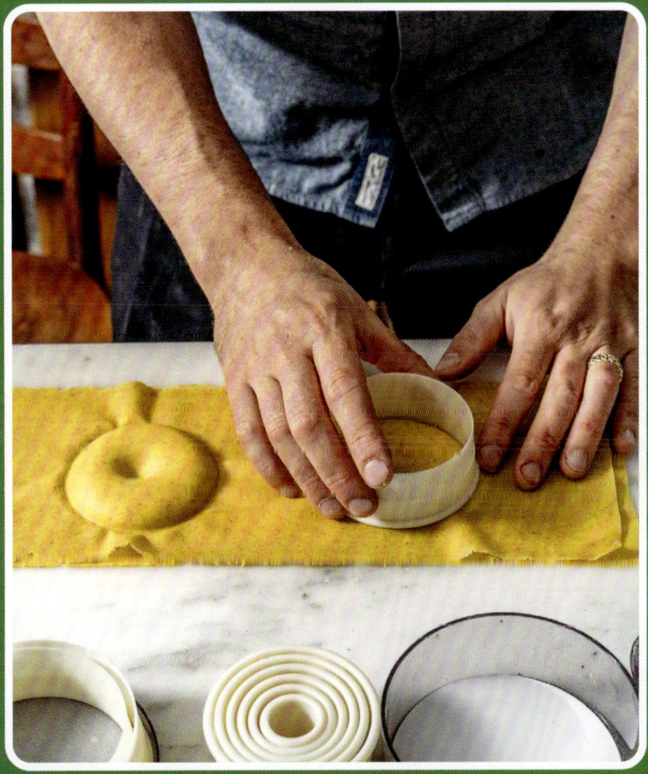

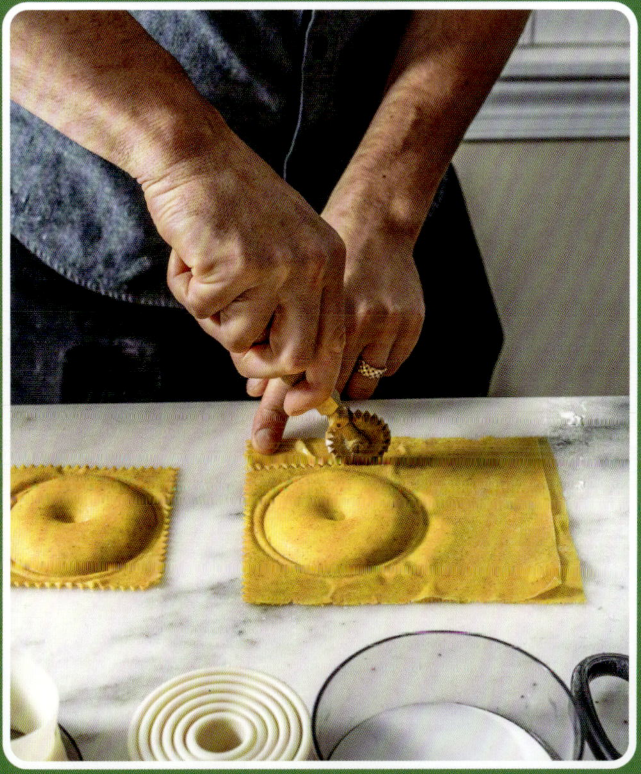

BRANDADE AGNOLOTTI

with chives

Potatoes and salt cod are one of those timeless combinations that always tastes good. That's what's in the pasta filling here, along with some leeks and anchovies to bump up the flavor, and egg to bind it all together. The sauce is just butter, pasta water, and chives, making the whole thing pretty simple in the end. But if, somehow, you mess up the pasta rolling part of the recipe, just toast some good bread, and schmear on the filling. It's so good, that alone could be your dinner! Keep in mind, you have to soak salt cod to get out the excess salt, so start this one a couple of days before serving it. Or look for presoaked Spanish bacalao, which saves loads of time! In that case, use the same amount as dried salt cod. To watch a video of making agnolotti, scan the QR code on page 175.

SERVES 6

Brandade Filling

- 4½ ounces Spanish bacalao (salt cod)
- 8 tablespoons (4 ounces) unsalted butter, cut into pieces
- ½ medium leek, white and light green parts only, cleaned and thinly sliced (about ⅔ cup)
- ½ medium yellow onion, diced (about ⅔ cup)
- 2 large garlic cloves, minced
- 1 teaspoon anchovy paste
- 8 ounces Yukon Gold potatoes (about 2 medium), very finely chopped

Soak the salt cod: To remove excess salt from the salt cod, soak it in water to cover in the refrigerator for 2 days, changing the soaking water twice a day. Drain the soaked salt cod, remove and discard any skin and bones, and then finely chop the meat. Set aside. You should have about 1 cup.

Make the brandade filling: In a large saucepan, melt the butter over medium heat. Stir in the leek, onion, garlic, and anchovy paste and sweat until the onions are translucent but not browned, 4 to 5 minutes. Add the chopped potatoes and cook, stirring to prevent sticking, until they are beginning to get tender when pierced with a fork, about 10 minutes.

Add the milk and salt cod and cook until the pan is nearly dry and the mixture is thick enough to stand slightly stiff on a spoon while still hot, 10 to 15 minutes. The texture should be similar to medium peaks when making meringue.

Remove from the heat and pass the mixture through the fine holes of a food mill into a medium bowl. Add salt until the filling tastes good to you and then stir in the egg until evenly incorporated. Spoon the mixture into a piping bag or zipper-lock bag, seal, and use immediately. (Or seal and refrigerate for up to 4 hours.)

⅔ cup whole milk

Kosher salt

1 large egg, beaten

Agnolotti

All-purpose flour, for dusting

8 ounces Egg Yolk Dough (page 74), rolled into sheets about 1/32 inch (0.8mm) thick

Kosher salt

8 tablespoons (4 ounces) unsalted butter, cut into pieces

1 cup chopped fresh chives

Make the agnolotti: Lightly dust a work surface with flour and follow the directions in Spring Pea Agnolotti with Mint and Butter (page 135) for cutting and filling the dough, but pipe a ¾-inch-wide line of brandade filling down the length of the pasta sheets.

Cook the agnolotti: Bring a large pot of water to a boil and add salt until it tastes like well-seasoned broth. Drop in all the agnolotti, give them a stir, and cover the pot to quickly return the water to a boil. Uncover or partially cover to maintain the boil and boil the pasta, stirring occasionally, until it is tender but still a little chewy when bitten, 3 to 4 minutes.

Right after dropping the pasta, in a deep 12-inch sauté pan, melt the butter over high heat. Add 1 cup of the hot pasta water or saved pasta water (see page 31) and boil the mixture until it thickens slightly into a thin velvety sauce, 2 to 3 minutes.

Using a spider strainer or a large slotted spoon, scoop the cooked agnolotti from the water and transfer them straight to the pan. Add the chives, crank the heat to high, and shake and swirl the pan until the sauce begins to get creamy and hug the pasta, about 1 minute (keep the pasta moving, adding a little more pasta water if necessary to create a lightly thickened, creamy sauce). Taste the sauce, adding salt until it tastes good to you. Toss gently until the pasta and sauce marry, leaving just a few spoonfuls of sauce in the pan.

Using a spider strainer or large spoon, dish out the agnolotti onto warmed plates. Spoon any remaining sauce evenly over each serving.

Scan this code to watch a video of making agnolotti.

SEAFOOD PASTA

POU
AND

> Start by doing what's necessary, then do what's possible, and suddenly you are doing the impossible.
>
> **—SAINT FRANCIS OF ASSISI,**
> ITALIAN CATHOLIC FOUNDER OF THE ORDER OF FRANCISCANS

LTRY
GAME

PASTA

Imagine it's September 1998, and you walk into an Italian restaurant in Philadelphia. This city has the second largest Italian American population in the US, and there's no meatball on the menu. There's no chicken parm. There's no red gravy and no red-and-white checkered tablecloths. The food is not familiar and the look is just not the Italian American restaurant you grew up with. You might think, "This is not an Italian restaurant!"

In the early days of Vetri Cucina, we had a lot of people with bewildered looks on their faces. But the restaurant had rustic wood floors, Venetian plaster walls, an antique espresso machine, and a vintage meat slicer. In the dining room, the Italian singers Pino Daniele and Francesco DeGregori set a captivating mood that mingled with the aromas of rosemary and ragù. So what if the ragùs weren't all red meat sauces? Some were made with duck or guinea hen. Some were made with rabbit. The pastas were made with not just the usual semolina or "00" flour. We added cocoa powder to the dough for tagliatelle and served it with squab ragù. At the time, these were not common flavor combinations in America, but you would certainly have seen them at restaurants in Tuscany, Lombardy, and elsewhere in Italy. Philadelphia already had plenty of red sauce joints. I felt that it was time for the city to taste some other facets of Italian cuisine.

That trailblazing spirit continues in my cooking to this day. In this book, I hope you discover even more of Italy's incredible food in dishes you may have never tried. That's why this chapter of "poultry pastas" doesn't call for boneless, skinless chicken breasts. Instead, experience the joy of Tagliolini with Chicken Liver Ragù (page 180). For all the liver haters out there, this one might change your mind! Expand your palate and taste the simple beauty of Tajarin with Rabbit Bolognese (page 187). Try the amazing flavor combination of Pumpernickel Pappardelle with Duck Ragù (page 182). In this dish, rye flour gives the pasta ribbons a spicy note, and when they absorb the rich ragù, it's a beautiful marriage of duck, bacon, red wine, juniper, and mustard. Like the sound of that? Then you'll love the Buckwheat Maltagliati with Duck and Espresso Ragù (page 184). The noodles incorporate the bittersweet and slightly grassy taste of buckwheat flour, which makes a surprisingly good complement to duck, espresso, and sautéed apples.

Rye and buckwheat in Italian food? How is this possible?! I know . . . buckwheat pasta with duck and espresso ragù is not spaghetti and meatballs, nor is it fettuccine Alfredo. But it is thoroughly Italian. These ingredients and the dishes in this chapter (and the rest of the book) reflect the many regions of Italy in various seasons throughout its history. Italian cuisine is unbelievably diverse—from the swordfish and blood oranges of Sicily to the bresaola and blue potatoes of Valtellina. Remember, it was only five hundred years ago that tomatoes arrived in Italy from the Americas. Sure, today, spaghetti and tomato sauce is synonymous with Italian food, but the country's first tomato sauces were only made in the late 1600s. Buckwheat actually predates tomatoes in Italy by at least 150 years, arriving from China in the 1400s. Now buckwheat is a staple food throughout Lombardy and the mountains of Trentino–Alto Adige. To this day, pizzoccheri remains a signature pasta of Valtellina, the northern Italian valley that borders Switzerland and the Alps. Cooks there pair buckwheat noodles with potatoes, greens like Swiss chard, and Parmesan cheese, a comforting meal for chilly nights in the mountains. In this context, buckwheat noodles with duck and espresso makes perfect sense—and is thoroughly Italian.

For me, unexpected flavor pairings like these are what drive the best dishes in this book. In this chapter, the pastas may seem unfamiliar to you, but they are infused with Italian history and deliver layer upon layer of flavor. Dishes like Potato Ravioli with Escargots and Castelrosso Fonduta (page 197) bring Italy's lesser-known pleasures to the table. These are some of the pastas I'm most excited to share with you now, just as I was excited to share combinations like peaches and porcini with Vetri Cucina guests back in 1998.

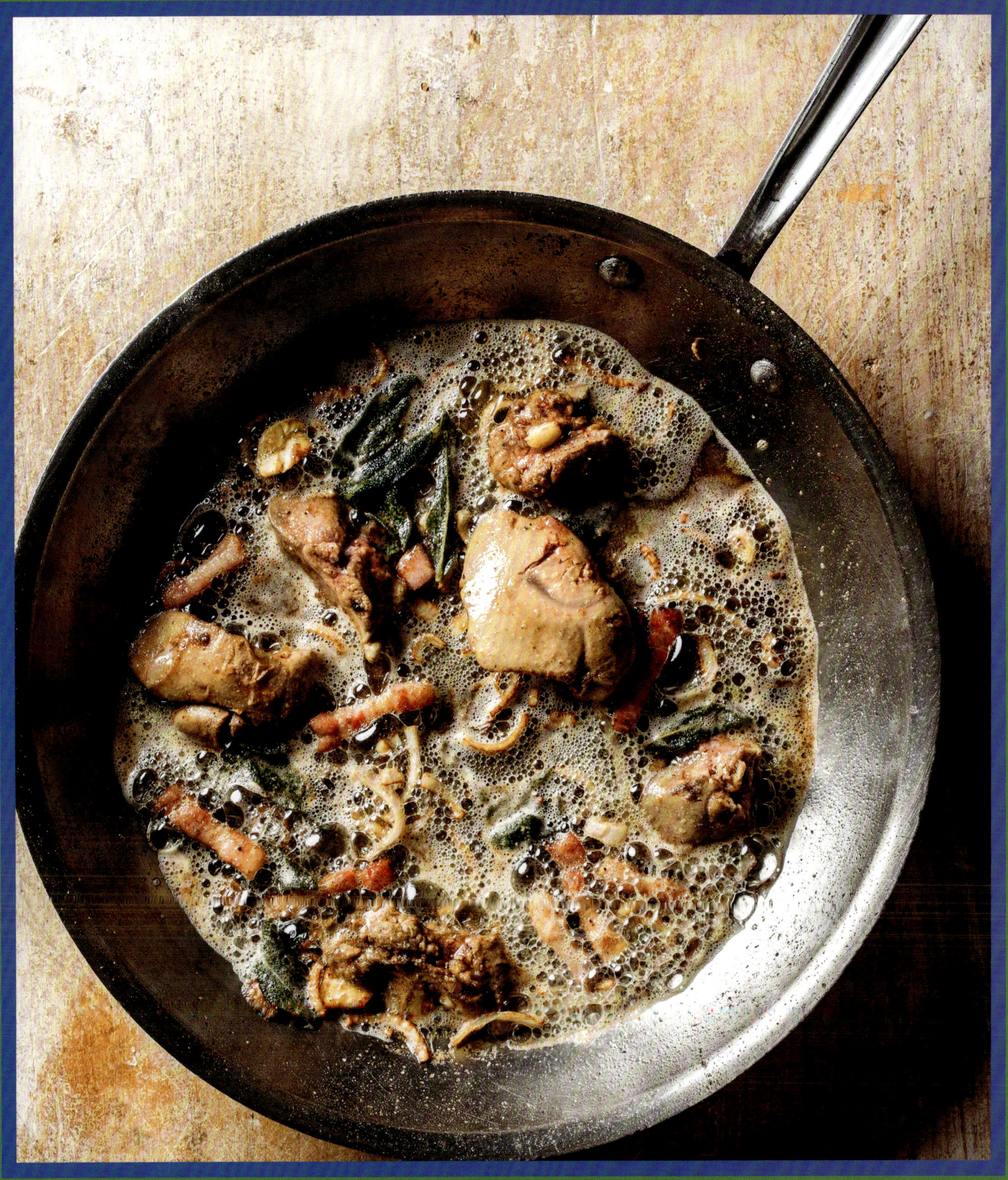

TAGLIOLINI WITH CHICKEN LIVER RAGÙ

LEVEL UP **Use fresh instead of dried tagliolini:** Replace the 12 ounces dried tagliolini with 1 pound fresh Chitarra Dough Tagliolini (page 68). Reduce the pasta boiling time to 2 to 3 minutes.

Straw and Hay Tagliolini with Chicken Liver Ragù: Make a classic Tuscan called *paglia e fieno* ("straw and hay"), as shown in the photograph. The "straw" is yellow egg pasta and the "hay" is green spinach pasta. Use 8 ounces Chitarra Dough (page 67) and 8 ounces Hay Dough (page 67) to make your tagliolini, rolling them together if you like.

On crostini or with pasta, chicken liver ragù is a Tuscan classic, an ingenious use of humble ingredients. We bump up the flavor with pancetta, mushrooms, and Marsala. If you're new to chicken liver, make this pasta your introduction! Once you toss the ragù and tagliolini with butter and Parmesan, there's no weird "liver-y" flavor at all. **SERVES 4 TO 6**

Chicken Liver Ragù

- 18 ounces chicken livers, cleaned of sinew and fat (about 1 pound cleaned)
- Kosher salt and freshly ground black pepper
- 2 tablespoons grapeseed oil or canola oil
- 1 (4-ounce) piece pancetta, guanciale, or thick-cut bacon, small diced (about ⅔ cup)
- 4 cremini (Baby Bella) mushrooms, trimmed and small diced
- 3 medium shallots, small diced
- 2 garlic cloves, smashed
- 8 fresh sage leaves
- 1 cup dry Marsala wine, such as Florio
- 2½ cups Chicken Stock (page 294)

Tagliolini

- Kosher salt
- 12 ounces store-bought dried tagliolini
- 5 tablespoons (2½ ounces) unsalted butter, cut into pieces
- 2 to 3 teaspoons sherry vinegar
- ½ cup finely grated Parmesan cheese, plus more for garnish

Make the chicken liver ragù: Season the chicken livers with about ½ teaspoon salt and several grinds of black pepper. In a deep 12-inch sauté pan, heat the oil over medium-high heat. When the oil is hot, carefully add the livers in a single layer (they may splatter) and sear until lightly browned all over, 6 to 8 minutes total, using a spatula to turn occasionally. Remove the livers to a cutting board.

Reduce the heat to medium and add the pancetta and cook, stirring now and then, until the meat is crispy and the fat renders, 6 to 8 minutes, reducing the heat if necessary to prevent burning. Add the diced mushrooms and cook, stirring a few times, until they shrink, the moisture evaporates, and they begin to brown, 3 to 4 minutes. Add the shallots, garlic, and sage and cook, stirring a couple times, until the shallots look translucent and soft, about 3 minutes. Pour in the Marsala and simmer until the pan bottom is dry, 4 to 6 minutes, scraping the browned bits from the pan bottom. Scrape the mixture over the chicken livers on the cutting board and finely chop everything.

Return the mixture to the pan and pour in the stock. Simmer over medium heat until the mixture thickens to a ragù consistency, 10 to 15 minutes. Remove from the heat, taste, and season with salt and pepper until it tastes good to you.

Cook the tagliolini: Bring a large pot of water to a boil and add salt until it tastes like well-seasoned broth. Drop in the tagliolini, give it a stir, and cover the pot to quickly return the water to a boil. Uncover or partially cover to maintain the boil and boil the pasta, stirring occasionally, until it is tender yet chewy when bitten, 10 to 12 minutes.

Right after dropping the pasta, return the sauté pan of chicken liver ragù to high heat. Add the butter along with 1 cup of the hot pasta water or saved pasta water (see page 31). Simmer and stir the mixture over high heat until it thickens slightly, 3 to 4 minutes. Add the sherry vinegar, a teaspoon at a time, seasoning the mixture until it tastes good to you. The vinegar should wake up the chicken liver, balancing its richness but not dominate as a flavor.

When the pasta is ready, use tongs or a spider strainer to scoop the tagliolini from the water and transfer it straight to the pan. Shake and swirl the pan until the sauce reduces more and begins to hug the pasta, 1 to 2 minutes. Remove from the heat, add the Parmesan, and toss until the pasta and sauce marry, leaving little to no sauce in the pan.

Using tongs or a pasta fork, dish out the pasta onto warmed plates, creating some volume by twirling it into a mound. Garnish with additional grated Parmesan.

PUMPERNICKEL PAPPARDELLE WITH DUCK RAGÙ

When we were developing the menu for Fiorella in Philly, this dish started out as a play on Alsatian choucroute, which is braised sauerkraut with mixed pork cuts and sausage. Our executive chef, Matt Rodrigue, had the inspiration to use duck instead of pork, which worked, and he added cream to the sauerkraut, which didn't work. Five versions later we arrived at this pasta, which is lighter, tighter, and straight to the point: duck, red wine, and rye noodles (no kraut, but cabbage is in there). To add a burst of acidity, throw in a handful of black huckleberries when tossing the pasta and sauce. SERVES 4 TO 6

Duck Ragù

- 3 pounds whole duck legs (3 to 5 legs)
- 3 slices thick-cut bacon (about 2 ounces each), cut into short ¼- to ½-inch-thick strips (lardons)
- ¼ small head green cabbage, finely chopped (about 2 cups)
- 1 large yellow onion, small diced
- ¼ large leek, white part only, cleaned and thinly sliced
- ¼ medium fennel bulb, cored, trimmed, and small diced
- 5 juniper berries
- 1 large sprig fresh rosemary
- 1 large sprig fresh thyme
- 3 large garlic cloves, smashed
- 1 small dried bay leaf
- 1½ cups dry red wine, such as Chianti

Make the duck ragù: Put the duck legs, skin-side down, in a large Dutch oven and set over medium-low heat. If the legs won't fit comfortably, brown them in batches. Cook, without flipping the legs, until the fat renders from under the skin and the skin becomes golden brown and releases easily from the pan, 30 to 40 minutes per batch. As the duck fat renders, spoon it off into a small bowl. Reserve the duck fat for use later in the recipe. (It keeps frozen for months and makes fantastic French fries and roasted potatoes!)

When the fat is rendered and the skin is golden brown, flip the legs and sear the leg meat over medium-high heat until golden brown, 5 to 6 minutes. Remove the legs to a platter.

Add the bacon to the pan and cook over medium heat until it starts to crisp up and the fat renders, about 5 minutes. Stir in the cabbage, onions, leek, and fennel and cook, stirring now and then, until the vegetables start to become tender, 6 to 8 minutes. If the pan looks dry, stir in some of the reserved duck fat and then shake the vegetables into an even layer in the pan. Let the vegetables cook until lightly browned on the bottom, 2 to 3 minutes more, adjusting the heat if necessary to prevent burning. Tie the juniper berries, rosemary, thyme, garlic, and bay leaf in cheesecloth (or a coffee filter) with kitchen twine to make a sachet. Add the sachet to the pan, along with the seared duck legs, skin-side up. Pour in the wine. Reduce the heat to low, cover, and braise over low heat until the leg meat is tender but not quite falling off the bone, 1½ to 2 hours. Check the pan every 30 minutes, as it may go dry. If it does, add ¼ cup water whenever necessary to keep the vegetables from burning.

1½ tablespoons Dijon mustard

Kosher salt and freshly ground black pepper

Pumpernickel Pappardelle

Kosher salt

1 pound fresh Pumpernickel Pappardelle (page 80)

6 tablespoons (3 ounces) unsalted butter, cut into pieces

1 to 3 teaspoons sherry vinegar

½ cup finely grated Parmesan cheese, plus more for garnish

Remove from the heat and let cool in the pan. When cool enough to handle, remove the skin from the duck, mince the skin, and transfer it to a deep 12-inch sauté pan. Crisp the skin over medium heat until browned all over, 3 to 4 minutes, stirring a few times.

Shred the meat, discarding the bones. Discard the sachet and pass the braised vegetables and braising liquid through the medium holes of a food mill or briefly pulse in a food processor to a coarse puree. Transfer to the pan with the skin. Stir in the shredded meat and the mustard, taste the ragù, and season it with salt, pepper, and additional mustard until it tastes good to you. Keep warm over low heat until ready to use. Or refrigerate it in an airtight container for up to 3 days. You can also freeze it for up to 1 month. Gently reheat over low heat before using.

Cook the pappardelle: Bring a large pot of water to a boil and add salt until it tastes like well-seasoned broth. Drop in the pappardelle, give it a stir, and cover the pot to quickly return the water to a boil. Uncover or partially cover to maintain the boil and boil the pasta until it is barely tender, about 2 minutes.

Just before dropping the pasta, add the butter to the ragù and bring to a simmer over high heat. Add 1 cup of the hot pasta water or saved pasta water (see page 31). Simmer and stir the mixture over high heat until it thickens slightly, just a minute or two. Add the sherry vinegar, a teaspoon at a time, seasoning the mixture until it tastes good to you.

Use tongs and/or a spider strainer to scoop the cooked pappardelle from the water and transfer it straight to the pan. Shake and swirl the pan until the sauce thickens a bit and begins to hug the pasta, 1 to 2 minutes (keep the pasta moving, adding a little more pasta water if necessary to create a loose, lightly thickened sauce). Remove from the heat, add the Parmesan, and toss until the pasta and sauce marry, leaving little to no sauce in the pan.

Dish out the pasta onto warmed plates, creating some volume by building it into a mound. Garnish with additional grated Parmesan.

Buckwheat Maltagliati with Duck and Espresso Ragù

Our chef Jacob Rozenberg has an obsession with cooking meat in coffee—just one of his many obsessions! I can't tell you how many times he's made some kind of al latte style ragù (pork or lamb braised in milk) and added coffee to make it like a cappuccino braise. It always tastes muddy to me, and after sampling umpteen versions, I said to him, "Not another coffee braise. Come on, Chef, I thought we moved on." Then he ditched the milk, boiled down the coffee, and added some coffee liqueur, which focused and intensified all the flavors. The coffee taste mostly cooks out, leaving only a dark roasted flavor in the ragù that really won me over with its depth. Buckwheat pasta adds a sharp edge that complements both the duck and the coffee. At the end, a little apple and scallion sautéed in the duck fat totally sends it. **SERVES 4 TO 6**

Duck and Espresso Ragù

3½ pounds whole duck legs (4 or 5 legs)

2 cups strong brewed coffee, hot or cold

⅔ cup espresso liqueur or coffee liqueur, such as Kahlúa

4 to 6 cups reduced Duck Stock (page 295) or store-bought duck demi-glace

½ small fennel bulb, cored and finely diced

1 thick negi scallion, or 4 to 5 standard scallions (2 to 3 ounces), finely chopped

Make the duck and espresso ragù: Put the duck legs, skin-side down, in a large Dutch oven and set over medium-low heat. If the legs won't fit comfortably, brown them in batches. Cook, without flipping the legs, until the fat renders from under the skin and the skin becomes golden brown and releases easily from the pan, about 30 minutes per batch. As the duck fat renders, spoon it off into a small bowl. Reserve about ¼ cup of the duck fat for use later in the recipe. (Save the rest. It keeps frozen for months and makes fantastic French fries or roasted potatoes!)

Preheat the oven to 400°F.

Meanwhile, in a small saucepan, bring the brewed coffee and espresso liqueur to a simmer over medium-high heat and cook until reduced in volume by almost half (to about ⅔ cup), 15 to 20 minutes.

When the fat is rendered and the skin is golden brown, flip the legs skin-side up and sear the leg meat over medium-high heat until golden brown, 5 to 6 minutes. Your goal here is to keep the skin nice and crispy. Pour the reduced coffee mixture into the pan around the duck legs. Pour in just enough of the reduced duck stock to come up to the skin on the legs.

RECIPE CONTINUES

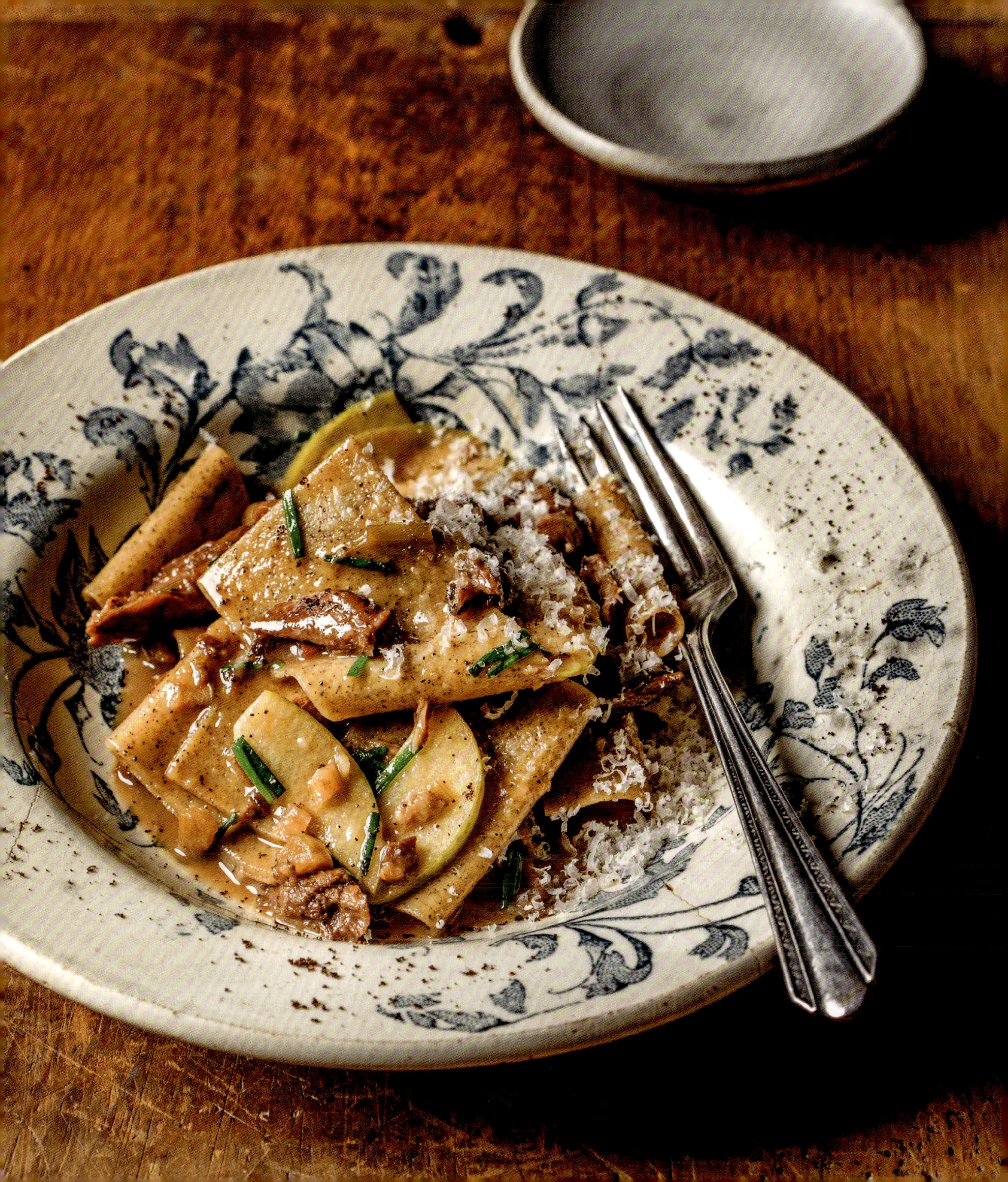

Buckwheat Maltagliati

Kosher salt

1 pound fresh Buckwheat Maltagliati (page 81)

4 tablespoons (2 ounces) unsalted butter, cut into pieces

1 thick negi scallion, or 4 to 5 standard scallions (2 to 3 ounces), finely chopped

1 large Honeycrisp apple, unpeeled, cored and finely diced

1 or 2 teaspoons sherry vinegar

¼ cup finely grated Parmesan cheese, plus more for garnish

Transfer to the oven and braise, uncovered, until the meat can be pulled easily from the bones and is fall-apart tender, about 1½ hours, adding more duck stock to the pan every 20 minutes or so to keep the pan from going dry and to prevent burning.

Remove from the oven and let cool in the pan. When cool enough to handle, transfer the duck legs to a cutting board. Remove the skin from the duck and mince it finely. If any of the skin is wobbly and not crispy, discard it. Shred the meat and discard the bones. Pour the braising liquid into a 2-cup glass measure and let cool a few minutes until the fat rises. Spoon off and discard the fat from the surface of the braising liquid.

Pour a couple tablespoons of the reserved duck fat into a large sauté pan. Add the fennel and scallion and sauté over medium heat, stirring now and then, until softened, 4 to 5 minutes. Stir in the shredded duck leg meat, minced skin, and the defatted braising liquid to make a ragù. Keep warm until needed. (Or refrigerate it in an airtight container for up to 3 days. Reheat gently before using.)

Cook the buckwheat maltagliati: Bring a large pot of water to a boil and add salt until it tastes like well-seasoned broth. Drop in the maltagliati, give it a stir, and cover the pot to quickly return the water to a boil. Uncover or partially cover to maintain the boil and boil the pasta, stirring occasionally, until it is tender but still a little chewy when bitten, 2 to 3 minutes.

While the pasta water comes to a boil, heat the butter and a couple tablespoons of the reserved duck fat over medium heat in a very large, deep sauté pan big enough to hold the pasta (a 12-inch high-sided pan works well). Add the chopped scallions and diced apples and sauté until just tender, 4 to 5 minutes, stirring a few times. After dropping the pasta, add the ragù to the pan along with 1 cup of the hot pasta water or saved pasta water (see page 31). Simmer and stir over high heat until the mixture thickens slightly, 1 to 2 minutes. Add the sherry vinegar, a teaspoon at a time, seasoning the mixture until it tastes good to you.

Using a spider strainer and/or tongs, scoop the maltagliati from the water and transfer it straight to the pan. Shake and swirl the pan until the sauce begins to hug the pasta, 1 to 2 minutes (keep the pasta moving, adding a little more pasta water if necessary to create a loose, creamy sauce). Remove from the heat, add the Parmesan, and toss until the pasta and sauce marry, leaving little to no sauce in the pan.

Using tongs or a pasta fork, dish out the pasta onto warmed plates, creating some volume by twirling it into a mound. Garnish with additional Parmesan.

Tajarin with Rabbit Bolognese

Bolognese sauce is usually made by searing meat at the beginning of cooking, but rabbit is so lean that it stays juicier if you poach it at the end of cooking instead. Here, a bacon sofrito provides a solid flavor foundation in the pan before you add the rabbit. We get our rabbit from a local farmer. Check your local farmers' market or buy it online from places like Blue Ridge Rabbit and D'Artagnan. This Bolognese tosses best with long, thin noodles, but you could make it with a variety of shapes. **SERVES 4 TO 6**

Rabbit Bolognese

2 big slices thick-cut bacon (about 2 ounces each), cut into short ¼- to ½-inch-thick strips (lardons)

½ medium yellow onion, finely diced

½ carrot, finely diced

½ celery stalk, finely diced

1 garlic clove, minced

Kosher salt and freshly ground black pepper

1 cup dry white wine, such as pinot grigio

1 pound ground rabbit or, in a pinch, ground dark-meat chicken

2 cups Chicken Stock (page 294)

Tajarin

Kosher salt

12 ounces fresh Tajarin (page 76)

4 tablespoons (2 ounces) unsalted butter, cut into pieces

¼ cup extra-virgin olive oil

½ cup finely grated Parmesan cheese, plus more for garnish

5 tablespoons finely chopped fresh flat-leaf parsley

3 tablespoons finely chopped or snipped fresh chives

Make the rabbit Bolognese: Set the bacon lardons in a single layer in a deep 12-inch sauté pan. Set the pan over medium heat and cook, stirring now and then, until the bacon is crisp and browned, 5 to 8 minutes. Add the onion, carrot, celery, and garlic and season everything lightly with about ½ teaspoon salt and a few grinds of pepper. Cook until the vegetables are soft, 6 to 8 minutes, stirring a few times. Pour in the wine and simmer until the pan bottom is dry, about 10 minutes, stirring a few times.

Add the ground rabbit and use a sturdy whisk to mash and break it up into fine pieces in the pan as it cooks (the whisk helps prevent large clumps of meat). When the meat is lightly browned, pour in the stock and simmer until the liquid reduces enough to create a thick, saucy consistency, 10 to 12 minutes. Taste the Bolognese and season with salt and pepper until it tastes good to you.

Cook the tajarin: Bring a large pot of water to a boil and add salt until it tastes like well-seasoned broth. Drop in the tajarin, give it a stir, and cover the pot to quickly return the water to a boil. Uncover or partially cover to maintain the boil and boil the pasta, stirring occasionally, until it is tender yet chewy when bitten, 2 to 3 minutes.

Right after dropping the pasta, add the butter and oil to the Bolognese along with 1 cup of the hot pasta water or saved pasta water (see page 31). Simmer and stir the mixture over high heat until it thickens slightly, 2 to 3 minutes.

When the pasta is ready, use tongs to scoop the tajarin from the water and transfer it straight to the Bolognese. Shake and swirl the pan until the sauce reduces a bit more and begins to hug the pasta, 1 to 2 minutes (keep the pasta moving, adding a little more pasta water if necessary to create a loose, creamy sauce). Remove from the heat, add the Parmesan, parsley, and chives and toss until the pasta and sauce marry, leaving little to no sauce in the pan.

Using tongs or a pasta fork, dish out the tajarin onto warmed plates, creating some volume by twirling it into a mound. Garnish with additional grated Parmesan.

RASCHIATELLI
WITH GUINEA HEN BOLOGNESE

LEVEL UP **Add crispy chicken skin:** Bake the chicken skin as directed in the first step of Smoked Potato Culurgiones (page 263). Season the crispy chicken skin with salt and pepper and then break it into shards or crush it between your fingers to garnish each serving.

I don't eat much chicken. Game birds like guinea hen and pheasant have so much more flavor. And they're easier to get these days. Made into a ragù with some pork belly for richness, the meat of these birds makes a fantastic complement to short, handmade pastas like raschiatelli, andarinos, and garganelli. We stuck with the classic Bolognese technique here by stirring in a little milk at the end, which gives this ragù a chicken potpie vibe. **SERVES 4 TO 6**

Guinea Hen Bolognese

1½ pounds boneless, skin-on guinea hen parts (or chicken thighs), coarsely chopped

6 ounces skin-on pork belly, coarsely chopped

1 tablespoon kosher salt

½ medium yellow onion, finely diced

½ small fennel bulb, finely diced

½ small carrot, finely diced

½ cup dry white wine, such as pinot grigio

2-inch Parmesan rind

1 medium sprig fresh rosemary

1 medium sprig fresh thyme

1 small garlic clove, smashed

1 dried bay leaf

¼ cup whole milk

Freshly ground black pepper

Raschiatelli

Kosher salt

1 pound fresh Raschiatelli (page 61)

4 tablespoons (2 ounces) unsalted butter, cut into pieces

2 or 3 teaspoons sherry vinegar

½ cup finely grated Parmesan cheese, plus more for garnish

Make the guinea hen Bolognese: Place the chopped guinea hen and pork belly on a sheet pan and sprinkle with the salt. Freeze, uncovered, for 20 minutes to chill and firm up the meat. Then grind all the meat through the large holes of a meat grinder or pulse in a food processor. (You could also have your butcher grind the meat. In that case, add the salt when you brown the ground meat in the next step.)

Add the ground meat to a deep 12-inch sauté pan and spread it in a single, even layer. Set over medium-high heat and let the meat sear, without stirring, until browned on the underside, 6 to 8 minutes. Stir in the onion, fennel, and carrot and cook until the vegetables are tender, 5 to 6 minutes. Stir in the wine and simmer, scraping up the browned bits, until the wine nearly evaporates, 3 to 4 minutes. Tie the Parmesan rind, rosemary, thyme, garlic, and bay leaf in cheesecloth (or a coffee filter) with kitchen twine to make a sachet. Add the sachet to the Bolognese and pour in enough water to almost cover the meat (about ½ cup). Braise over low heat, uncovered, until the liquid evaporates, 15 to 20 minutes.

Remove from the heat and let cool until warm, about 20 minutes. Squeeze the sachet to extract any juices and then discard it. Stir the milk into the Bolognese, taste it, and season with salt and pepper until it tastes good to you. Keep warm over low heat until needed.

Cook the raschiatelli: Bring a large pot of water to a boil and add salt until it tastes like well-seasoned broth. Drop in the raschiatelli, give it a stir, and cover the pot to quickly return the water to a boil. Uncover or partially cover to maintain the boil and boil the pasta, stirring occasionally, until it is tender but still a little chewy when bitten, 2 to 3 minutes.

Right after you drop the pasta, add the butter to the pan of ragù. Crank the heat to high and add about 1 cup of the hot pasta water or saved pasta water (see page 31). Simmer until the mixture thickens slightly, 1 to 2 minutes.

Using a spider strainer or slotted spoon, scoop the raschiatelli from the water and transfer it straight to the pan of ragù. Shake and swirl the pan until the sauce begins to hug the pasta, 1 to 2 minutes. Add the sherry vinegar, a teaspoon at a time, until the sauce tastes good to you. Season with a little salt, too, if you think it needs it (keep in mind that Parmesan will be added as well). Remove from the heat, add the Parmesan, and toss until the pasta and sauce marry, leaving little to no sauce in the pan.

Using a large spoon, dish out the pasta onto warmed plates, creating some volume by building it into a mound. Garnish with additional grated Parmesan.

ANDARINOS

Jacob Rozenberg, the chef de cuisine at Vetri Philly, told me that his mom always made braised chicken thighs with currants and apricots for Rosh Hashanah. When he did a spin on that using pistachios instead of currants and capon for the bird, it caught my eye. The nuts braise right along with the meat and white wine, becoming soft and tender like cooked beans. Such a cool texture in ragù! I highly recommend using Sicilian pistachios here—they're smaller, deep green, and taste better than the California ones. Same goes for seeking out capon. It's juicier, more tender, and richer-tasting than your average chicken. **Serves 4 to 6**

Capon Ragù

- 2 pounds capon or chicken leg quarters (about 2 capon or 4 to 6 chicken leg quarters)
- Kosher salt and freshly ground black pepper
- 2 tablespoons (1 ounce) unsalted butter, cut into pieces
- 1½ teaspoons canola oil
- 4 to 6 small cippolini onions, peeled and left whole or halved if large
- 2 garlic cloves, peeled
- ½ cup slightly sweet white wine, such as Riesling or Gewürztraminer
- 1½ cups Chicken Stock (page 294)
- ¼ cup shelled raw pistachios, preferably Sicilian
- 1 large sprig fresh thyme
- 5 dried apricots, finely diced (¼ cup)

Make the capon ragù: Preheat the oven to 350°F.

Season the capon leg quarters all over with salt and pepper (about 1 tablespoon salt). In a large Dutch oven, melt the butter and oil over medium-high heat. When hot, working in batches to avoid overcrowding, add the capon leg quarters skin-side down. Cook until the capon is evenly browned all over, 6 to 8 minutes per side. To help get even browning, spoon the hot fat over the capon as it cooks. Adjust the heat if necessary to keep the butter from burning. Remove the seared and browned capon to a platter.

Add the cippolini onions to the pan. Cook over medium heat until the onions begin to brown in spots, shaking the pan to help capture some flavorful browned bits from the pan bottom, 4 to 5 minutes. Spoon off and discard most of the fat from the pan. Add the garlic and cook until fragrant, about 30 seconds. Add the wine and simmer over medium-high heat, scraping the pan bottom now and then, until the wine evaporates, 5 to 8 minutes. Add the chicken stock, pistachios, and thyme sprig, along with the reserved capon and any accumulated juices. Turn the capon parts skin-side up, cover, and transfer to the oven.

Braise for 30 minutes. Add the apricots to the pan and braise, uncovered, until an instant-read thermometer registers 165°F in the thickest part of a thigh, 10 to 15 minutes.

Remove from the oven and let cool in the pan, 20 to 30 minutes.

When cool enough to handle, remove the capon to a cutting board. Remove the skin, mince it finely, and transfer it to a medium sauté pan. Crisp up the skin pieces over medium heat until browned all over, 3 to 4 minutes, stirring once or twice.

Di Usini with Capon Ragù, Pistachios, and Apricots

Andarinos di Usini

Kosher salt

1 pound fresh Andarinos di Usini (page 64)

5 tablespoons (2½ ounces) unsalted butter, cut into pieces

Freshly ground black pepper

½ cup finely chopped fresh flat-leaf parsley

5 tablespoons finely grated Parmesan cheese, plus more for serving

Pick the meat from the bones, discard the bones, and shred the meat. Stir the shredded meat and crisped skin back into the ragù. Taste the ragù and season with salt and pepper until it tastes good to you. Keep warm over low heat until ready to serve. (Or refrigerate in a covered container for up to 3 days and reheat gently over low heat when needed.) Remove the garlic and thyme sprig before using.

Cook the andarinos di usini: Bring a large pot of water to a boil and add salt until it tastes like well-seasoned broth. Drop in the andarinos, give them a stir, and cover the pot to quickly return the water to a boil. Uncover or partially cover to maintain the boil and boil the pasta, stirring occasionally, until it is tender but still a little chewy when bitten, 2 to 3 minutes.

While the pasta water comes to a boil, in a deep 12-inch sauté pan, melt the butter over high heat. Add the ragù and about ¾ cup of the hot pasta water or saved pasta water (see page 31) and simmer over high heat until the mixture thickens slightly, 1 to 2 minutes.

Using a spider strainer or slotted spoon, drain the andarinos by transferring them to the pan. Shake and swirl the pan until the sauce thickens a bit and begins to hug the pasta, 1 to 2 minutes (keep the pasta moving, adding a little more pasta water if necessary to create a loose, lightly thickened sauce). Taste the sauce, adding salt and pepper until it tastes good to you. Remove from the heat, add the parsley and Parmesan, and toss until the pasta and sauce marry, leaving little to no sauce in the pan.

Using a large spoon, dish out the pasta onto warmed plates, creating some volume by building a mound. Garnish with additional grated Parmesan.

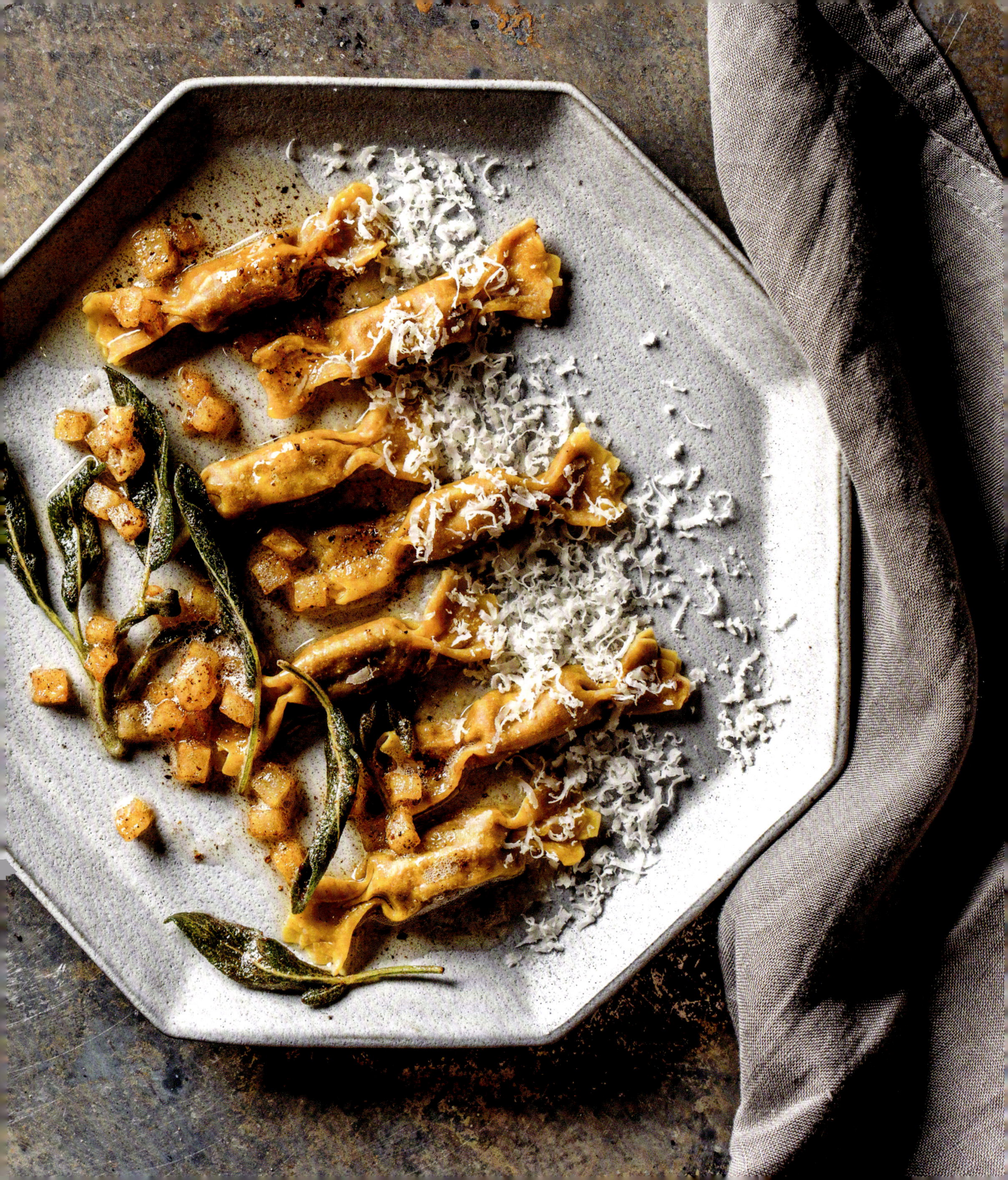

Chicken Liver Caramelle with Apples and Sage

This shape is fun to make, as simple as twisting the wrapper on a piece of candy. But the "candy" inside this pasta is a smooth chicken liver mousse with bacon, brandy, apples, and sage! The sugar in the apple really helps balance out the richness of the chicken liver. The sauce is mostly brown butter, which is all you need, plus a little more apple and sage to drive the point home. To watch a video of making this pasta, scan the QR code on page 196. **SERVES 8 TO 10**

Chicken Liver Filling

2 tablespoons canola oil

18 ounces chicken livers, cleaned of sinew and fat (about 1 pound cleaned)

1 slice thick-cut bacon, finely chopped

1 small yellow onion, small diced (about ¾ cup)

1 slice (about ¼-inch-thick) unpeeled Honeycrisp apple, small diced (about 1 tablespoon)

4 fresh sage leaves

¼ cup brandy

½ cup heavy cream, plus more as needed

Kosher salt

1 small egg yolk

Make the chicken liver filling: Heat a large sauté pan over high heat. When hot, swirl in the oil and add the chicken livers. Sear the livers, turning now and then, until browned all over, 5 to 6 minutes. Remove to a plate.

Reduce the heat to medium and add the chopped bacon to the pan. Cook until the bacon is crispy and the fat renders, 3 to 4 minutes, flipping halfway through. Add the onion, diced apple, and the sage leaves and cook, stirring now and then, until the vegetables are soft, about 5 minutes. Pour in the brandy, stand back (because there will be a huge whoosh of flame) and light (flambé) the brandy with a long-handled lighter or long match. It will flare up at first and then quickly die down. You could flambé off the heat if you prefer. When the flames die down, stir in the cream and cook until the liquid thickens enough to glaze the vegetables. Remove from the heat and let the mixture cool until warm.

In an upright blender, puree the chicken livers (save any juices on the plate) and the vegetable mixture (or transfer to a tall container and blend using a stick blender). If necessary, add enough of the reserved chicken liver juices so that the mixture purees easily into a thick, smooth filling. If there were no juices, add just enough additional heavy cream to get the mixture to puree. For a super-silky texture, press the mixture through a fine-mesh sieve with a spoon into a bowl. Taste it and season with salt until it tastes good to you. Mix in the egg yolk. Spoon the mixture into a piping bag or zipper-lock bag, seal, and use immediately. (Or refrigerate until you're ready to fill the pasta, up to 8 hours.)

RECIPE CONTINUES

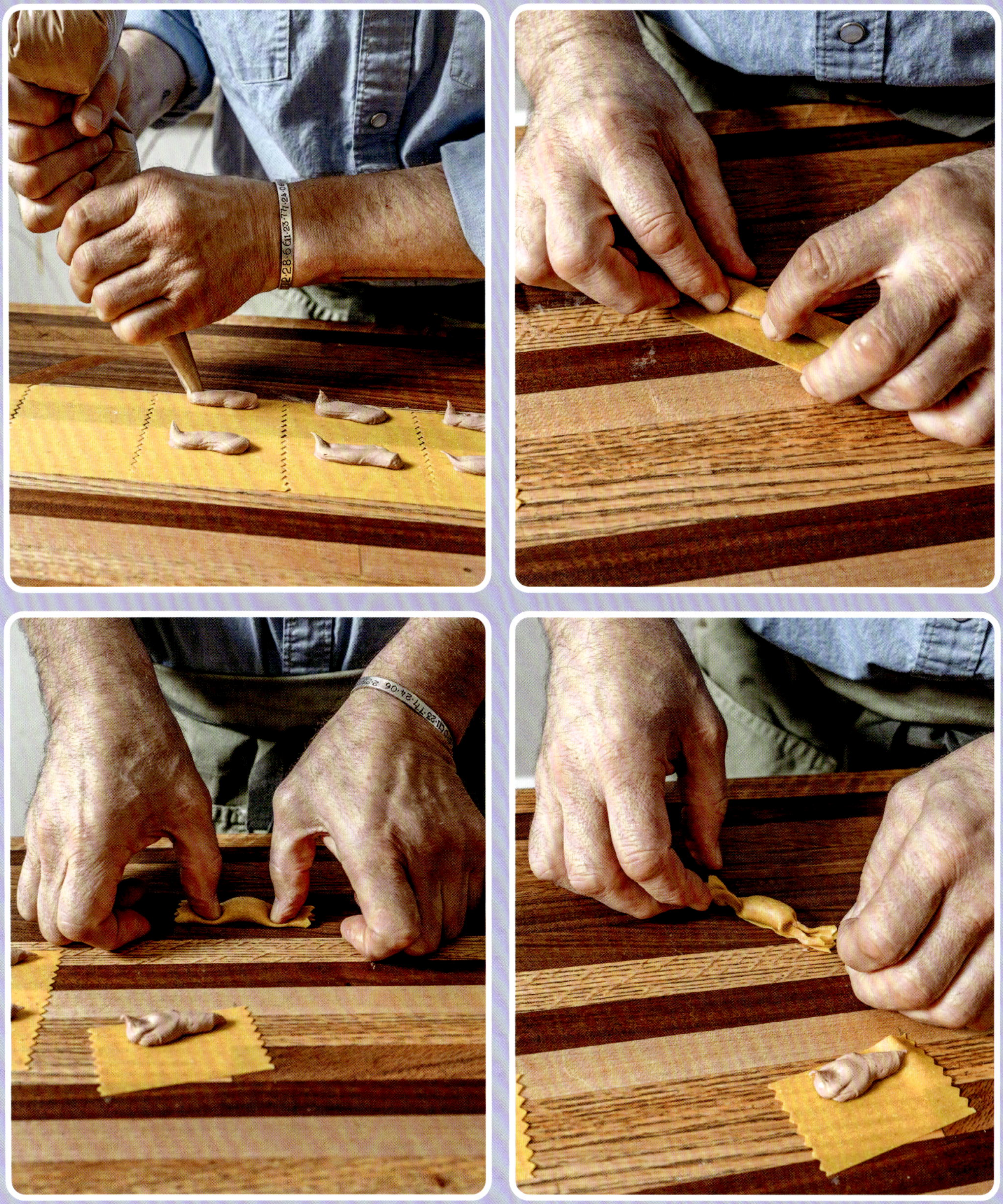

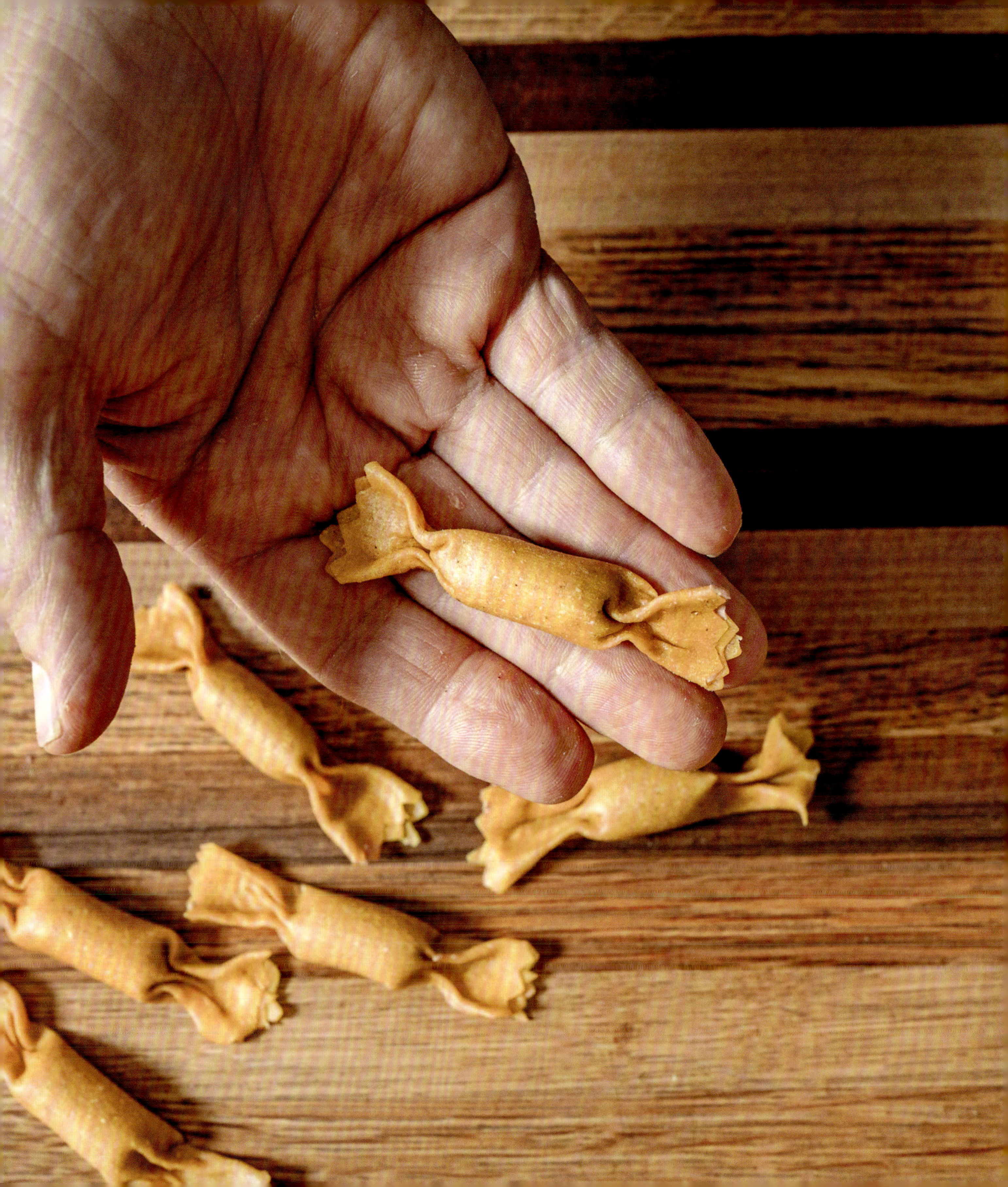

Caramelle

1 pound Egg Yolk Dough (page 74), rolled into super-thin sheets about 1/32 inch (0.8mm) thick

Kosher salt

16 tablespoons (8 ounces) unsalted butter, cut into pieces

1 small Honeycrisp apple, unpeeled, finely diced (about ½ cup)

20 fresh sage leaves

Finely grated Parmesan cheese, for garnish

Make the caramelle: Place a spray bottle of water next to your work area. Lay a pasta sheet on a lightly floured work surface and trim the ends square. Keep the remaining pasta covered as you work. Lightly mist the dough with water to keep it from drying out and then cut the dough into 2 × 3-inch rectangles, preferably with a fluted cutter on the short ends. Cut off the tip of the piping bag (or one corner if using a zipper-lock bag) to make a ½-inch-diameter hole. Pipe about ½ teaspoon filling in a line along the bottom third of each rectangle, about 1 inch long and ½ inch wide, leaving ¼ to ½ inch of empty space on either side.

Wet your fingers and moisten the edges of a rectangle. Lift the bottom of the pasta over the filling so the edge just covers the filling, then continue folding until the filling is enclosed and the pasta forms a small rectangle. Press down on the dough on both sides of the filling to seal the filling inside. Using both hands, pinch the dough on both sides of the filling, pinching the dough around the filling to plump up the filling so the pasta resembles a sort of long wrapped candy. As the caramelle are formed, transfer them to floured sheet pans. Repeat with the remaining pasta and filling. You should have about 150 caramelle. Light dust the caramelle with flour and use immediately. (Or refrigerate them until needed, up to 2 hours. Or freeze them in a single layer on floured sheet pans, transfer them to zipper-lock bags, and freeze them for up to 3 days. Take the pasta straight from the freezer to the pasta water.)

Cook the caramelle: Bring a large pot of water to a boil and add salt until it tastes like well-seasoned broth. Drop in the caramelle, give it a stir, and cover the pot to quickly return the water to a boil. Uncover or partially cover to maintain the boil and boil the pasta, stirring occasionally, until it is tender yet chewy when bitten, 2 to 3 minutes.

While the pasta cooks, in a large sauté pan, melt the butter over medium-high heat. As it melts, season it with a little salt. It will sizzle at first, and when that stops it will start to brown. When the butter looks golden brown and smells nutty, after 4 to 5 minutes, add the diced apple and sage leaves, shaking the pan to coat with the brown butter. Remove from the heat.

Using a spider strainer or slotted spoon, scoop the caramelle from the water, letting it drip almost dry. Transfer the drained pasta to warmed plates, creating some volume by building it into a tall mound. Spoon some brown butter with apples and sage over each serving and finish with grated Parmesan.

Scan this code to watch a video of making Chicken Liver Caramelle.

POTATO RAVIOLI
WITH ESCARGOTS AND CASTELROSSO FONDUTA

Save this one for a special occasion—it's got a few steps to it! But the flavors are pretty straightforward. Our chef, Matt Rodrigue, sticks to the rule of three (see page 18): potato, snails, cheese. These ingredients blend seamlessly in the dish—with a few special touches, of course. Snails always come to life with a little alcohol, and Chartreuse does the job here, adding some botanical aromas. For the potatoes, instead of plain butter, brown butter takes them to another level. And for the cheese, Castelrosso is one of those Piemonte gems, a cow's-milk cheese that's both creamy and crumbly and somehow tastes like toasted pine nuts and lemon. To watch a video of making a similar ravioli, scan the QR code for Corn Anolini on page 272. **SERVES 6 TO 8**

Potato Filling

- 2 medium Yukon Gold potatoes (12 to 14 ounces), unpeeled
- ⅓ cup whole milk
- 1 small sprig fresh rosemary
- 1 small sprig fresh thyme
- ½ small garlic clove
- 1 tablespoon extra-virgin olive oil
- ¼ medium yellow onion, small diced (about ¼ cup)
- ⅛ medium leek, white part only, cleaned and thinly sliced (2 to 3 tablespoons)
- 3 tablespoons (1½ ounces) unsalted butter
- ½ cup shredded Fontina cheese
- ⅓ cup finely grated Piave or Grana Padano cheese
- ¼ cup finely grated Parmesan cheese
- Kosher salt
- 1 large egg, beaten

Make the potato filling: In a medium saucepan, combine the potatoes with cold water to cover by 1 inch. Cover and bring to a boil over high heat. Uncover and boil the potatoes until very tender, 30 to 35 minutes. Remove the potatoes to a cutting board and coarsely chop with the skin. (If you don't have a food mill and will be using a ricer instead, peel the potatoes first.)

While the potatoes are cooking, in a small saucepan, combine the milk, rosemary, thyme, and garlic. Bring just to a simmer over medium heat, then cut the heat to low and cook for 5 minutes. Remove from the heat and let steep until the milk is infused with flavor, about 30 minutes.

Meanwhile, in a small sauté pan, heat the oil over medium heat. Add the onion and leek and cook, stirring a few times, until soft but not browned, 4 to 5 minutes.

Pass the boiled potatoes and the sautéed onion mixture through the fine holes of a food mill into a medium bowl, discarding the solids. (If you don't have a food mill, peel the potatoes and pass them through a potato ricer into a bowl. Puree the sautéed onion mixture in a mini chopper and combine it with the potatoes in the bowl.)

Rinse out the small sauté pan and then melt the butter in it over medium-high heat. Let cook until the butter looks golden brown and smells nutty (browned butter), 4 to 5 minutes.

RECIPE CONTINUES

Snail Ragù

1 (28-ounce) can extra-large snails, drained (about 1 pound drained)

2 tablespoons extra-virgin olive oil

½ large yellow onion, finely diced

½ medium fennel bulb, trimmed, cored, and finely diced

½ large carrot, finely diced

2 garlic cloves, minced

2 tablespoons green Chartreuse or dry vermouth

1 small sprig fresh rosemary

1 sprig fresh thyme

1 small dried bay leaf

2½ teaspoons unflavored gelatin powder

Kosher salt

Ravioli and Castelrosso Fonduta

1 pound Egg Yolk Dough (page 74), rolled into super-thin sheets about 1/32 inch (0.8mm) thick

All-purpose flour, for dusting

1 cup heavy cream

4 ounces Castelrosso cheese, small diced or crumbled

Kosher salt

6 tablespoons (3 ounces) unsalted butter, cut into pieces

Finely grated Parmesan cheese, for garnish

Pour the steeped milk through a sieve into the potato bowl (discard the solids). Add the browned butter and fold the milk and browned butter into the potato mixture. Fold in the Fontina, Piave, and Parmesan cheeses until incorporated. Taste the mixture and add salt until it tastes good to you (¼ to ½ teaspoon should do it). Measure out half the beaten egg, about 1½ tablespoons, and fold the egg into the filling (discard the remaining egg). Spoon the mixture into a piping bag or zipper-lock bag, seal, and refrigerate until needed, up to 8 hours.

Make the snail ragù: Chop the snails into fork-friendly pieces and rinse in a colander under cold running water for several minutes until the snails are completely free of grit. Taste one to make sure all grit has been removed.

In a large, deep sauté pan, heat the oil over medium heat. Add the onions, fennel, and carrot and cook, stirring a few times, until the vegetables are soft but not browned, 6 to 8 minutes. Add the garlic and cook until fragrant, about 30 seconds. Pour in the Chartreuse and simmer until the liquid evaporates, about a minute. Tie the rosemary, thyme, and bay leaf in cheesecloth (or a coffee filter) with kitchen twine and add to the pan.

Add the snails and pour in enough water to barely cover the ingredients, 1 to 1½ cups, depending on the size of your pan. Reduce the heat to low, cover, and braise the ragù gently until the flavors marry, about 20 minutes.

When the ragù is nearly done, stir the gelatin into ¼ cup cold water until dissolved and let stand 5 minutes. Remove the ragù from the heat and stir in the gelatin mixture until evenly distributed. Taste the ragù and season with salt until it tastes good to you (you may need as much as 2 teaspoons). Cover and let stand until ready to use. (Or cool completely, and refrigerate in an airtight container for up to 1 day.)

Make the ravioli: Keep a spray bottle of water next to your work area. Lay a pasta sheet on a lightly floured work surface and trim the edges square. Fold the sheet over itself from left to right (or right to left), lining up the ends, and mark the halfway point with a small notch in the dough. Unfold the dough so it's flat again on your work surface. Pipe 1-inch balls of filling in rows along half of the dough to the halfway mark, leaving ¼ to ½ inch of space around each ball of filling. You should be able to get 3 rows of filling on each pasta sheet. Lightly mist the filled side of the dough with water. Lift the empty half of the dough up and drape it over the filled half, lining up all the edges. Gently press the dough around each ball of filling to form a sealed dome over the filling (if you have a 1¼- to 1½-inch ring mold or biscuit cutter, it's easier and faster to use the blunt side of the mold to gently seal the domes, rather than using your hands).

RECIPE CONTINUES

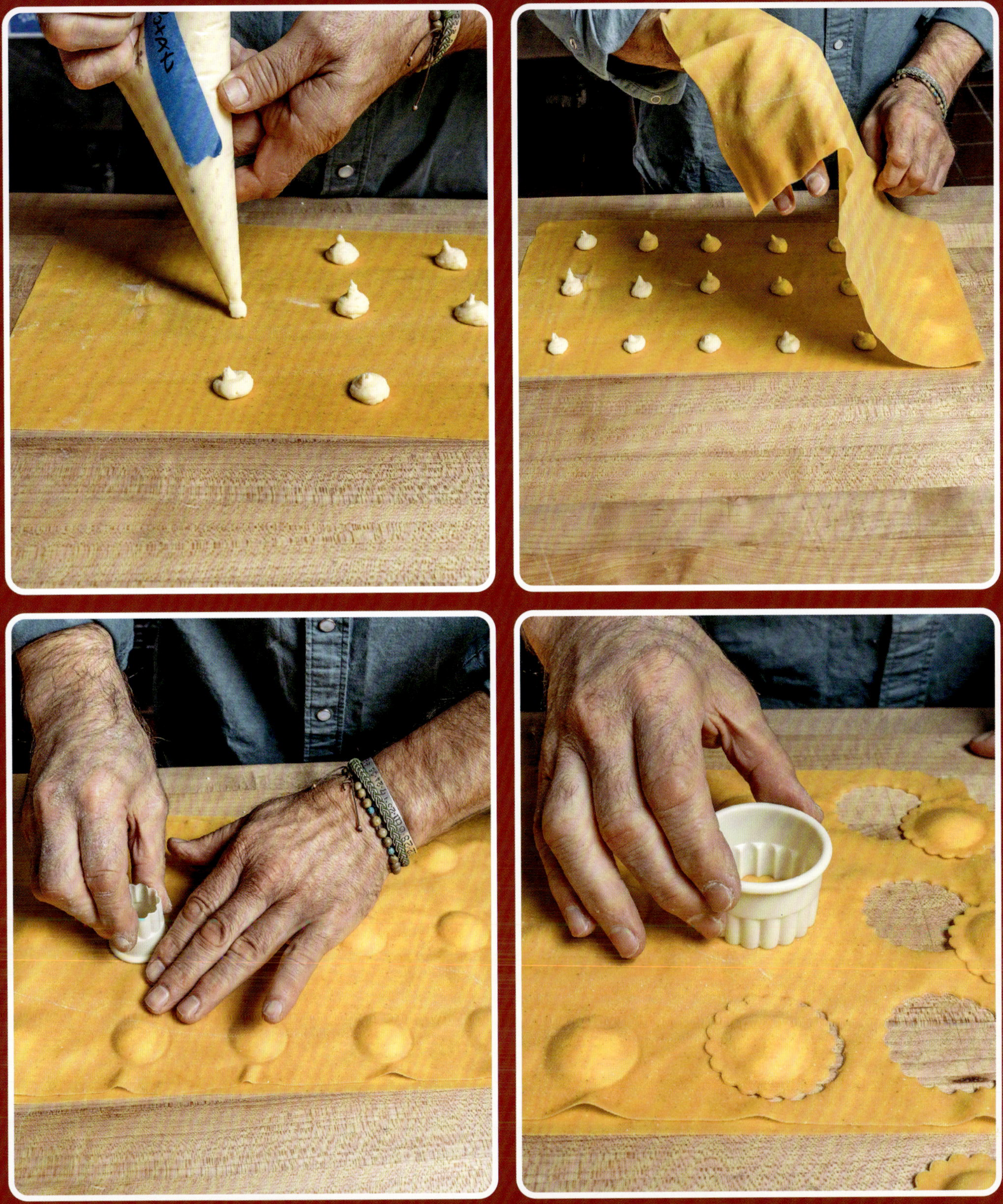

Next, use a 2-inch round pasta cutter (preferably fluted) to punch out round domed ravioli with a small border of pasta. Transfer the ravioli to floured sheet pans. Repeat the process with the remaining pasta and filling. You should have 80 to 90 ravioli. Cover the ravioli and use them within 1 hour. (Or refrigerate them for up to 4 hours. You can also freeze the ravioli in a single layer, then transfer them to zipper-lock bags and freeze them for up to 3 days. Take the ravioli straight from the freezer to the pasta water.)

Make the Castelrosso fonduta: In a small saucepan, bring the cream to a boil. Reduce the heat to low and gradually whisk in the Castelrosso, stirring constantly and mashing the cheese a bit to break it up. Let the mixture cook over low to medium-low heat until slightly thickened to a medium-thin cheese sauce, 10 to 12 minutes. For a super-silky texture, strain the sauce through a medium-mesh sieve, pressing on the solids, and then return it to the pan. Keep warm over low heat.

Cook the ravioli: Bring a large pot of water to a boil and add salt until it tastes like well-seasoned broth. Drop in the ravioli, give them a stir, and cover the pot to quickly return the water to a boil. Uncover or partially cover to maintain the boil and boil the pasta, stirring occasionally, until it is tender yet chewy when bitten, 2 to 3 minutes. You can also squeeze a corner of the pasta to see if it is tender.

Right after dropping the pasta, in a deep 12-inch sauté pan, melt the butter. Add about 2 cups of the ragù and ½ cup of the hot pasta water or saved pasta water (see page 31). Reserve any remaining ragù for another use—it's fantastic served with risotto. Simmer and stir the mixture over high heat until it thickens slightly, just a minute or two.

Using a spider strainer, scoop the cooked ravioli from the water and transfer it straight to the pan. Shake and swirl the pan until the sauce thickens a bit and begins to hug the pasta, 1 to 2 minutes (keep the pasta moving, adding a little more pasta water if necessary to create a loose, lightly thickened sauce). Remove from the heat and toss until the pasta and sauce marry, leaving just a little sauce in the pan.

Using a large spoon, dish out the pasta onto warmed plates, creating some volume by building it into a mound. Garnish with grated Parmesan and a spoonful of the Castelrosso fonduta.

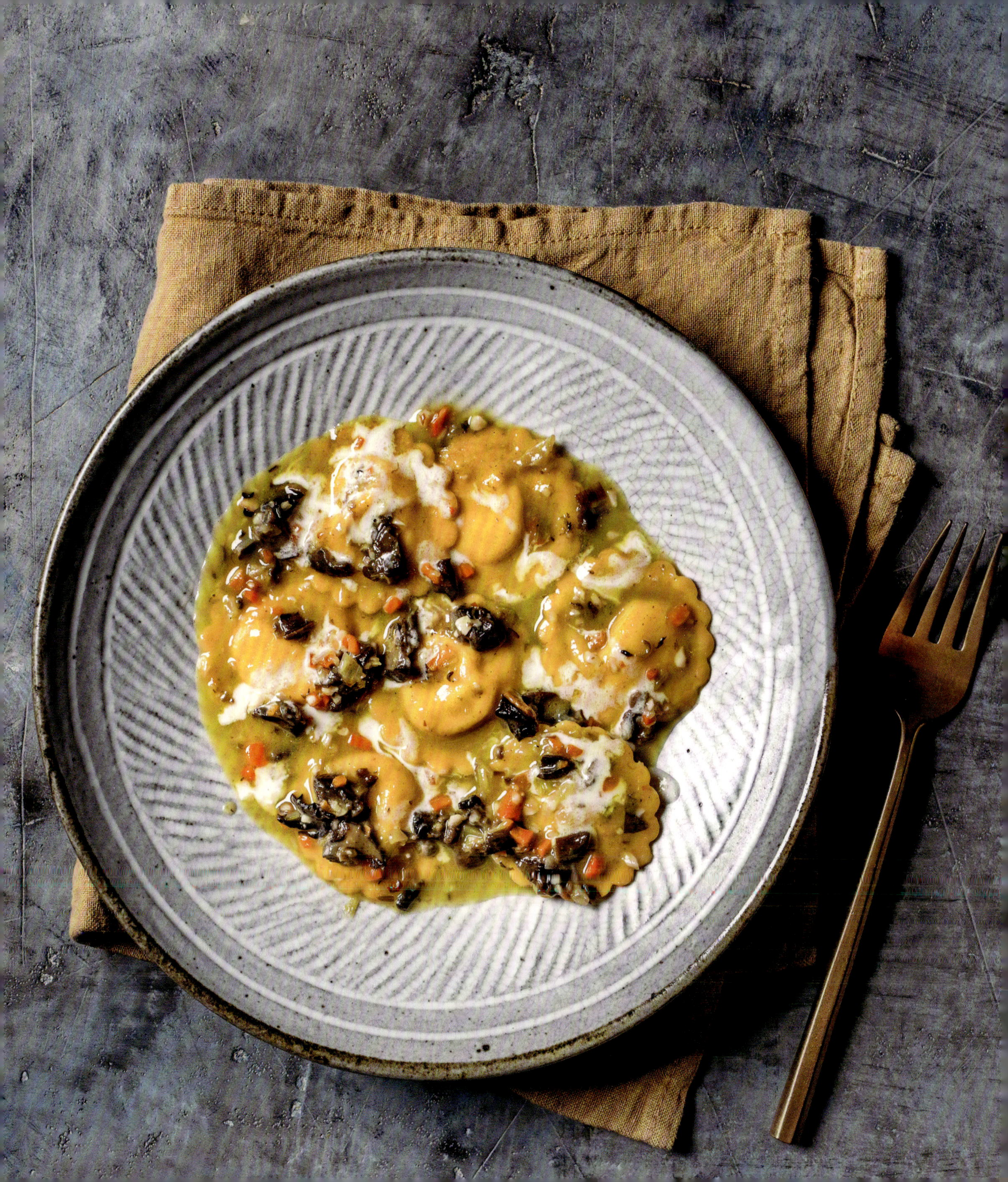

PO

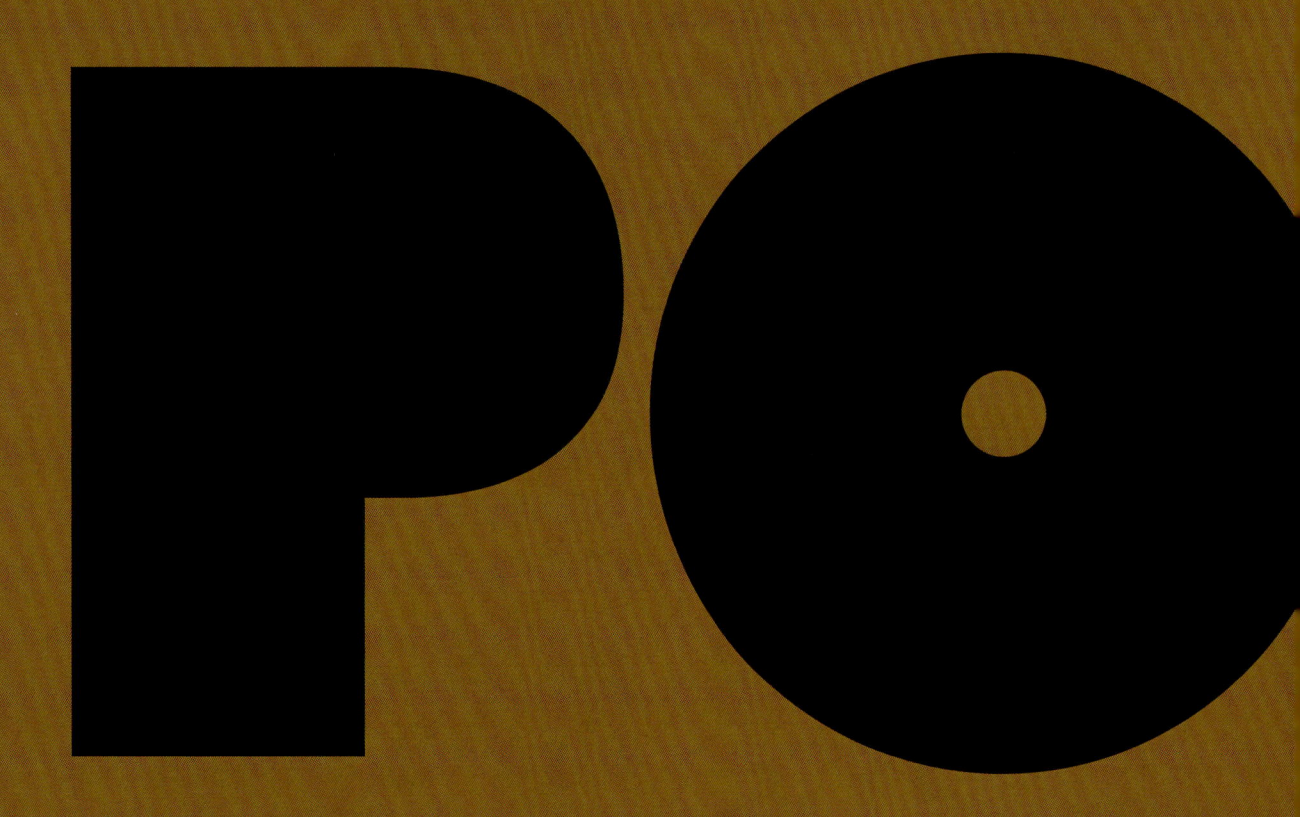

> Salsiccia is a food of the people, an everyday indulgence that can be transformed with a few ingredients—proof that good cooking doesn't need extravagance.
>
> **—PELLEGRINO ARTUSI,** IN *SCIENCE IN THE KITCHEN AND THE ART OF EATING WELL*

RK
PASTA

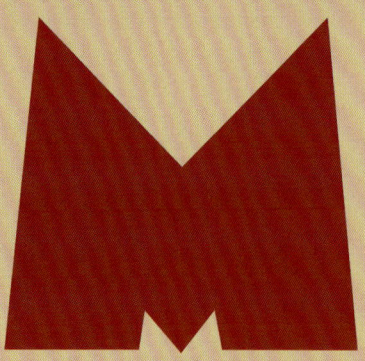

My father, Sal Vetri, grew up at 7th and League Streets in the heart of South Philadelphia. This was back in the 1940s. His grandfather, Paul Savarese, owned a "barber shop" in the neighborhood. The business is in quotes because no one ever got a haircut there. It was more of a front for . . . well . . . never mind. My dad's father, Mario, wanted nothing to do with that business. As a South Philly kid in the 1920s, my grandfather Mario had no skills to speak of, but he loved music. He taught himself to play the oboe and eventually earned a seat with the Philadelphia orchestra.

His son, my father, Sal, also went in a different direction. Like most Italians, Sal always liked food and cooking. As a teenager, he made a few bucks in the slaughterhouse at Esposito's, a family butcher around the block on 9th Street in the Italian Market. Lots of neighborhood families had stalls on the sidewalk under the awnings there. Some sold fresh meat, fish, and vegetables. Others ran specialty shops, selling things like Italian cheeses, olive oil, and Carnaroli rice. Word on the street was that the best sausage was around the corner on Christian Street, between 8th and 9th. The Fiorella family had been running their sausage shop since 1904, and Mario would tell Sal to grab sausages there on the way home for dinner. For as long as I can remember, there were 2-inch pieces of well-seasoned, ground, and cased meats floating in my grandmother's Sunday gravy with meatballs and hard-boiled eggs. (Yes, hard-boiled eggs in gravy!) The sausage was so good I'd pray to get a few pieces on my plate, giving my grandmother Jenny all the charming looks I could muster!

For over one hundred years, Fiorella made only four kinds of sausage: sweet fennel sausage, spicy fennel sausage, cheese sausage, and pork liver and orange sausage. Then, in 2018, Dan Fiorella fell ill, his mother passed away, and there was no one left in the family who wanted to take over the business. Sadly, they put the sausage shop up for sale. It was the end of an era for South Philly. At the time, I had this crazy idea of opening a pasta bar, a small restaurant with counter seating where guests could watch the cooks tossing pasta right in front of them. When I found out about this building in the Italian Market, I called up the Fiorellas right away. Dan Fiorella gave me his blessing to keep their family name alive, and that's when everything started to click.

My dad, Sal, overhead me planning out the restaurant and started telling me stories. "I used to stop in Fiorella's all the time to get their spicy fennel sausage," he went on, "and their pork liver and orange sausage." As he was talking, his story stopped me in my tracks. "What?! You got the sausage from Fiorella?!" I had no idea that this was the same sausage I grew up loving at my grandparents' Sunday dinner! And now I owned the place. The world works in mysterious ways!!

After that, all I could think about was putting pastas on the menu that somehow told this amazing story. It sounds like a tall task, but if you sit and talk with me long enough, you'll see that every little decision made for all the dishes at my restaurants—and in this book—tells a story of South Philadelphia.

First, we worked on the Fiorella Sausage Ragù (page 208). We did a super-coarse grind on the meat, just like Dan Fiorella did for all his sausage. We used the same spices he did—whole fennel seeds and crushed chile flakes—ground right along with the meat. To highlight the fennel that Fiorella was so well known for, we added fresh fennel to the sofrito along with the basic mirepoix (onion and carrot). We simmered the sausage ragù in a good red wine and then added milk at the end to make it creamy like a classic Bolognese. The finishing touch was a garnish of grated Locatelli pecorino cheese, which was *the* alternative to the more expensive Parmesan back in the day. It still tastes fantastic.

Rigatoni was (and still is) the ideal noodle for this Fiorella sausage ragù. You get lots of flavor in every bite as bits of meat and sautéed vegetables get stuck in the big tubes. Plus, it's a special noodle for me. At Sunday dinner with my grandmother, it was always rigatoni or spaghetti on the table. Spaghetti was like the normal pasta, and rigatoni was, for some reason, more special. Whenever she chose rigatoni over spaghetti, I thought it was because someone did something good, so we got rigatoni that week instead of spaghetti. The rigatoni was like a little treat.

The next pasta we created featured Fiorella's famous sausage with pork liver and orange. So many people from South Philly tell me stories about that sausage.

Dan ground the orange rind right into the meat along with the pork liver and everything else. The first thing that popped into my head was a chicken liver dish with rigatoni I made when I opened Osteria on North Broad Street in Philadelphia. That pasta was a crowd favorite. For Fiorella, I used the same method but with pork liver and orange sausage. The noodle needed to be a bit thinner, though, and more delicate, so I went with ziti. With the citrusy orange rind, musky sage, and spicy chile flakes, it came out perfect—check out the recipe on page 216.

These pasta dishes are my way of honoring the history of Fiorella sausage and continuing some of the traditions the family inspired in South Philadelphia. Of course, there's more than sausage in this chapter. Like Anthony Bourdain said, "The pig is a magical animal!" You'll find guanciale (cured pork jowl) in everyday pastas like Spaghetti alla Carbonara (page 206), dry-cured ham in Friulian Spaghetti alla Chitarra with Basil, Poppy Seed, and Prosciutto (page 215), and the modern pig's predecessor in the timeless Tuscan classic Chestnut Fettuccine with Wild Boar Ragù (page 211). When you're ready for something really adventurous, try the Masa Ferricelli with Pork Shank Ragù (page 222). Masa harina in pasta dough is a revelation!

As for my grandmother's traditional Sunday gravy with sausage, meatballs. and hard-boiled eggs . . . it has plenty of pork in it, but I can't give you that recipe. I'd get my knees broken! The meatball itself, however, is in my book *Rustic Italian Food,* and you can also find it online (search for Sal's Old School Meatballs). My dad, Sal, learned how to make those meatballs by watching his mother make them. "Always use pork, veal, and beef in meatballs," he used to say. Sal taught me how to make them, he taught my kids how to make them, and he served them to thousands of Vetri cooks and staffers over the years. This is how food traditions are passed on. Like Fiorella's sausage, Sal's meatballs now have a life of their own. And they are forever imprinted on my father's soul. Rest in peace, Pop.

PORK PASTA 205

SPAGHETTI
ALLA CARBONARA

At one of my pasta classes, there was a sweet couple that had just returned from Rome. The gentleman told me he loved carbonara so much he ordered it at every restaurant they visited. He said that no one in America can make that pasta correctly and almost sheepishly asked if I had a good recipe. I said to him, "Let's make it right now!" I showed everyone how to sear the bacon (we didn't have guanciale, so I used pancetta); how to mix the eggs and grated cheese into a slurry; and then how to slowly combine the cooked pasta and slurry off the heat so the eggs don't scramble. After everyone enjoyed their creamy pasta with *oohs* and *aahs*, the gentleman looked up and said, "I guess there *is* good carbonara in America!" **SERVES 4 TO 6**

Kosher salt

12 ounces dried spaghetti

2 large eggs

3 large egg yolks

6 generous tablespoons finely grated Parmesan cheese, plus more for garnish

6 generous tablespoons finely grated pecorino cheese, plus more for garnish

1 tablespoon coarsely cracked black pepper

11 tablespoons (5½ ounces) unsalted butter, cut into pieces

3 ounces guanciale, pancetta, or thick-cut bacon, cut into short ¼- to ½-inch-thick strips (lardons)

Scan this code to watch a video of making Spaghetti alla Carbonara.

Cook the spaghetti: Bring a large pot of water to a boil and add salt until it tastes like well-seasoned broth. Drop in the spaghetti, give it a stir, and cover the pot to quickly return the water to a boil. Uncover or partially cover to maintain the boil and boil the pasta, stirring occasionally, until it is tender but still a little chewy when bitten, 10 to 12 minutes.

While the pasta water comes to a boil, in a medium bowl, lightly beat the whole eggs and egg yolks. Stir in the Parmesan, pecorino, and pepper. Set aside.

In a deep 12-inch sauté pan, melt the butter over medium heat. Add the guanciale and cook, stirring occasionally, until the fat renders and the guanciale is golden brown, 3 to 4 minutes, managing the heat to keep the butter from burning. If the butter begins to burn, quickly pour it off and add fresh butter to the pan. After dropping the pasta, add 1¼ cups pasta water or saved pasta water (see page 31) to the pan. Bring to a simmer over high heat and simmer until it reduces in volume a bit, 1 to 2 minutes.

When the pasta is ready, use tongs or a spider strainer to scoop the cooked spaghetti from the water and transfer it straight to the pan. Add another 1¼ cups hot pasta water or saved pasta water and shake and swirl the pan until the sauce thickens a bit more and begins to hug the pasta, 1 to 2 minutes (keep the pasta moving, adding a little more pasta water if necessary to create a loose, somewhat thin sauce). When the liquid in the pan is still pretty loose, take the pan off the heat and toss while gradually adding the egg mixture a little at a time. Continue tossing until the egg mixture thickens, adding more pasta water if necessary to create a creamy sauce. You may need to put the pan back over low heat very briefly to gently cook and thicken the egg mixture, but do not let it simmer or it will scramble. When it begins to thicken, remove from the heat, taste the sauce, and add a little salt if you think it needs it. Keep tossing until the pasta and sauce marry, leaving little to no sauce in the pan.

Using tongs or a pasta fork, dish out the pasta onto warmed plates, twirling it into a mound to create some volume. Garnish with a little more grated Parmesan and pecorino if you like.

PORK PASTA

RIGATONI with FIORELLA SAUSAGE RAGÙ

This is the recipe that started it all for the Fiorella pasta bar! It inspired every other dish on the menu and carries on the traditions started back in 1904 by the Fiorella family in South Philadelphia. The warm, spicy taste of fennel seed with a hint of heat from chile flakes softened by the creamy mouthfeel of milk in the ragù make it a crowd-pleaser. A grating of sharp aged Locatelli pecorino on top ties it all together. If you start with sweet Italian sausage, add some chile flakes to give it that extra oomph. To watch a video of making this pasta, scan the QR code on page 210. **SERVES 6**

Fiorella Sausage Ragù

1 pound hot Italian fennel sausage, preferably loose

½ medium yellow onion, finely diced

¼ small fennel bulb, cored, trimmed, and finely diced

¼ medium carrot, finely diced

¾ cup dry red wine, such as Chianti

1 small sprig fresh rosemary

1 small sprig fresh thyme

1 small dried bay leaf

1 small garlic clove, smashed

1 small Parmesan rind (about 1 inch square)

2½ cups chopped canned tomatoes, with their juice

¾ cup whole milk

Kosher salt

Make the Fiorella sausage ragù: If the sausage is in links, remove them from the casings. Heat a deep 12-inch sauté pan over medium-high heat. Scatter the loose sausage over the pan and bust up the meat into small pieces with a spatula. Make a fairly even layer in the pan and then let the sausage cook until the underside is deeply browned, 6 to 8 minutes. Don't worry about browning the top side; it will cook through and remain tender, while the browned underside delivers deep flavors.

Once the underside is browned, stir in the onion, fennel, and carrot, breaking up the sausage even more. The sausage will be stuck to the pan here and there but should start to loosen up as the vegetables release moisture. Cook over medium heat until the vegetables are beginning to soften, 4 to 6 minutes, stirring now and then to loosen the sausage from the pan. Check a carrot for tenderness; it should have lost most of its crunch. When it has, stir in the red wine, scrape up the browned bits from the pan bottom, and let simmer until the liquid reduces in volume by about two-thirds, about 5 minutes.

Meanwhile, tie the rosemary, thyme, bay leaf, garlic, and Parmesan rind in cheesecloth (or a coffee filter) with kitchen twine to make a sachet. Add the sachet to the pan along with the tomatoes (and juice), stirring until the tomatoes are evenly distributed. Once the mixture returns to a simmer, reduce the heat to medium-low and simmer gently until the pan goes dry, about 15 minutes.

RECIPE CONTINUES

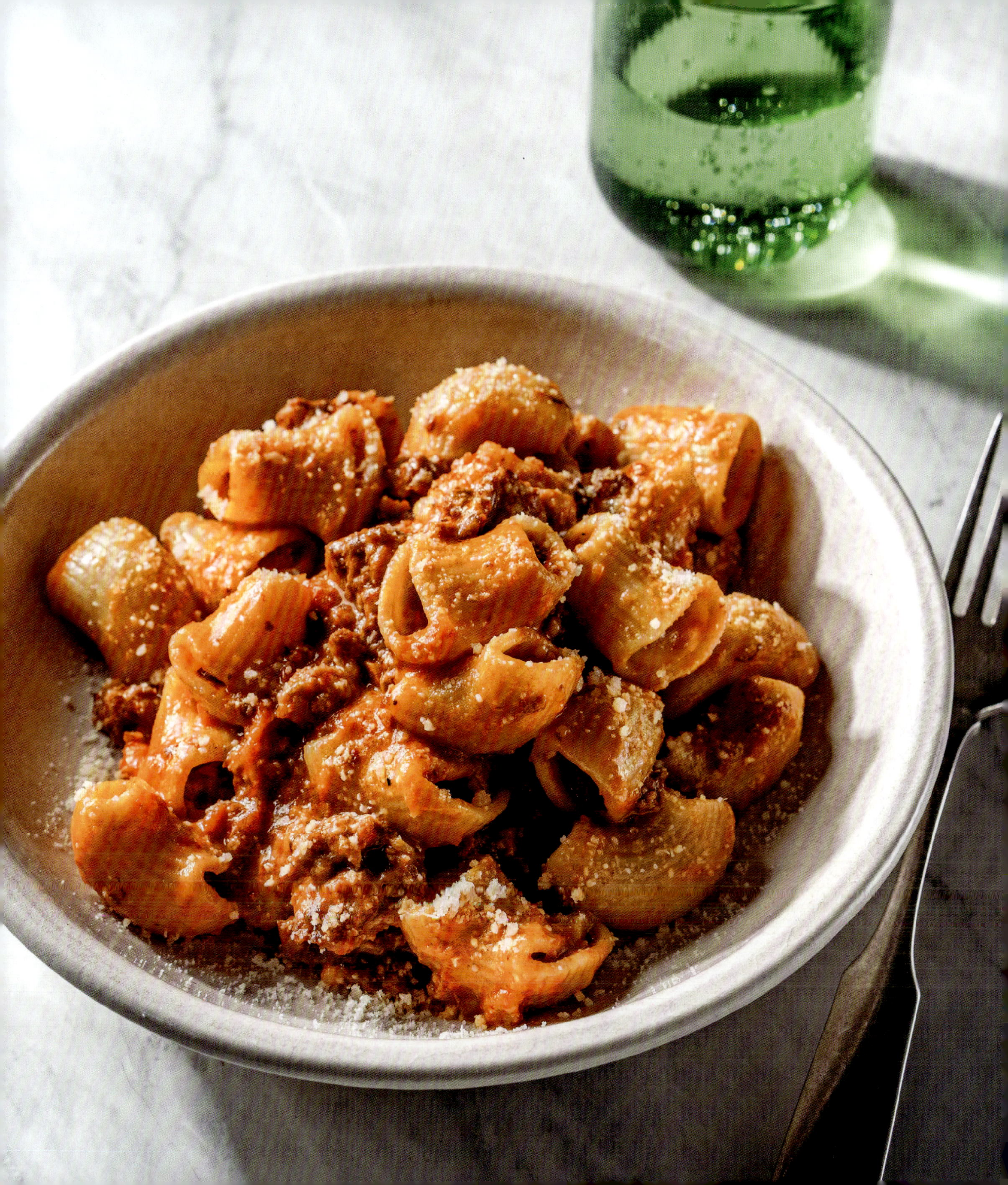

Rigatoni

Kosher salt

1 pound dried rigatoni

6 tablespoons finely grated Parmesan cheese

Grated pecorino cheese, preferably Locatelli, for garnish

3 tablespoons (1½ ounces) unsalted butter, cut into pieces

3 tablespoons extra-virgin olive oil

Remove from the heat and let cool for 5 to 10 minutes. When the sachet is cool enough to handle, squeeze it over the ragù to extract its flavors and then discard. Stir in the milk and taste the ragù, adding salt if you think it needs it. Use the ragù immediately. (Or refrigerate it in an airtight container for 3 to 4 days, or freeze for up to 1 month. Reheat gently over low heat before using.)

Cook the rigatoni: Bring a large pot of water to a boil and add salt until it tastes like well-seasoned broth. Drop in the rigatoni, give it a stir, and cover the pot to quickly return the water to a boil. Uncover or partially cover to maintain the boil and boil the pasta, stirring occasionally, until it is tender but still a little chewy when bitten, 10 to 12 minutes.

Right after dropping the pasta, add the butter and oil to the ragù and reduce the heat to low.

When the pasta is ready, use a spider strainer or slotted spoon to scoop the cooked rigatoni from the water and transfer it straight to the pan. Increase the heat to medium-high and add about ¾ cup of the hot pasta water or saved pasta water (see page 31) to the pan. Shake and swirl the pan until the sauce begins to get creamy and hug the pasta, 1 to 2 minutes (keeping the pasta moving, adding a little more pasta water if necessary to create a loose sauce). Taste the pasta and add salt until it tastes good to you. Remove from the heat, add the Parmesan, and toss until the pasta and sauce marry, leaving little to no sauce in the pan.

Using tongs or a pasta fork, dish out the pasta onto warmed plates, creating some volume by building it into a mound. Garnish with pecorino.

Scan this code to watch a video of making Rigatoni with Fiorella Sausage Ragù.

CHESTNUT FETTUCCINE WITH WILD BOAR RAGÙ

It doesn't get more classic than this, a thick, Tuscan-style ragù served with big ribbons of pasta to soak up the sauce. Wild boar has tons of flavor, but it's lean, so I like to marinate it overnight in oil, rosemary, and garlic. After you sear and braise the meat, a little cocoa powder and sherry vinegar complement it so well. You can buy wild boar shoulder online from places like Broken Arrow Ranch and D'Artagnan. Pork shoulder works in a pinch, but if it were me, I'd go for the boar! To watch a video of making this pasta, scan the QR code on page 212. **SERVES 6**

Wild Boar Ragù

1 pound boneless wild boar shoulder or pork shoulder, cut in ¼- to ½-inch cubes

1¼ cups extra-virgin olive oil, plus more as needed

2 large sprigs fresh rosemary

2 garlic cloves, smashed

¼ cup tipo "00" flour or all-purpose flour, plus more for dusting

½ large white onion, finely diced

2 small carrots, finely diced

1 cup dry red wine, such as Chianti

1½ cups Beef Stock (page 295), plus more as needed

2 tablespoons unsweetened cocoa powder, preferably Dutch-process, plus more for garnish

Make the wild boar ragù: Put the meat, olive oil, 1 sprig of the rosemary, and the garlic in a large zipper-lock plastic bag, seal closed, and marinate in the refrigerator for 24 hours.

Drain the meat by pouring it into a sieve set over a medium bowl. Reserve the oil in the bowl (discard the rosemary and garlic). Once the meat has drained well, toss the cubes in the flour in another medium bowl, coating them evenly.

Measure out 2 to 3 tablespoons of the marinating oil (discard the rest), pour into a medium Dutch oven, and heat over medium heat. Add the boar and cook, turning now and then, until browned all over, 8 to 10 minutes.

Add the onions and carrots and sauté until tender and beginning to brown, 5 to 7 minutes, stirring a few times. Increase the heat to medium-high, pour in the wine, and bring to a simmer, scraping the pan bottom to loosen the browned bits. Simmer until the liquid reduces in volume by about one-third, 3 to 4 minutes. Add enough stock to come about two-thirds of the way up the sides of the meat, reduce the heat to low, cover, and simmer gently until the meat is fall-apart tender, 1½ to 2 hours, stirring every 20 minutes or so. During the last 30 minutes, cook with the pan partially uncovered and add more stock if the pan begins to go dry.

RECIPE CONTINUES

1 tablespoon sherry vinegar

Kosher salt and freshly ground black pepper

Chestnut Fettuccine

Kosher salt

1 pound fresh Chestnut Fettuccine (page 80)

4 tablespoons (2 ounces) unsalted butter, cut into pieces

⅓ cup finely grated Parmesan cheese, plus more for garnish

Remove the pan from the heat and stir in the cocoa powder and vinegar. Bury the remaining rosemary sprig in the ragù, taste the ragù, and season with salt and pepper until it tastes good to you (about 1½ teaspoons salt). Let cool to room temperature. (Or refrigerate in an airtight container for up to 3 days. Reheat gently just before serving. If the ragù thickened considerably, add a little stock to thin it to a thick ragù consistency.)

Cook the chestnut fettuccine: Bring a large pot of water to a boil and add salt until it tastes like well-seasoned broth. Drop in the fettuccine, give it a stir, and cover the pot to return the water quickly to a boil. Uncover or partially cover to maintain the boil and boil the pasta, stirring occasionally, until it is tender but still a little chewy when bitten, 2 to 3 minutes.

Right after dropping the pasta, in a deep 12-inch sauté pan, melt the butter over high heat. Add the ragù and about 1 cup of the hot pasta water or saved pasta water (see page 31). Simmer the mixture over high heat until it thickens slightly, just a minute or two. Drizzle in a little olive oil if necessary to help emulsify and thicken the ragù. Taste it, adding salt and pepper until it tastes good to you.

When the pasta is ready, use tongs or a spider strainer to transfer the pasta from the water straight to the pan of ragù. Shake and swirl the pan until the ragù thickens a bit and begins to hug the pasta, 1 to 2 minutes (keep the pasta moving, adding a little more pasta water if necessary to create a loose, slightly thickened sauce). Remove from the heat, add the Parmesan, and toss until the pasta and sauce marry, leaving little to no sauce in the pan.

Using tongs or a pasta fork, dish out the pasta onto warmed plates, creating some volume by twirling the pasta into a mound. Garnish with a dusting of cocoa powder and a little grated Parmesan.

Scan this code to watch a video of making Chestnut Fettuccine with Wild Boar Ragù.

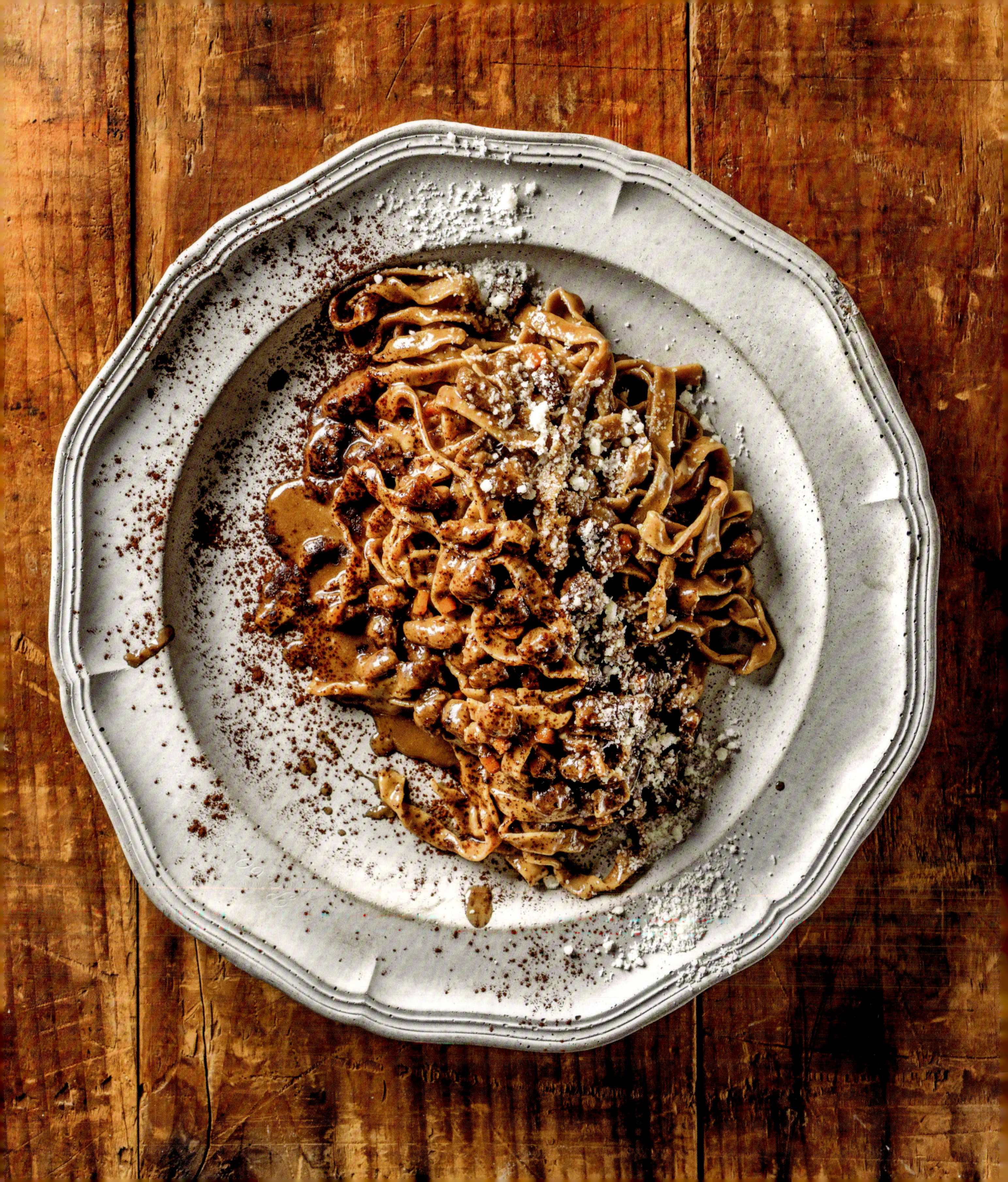

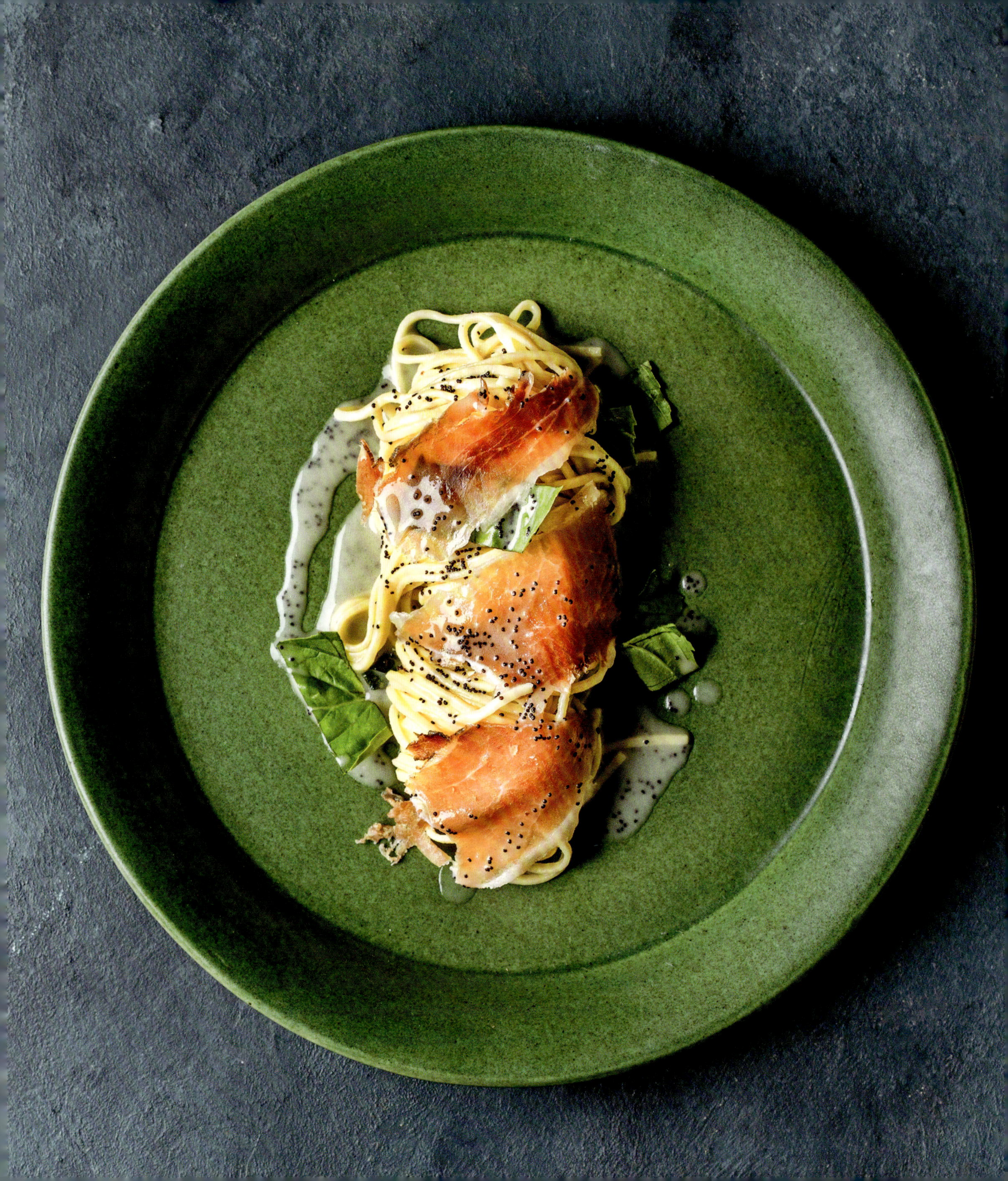

Spaghetti alla Chitarra with Basil, Poppy Seed, and Prosciutto

In Friuli, the hilltop town of San Daniele is world famous for its dry-cured ham. There, they sprinkle the prosciutto with poppy seeds in a few different versions of this pasta dish. It's a unique flavor combination that works surprisingly well. A simple butter sauce and fresh basil bring together the chewy noodles, crunchy poppy seeds, and savory ham in a dish that's far greater than the sum of its parts. Plus, it comes together fast. Pro tip: If you have a big bag of poppy seeds, keep them in the freezer. They'll last a lot longer that way! **SERVES 4**

Kosher salt

1 pound fresh Spaghetti alla Chitarra (page 69)

12 tablespoons (6 ounces) unsalted butter, cut into pieces

1 cup loosely packed fresh basil leaves (about 35 leaves)

2½ tablespoons poppy seeds

Juice of 1 lemon (about 2½ tablespoons), plus more as needed

¾ cup finely grated Parmesan cheese, plus more for garnish

8 paper-thin slices prosciutto

Cook the spaghetti: Bring a large pot of water to a boil and add salt until it tastes like well-seasoned broth. Drop in the spaghetti, give it a stir, and cover the pot to quickly return the water to a boil. Uncover or partially cover to maintain the boil and boil the pasta, stirring occasionally, until it is tender but still a little chewy when bitten, 2 to 3 minutes.

While the pasta water comes to a boil, in a deep 12-inch sauté pan, melt the butter over low heat. After dropping the pasta, add 2½ cups of the hot pasta water or saved pasta water (see page 31) and bring the mixture to a boil over high heat. Simmer until slightly reduced in volume, 3 to 4 minutes.

When the pasta is ready, use tongs or a spider strainer to scoop the cooked spaghetti from the water and transfer it straight to the pan. Add the basil, poppy seeds, and lemon juice and shake and swirl the pan until the sauce thickens a bit more and begins to hug the pasta, 1 to 2 minutes (keep the pasta moving, adding a little more pasta water if necessary to create a loose, slightly creamy sauce). Taste the sauce, adding more lemon juice if you think it needs it (the sauce should taste fairly mild with just a spark of lemon). Remove from the heat, add the Parmesan, and toss until the pasta and sauce marry, leaving little to no sauce in the pan.

Using tongs or a pasta fork, dish out the pasta onto warmed plates, creating some volume by twirling it into a mound, and finish with grated Parmesan. Artfully drape and fold 2 slices of prosciutto over each serving.

ZITI WITH FIOR

For more than one hundred years, the Fiorella family sold just four sausage recipes in their South Philly sausage shop. The most famous was pork liver and orange sausage. After I bought the building from Dan Fiorella, everyone who came by talked about that sausage. To carry on the Fiorella legacy, I worked it into a pasta dish. Pork liver isn't as common these days, so we call for chicken livers. But if you can find pork liver, I highly recommend it. You'll taste a piece of South Philly history! To watch a video of making this pasta, scan the QR code on page 217. **SERVES 4**

Liver and Orange Sausage

12 ounces chicken livers or pork liver, cleaned of sinew and fat (about 10½ ounces cleaned)

5½ ounces ground pork shoulder or unseasoned pork sausage

3¼ teaspoons kosher salt

1½ teaspoons crushed red pepper flakes

½ garlic clove, minced to a paste

Finely grated zest of ½ large orange

Ziti

Kosher salt

12 ounces dried ziti

Make the liver and orange sausage: In a food processor, pulse the chicken livers until finely chopped (or if you have a meat grinder, you'll get a nicer texture by grinding the liver through the large die). Scrape into a bowl and add the ground pork. Scatter on the salt, pepper flakes, garlic, and orange zest. Put on some gloves and mix everything together by hand until thoroughly combined. The mixture will be loose and wet.

Cook the ziti: Bring a large pot of water to a boil and add salt until it tastes like well-seasoned broth. Drop in the ziti, give it a stir, and cover the pot to quickly return the water to a boil. Uncover or partially cover to maintain the boil and boil the pasta, stirring occasionally, until it is tender but still a little chewy when bitten, 10 to 12 minutes.

Make the ragù: While the pasta water comes to a boil, in a deep 12-inch sauté pan, heat the oil and 2 tablespoons of the butter over medium-high heat. When the butter foams, add the onions and sage and cook over medium-high heat, shaking the pan frequently, until the onions are deep mahogany brown and the sage is crisp, 4 to 6 minutes. Add the sausage to the pan, breaking it up and smearing it across the pan bottom in an even layer to maximize the surface area for better browning and more flavor. Cook until the sausage is browned and seared on the bottom, 5 to 6 minutes (don't worry about stirring and cooking the top of the sausage just yet).

After dropping the pasta, carefully add 1 cup of the hot pasta water or saved pasta water (see page 31) to the pan, scraping the pan bottom to capture the browned bits and stirring everything together. Break up the pork sausage into fork-friendly pieces as you stir.

...ELLA LIVER AND ORANGE SAUSAGE RAGÙ

Ragù

- 2 tablespoons extra-virgin olive oil
- 5 tablespoons (2½ ounces) unsalted butter, cut into pieces
- 2 medium or 4 small cippolini onions (about 4 ounces), peeled and thinly sliced
- 6 fresh sage leaves
- Kosher salt
- 1 teaspoon sherry vinegar, or more to taste
- ¼ cup finely grated Parmesan cheese, plus more for garnish
- Finely grated fresh orange zest, for garnish

When the pasta is ready, use a spider strainer or slotted spoon to scoop the cooked ziti from the water and transfer it straight to the pan. Add the remaining 3 tablespoons butter and shake and swirl the pan over medium-high heat until the sauce begins to get creamy and hug the pasta, 1 to 2 minutes (keep the pasta moving, adding a little more pasta water if necessary to create a loose, slightly creamy sauce). Stir in the sherry vinegar. Taste the pasta, adding salt and/or sherry vinegar until it tastes good to you. The vinegar should wake up all the flavors but the sauce should not taste like vinegar. Remove from the heat, add the Parmesan, and toss until the pasta and sauce marry, leaving little to no sauce in the pan.

Using tongs or a pasta fork, dish out the pasta onto warmed plates, creating some volume by building it into a mound. Garnish with Parmesan cheese and some finely grated orange zest.

Scan this QR code to watch a video of making Ziti with Fiorella Liver and Orange Sausage Ragù.

FARFALLE WITH GUANCIALE, PEAS, AND TARRAGON

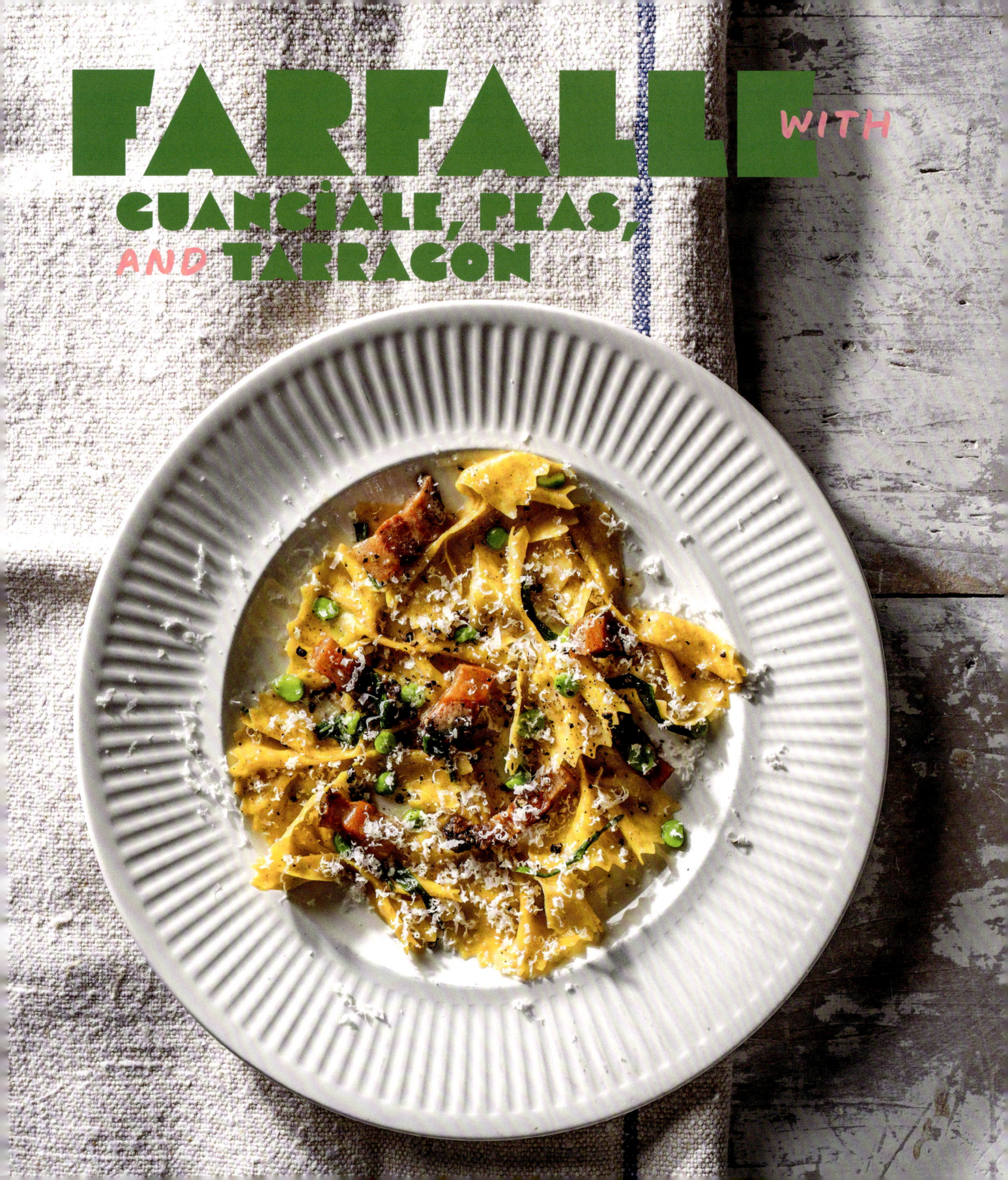

This is one of the simplest dishes in the book. What makes it special is handling each ingredient thoughtfully. The guanciale needs to be thoroughly rendered and browned, but if it burns, it will taste bitter; if it's undercooked, it will taste chewy and lack flavor. The peas will ideally be fresh from your local farmers' market and shucked right from the pods. (You'll need about 12 ounces peas in the pod to get the right amount of peas here.) When all of the ingredients are handled with care and thoroughly married in the pan, bits of guanciale and peas get caught in the folds of the farfalle, and the pasta manages to taste both rich and light at the same time. **SERVES 4 TO 6**

Kosher salt

⅔ cup shelled green peas, fresh or frozen

1 tablespoon extra-virgin olive oil

8 ounces guanciale, pancetta, or thick-cut bacon, cut into short ¼- to ½-inch-thick strips (lardons)

1 pound fresh Farfalle (page 77)

⅓ cup chopped fresh tarragon

Juice of ½ lemon, plus more as needed

½ cup finely grated Parmesan cheese, plus more for garnish

Blanch the peas: Have ready a bowl of ice water. Bring a large pot of water to a boil and add salt until it tastes like well-seasoned broth. (You can use the same pot of water to cook the pasta.) Drop in the peas and blanch them until they are bright green, about 30 seconds. Scoop out the peas with a spider strainer or slotted spoon and transfer them to the ice water to stop the cooking. Set aside.

Brown the guanciale: In a deep 12-inch sauté pan, heat the oil over medium heat. Add the guanciale and cook, stirring now and then, until the fat renders and the guanciale is crispy and browned all over, about 20 minutes. We like to save all the fat in the pan. But if you prefer less fat, pour it off, leaving at least ¼ cup in the pan.

Cook the farfalle: Drop the farfalle into the boiling salted water and give it a stir. Cover the pot to quickly return the water to a boil. Uncover or partially cover to maintain the boil and boil the pasta, stirring occasionally, until it is tender but still a little chewy when bitten, 3 to 4 minutes.

Soon after dropping the pasta, scoop about 2 cups of the hot pasta water or saved pasta water (see page 31) into the guanciale pan to stop the rendering process.

When the pasta is ready, use a spider strainer or slotted spoon to scoop the cooked farfalle from the water and transfer it straight to the pan. Use a spider strainer or slotted spoon to drain the peas from the ice water and transfer them to the pan as well. Add the tarragon and lemon juice and bring the mixture to a boil over high heat. Shake and stir the pan until the sauce thickens a bit and begins to hug the pasta, 2 to 3 minutes (keep the pasta moving, adding a little more pasta water if necessary to create a loose, slightly thickened sauce). Taste the pasta and add salt and/or lemon juice until it tastes good to you. Remove from the heat, add the Parmesan, and toss until the pasta and sauce marry, leaving little to no sauce in the pan.

Using tongs or a pasta fork, dish out the pasta onto warmed plates, creating some volume by building it into a mound. Garnish with additional Parmesan.

FENNEL SAUSAGE RICOTTA GNOCCHI WITH ZUCCHINI CREMA

In 2017, I was in Naples doing research for my book *Mastering Pizza* and tasted the most incredible pizzas of my life at Pepe in Grani, north of the city. Franco Pepe's signature pizza is what he calls *margherita sbagliata* or "margherita done wrong." The flavors are classic—tomato, basil, and mozzarella—but he bakes the dough with only mozzarella on it and then spoons on stripes of tomato passata and dots of basil pesto on top. Franco's margherita is ethereal, and if you ask me, totally right. Not wrong at all! That's exactly his point with the name "sbagliata." So here we have what you might call *gnocchi sbagliati* or "gnocchi done wrong." It's classic Italian ricotta gnocchi, but I put sausage in it. This is my way of making it. You might think, "Blasphemy!" But taste before you judge. With a creamy puree of zucchini underneath and a shower of Parmesan on top, I think it's absolutely the right way to make gnocchi. SERVES 4 TO 6

Fennel Sausage Ricotta Gnocchi

- 1 cup ricotta impastata (see page 93)
- Scant ¾ cup all-purpose flour, plus 2 cups for shaping
- ⅔ cup finely grated Parmesan cheese
- ⅛ teaspoon freshly grated nutmeg
- Kosher salt
- 2 large eggs
- 3 ounces loose Italian fennel sausage (about 1 small link, casing removed)

Zucchini Crema

- 2 tablespoons extra-virgin olive oil
- 1 medium shallot, small diced
- 1 medium zucchini, small diced
- Kosher salt and freshly ground black pepper
- Finely grated Parmesan cheese, for garnish

Mix the gnocchi batter: In the bowl of a stand mixer fitted with the paddle attachment, combine the ricotta, ¾ cup flour, Parmesan, and nutmeg and mix on medium-low speed until blended, 1 to 2 minutes. Taste the mixture, adding salt until it tastes good to you (about ¼ teaspoon; when the salt level is perfect, it should bring the Parmesan alive!). Add the eggs and sausage and continue mixing until the sausage is evenly blended throughout the batter. Spoon the mixture into a piping bag or zipper-lock bag, seal, and use immediately. (Or seal and refrigerate for up to 4 hours.)

Form the gnocchi: Dump the 2 cups flour onto a sheet pan, shaking it to cover the pan bottom. This is your landing zone for the piped balls of gnocchi. Follow the directions in Spinach Gnocchi with Brown Butter and Shaved Ricotta Salata (page 123) for how to form the gnocchi. To watch a video of forming the gnocchi, scan the QR code on page 124.

Make the zucchini crema: In a small saucepan, heat the oil over medium heat. Add the shallot and cook, stirring now and then, until translucent but not browned, 2 to 3 minutes. Add the zucchini and cook, stirring a couple times, until the zucchini is very tender but not browned, 5 to 6 minutes more. Puree the mixture right in the pot with a stick blender, trickling in a little water if necessary to get the mixture to blend. (Or puree in an upright blender and then return the puree to the pot). Taste it and season with salt and pepper until it tastes good to you (about ¼ teaspoon salt should do it). Keep warm over low heat.

Cook the gnocchi: Bring a large pot of water to a boil and add salt until it tastes like well-seasoned broth. Drop in the gnocchi, give them a gentle stir, and cover the pot to return the water quickly to a boil. Uncover or partially cover to maintain the boil and boil the gnocchi until they begin to float, 3 to 5 minutes. When they float, the gnocchi will be 20 to 30 seconds from being finished.

At this point, quickly spread a generous 2 tablespoons of the crema over the bottom of warmed pasta bowls.

Using a spider strainer or slotted spoon, remove one gnoccho from the water and test its doneness by gently squeezing it. The outside "walls" of the sphere should feel firm and set, while the middle of the ball should feel "squishy." This is the desired doneness, as the gnocchi should be molten and oozy when split in half with a fork. When the gnocchi are done, scoop them from the water with the spider or slotted spoon, let them drain briefly over the pot, and divide them among the bowls, serving 6 to 8 gnocchi over the crema in each bowl. Garnish each serving generously with Parmesan.

MASA FERRICELLI
with Pork Shank Ragù

This pasta really sums up what Philly's Italian Market is all about these days. It's a mix of old-school Italian and Mexican flavors reflecting the immigrant population as it stands today. There's corn in the pasta, lime in the sofrito, and chile-laced pork in the ragù. Welcome to America, baby! Sometimes flavored doughs bring more color than flavor (looking at you, spinach pasta), but if you use a good masa harina here, you can really taste the corn. You should be able to make the pasta while the pork shanks braise, and I highly recommend leveling it up with the garnish of black lime powder (see Level Up, on the facing page). **SERVES 6 TO 8**

Pork Shank Ragù

3 pounds skinless pork shanks (2 to 3 shanks)

Kosher salt

1 tablespoon grapeseed oil or canola oil

½ large yellow onion, small diced

1 medium carrot, small diced

1 medium celery stalk, small diced

1 large garlic clove, minced

2 red Fresno or jalapeño peppers, seeded and small diced

½ cup dry white wine, such as pinot grigio

3 cups Pork Stock (page 295) or Chicken Stock (page 294), plus more as needed

Sofrito

1 tablespoon extra-virgin olive oil

¼ medium leek, small diced

¼ medium shallot, small diced

¼ medium carrot, small diced

¼ medium celery stalk, small diced

Braise the pork shanks: Preheat the oven to 325°F.

Sprinkle the shanks all over with salt (about 2 teaspoons). In a 5-quart Dutch oven, heat the oil over medium-high heat. Add the shanks and sear them, turning frequently, until deeply browned all over, 15 to 18 minutes, adjusting the heat if necessary to prevent burning. Remove the shanks to a platter.

Reduce the heat to medium, add the onion, carrot, and celery to the pot and sauté, stirring a few times, until softened, about 4 minutes. Add the garlic and Fresno peppers and cook until fragrant, another 2 minutes. Return the seared shanks to the pan along with any accumulated juices and cook until the pan is dry, 1 to 2 minutes. Pour in the wine and cook, turning the shanks once or twice, until the pan is nearly dry again and the wine glazes the meat, 6 to 8 minutes. Pour in enough stock to come about three-quarters of the way up the meat. Cover and transfer to the oven.

Braise until the meat is fork-tender, about 3 hours, checking on the meat once or twice. If the pan goes dry during that time, add more stock as necessary to keep about 1 inch of liquid in the pan. When the pork shanks are tender, remove the pot from the oven and let the meat cool in the pan (there should still be some liquid left in the pan).

While the shanks are cooling, make the sofrito: In a deep 12-inch sauté pan, heat the oil over medium heat. Add the leek, shallot, carrot, celery, and Fresno pepper and cook, stirring once or twice, until the vegetables are tender but not browned, 4 to 5 minutes. Finely grate the zest from the lime and reserve half of the lime zest for garnish. Add the other half of the lime zest to the pan and squeeze in the juice from half the lime. Taste the sofrito, adding salt and additional lime juice until it tastes good to you. Remove from the heat and set aside.

½ medium red Fresno or jalapeño pepper, seeded and small diced

1 medium lime

Kosher salt

Masa Ferricelli

Kosher salt

1 pound fresh Masa Ferricelli (page 60)

5 tablespoons (2½ ounces) unsalted butter, cut into pieces

5 tablespoons finely grated Parmesan cheese, plus more for garnish

LEVEL UP **Garnish with black lime powder:** Instead of fresh lime zest, use black limes (dried limes). We buy whole black limes and finely grate them over the top of each dish to add a subtle funky/sour flavor. You can do the same, or buy preground black lime powder and sprinkle a little over the top.

When the meat is cool, transfer the shanks to a cutting board and remove the meat from the bones. Discard the bones (or save them for Pork Stock, page 295) and shred or dice the meat into fork-friendly pieces. Run the braised vegetables and liquid through the medium holes of a food mill (or puree with brief pulses in a blender or food processor). Add the puree and the diced meat to the sofrito, stirring them together. Taste the ragù and season with salt until it tastes good to you. Keep warm over low heat until ready to use. (The ragù can also be made a few days ahead and refrigerated in an airtight container or frozen up to 1 month. Reheat gently over low heat when you cook the pasta.)

Cook the ferricelli: Bring a large pot of water to a boil and add salt until it tastes like well-seasoned broth. Drop in the ferricelli, give it a stir, and cover the pot to quickly return the water to a boil. Uncover or partially cover to maintain the boil and boil the pasta, stirring occasionally, until it is tender but still a little chewy when bitten, 2 to 3 minutes.

Right after dropping the pasta, add the butter to the ragù along with about 1½ cups of the hot pasta water or saved pasta water (see page 31). Bring the mixture to a simmer over medium-high heat and cook until slightly reduced in volume, 1 to 2 minutes.

When the pasta is ready, use a spider strainer or slotted spoon to scoop the cooked ferricelli from the water and transfer it straight to the pan. Shake and swirl the pan until the sauce begins to get creamy and hug the pasta, 1 to 2 minutes (keep the pasta moving, adding a little more pasta water if necessary to create a loose, slightly creamy sauce). Taste the pasta and add salt until it tastes good to you. Remove from the heat, add the Parmesan, and toss until the pasta and sauce marry, leaving little to no sauce in the pan.

Dish out the pasta onto warmed plates, creating some volume by building it into a mound. Garnish with the reserved lime zest and additional Parmesan.

BEEF AN

> The important thing is that we are not wasting anything. Because we can't kill an animal for one filet.
>
> **—DARIO CECCHINI,**
> EIGHTH-GENERATION ITALIAN BUTCHER

D LAMB

PASTA

I never loved beef as a kid. Like most Italian American Jews, my siblings and I grew up with dry, nasty braised brisket served at Passover. My mom, Barbara, was not much of a cook. She was so bad that when it was her turn to do dinner, we would hand her the phone to order it! Most of the traditional Jewish holiday foods were decent—apples and honey, matzo ball soup, potato kugel, and orange-scented sweet potatoes with raisins (tzimmes). But the sweet and sour beef brisket was inedible, like dry pieces of cardboard soaked in evil. Sometimes we had short ribs instead of brisket. Tragically, they also tasted like cardboard. After Passover dinner, my father, Sal, and I would sometimes grab a Lee's hoagie just so we'd have something to eat! Honestly, aside from the occasional braciole (meat roulade) that my Sicilian grandparents made, and a decent burger here and there, my entire childhood was plagued with horrible beef meals.

I never really knew good beef until I got to Italy. When I moved to Bergamo in 1994, I had my first real experience with it. There was always a side of beef hanging in the walk-in refrigerator at Taverna del Colleoni, where I started my apprenticeship. It looked so foreign to me. I didn't understand how meat could just hang for weeks and not go bad. In fact, it got better with age. And we used all of it . . . the brisket, chuck, and round plus the oxtail, tongue, and tripe . . . everything, right down to the bone marrow. With the less popular cuts, we made ragùs and pasta stuffings. One time we turned beef short ribs into a filling for ravioli and it completely blew my mind. I couldn't believe how tender it was. Nothing like what I grew up eating! Taste that short rib for yourself in Francobolli with Short Ribs and Celery Root (page 249). At Taverna, I learned that beef, properly cooked with just the right seasoning, was awesome! I also learned to use lesser-known cuts so none of the animal went to waste. We made beef shanks into ragù and even used the beef heart in Bolognese. You can taste both of those in Busiati Grano Arso with Beef Shank and Peaches (page 236) and Ferricelli with Beef Heart Bolognese (page 234).

The other key moment in my beef education happened long after I returned from Italy. In 2006, I started the Great Chefs Event, a fundraiser with Alex's Lemonade Stand to help fight childhood cancer. I brought together chef friends to serve bites of their signature dishes and help raise money to fight this horrible disease. Over the years, the Great Chefs Event has evolved into something truly remarkable. From Philly to Los Angeles, New York City to Chicago, and Miami to Jackson Hole, Wyoming, we've held Great Chefs Events all over the country, raising millions of dollars every year. After dozens of events over twenty years where I've tasted hundreds of incredible dishes from chefs at the top of their game, the one bite that I remember most is a piece of beef from Adam Perry Lang.

It was our fourth or fifth year of Great Chefs when I first asked APL to come. Adam was always doing interesting collaborations with big-name chefs like Jamie Oliver. He would handle their meat programs, sourcing and dry-aging the perfect cuts for their restaurants and pop-up events. APL had a reputation as a meat savant. The two of us had known each other for a while, so I thought it would be fun for him to do a dish at Great Chefs Philadelphia. In true APL fashion, he had a buddy drive a smoker rig down from New York City for the after-party. We always hold an after-party for the participating chefs, and VIP guests also attend because after a huge, daylong, star-studded food event, what do you wanna do first? Eat more, of course.

Adam smoked a mountain of beef short ribs for hours on the smoker, and then sprinkled chunks of the meat with coarse salt and served them simply on white bread with homemade pickles. It was the perfect bite—nothing like the dry, leathery short ribs I grew up eating! Every year after that, I invited him back, and every year I would look forward to the after-party so I could get another bite of APL's smoked short ribs. To be fair, the great meat isn't the only thing that makes those short ribs stick in my memory. At the after-party, all the chefs would sit around APL's smoker in lawn chairs, drinking beer and decompressing after the day's craziness. It was just chefs talking shop and enjoying one another's company like we rarely get to do. And that's what made it magical.

These two experiences—one in Italy and one in America—really kicked my obsession with beef into high gear. I guess I was starved for beef because nothing I'd eaten growing up was very good. Now I always source the best I can, which is often more expensive, and I use every part of the animal in creative ways. If you usually stick with just one or two familiar cuts of beef, try branching out. You'll be pleasantly surprised. The lesser-known cuts tend to be easier on the wallet, and they're no less delicious. If you've never had oxtail, get ready for the beefiest tasting beef you've ever had! Taste it in Cannelloni with Oxtail and Cipollini (page 244). And if you've never had lamb or were never a fan, try Orecchiette with Lamb Merguez and Fiore Sardo (page 229). This dish comes together pretty fast and is bursting with the flavors of spicy lamb sausage, Sicilian sun-dried tomatoes, red wine, and sharp Sardinian pecorino. Like the other chapters in this book, the easier dishes come first, and the more complicated ones are near the end. Start at the beginning and work your way through!

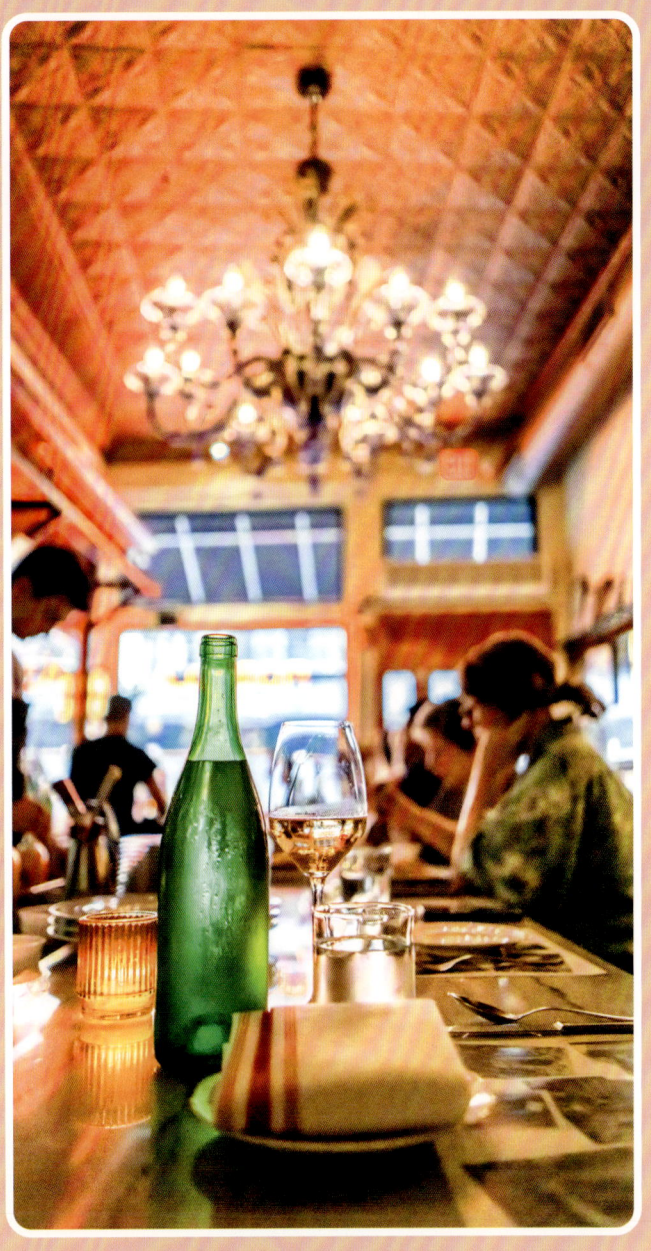

BEEF AND LAMB PASTA **227**

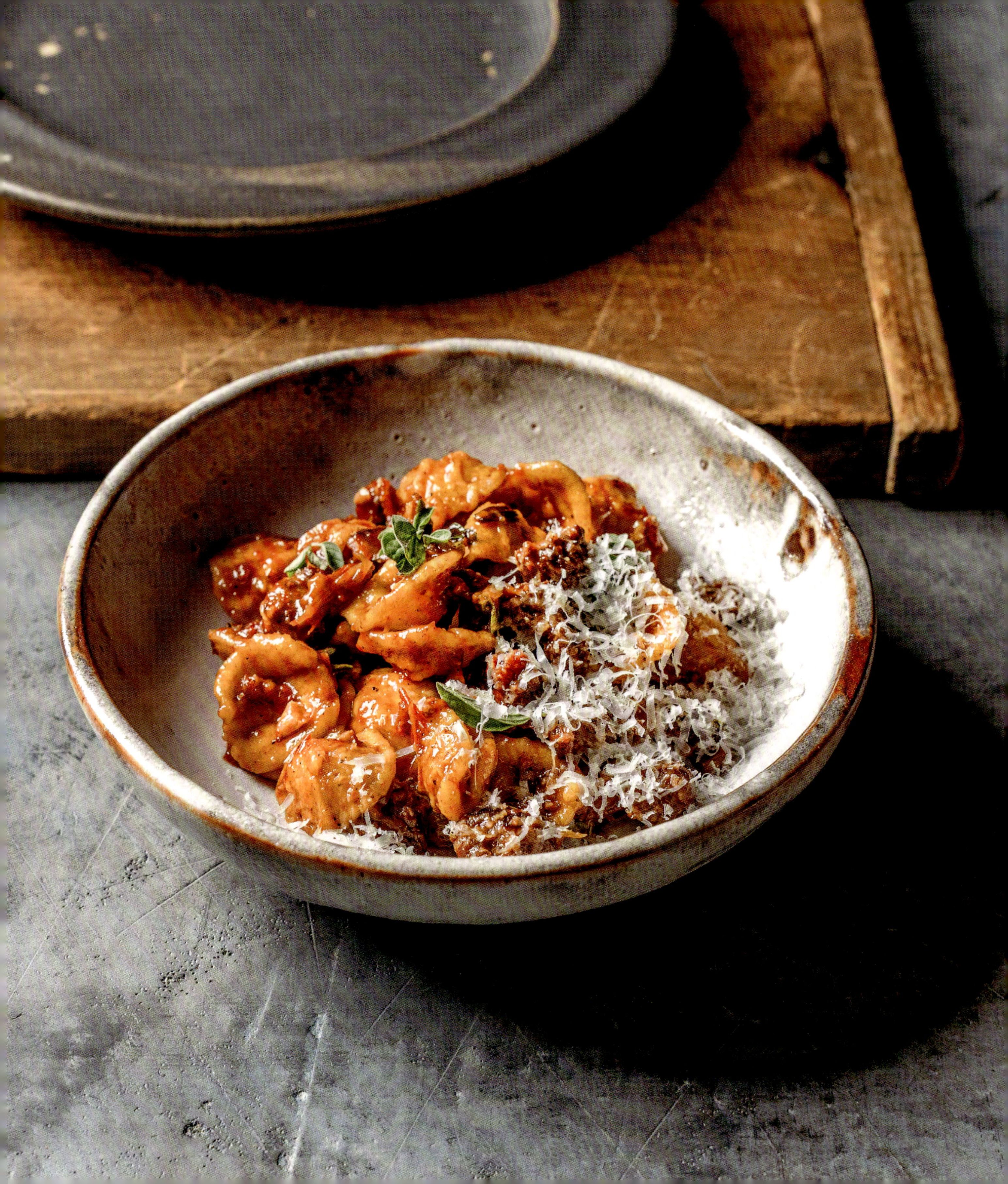

Orecchiette with Lamb Merguez and Fiore Sardo

In the Sicilian town of Pachino, they grow the best cherry and plum tomatoes, and after sitting under the summer sun for weeks, the tomatoes darken to an almost black color and have an intense, savory, sweet taste. This pasta was completely inspired by those sun-dried tomatoes, so try to buy Pachino sun-dried tomatoes! We built a pretty simple sauce around them with merguez (spicy Algerian lamb sausage), red wine, and Sardinian pecorino cheese. The orecchiette catches bits of sun-dried tomato and sausage in the hollows, marrying pasta and sauce perfectly. If you're short on time, you could buy the merguez instead of making it yourself. **SERVES 4 TO 6**

Lamb Merguez

1 pound ground lamb, preferably leg or shoulder

2¾ teaspoons Aleppo pepper (or 2½ teaspoons paprika plus ¼ teaspoon cayenne pepper)

2½ teaspoons kosher salt, plus more to taste

2 large garlic cloves, minced and mashed into a paste (about 1½ teaspoons)

1½ teaspoons Urfa pepper flakes or crushed red pepper flakes

½ teaspoon ground cardamom

½ teaspoon ground fennel

Generous ¼ teaspoon ground coriander

Generous ¼ teaspoon ground caraway

Generous ¼ teaspoon freshly ground black pepper

Make the lamb merguez: Put the lamb in a medium bowl and scatter on the Aleppo pepper, salt, garlic, Urfa pepper, cardamom, fennel, coriander, caraway, and black pepper. Using clean hands, mix it so the spices are evenly distributed. (Or, to grind the meat yourself, buy lamb shoulder, and scatter the spices over the cubed meat before grinding.) Use immediately. Or cover tightly and refrigerate for up to 8 hours.

Make the merguez sauce: In a deep 12-inch sauté pan, heat the oil over medium-high heat. Add the merguez and cook until it is no longer pink, 3 to 4 minutes, using a spatula to break up the meat into small pieces as it cooks. Stir in the sun-dried tomatoes, onion, and garlic and cook until fragrant, 1 to 2 minutes. Pour in the red wine, scraping the pan bottom to release the tasty bits, and cook until the pan goes dry, 2 to 3 minutes. Stir in the stock and simmer over medium-low heat to a thick, saucy consistency, 10 to 12 minutes. Taste and add salt and Urfa pepper until it tastes good to you. Keep warm over low heat.

Cook the orecchiette: Bring a large pot of water to a boil and add salt until it tastes like well-seasoned broth. Drop in the orecchiette, give it a stir, and cover the pot to quickly return the water to a boil. Uncover or partially cover to maintain the boil and boil until the pasta is tender but still a little chewy when bitten, 10 to 12 minutes.

RECIPE CONTINUES

Merguez Sauce

1 tablespoon extra-virgin olive oil

8 ounces oil-packed Sicilian sun-dried tomatoes, drained and minced

1 small yellow onion, small diced

4 garlic cloves, minced (about 1 tablespoon)

½ cup dry red wine, such as Chianti

2 cups Lamb Stock (page 295) or Beef Stock (page 295)

Kosher salt

Urfa pepper

Orecchiette

Kosher salt

12 ounces store-bought dried orecchiette

3 tablespoons extra-virgin olive oil

¼ cup minced fresh flat-leaf parsley, plus more for garnish

⅓ cup finely grated Fiore Sardo (Sardinian pecorino) cheese, plus more for garnish

Right after dropping the pasta, add the 3 tablespoons oil to the merguez pan along with about ¾ cup of the hot pasta water or saved pasta water (see page 31). Crank the heat to high and simmer and stir the mixture over high heat until it thickens slightly, about 2 minutes.

When the pasta is ready, use a spider strainer or slotted spoon to scoop the cooked orecchiette from the water and transfer it straight to the pan. Shake and swirl the pan until the sauce thickens a bit and begins to hug the pasta, 1 to 2 minutes (keep the pasta moving, adding a little more pasta water if necessary to create a loose, lightly thickened sauce). Remove from the heat, add the parsley and Fiore Sardo, and toss until the pasta and sauce marry, leaving little to no sauce in the pan.

Dish out the pasta onto warmed plates, creating some volume by building it into a mound. Garnish with additional grated Fiore Sardo and minced parsley.

> **LEVEL UP** **Use fresh pasta:** Replace the 12 ounces dried orecchiette with 1 pound fresh Orecchiette (page 57).
>
> **Add sweetbreads:** They add a beautiful richness to the merguez. Add 3½ ounces ground or minced sweetbreads to the ground lamb before adding the spices.

Mint Fazzoletti with Lamb al Latte Ragù

The first time our chef Jacob Rozenberg made this ragù, he was certain that he ruined $300 worth of lamb. He didn't! It's an al latte–style braise with milk in it, and after you braise the meat, the milk curdles and looks clumpy in the pot. Not to worry. You just buzz the liquid in a blender to make it creamy again. With mint in the pasta and pecorino in the ragù, it's a beautiful combination. Borlotti beans make a surprisingly good complement to the lamb. I like a little extra black pepper in this ragù, but you be the judge when you taste it. **SERVES 4 TO 6**

- 1 cup dried borlotti beans
- 3 pounds bone-in lamb shanks (about 2 shanks)
- Kosher salt and freshly ground black pepper
- 2 tablespoons grapeseed oil or canola oil
- ½ large leek, cleaned and sliced
- 1 cup whole milk
- 2 cups Lamb Stock (page 295) or Beef Stock (page 295), plus more as needed
- 1 pound fresh Mint Fazzoletti (page 79)
- 2 tablespoons extra-virgin olive oil
- 2 tablespoons (1 ounce) unsalted butter, cut into pieces
- 6 tablespoons finely grated pecorino cheese, plus more for garnish
- 3 tablespoons minced fresh mint, plus more for garnish

Make the ragù: Soak the dried beans in water to cover for 8 hours or overnight.

Preheat the oven to 300°F.

Season the lamb all over with about 1½ teaspoons salt and several grinds of black pepper. In a large Dutch oven, heat the oil over medium-high heat. Add the lamb and sear, turning for even browning, until deeply browned all over, about 15 minutes. Remove to a platter and keep warm.

You will be left with a brown glaze, or fond, in the pan that will create a deeply flavorful base for the ragù. There will be some fat, too. Discard all but 2 tablespoons fat, add the sliced leeks to the pan, and sauté over medium heat until soft, 3 to 4 minutes, stirring up the fond with a wooden spoon. Drain the beans and add to the pan along with the seared lamb, any accumulated juices, and the milk. Add enough stock to come about three-quarters of the way up the meat. Cover and transfer to the oven.

Braise until the meat and beans are fork-tender, 3 to 4 hours. After 2 hours and again at 3 hours, check the liquid level in the pan; if the pan looks like it may go dry, add another 1 cup stock.

RECIPE CONTINUES

Remove from the oven and let cool for 30 minutes, covered. When you remove the lid, don't be alarmed if the liquid looks curdled; that's supposed to happen. Once cooled, use tongs to remove the meat from the pot to a cutting board. Remove and discard the bones (or save them to make more Lamb Stock, page 295) and cut the meat into fork-friendly pieces. Use a spider strainer or slotted spoon to lift out and strain the beans from the braising liquid and hold the beans with the meat.

Using a stick blender (or upright blender or food mill), puree the rest of the braise (liquid, fat, curdled bits, vegetables, and all) into a nice thick ragù. Taste the ragù and season with salt and pepper until it tastes good to you. Fold the lamb and beans back into the ragù and keep warm over low heat. (Or refrigerate in an airtight container for up to 3 days.)

Cook the fazzoletti: Bring a large pot of water to a boil and add salt until it tastes like well-seasoned broth. Drop in the fazzoletti, give it a stir, and cover the pot to return the water quickly to a boil. Uncover or partially cover to maintain the boil and boil the pasta, stirring occasionally, until it is tender but still a little chewy when bitten, about 2 minutes.

While the pasta water comes to a boil, pour the ragù into a deep 12-inch sauté pan. Stir in the olive oil, butter, and a few grindings of black pepper and simmer gently over medium-low heat. Right after dropping the pasta, add about 1 cup of the hot pasta water or saved pasta water (see page 31) to the pan and crank the heat to high. Simmer and stir the mixture until it thickens slightly, 2 to 3 minutes.

When the pasta is ready, use a spider strainer or slotted spoon to scoop the fazzoletti from the water and transfer it straight to the pan of ragù. Shake and swirl the pan until the sauce thickens a bit more and begins to hug the pasta, 1 to 2 minutes (keep the pasta moving, adding a little more pasta water if necessary to create a loose, creamy sauce). Remove from the heat, add the pecorino and mint, and toss until the pasta and sauce marry, leaving little to no sauce in the pan.

Using a large spoon, dish out the pasta onto warmed plates, creating some volume by spooning it into a mound. Top with a grating of pecorino and minced fresh mint.

SIMPLIFY IT

Use canned borlotti beans: Replace the 1 cup dried beans with 2½ cups canned borlotti beans (about one and a half 15-ounce cans). Goya sells borlotti beans as "Roman beans." Others call them cranberry beans. Rinse and drain the canned beans and then fold them into the ragù along with the cut braised lamb. Heat over medium-low heat until the flavors meld, about 20 minutes, and then cut the heat to low and keep warm.

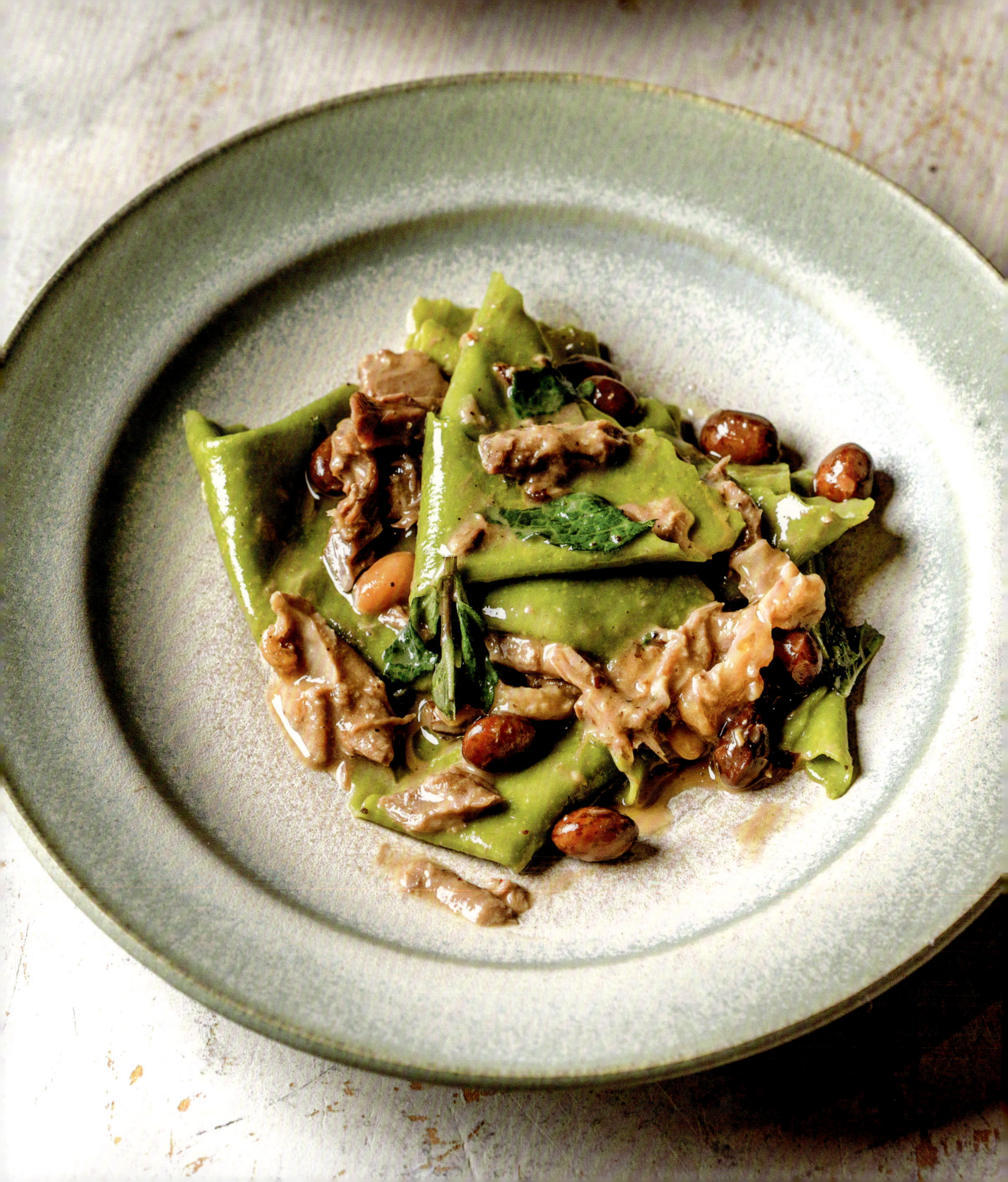

FERRICELLI with BEEF HEART BOLOGNESE

In 2018 at Vetri Philly, we did a dinner with chef Chris Cosentino for his book *Offal Good*. He set up a meat grinder and served beef heart tartare, a dish made famous at his San Francisco restaurant, Cockscomb. After the dinner, we had some extras and made Bolognese for a staff family meal. This pasta was so good we decided to put it on the Vetri menu. This dish also demonstrates the principle of using *all* parts of any animal and not letting anything go to waste. Sure, you could use another kind of ground beef here and follow the recipe as a template, but the texture of beef heart is so much richer, and I highly recommend using it. **SERVES 4 TO 6**

Beef Heart Bolognese

- 1 pound beef heart (about 1 medium)
- 3 ounces pancetta
- 2 tablespoons grapeseed oil or canola oil
- ½ large yellow onion, small diced (about ⅔ cup)
- 1 medium carrot, small diced (about ⅔ cup)
- 2 medium celery stalks, small diced (about ⅔ cup)
- ¾ cup dry white wine, such as pinot grigio
- 3 cups reduced Veal Stock (page 295) or store-bought veal demi-glace
- 2 cups canned tomato puree
- 2-inch Parmesan rind
- ½ cup whole milk

Make the beef heart Bolognese: If your knife skills are good, very finely mince the beef heart and pancetta. Otherwise, pulse it in a food processor until finely minced (careful, you don't want meat puree!).

In a deep 12-inch sauté pan, heat the oil over medium heat. Add the ground beef heart and pancetta and use a whisk or wooden spoon to vigorously break the meat up into tiny pieces as it cooks. This will create the most tender, flavorful Bolognese possible. Cook until the meat is lightly seared and broken up, 5 to 7 minutes. Add the onion, carrot, and celery and cook, stirring a few times, until the vegetables are soft and translucent, 6 to 8 minutes. Pour in the wine, scraping up any browned bits from the pan bottom. Simmer until the liquid reduces in volume by about two-thirds, 3 to 4 minutes. Add the stock, tomato puree, and Parmesan rind. Bring to a vigorous simmer. Cut the heat to medium-low, cover, and simmer gently until the meat is extremely tender, 2 to 3 hours. Taste it to test the tenderness.

Stir in the milk and simmer until it cooks down a bit, another 15 minutes. Taste the Bolognese and add salt and pepper until it tastes good to you. Remove from the heat and sink the cinnamon stick and bay leaf in the sauce. Let stand, covered, at room temperature until ready to use, up to 1 hour. (Or refrigerate for up to 3 days.)

Kosher salt and freshly ground black pepper

1 small cinnamon stick (about 2 inches long)

1 large dried bay leaf

Ferricelli

Kosher salt

1 pound fresh Ferricelli (page 60)

¾ cup finely grated Parmesan cheese, plus more for garnish

½ cup finely chopped fresh flat-leaf parsley

4 tablespoons (2 ounces) unsalted butter, cut into pieces

Cook the ferricelli: Bring a large pot of water to a boil and add salt until it tastes like well-seasoned broth. Drop in the ferricelli, give it a stir, and cover the pot to quickly return the water to a boil. Uncover or partially cover to maintain the boil and boil the pasta, stirring occasionally, until it is tender and a little chewy when bitten, 2 to 3 minutes.

While the pasta water comes to a boil, reheat the Bolognese over medium heat in the pan you cooked it in, 2 to 3 minutes, stirring a couple times. Right after dropping the pasta, discard the cinnamon and bay leaf from the Bolognese and stir in 1 cup of the hot pasta water or saved pasta water (see page 31). Crank the heat to high and simmer until the mixture thickens slightly, just a minute or two.

When the pasta is ready, use a spider strainer or slotted spoon to scoop the cooked ferricelli from the water and transfer it straight to the pan. Shake and swirl the pan until the sauce thickens a bit and begins to hug the pasta, 1 to 2 minutes (keep the pasta moving, adding a little more pasta water if necessary to create a loose, lightly thickened sauce). Remove from the heat, add the Parmesan, parsley, and butter and toss until the pasta and sauce marry, leaving little to no sauce in the pan.

Dish out the pasta onto warmed plates, creating some volume by building it into a mound. Garnish with additional Parmesan.

LEVEL UP **Grind the meat:** Instead of chopping the beef heart and pancetta, you'll get an even more luxurious texture in the Bolognese if you double-grind the meats as you would sausage. Pass the beef heart and pancetta through the medium holes of a meat grinder twice, and then proceed with the recipe. You can also have your butcher do this for you.

BUSIATI
GRANO ARSO WITH BEEF SHANK AND PEACHES

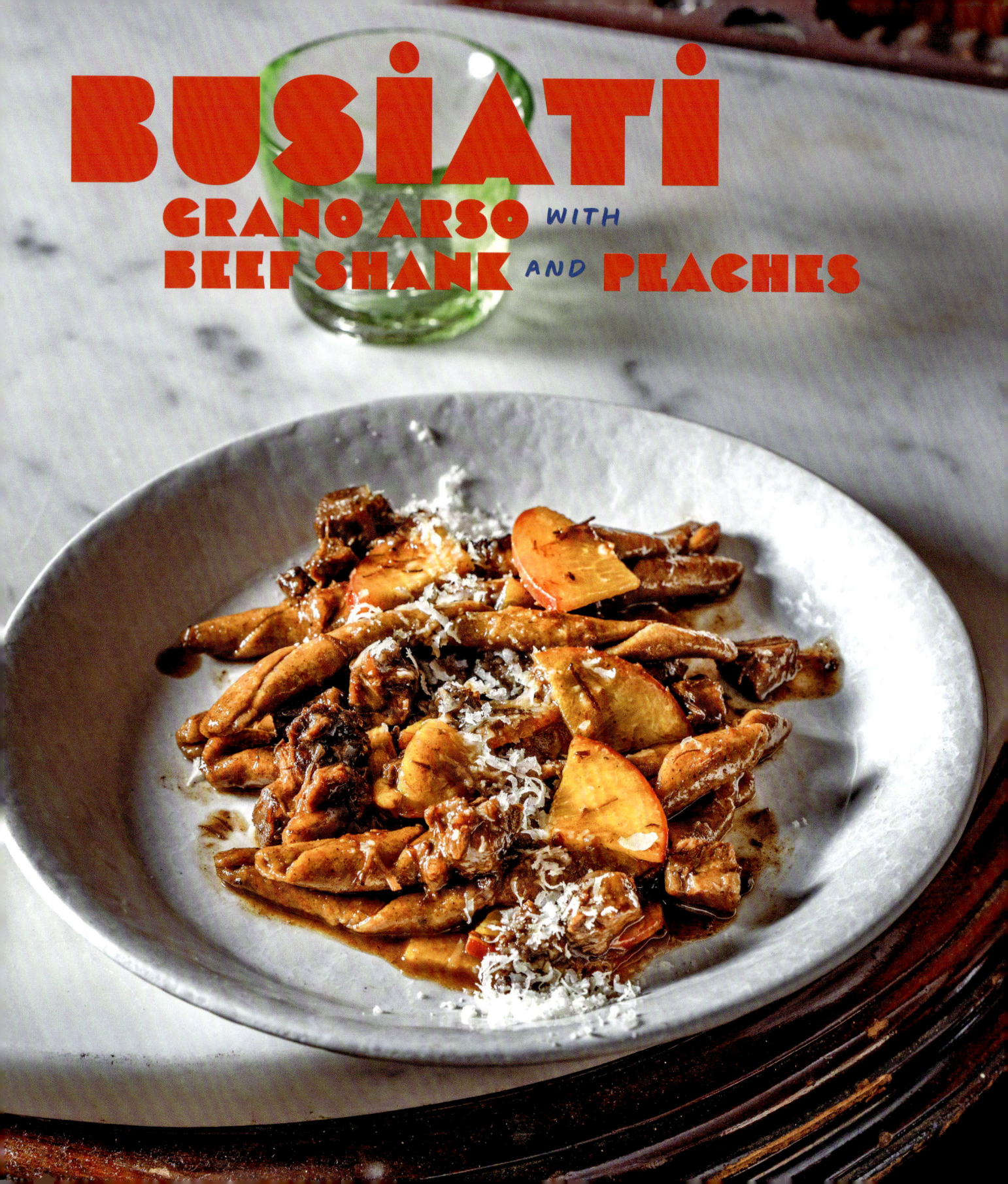

Like a lot of pastas in this chapter, this one starts with braised bone-in meat, and ends with one of the most satisfying meals you'll ever taste. A little dried porcini and Parmesan rind in the meat braise gives the ragù such a deep, savory flavor. And you'll be surprised how well beef and peaches go together. The burnt flour in the pasta really brings them together. If nectarines look fresher at your market, you could use them instead. **SERVES 6**

Beef Shank Ragù

4½ pounds cross-cut beef shanks (about 5 pieces, 1 to 1½ inches thick)

Kosher salt and freshly ground black pepper

3 tablespoons grapeseed oil or canola oil

3 tablespoons (1½ ounces) unsalted butter, cut into pieces

1 large yellow onion, coarsely chopped (about 1½ cups)

½ medium fennel bulb, cored, trimmed, and coarsely chopped (about ⅔ cup)

¾ cup dry white wine, such as pinot grigio

A few sprigs fresh rosemary and/or thyme

1 large garlic clove, smashed

2-inch Parmesan rind

1 large dried bay leaf

2 tablespoons (0.12 ounce) broken-up dried porcini mushrooms

Braise the beef shanks: Preheat the oven to 300°F.

Season the beef shanks all over with about 1 tablespoon salt and several grinds of black pepper. Heat a large Dutch oven over medium-high heat. When hot, add the oil and sear the shanks in the oil in two batches until deeply browned on both sides, 8 to 10 minutes per batch, adjusting the heat if necessary to prevent burning. Remove the seared meat to a platter.

Reduce the heat under the pan to medium-low. Add the butter and when melted, add the onion and fennel and sweat the vegetables, stirring frequently, until tender but not browned, 5 to 8 minutes, scraping up the browned bits on the pan bottom. Pour in the white wine and simmer until the liquid is reduced in volume by about half, 6 to 8 minutes.

Meanwhile, tie the rosemary and/or thyme, garlic, Parmesan rind, bay leaf, and porcini in a large piece of cheesecloth (or a coffee filter) with kitchen twine to make a sachet.

Return the meat and accumulated juices to the pan, burying it among the vegetables. Pour in enough water to almost cover the shanks (2 to 3 cups). Sink the sachet in the liquid, cover, and transfer to the oven.

Braise until the meat is fork-tender, about 3 hours. Let cool in the pan, covered, for 30 minutes.

Make the ragù: Transfer the shanks from the braising liquid to a cutting board. Remove the meat from the bones and cut the meat into small cubes. Discard the sachet and bones (or save the bones for stock). Run the vegetables and liquid through the medium holes of a food mill (or pulse to a coarse puree in a blender or food processor). Taste the pureed ragù, adding salt and pepper until it tastes good to you. Stir in the cubed meat and keep warm over low heat. (Or cover and refrigerate for up 3 days.)

Cook the busiati: Bring a large pot of water to a boil and add salt until it tastes like well-seasoned broth. Drop in the busiati, give it a stir, and cover the pot to quickly return the water to a boil. Uncover or partially cover to maintain the boil and boil until the pasta is tender yet chewy when bitten, 2 to 3 minutes.

RECIPE CONTINUES

Busiati

Kosher salt

1½ pounds fresh Busiati Grano Arso (page 65)

8 tablespoons (4 ounces) unsalted butter, cut into pieces

2 peaches, pitted and thinly sliced

Finely grated Parmesan cheese, for garnish

While the pasta water comes to a boil, in a deep 12-inch sauté pan, melt the butter over medium heat. Add the ragù, stir until combined, and simmer until slightly thickened. Right after dropping the pasta, add about 1½ cups of the hot pasta water or saved pasta water (see page 31) to the ragù. Crank the heat to high and simmer until the mixture thickens slightly, 2 to 3 minutes.

When the pasta is ready, use a spider strainer or slotted spoon to scoop the cooked busiati from the water and transfer it straight to the pan. Shake and swirl the pan until the sauce thickens a bit and begins to hug the pasta, 1 to 2 minutes (keep the pasta moving, adding a little more pasta water if necessary to create a lightly thickened sauce). Remove from the heat, add the sliced peaches, and toss until the peaches are heated through and the pasta and sauce marry, leaving little to no sauce in the pan.

Dish out the pasta onto warmed plates and garnish with grated Parmesan.

LAMB TORTELLINI
IN BRODO

If you like beef tortellini, you'll love this lamb version. We braise bone-in lamb shoulder (or shanks) in dry white wine with rosemary and garlic, and then whip the meat with Parmesan and egg to make the tortellini filling. Served in a rich broth made from the braise, it makes a fantastic starter course. The lamb filling needs to firm up in the fridge for an hour, or even a day, so you might want to start this one the day before you plan to serve it. We like to garnish this dish with steamed fresh peas and pea shoots. To watch a video of making tortellini, scan the QR code on page 240. **SERVES 8 TO 10**

Braised Lamb

3 pounds bone-in lamb shanks (about 2 shanks)

Kosher salt and freshly ground black pepper

2 tablespoons grapeseed oil or canola oil

2 tablespoons (1 ounce) unsalted butter, cut into pieces

1 large yellow onion, small diced (about 1½ cups)

½ small fennel bulb, cored, trimmed, and small diced (about ½ cup)

¾ cup dry white wine, such as pinot grigio

A few sprigs fresh rosemary and/or thyme

1 garlic clove, smashed

2-inch Parmesan rind

1 small dried bay leaf

1 to 2 tablespoons (0.12 ounce) broken-up dried porcini mushrooms

Braise the lamb: Preheat the oven to 300°F.

Season the lamb all over with about 1½ teaspoons salt and several grinds of black pepper. In a large Dutch oven, heat the oil over medium-high heat. Add the lamb and sear, turning for even browning, until deeply browned all over, about 15 minutes. Remove to a platter and keep warm (discard any fat in the pan).

You will be left with a brown glaze (fond) in the pan that will create a deeply flavorful base for the ragù. Reduce the heat to medium-low, add the butter to the pan, and when melted, add the onion and fennel and sweat the vegetables, stirring frequently, until tender but not browned, 5 to 8 minutes. Pour in the white wine and simmer until the liquid is reduced in volume by about half, 5 to 8 minutes.

Meanwhile, tie the rosemary and/or thyme, the garlic, Parmesan rind, bay leaf, and porcini in a large piece of cheesecloth (or a coffee filter) with kitchen twine to make a sachet.

Return the meat and accumulated juices to the pan, burying it among the vegetables, then pour in the stock. Sink the sachet in the liquid, cover, and transfer to the oven.

Braise until the meat is fork-tender, 3 to 4 hours. Remove from the oven and let cool for 30 minutes, covered.

RECIPE CONTINUES

6 cups Lamb Stock or Beef Stock (page 295)

¼ cup finely grated Parmesan cheese

1 large egg, beaten

Lamb Brodo and Tortellini

Sherry vinegar

Kosher salt

All-purpose flour, for dusting

12 ounces Egg Yolk Dough (page 74), rolled into sheets about 1⁄32 inch (0.8mm) thick

Once cooled, use tongs to remove the meat from the pot to a cutting board. Remove and discard excess fat, gristle, and the bones (or save the bones to make Lamb Stock, page 295). Coarsely chop the meat into 1- to 2-inch pieces (they will get whipped later, so don't worry about the exact size). Discard the sachet and pass the braising liquid and vegetables through the medium holes of a food mill set over a large bowl to make a puree (or use a stick blender or upright blender to puree). Return the chopped lamb to the puree and let cool completely, about 1 hour. (Or cover and refrigerate it for up to 1 day.) When cool, skim and discard the cooled lamb fat from the top.

Pick the cooled meat from the braise and transfer it to a food processor or, better yet, a meat grinder. Reserve the cooled braising liquid. Add the Parmesan to the processor (or grinder) and pulse briefly (or grind through the large die and then the small die) until the meat is finely chopped or ground. Taste the mixture, adding salt until it tastes good to you. Measure out half the beaten egg, about 1½ tablespoons, and add the egg to the processor (discard the remaining egg). Pulse in the egg and just enough of the braising liquid (maybe a tablespoon or two) to create a whipped meat filling that holds together nicely on a spoon like a mousse. Spoon the filling into a piping bag or zipper-lock bag, seal, and refrigerate while you make the brodo (it keeps for up to 3 days).

Make the lamb brodo: Strain the lamb braising liquid through a fine-mesh sieve into a medium saucepan. Taste the brodo and season with sherry vinegar and salt until it tastes good to you. Use immediately. Or transfer to a covered container and refrigerate for up to 1 week.

Assemble the tortellini: Dust a work surface with flour. Cut, fill, and shape the tortellini as described in Almond Tortellini with Truffle and Parmesan (page 131), but make the tortellini a little smaller, piping ½-inch balls of filling onto 2-inch squares of pasta.

Cook the tortellini: Bring a large pot of water to a boil and add salt until it tastes like well-seasoned broth. Working in batches if necessary to prevent crowding, drop in the tortellini, give them a stir, and cover the pot to quickly return the water to a low boil. Uncover or partially cover to maintain the boil and boil the tortellini until they are tender but still a little chewy when bitten, 2 to 3 minutes. Using a spider or slotted spoon, drain the pasta by transferring them to warmed pasta plates or soup bowls.

While the pasta water comes to a boil, heat the brodo over medium heat in a medium pot with a pour spout until it reaches a simmer. Pour ¼ to ⅓ cup of brodo into each bowl around the tortellini. Serve warm.

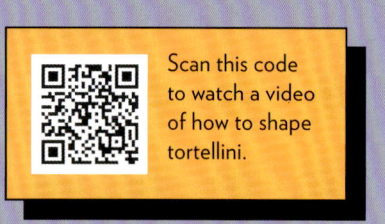

Scan this code to watch a video of how to shape tortellini.

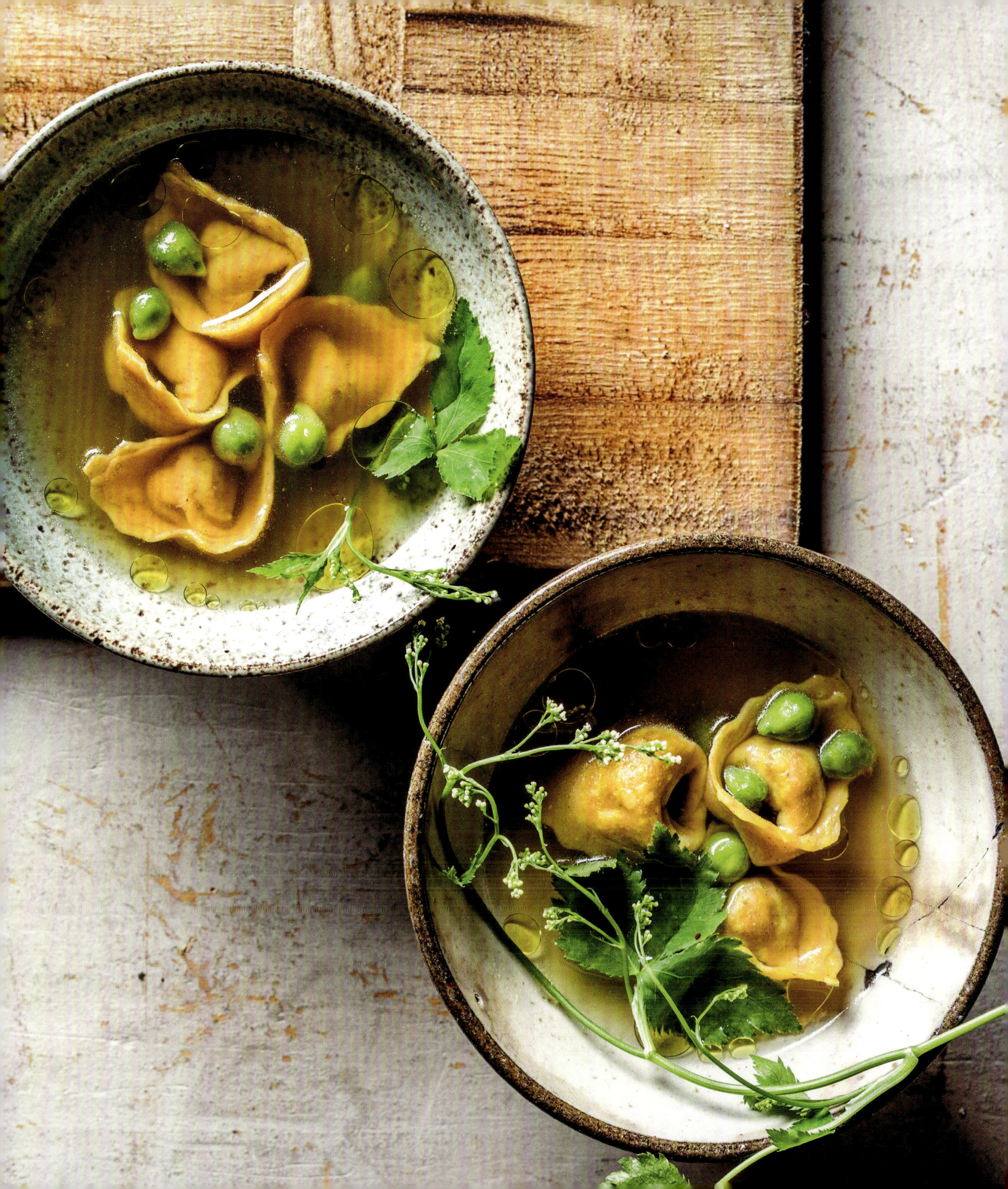

Ricotta Cavatelli with Veal Shank Ragù

If you haven't made ricotta cavatelli at home, give them a shot. They come out so tender and beautiful, completely different from the commercial frozen cavatelli a lot of people buy. The veal ragù adds deep, savory flavors sharpened by lemon and brightened with fresh celery and parsley tossed in at the end. **SERVES 6 TO 8**

Veal Shank Ragù

2½ pounds cross-cut (osso buco) veal shanks (about 3 pieces), trimmed of excess fat and membrane

Kosher salt and freshly ground black pepper

All-purpose flour, for dusting

2 tablespoons grapeseed oil or canola oil

½ large yellow onion, coarsely chopped (about ½ cup)

1 large celery stalk, coarsely chopped (about ½ cup)

1 medium carrot, coarsely chopped (about ½ cup)

4 oil-packed anchovy fillets, or 1 generous tablespoon anchovy paste

Finely grated zest of 1 small lemon

½ cup dry white wine, such as pinot grigio

2 to 3 cups Veal Stock or Beef Stock (page 295)

Braise the veal shanks: Preheat the oven to 350°F.

Season the veal shanks generously with salt and pepper (1½ to 2 teaspoons salt) and then roll in flour to coat all over. Shake off the excess flour.

In a large Dutch oven, heat the oil over medium-high heat until hot. Working in batches to avoid overcrowding, add the veal shanks and cook, turning now and then to avoid burning, until the shanks are seared and deeply browned all over, 15 to 20 minutes total per batch, adjusting the heat as necessary to avoid burning the flour. Remove the shanks to a platter or plate. You will be left will a brown glaze (fond) in the pan that will create a deeply flavorful base for the ragù.

Pour off all but a few tablespoons of fat from the pan. Add the onion, celery, and carrot and cook over medium heat until the vegetables are soft, 5 to 8 minutes, scraping the pan with a wooden spatula occasionally to loosen the fond. Stir in the anchovies and lemon zest and cook and scrape again until the anchovies disappear, about 3 minutes. Stir in the wine, crank the heat to medium-high, and simmer until it has a syrupy consistency, about 5 minutes. Stir in 2 cups of the veal stock and simmer until the liquid reduces in volume by about one-quarter, 8 to 10 minutes.

Return the veal shanks and accumulated juices to the pot, nestling them in the braising liquid. They should be almost covered by liquid. If they're not, add enough stock to barely cover them. Cover the pot and transfer to the oven.

Braise until fork-tender, about 2 hours. Remove from the oven and let cool for 30 minutes, covered.

Ricotta Cavatelli

Kosher salt

1¼ pounds fresh Ricotta Cavatelli (page 93)

2 tablespoons extra-virgin olive oil

4 tablespoons (2 ounces) unsalted butter, cut into pieces

2 large celery stalks, small diced (about 1 cup)

¾ cup minced fresh flat-leaf parsley

4 large garlic cloves, minced and mashed into a paste (about 2 teaspoons)

Freshly ground black pepper

¾ cup finely grated Parmesan cheese, plus more for garnish

Use tongs to remove the meat from the pot to a cutting board. Remove the meat from the bones, discarding excess fat and wobbly bits, and return the trimmed meat to the braising liquid (it should still be in large pieces). Remove the marrow from the bones while still warm and add it to the braising liquid (discard the bones). Let the meat rest in the braising liquid until completely cooled, about 30 minutes more. Then remove the meat from the liquid and cut it into ¼-inch pieces.

Make the ragù: Pour the braising liquid and solids into a sieve set over a bowl and reserve the braising liquid. Puree the solids by passing them through a food mill fitted with the medium-hole disk (or puree with a blender or food processor). Add just enough of the braising liquid to create a nice, thick ragù. Taste the ragù and season until it tastes good to you, using some restraint to avoid overseasoning (the Parmesan added later will add some saltiness). Fold the veal into the ragù and use immediately. Or refrigerate in an airtight container for up to 1 week or freeze it for up to 1 month.

Cook the ricotta cavatelli: Bring a large pot of water to a boil and add salt until it tastes like well-seasoned broth. Drop in the cavatelli, give it a stir, and cover the pot to quickly return the water to a boil. Uncover or partially cover to maintain the boil and boil the pasta, stirring occasionally, until it is tender but still a little chewy when bitten, 2 to 3 minutes.

While the pasta water comes to a boil, in a deep 12-inch sauté pan, heat the oil and 1 tablespoon of the butter over medium heat until hot. Add the celery and sauté, stirring a few times, until soft, 5 to 6 minutes. Stir in the parsley and garlic paste and season with pepper. Sauté until fragrant, about 30 seconds. Add the veal ragù and keep warm over low heat.

When the pasta is ready, use a spider strainer or slotted spoon to scoop the cook cavatelli from the water and transfer it straight to the pan. Add the remaining 3 tablespoons butter and 1 cup of the hot pasta water or saved pasta water (see page 31). Crank the heat to high and shake and swirl the pan until the sauce thickens a bit and begins to hug the pasta, 1 to 2 minutes (keep the pasta moving, adding a little more pasta water if necessary to create a loose, lightly thickened sauce). Remove from the heat, add the Parmesan, and toss until the pasta and sauce marry, leaving little to no sauce in the pan.

Dish out the pasta onto warmed plates, garnishing with a little grated Parmesan.

Cannelloni with Oxtail and Cipollini

You can't go wrong with the classic steakhouse flavors of seared beef, onions, and beef jus. Here you get them in pasta form. We use oxtail because it tastes even more beefy than tenderloin and rib eye, and we pan-roast small cipollini onions, leaving them whole so each person gets a few on their plate. We also give the beef jus some love by simmering cranberries in it to deepen the flavor, and then we enrich the jus with butter for a silkier texture. You get all that in this dish, plus a tube of tender pasta stuffed with oxtail ragù, creamy béchamel, and Parmesan. It's pretty special!

Serves 6 to 8

Oxtail

- 5 pounds oxtail, trimmed of fat
- Kosher salt and freshly ground black pepper
- 2 tablespoons grapeseed oil or canola oil
- 1 large yellow onion, diced (about 1½ cups)
- 1 medium fennel bulb, cored, trimmed, and diced (about 1½ cups)
- A few sprigs fresh rosemary and thyme
- 1 garlic clove, peeled
- 1 small dried bay leaf
- 4 cups dry red wine, such as Chianti
- 2 to 3 tablespoons sherry vinegar
- 1 cup fresh cranberries

Prepare the oxtail: Season the oxtail generously with about 2½ teaspoons salt and several grinds of pepper. In a large Dutch oven, heat the oil over medium-high heat. Working in batches to avoid overcrowding, add the oxtail and sear them hard (until dark brown) on both sides, 8 to 10 minutes per side. Remove the meat to a platter.

Drain off all but a few tablespoons of fat from the pan. Reduce the heat to medium, stir in the onion and fennel, and cook until tender but not too browned, 4 to 5 minutes, stirring to scrape up the browned bits from the pan bottom. Tie the rosemary and thyme, garlic, and bay leaf in a large piece of cheesecloth (or a coffee filter) with kitchen twine to make a sachet.

Return the meat to the pan, burying it among the vegetables, and pour in enough wine to barely cover the ingredients (about 2 cups). Sink the sachet in the liquid and bring to a boil over high heat. Reduce the heat to low, cover, and cook very gently until the meat is fork-tender, about 4 hours.

Remove from the heat and let cool in the pan for 30 minutes, covered. Lift the lid, then spoon off and discard the fat from the surface of the braise. Use tongs to transfer the oxtails to a cutting board and pick the oxtail meat off the bones, being very careful to discard any cartilage and bone bits. Shred the meat with a fork and place in a large bowl (or shred it in the bowl of a stand mixer fitted with the paddle attachment on low to medium-low speed). Strain the braising

Pan-Roasted Cipollini

12 ounces small fresh cipollini onions (12 to 15)

3 tablespoons (1½ ounces) unsalted butter, cut into pieces

2 or 3 sprigs fresh thyme

2 tablespoons sherry vinegar, plus more as needed

Cannelloni and Assembly

1 pound Egg Yolk Dough (page 74), rolled into sheets a little less than ⅛ inch thick

All-purpose flour, for dusting

Kosher salt

2 cups Béchamel (page 247)

Softened butter, for the baking dish

½ cup finely grated Parmesan cheese

6 tablespoons (3 ounces) unsalted butter, cut into pieces

liquid through a fine-mesh sieve set over a medium bowl (reserve the braising liquid). Discard the sachet and pass the vegetable solids through a food mill fitted with the medium-hole disk set over another medium bowl (or puree the solids in a blender or food processor). Transfer the vegetable puree to the bowl with the meat and mix well. Taste the mixture and season with salt and sherry vinegar until it tastes good to you.

Measure the reserved oxtail braising liquid. For every 1 cup braising liquid, measure out ⅔ cup red wine and ⅓ cup cranberries (you should have about 2 cups braising liquid, which means measuring out 1⅓ cups wine and ⅔ cup cranberries). Pour the wine into a small saucepan, bring to a simmer, and cook until the volume is reduced by about half, 8 to 10 minutes.

Add the cranberries and braising liquid and bring to a boil. Reduce the heat to medium-low and simmer until the cranberries soften considerably and you're left with about 1½ cups liquid, about 25 minutes. Strain through a medium-mesh sieve into a 2-cup glass measure without pressing on the solids. Discard the cranberries. The liquid is your oxtail jus. Pour it into a medium saucepan and set aside.

Pan-roast the cipollini: Trim off the root side and top side of each onion and remove the skin. In a medium sauté pan, melt the butter over medium heat. Toss in the thyme sprigs and when the butter bubbles, add the cipollini onions. Reduce the heat to medium-low and let the cipollini cook gently, without moving them, until they take on a strong golden-brown color on the bottom, 10 to 15 minutes. Flip them individually and cook until the other side is deep golden brown and the onions are tender to the touch, another 8 to 10 minutes. Pour in the sherry vinegar, shaking the pan to deglaze the browned bits from the pan bottom. Cover, remove from the heat, and set aside.

Preheat the oven to 400°F.

Cut and blanch the pasta: Keep a spray bottle of water next to your work surface. Lay the pasta sheets on a lightly floured work surface and cut them into 4-inch squares. As you work, lightly mist the pasta to prevent it from drying out, or cover it with a damp kitchen towel.

Set up a large bowl of ice water. Bring a large pot of water to a boil and add salt until it tastes like well seasoned broth. Working in batches to prevent overcrowding, drop the pasta in the boiling water and blanch the squares for 30 seconds, stirring gently to prevent sticking. Using a spider strainer or slotted spoon, transfer the squares to the ice water, swishing them around to cool them quickly. When cool, transfer the squares to damp kitchen towels, separating the squares, laying them flat, and patting them dry. The pieces will be delicate and some may stick, but you should have plenty.

RECIPE CONTINUES

Assemble the cannelloni: (For photos, see Crab Cannelloni with Saffron on page 167.) Spoon the béchamel into a piping bag or zipper-lock bag and snip off one of the bottom corners to make a ½-inch-diameter hole. Butter a 4-quart (about 15 × 10-inch) baking dish or 6 to 8 individual 2-cup (8-ounce) baking dishes. To fill each cannelloni, pipe a line of béchamel about ½ inch in diameter along the bottom of the square that is closest to you, leaving about ½ inch on the left and right sides of the square. Spoon about 3 tablespoons of the oxtail filling over the béchamel so it completely covers the béchamel. Grate some Parmesan over the oxtail until covered lightly (1 to 2 teaspoons). Roll the sheet onto itself, rolling away from you, so that the pasta resembles a cigar. Place the cannelloni seam-side down into the baking dish(es) as they are done. Repeat until all the cannelloni are filled, and then top the cannelloni with a nice grating of Parmesan.

Bake until the filling is heated through and the top is lightly golden brown, about 10 minutes.

Finish the jus: While the cannelloni are baking, set the saucepan of oxtail jus over medium heat and bring to a boil. Add the 6 tablespoons butter and the cipollini onions to the jus. Simmer the sauce until it thickens and takes on a glossy appearance, 4 to 6 minutes, stirring a few times. Taste the sauce and season it with sherry vinegar and salt until it tastes good to you.

Transfer a few cannelloni to each plate (if baking in a single dish) and spoon the sauce over the top, serving a few cipollini per person.

Scan this code to watch a video of making cannelloni.

BÉCHAMEL

Besciamella, salsa bianca, white sauce . . . whatever you want to call it, this sauce has a thousand uses. It's part of the creamy filling in cannelloni, it gets layered into lasagna Bolognese, and it gets ladled on crespelle (like cannelloni but with Italian crepes). It can also be the base for homemade mac and cheese. They don't call it a mother sauce for nothing! **MAKES ABOUT 4 CUPS**

4 tablespoons (2 ounces) unsalted butter, cut into pieces
½ cup tipo "00" flour or all-purpose flour
4⅓ cups whole milk
Kosher salt

In a medium saucepan, melt the butter over medium heat. Whisk in the flour to make a roux (it will look like lumpy batter) and let it cook for 1 minute to cook out the raw flour taste. This is called a blond roux. If you keep cooking until the flour is dark amber brown, it's called a brown roux and has a deeper, toasted flavor but less thickening power.

When the roux is ready, whisk the milk into the roux until it is fully incorporated and the mixture is free of lumps. Simmer the mixture gently over medium-low heat, whisking frequently, until it thickens and tastes sweeter and less like flour, 15 to 20 minutes.

Remove from the heat. For a silkier texture, strain the béchamel through a fine-mesh sieve. Taste it and season with salt until it tastes good to you (about 1 teaspoon should do it). Use the béchamel within 20 or 30 minutes; it will thicken as it stands. (Or let it cool completely, cover it with plastic wrap pressed directly onto the surface to prevent a skin from forming, and refrigerate it for up to 2 days. Reheat the béchamel in a saucepan over low heat before using.)

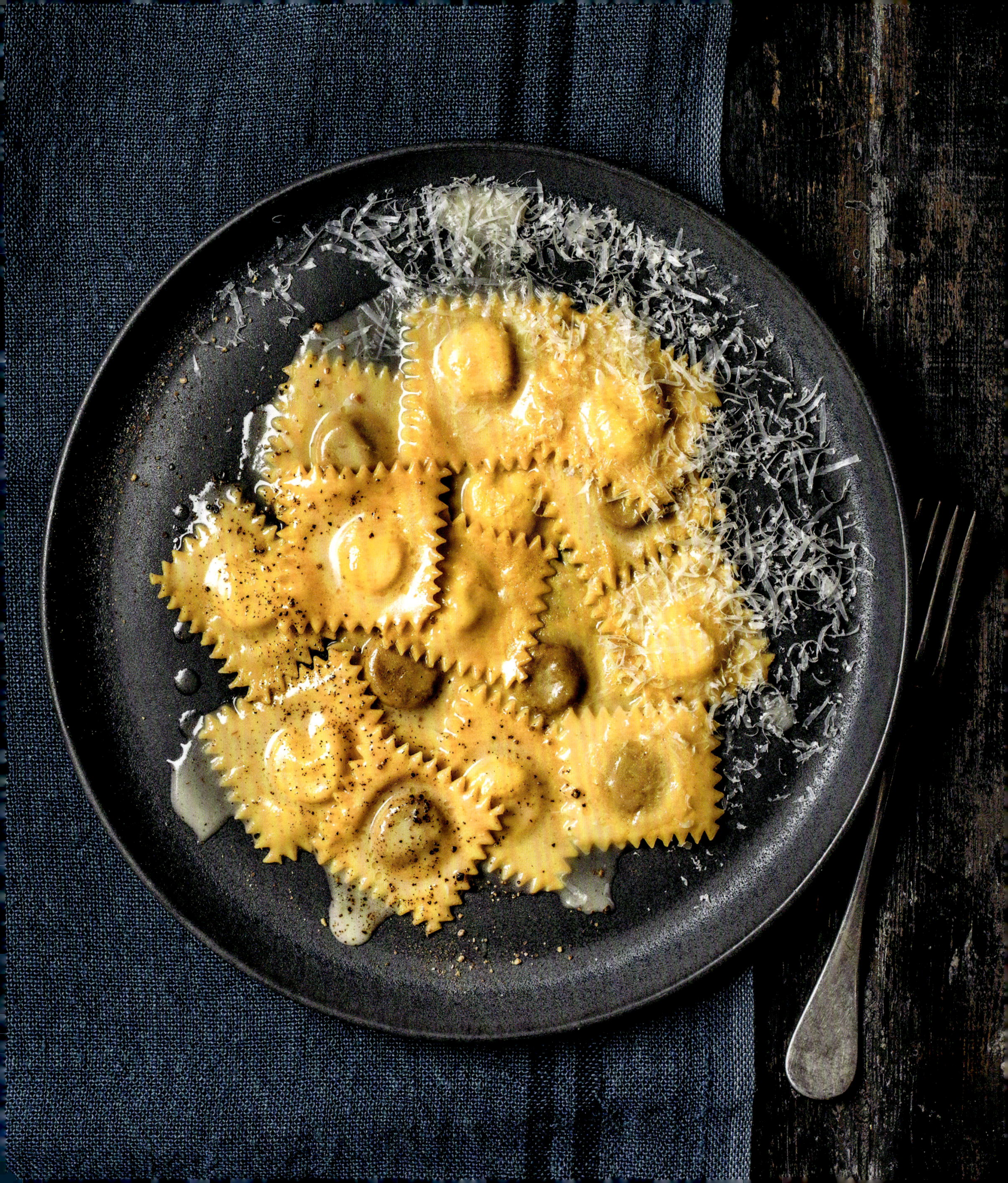

FRANCOBOLLI WITH SHORT RIBS AND CELERY ROOT

Short ribs with celery root is a can't-miss combination. Add some pasta, and I'm in heaven. Here, we stuff half the francobolli with short rib and half with celery root filling. When you eat these little pasta squares, you never know which filling you're gonna get! With all that flavor, a simple butter sauce is all you need to finish it. And maybe some grated Parmesan. To watch a video of making this pasta, scan the QR code on page 250. **SERVES 6 TO 8**

Short Rib Filling

2 pounds bone-in beef short ribs (about 4 ribs)

Kosher salt and freshly ground black pepper

1 tablespoon grapeseed oil or canola oil

1 tablespoon unsalted butter, cut into pieces

½ large yellow onion, diced (about ⅔ cup)

¼ small fennel bulb, cored, trimmed, and diced (about ¼ cup)

½ cup dry white wine, such as pinot grigio

A couple sprigs fresh rosemary and/or thyme

1 small garlic clove, smashed

2-inch Parmesan rind

1 small dried bay leaf

1 tablespoon (0.06 ounce) broken-up dried porcini mushrooms

Braise the short ribs: Preheat the oven to 300°F.

Season the short ribs all over with about 1 tablespoon salt and a few grinds of pepper. In a large Dutch, heat the oil over medium-high heat. Working in batches to avoid overcrowding, sear the ribs in the oil until deeply browned all over, about 10 minutes total per batch. Turn the ribs for even browning and reduce the heat as necessary to prevent burning. Remove the seared meat to a platter.

Reduce the heat under the Dutch oven to medium-low. Add the butter and when melted, add the onion and fennel and sweat the vegetables, stirring frequently, until tender but not browned, 5 to 8 minutes. Pour in the white wine and simmer until the liquid is reduced in volume by about half, 5 to 8 minutes.

Meanwhile, tie the rosemary and/or thyme, the garlic, Parmesan rind, bay leaf, and porcini in a large piece of cheesecloth (or a coffee filter) with kitchen twine to make a sachet.

Return the meat and accumulated juices to the pan, burying the ribs among the vegetables, then pour in enough water to barely cover the ingredients (1 to 2 cups). Sink the sachet in the liquid, cover, and transfer to the oven.

Braise until the meat is fork-tender, 2 to 3 hours. Remove from the oven and let cool in the pan for 30 minutes, covered.

RECIPE CONTINUES

Celery Root Filling

9 tablespoons (4½ ounces) unsalted butter, cut into pieces

A couple sprigs fresh thyme

1 small dried bay leaf

2 large garlic cloves, peeled

1 medium celery root (about 1 pound), peeled and finely diced

½ cup finely grated Parmesan cheese

1 large egg yolk

Kosher salt

Francobolli

1 pound Egg Yolk Dough (page 74), rolled into sheets between 1/32 and 1/16 inch (0.8 and 1.5) thick

All-purpose flour, for dusting

Kosher salt

8 tablespoons (4 ounces) unsalted butter, cut into pieces

Finely grated Parmesan cheese

Scan this code to watch a video of making Francobolli with Short Ribs and Celery Root.

Use tongs to remove the meat from the braising liquid to a cutting board. Remove the meat from the bones and then discard the bones (or save them for Beef Stock, page 295). Discard excess fat, gristle, and nasty bits from the meat. Cut and/or shred the meat into small pieces. Discard the sachet and run the vegetables and liquid through the medium holes of a food mill (or puree them in a blender or food processor). Return the pureed ragù to the pan. Taste it, adding salt and pepper until it tastes good to you. Stir in the meat and mix vigorously with a rubber spatula to break up the meat and create a harmonious and somewhat smooth filling that can be piped. Let cool in the pan until just warm to the touch. Spoon into a piping bag or zipper-lock bag, seal, and use immediately. (Or refrigerate for up to 1 day.)

Make the celery root filling: In a very large sauté pan, melt the butter over medium heat and wait for it to bubble. Tie the thyme and bay leaf together with kitchen twine to make a bouquet and add it to the butter. Add the garlic and cook until it is fragrant, about 20 seconds. Add the celery root, cover, and cook over medium-low heat, stirring frequently, until it is very tender but not browned, about 20 minutes.

When tender, remove from the heat and use tongs to remove the bouquet, squeezing the bouquet into the butter, and then discarding it. Remove and discard the garlic. Use a slotted spoon to transfer only the celery root to a blender. Reserve the butter in the pan. Let the celery root cool until it stops steaming and then add the Parmesan and egg yolk to the blender. Blend until smooth, adding just enough of the reserved butter to create a nice thick pasta filling that holds its shape on a spoon. Taste it and season with salt until it tastes good to you. Spoon into a piping bag or zipper-lock bag, seal, and use immediately. (Or refrigerate for up to 1 day.)

Assemble the francobolli: Lay a pasta sheet on a lightly floured surface and trim the edges square. Mark the halfway point of the sheet and cover the left side with damp paper towels or kitchen towels to prevent it from drying out. You'll be using each filling to create two types of filled pasta. Use a 1-inch-diameter ring mold or glass (such as a small inverted vase) to mark a grid pattern on the pasta, leaving ½-inch spaces between the marks and without cutting all the way through. Pipe about ¾-inch balls of celery root filling inside of every other marking, leaving the rest empty. Repeat with the short rib filling, piping ¾-inch balls to fill the empty markings.

Remove the towels and carefully lay the reserved section of the pasta over the filling, gradually moving from left to right. Using the blunt side of the ring mold or glass (or your fingers), gently press the pasta over and around the fillings to form a domed seal over the fillings, without cutting through the pasta. Using a fluted pasta wheel, trim all four sides of the sheet. Then cut between the markings, left to right and top to bottom, to create pastas about 1½-inch square. Repeat with the remaining pasta and filling and use immediately. You should have 70 to 80 francobolli. (Or dust with flour and refrigerate in an airtight container for up to 4 hours. You can also freeze them in a single layer, transfer them to zipper-lock bags, and freeze for up to 3 days. Take the pasta straight from the freezer to the boiling pasta water.)

Cook the pasta: Bring a large pot of water to a boil and add salt until it tastes like well-seasoned broth. Working in batches to avoid overcrowding, drop in the francobolli (equal amounts of each filling), give them a stir, and cover the pot to return the water quickly to a boil. Uncover or partially cover to maintain the boil and boil the pasta, stirring occasionally, until it is tender but still a little chewy when bitten, 2 to 3 minutes.

While the pasta water comes to a boil, in a deep 12-inch sauté pan, melt the butter over medium heat. Right after dropping the pasta, add about 1 cup of the hot pasta water or saved pasta water (see page 31) to the melted butter. Crank the heat to high and boil until the sauce thickens slightly, 2 to 3 minutes.

When the pasta is ready, use a spider strainer or slotted spoon to scoop it from the water and transfer it straight to the pan. Shake and swirl the pan until the sauce thickens a bit and begins to hug the pasta, 1 to 2 minutes (keep the pasta moving, adding a little more pasta water if necessary to create a loose, lightly thickened sauce). Continue shaking the pan until the sauce thickens further and the pasta and sauce marry, leaving just a little sauce in the pan.

Dish out the pasta onto warmed plates, drizzling on the sauce from the pan and creating some volume by building the pasta into a mound. Garnish with grated Parmesan.

NEX
LI

> Details make perfection.
> And perfection is not a detail.
>
> **—LEONARDO DA VINCI,**
> ITALIAN ARTIST, SCIENTIST,
> ENGINEER, AND RENAISSANCE MAN

PASTA

I don't know exactly where it came from. I got it from Brad Spence, our chef and partner at Amis, our Roman trattoria in Philadelphia (now shuttered). Brad got it from chef Andy Nusser, when they cooked together at Casa Mono in New York City. Maybe Andy got it from somewhere else. I don't know. But ever since I heard it from Brad, I've used the phrase "Hee Hee on the Ha Ha."

When you're experimenting with a new dish, you typically make it a few times and usually it needs a little something, or something needs to be taken away. In our kitchens, after tinkering and adjusting a dish, when we finally get it right, we say, "That's the Hee Hee on the Ha Ha!" It's that final little detail that makes the dish perfect.

Often, that little something takes the dish to another level entirely. I love cooking traditional simple pastas like Spaghetti alla Carbonara (page 206) and Rigatoni with Fiorella Sausage Ragù (page 208). But at Vetri Cucina, we like to take things up a notch and really surprise guests with something special. That's what this chapter is all about.

The extra sparkle could come from almost anything. Sometimes it's an extravagant ingredient like the caviar in Corn Anolini with Buttermilk Espuma and Caviar (page 271) or the fine shavings of frozen foie gras on Sweet Potato Cappelletti with Granola and Foie Gras Torchon (page 276). Or maybe it's a unique flavor like the fermented citrus punch of yuzu kosho in Gnocchi Sardi with Lobster, Corn, and Yuzu Kosho (page 259). Other times, it's a special technique, and those are my favorite.

Fusilli with Clams, Cauliflower, and Speck Bread Crumbs (page 257) is a good example. At all my restaurants, we make the noodles in house. At Fiorella in Philadelphia, we had just gotten a new fusilli extruder die that cut the pasta a little thicker than your average fusilli. I told our executive chef, Matt Rodrigue, that it reminded me of thick, chewy paccheri, which I love pairing with seafood. When we started playing around with the thicker fusilli, we put clams with it. Instead of marrying the seafood and pasta with fat and starchy pasta water like we usually do, we made a cauliflower puree. That added the rich mouthfeel of cream but made the pasta taste lighter. It was beautiful, and we could have stopped right there. But we thought the dish would be even better with something crunchy to complement the creamy cauliflower. The initial thought was bread crumbs. We tried it and toasted bread crumbs tasted good. But we kept pushing, trying to come up something even better until we finally landed on . . . speck bread crumbs! We rendered some chopped speck in a pan until it got crispy and then crumbled it up like bacon. When mixed into the toasted bread crumbs, it added a smoky, savory taste that took the dish to another level entirely and perfectly balanced everything else. Plus, it inspired us to smoke the cauliflower crema, which amplified the smoky element in the dish even more.

Some of the dishes in this chapter are more complex than others in the book, but they are well worth the effort. I pulled together all the special pastas we've come up with over the years, including ideas that we bounced around at both Vetri Cucina and Fiorella in both Philadelphia and Las Vegas. These are the dishes that started out as exciting concepts and ended up as something truly extraordinary. That little touch of magic might be the hint of cranberries in Carrot and Brisket Doppio Ravioli with Brisket Jus and Red Pearl Onion Agrodolce (page 283); the special tomato preparations in Scallop Corzetti with Clarified Pomodoro, Tomato Powder, and Basil Oil (page 269); or the creative use of chicken skin in Smoked Potato Culurgiones with Lemon Butter and Chicken Skin Gremolata (page 263). All of these dishes were beautifully executed, but then someone said it could use a little something extra, and when we made that extra thing and tasted it, we all said, "Now, *that's* the Hee Hee on the Ha Ha!"

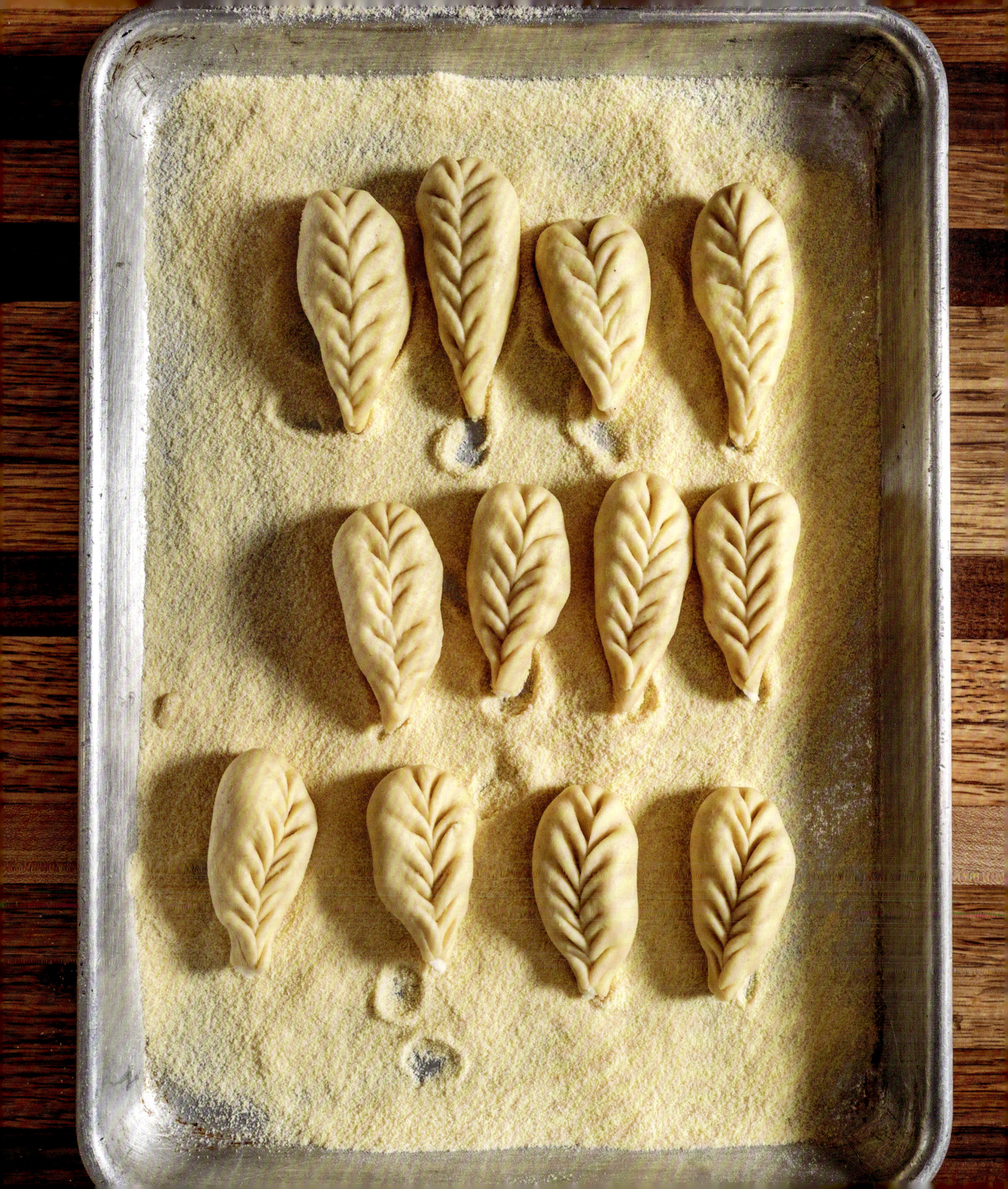

LEVEL UP **Smoke the cauliflower crema:** Set up a smoker for 225°F indirect heat. Spoon the pureed crema into a small heatproof pan (such as a disposable aluminum tray) and smoke with indirect heat until the crema picks up some smoke aroma, 30 to 40 minutes. If it becomes too thick, stir in water, a tablespoon at a time, until it returns to the consistency of a cream sauce.

FUSILLI WITH CLAMS, CAULIFLOWER, AND SPECK BREAD CRUMBS

Mantecare is an Italian verb we use to describe what happens when we combine pasta and sauce, when by stirring the water, starch, and fat together, it gets thicker and creamier and brings the pasta and sauce together as one. In this dish, instead of mantecare, a creamy cauliflower puree does the job. Fusilli is so perfect here because the twisted ridges of the corkscrew shape pick up the thick, creamy sauce. **SERVES 4**

Clams

- 2 tablespoons extra-virgin olive oil
- ½ medium yellow onion, small diced
- ½ small fennel bulb, cored, trimmed, and small diced
- Pinch of crushed red pepper flakes
- 2 cups dry white wine, such as pinot grigio
- 5 pounds small Manila or littleneck clams, scrubbed and purged of sand (see page 143)

Speck Bread Crumbs

- ½ small garlic clove, coarsely chopped
- 1 generous teaspoon extra-virgin olive oil
- Kosher salt
- 1 cup plain panko bread crumbs
- 1¼ ounces speck (or prosciutto in a pinch), sliced or whole

Steam the purged clams: In a deep 12-inch sauté pan with a lid, heat the oil over medium heat. Add the onion, fennel, and pepper flakes and sweat, stirring a few times, until the onion is translucent but not browned, 4 to 6 minutes. Add the wine and bring to a simmer. Add the clams, cover, and steam over medium heat until the clams open, 8 to 10 minutes. Remove the lid and discard any clams that do not open after 10 minutes. Pour the pan contents through a sieve set over a large bowl. Pick out and reserve the clam meat and steaming liquid (discard the shells and other solids). You can hold the picked clams and steaming liquid at room temperature for an hour or keep them in separate airtight containers in the refrigerator for up to 8 hours.

Make the speck bread crumbs: Preheat the oven (or toaster oven) to 350°F.

In a mini-chopper, buzz the garlic, oil, and a pinch of salt until finely chopped. Buzz in the panko briefly, just until everything is incorporated (not too finely chopped). Taste and add more salt if you think it needs it. Spread the seasoned bread crumbs in a single layer on a small sheet pan and bake until the bread crumbs are toasted golden brown, 6 to 8 minutes, stirring and shaking a few times for even browning.

Meanwhile, cut the speck into short, ¼- to ½-inch-thick strips (lardons), or skip this step if you bought pre-sliced speck. Place in a large, cold sauté pan and set the pan over medium-low heat. Cook slowly until the fat gradually renders from the meat and the meat shrinks and crisps like bacon, 8 to 10 minutes. Remove the rendered speck to paper towels to cool (it will crisp up more as it cools, like bacon).

RECIPE CONTINUES

Cauliflower Crema

3 tablespoons (1½ ounces) unsalted butter, cut into pieces

2 cups cauliflower florets (from ½ medium head), thinly sliced

1 garlic clove, thinly sliced

Kosher salt

Fusilli

Kosher salt

12 ounces store-bought dried fusilli

3 tablespoons (1½ ounces) unsalted butter, cut into pieces

A generous ¼ cup finely grated Parmesan cheese

About 1 tablespoon fresh lemon juice

3 tablespoons chopped fresh chives

Crush the speck to bits with your hands and combine with the toasted bread crumbs. Set aside until needed.

Make the cauliflower crema: In a medium saucepan, melt the butter over medium-low heat. Add the cauliflower and garlic, cover, and sweat, shaking the pan a few times, until the cauliflower is very tender but not browned, 10 to 12 minutes, lowering the heat if necessary to prevent browning. Transfer to a small food processor or blender (or use a stick blender), and puree until smooth, adding a little water, tablespoon by tablespoon, as necessary to get the mixture to puree (you don't want to dilute the flavor too much). The final consistency should be similar to mashed potatoes. Taste and season with salt until it tastes good to you.

Cook the fusilli: Bring a large pot of water to a boil and add salt until it tastes like well-seasoned broth. Drop in the fusilli, give it a stir, and cover the pot to quickly return the water to a boil. Uncover or partially cover to maintain the boil and boil the pasta, stirring occasionally, until it is tender but still a little chewy when bitten, 10 to 12 minutes.

About 5 minutes before the pasta is ready, in a deep 12-inch sauté pan, combine 1 cup of the clam steaming liquid and ¾ cup of the hot pasta water or saved pasta water (see page 31) and bring to a boil over high heat. Boil until reduced in volume by about half, 3 to 4 minutes.

When the pasta is ready, use a spider strainer or large slotted spoon to scoop it from the water and transfer it straight to the pan. Add the butter and about ½ cup of the cauliflower crema and shake and swirl the pan until the sauce begins to hug the pasta, 2 to 3 minutes (keep the pasta moving, adding a little more pasta water and/or cauliflower crema if necessary to create a lightly thickened sauce). Add the picked clams and toss just to heat through, about 30 seconds. Remove from the heat, add the Parmesan, and toss until the pasta and sauce marry, leaving little to no sauce in the pan. Add the lemon juice and chives, toss to mix, and then take a taste, adding salt until it tastes good to you.

Dish out the pasta onto warmed plates, creating some volume by building it into a mound. Top with the speck bread crumbs.

Gnocchi Sardi with Lobster, Corn, and Yuzu Kosho

Our chef at Fiorella, Matt Rodrigue, was on vacation in Portland, Maine, one summer and stopped by Eventide Oyster Company for a brown butter lobster roll. He got the crab roll, too. It came dressed in mayo spiked with yuzu kosho, a Japanese paste of fermented, chile-spiked yuzu peel. One of my favorite condiments! When he got back to Philly Matt made this dish to highlight that flavor. Once you cook the lobster, this pasta is pretty straightforward. It's the yuzu kosho that really sends it. **SERVES 4 TO 6**

3 large live Maine lobsters (1 to 1½ pounds each)

3 medium ears fresh sweet corn, shucked

Kosher salt

1 pound fresh Gnocchi Sardi (page 62)

8 tablespoons (4 ounces) unsalted butter, cut into pieces

5 tablespoons yuzu kosho

Juice of 2 large lemons, or more as needed

1 cup minced fresh chives

Cook the lobsters: Kill the lobsters, blanch the tail and claws, remove the tail and claw meat, and cut the meat into fork-friendly pieces as directed in Lobster Tagliolini with 'Nduja Bread Crumbs (page 150). You should have 2½ to 3 cups lobster meat.

Prep the corn: Be sure all the silken threads are removed from the shucked corn. Then cut the kernels off the cobs. You should have about 2 cups kernels. Set aside.

Cook the gnocchi sardi: Bring a large pot of water to a boil and add salt until it tastes like well-seasoned broth. Drop in the gnocchi sardi, give them a stir, and cover the pot to quickly return the water to a boil. Uncover or partially cover to maintain the boil and boil the gnocchi until they are tender but still a little chewy when bitten, 4 to 5 minutes.

When the pasta water has nearly come to a boil, in a deep 12-inch sauté pan, melt the butter over medium heat. Add the corn kernels, season lightly with salt, and cook until just tender, 2 to 3 minutes, stirring a couple times. Right after dropping the pasta, add 1 cup of the hot pasta water or saved pasta water (see page 31) to the pan. Bring to a boil over high heat and boil until the liquid thickens slightly, 4 to 5 minutes.

When the pasta is ready, use a spider strainer or slotted spoon to scoop the cooked gnocchi sardi from the water and transfer it straight to the pan. Shake and swirl the pan until the sauce begins to thicken and hug the gnocchi, 2 to 3 minutes (keep the gnocchi moving, adding a little more pasta water if necessary to create a lightly thickened sauce). Add the lobster meat and yuzu kosho and keep tossing just until the lobster is heated through, about 1 minute. Toss in the lemon juice and chives. Taste the sauce. It should be well seasoned at this point, but if you think it needs it, add more salt and lemon juice until it tastes good to you. Remove from the heat and toss until the gnocchi and sauce marry, leaving little to no sauce in the pan.

Using a large spoon, dish out the gnocchi onto warmed plates, creating some volume by building it into a mound and evenly distributing the lobster among the plates.

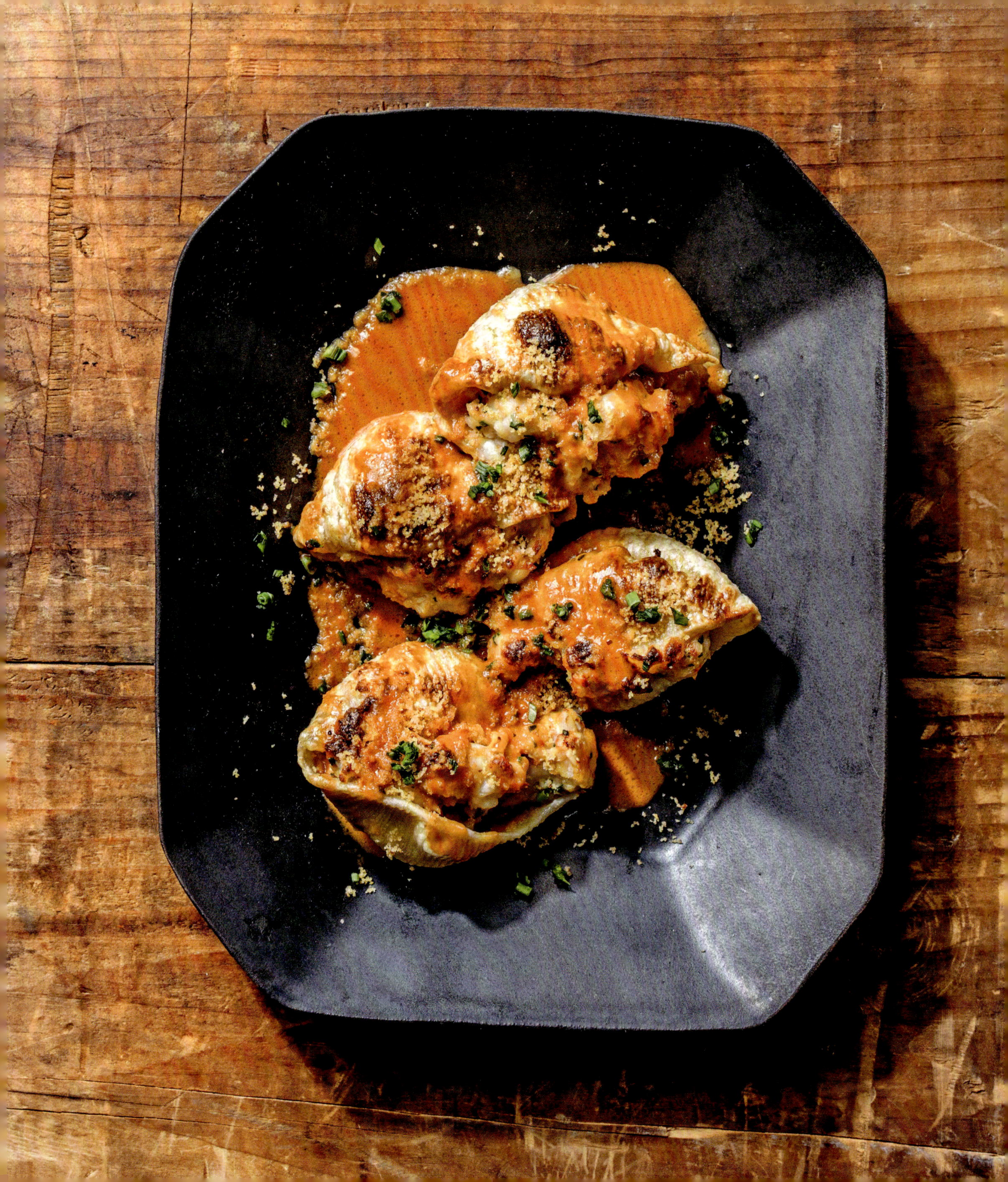

LOBSTER CONCHIGLIE
with sauce américaine

When we brought on chef Matt Rodrigue to help open Fiorella, he kept a notebook of menu ideas. He must have jotted down at least a hundred, and in his words, "maybe three of them were worth pursuing." This was one of them. It's like an ode to lobster. The lobster meat becomes a filling for stuffed baked pasta, and the lobster shells get transformed into a classic, velvety, red sauce on the plate. In his notebook, he'd written, "a cornucopia of lobster." Stuff as much filling as you can into the big conchiglie shells, and the dish literally looks like a cornucopia of lobster! **SERVES 4 TO 6**

Lobster Filling

2 live Maine lobsters (1 to 1½ pounds each)

2 tablespoons extra-virgin olive oil

½ (14.5-ounce) can peeled whole Italian plum tomatoes, preferably San Marzano, with their juice

1 cup dry white wine, such as pinot grigio

6 to 7 peeled and deveined large shrimp (about 2½ ounces)

1 large egg, separated

¼ cup heavy cream

4 ounces fresh buffalo mozzarella, shredded

¼ cup chopped fresh chives, plus more for garnish

Finely grated zest of 2 small lemons

Kosher salt

Make the lobster filling: Kill the lobster, blanch the tail and claws, remove the tail and claw meat, cut the meat into ½-inch pieces, and make reduced stock from the lobster head and body using the 2 tablespoons olive oil, the canned tomatoes and half the juice from the can, and the white wine. See Lobster Tagliolini with 'Nduja Bread Crumbs (page 150) for photos and a detailed description.

In a mini-chopper or small food processor, process the shrimp until smooth, 1 to 2 minutes, scraping down the sides as necessary. Add the egg white and process until fully combined, about 1 minute. Add the cream and process until fully combined, about 1 minute. Transfer the shrimp mousse to a medium bowl and use a rubber spatula to fold in the egg yolk, lobster meat, mozzarella, chives, and lemon zest. Season with salt (about 1 teaspoon). Transfer the lobster filling to an airtight container and refrigerate until needed, up to 8 hours.

Make the sauce Américaine: Add the cream to the reduced lobster stock and simmer until the liquid reduces in volume by about one-quarter (to about 1½ cups), 6 to 8 minutes. Use the sauce Américaine immediately. (Or cover and let stand for up to 1 hour. Or refrigerate in an airtight container for up to 3 days.)

Cook the conchiglie: Set up a large bowl of ice water. Bring a large pot of water to a boil and add salt until it tastes like well-seasoned broth. Drop the conchiglie into the boiling water, give it a stir, and cover the pot to quickly return the water to a boil. Uncover or partially cover to maintain the boil and

RECIPE CONTINUES

Sauce Américaine and Assembly

¼ cup heavy cream

Kosher salt

12 ounces store-bought dried conchiglie (jumbo pasta shells)

Cooking spray

3 tablespoons (1½ ounces) unsalted butter, cut into pieces

Sherry vinegar

Chopped fresh chives, for garnish

boil the pasta, stirring occasionally, until it is tender but still a little chewy when bitten, about 10 minutes. Use a spider strainer or slotted spoon to transfer the cooked conchiglie to the ice water. When cool to the touch, transfer the pasta to kitchen towels, and turn upside down to dry.

Bake the shells: About 40 minutes before you're ready to serve, preheat the oven to 450°F.

Fill the shells generously with the lobster filling and lay them face up on a sheet pan. Coat with cooking spray and transfer to the oven.

Bake until lightly browned and heated through, about 15 minutes. Remove and let cool a minute or two.

Meanwhile, finish the sauce: In a medium saucepan, heat the sauce Américaine over medium heat and whisk in the butter, a tablespoon at a time, until the sauce is smooth and slightly glossy. The consistency should be somewhat thin, like a silky cream sauce with a red hue. Taste it and add salt and sherry vinegar until it tastes good to you.

Spoon a small pool of sauce Américaine onto warmed plates. Arrange a few of the stuffed shells over the sauce and then top with additional sauce. Garnish with chopped fresh chives.

Smoked Potato Culurgiones with Lemon Butter and Chicken Skin Gremolata

At Vetri Cucina, chicken skin gremolata started out as one of those little twists on a classic condiment and has since become a staple in the home kitchens of our cooks. Maybe you'll fall in love with it, too! It's the perfect crispy topping for culurgiones, one of Sardinia's greatest and oldest stuffed pastas. They're traditionally filled with potatoes and served in tomato sauce. Our sous chef, Brian Paragas, put his own flair on the dumplings by smoking the potatoes for the filling. With a simple lemon-butter sauce and the savory, crunchy gremolata, this dish is a great example of how to get creative while respecting and honoring tradition. To watch a video of making this pasta, scan the QR code on page 264. **SERVES 6**

Chicken Skin Gremolata

Skin from ½ (about 5-pound) chicken

Leaves from ½ bunch fresh flat-leaf parsley (about ¾ ounce total), patted dry

Grated zest of 1 lemon

Maldon or other flaky sea salt

Freshly ground black pepper

Smoked Potato Filling

12 ounces Yukon Gold potatoes (about 2 large), scrubbed

1 cup heavy cream

⅓ cup finely grated Parmesan cheese, plus more for garnish

1 large egg yolk

Kosher salt

Make the gremolata: Preheat the oven to 350°F. Line a sheet pan with parchment paper.

Arrange the chicken skin in a single layer on the parchment. Lay another sheet of parchment over the chicken skin and top with ovenproof heavy weights, such as bricks or cast-iron pans, to keep the chicken skin pressed flat. Bake until browned and crispy, 30 to 35 minutes.

Remove from the oven, disassemble everything, and place the chicken skin on paper towels to dry. Top with additional paper towels, blotting the skin dry. Let stand until the skin is cooled and brittle.

Reduce the oven temperature to 150°F, or set a dehydrator to 125°F. Set the parsley and lemon zest on a Silpat (silicone baking mat) on a sheet pan. Bake or dehydrate until the parsley and lemon zest is dry and crispy, 1 to 1½ hours.

Crush the parsley and lemon zest between your fingers into a medium bowl. Crush the crispy chicken skin the same way and mix the gremolata until everything is evenly distributed. Season with Maldon salt and black pepper until it tastes good to you. Use immediately. (Or store in an airtight container at room temperature for up to 3 days.)

RECIPE CONTINUES

Culurgiones

18 ounces Culurgione Dough (page 54), rolled into sheets about 1/16 inch (1.5mm) thick

All-purpose flour, for dusting

Kosher salt

5 tablespoons (2½ ounces) unsalted butter, cut into pieces

Juice of 1 lemon

Freshly ground black pepper

Finely grated Parmesan, for garnish

Scan this code to watch a video of making Smoked Potato Culurgiones.

Smoke the potatoes: Put the unpeeled potatoes in a large saucepan and add cold water to cover by 1 inch. Add 2 big pinches of salt, cover, and bring to a boil over high heat. Uncover and boil the potatoes until very tender, 30 to 35 minutes.

Drain and then return the potatoes to the dry pot. Place the pot over medium heat and dry out the potatoes for about 5 minutes, turning a couple times. Pass the potatoes through the fine holes of a food mill into a medium bowl, discarding the skins.

Set up a smoker for 225°F indirect heat (we use oak and cherry woods but any hardwood will do). Spread out the mashed potatoes into a thin layer on a quarter-sheet pan and place the cream in a heatproof bowl. Place the sheet pan of potatoes and bowl of cream in the smoker and smoke until they get some smoke flavor on them, 20 to 30 minutes.

Make the potato filling: Transfer the potatoes and cream to a medium bowl and add the Parmesan, egg yolk, and a pinch of salt. Whip with a wire whisk until smooth and creamy, just a minute or two. Spoon into a piping bag or zipper-lock bag, seal, and use immediately. (Or refrigerate for up to 1 day.)

Shape the culurgiones: Lay a pasta sheet on a lightly floured work surface. Using a 3-inch round cutter, cut the dough into rounds. Cut off the tip of the piping bag (or one corner if using a zipper-lock bag) to make a ½-inch-diameter hole. Squeeze about 1 tablespoon of the potato filling in a ½-inch-thick line into the center of each round. To shape each culurgione, pick up the round of dough and filling and hold it in one hand like a taco. Rest the bottom of the "taco" on the side of your middle finger and hold the two sides of the taco gently between your thumb and index finger. At the open end of the taco opposite your palm, pinch the dough together near the bottom where the dough curves upward to form the taco shape. Pinch hard so the dough gets thinner, creating a seal.

Now, hold that pinched piece between your thumb and index finger and continue sealing in the filling by sort of "braiding" the dough over the top: To make the "braid," push the dough directly toward the center of the filling just enough to make the taco curve out on each side. From the top, it should look sort of like a pointy bracket—one of these: {. Take the pinched point of dough and press it into one curve of that bracket. Pinch those two pieces of dough together to form a new pinched piece. Then stretch that new thinner piece into the opposite curved part, sealing in the filling. Repeat the previous steps and continue pushing, pinching, stretching, and tucking the dough to opposite sides, working your way to the other end of the taco. When you reach the other end, pinch and twist the dough into a point. It's fine if a little filling squishes out when you're finished; that means the pasta will be nice and plump.

RECIPE CONTINUES

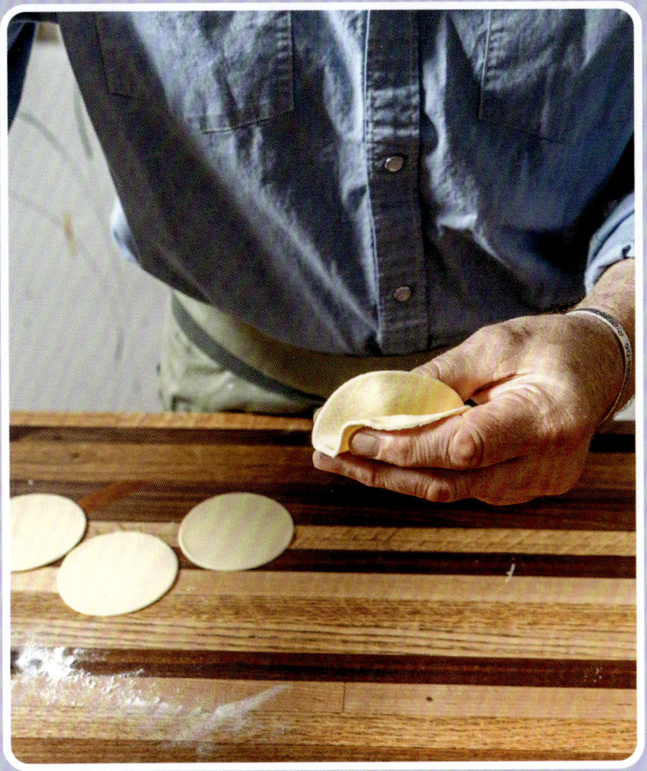
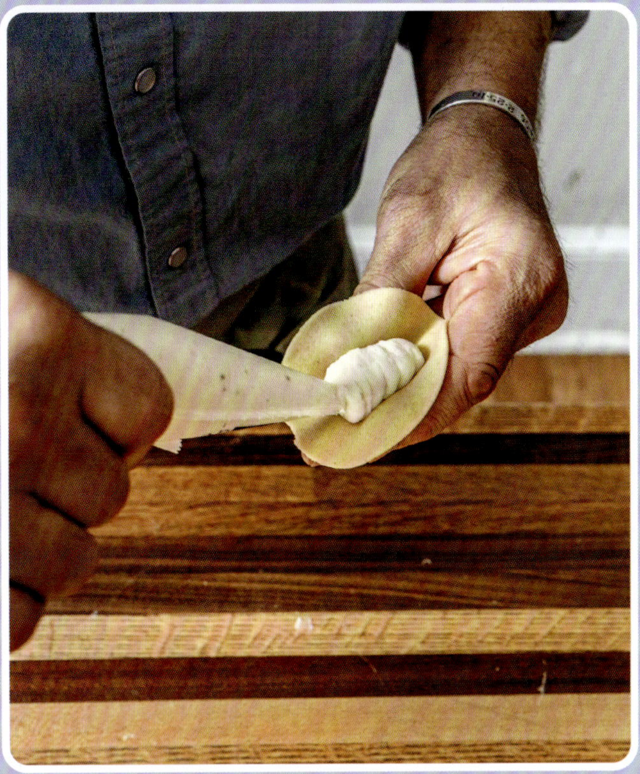
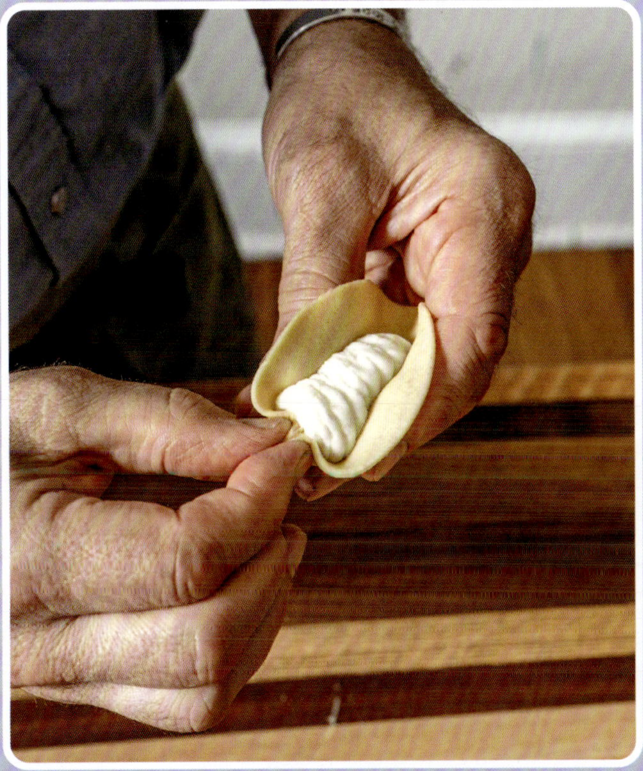
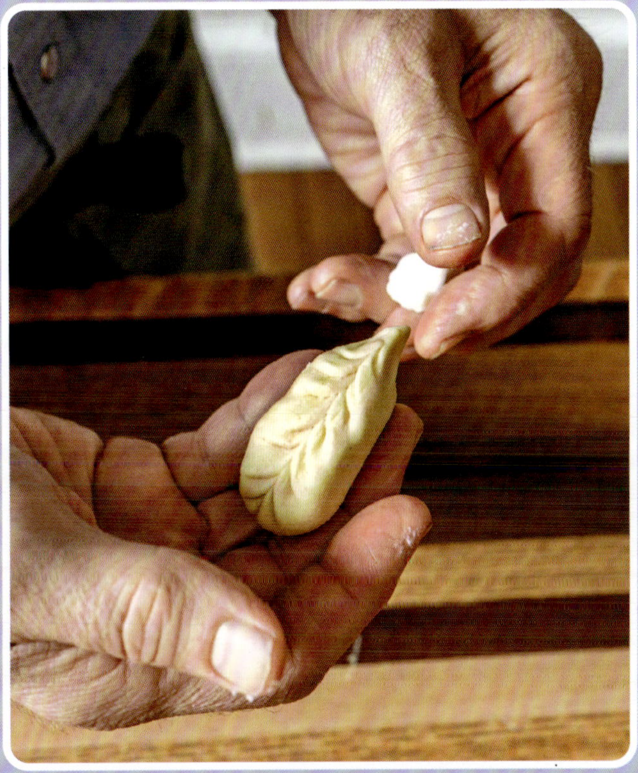

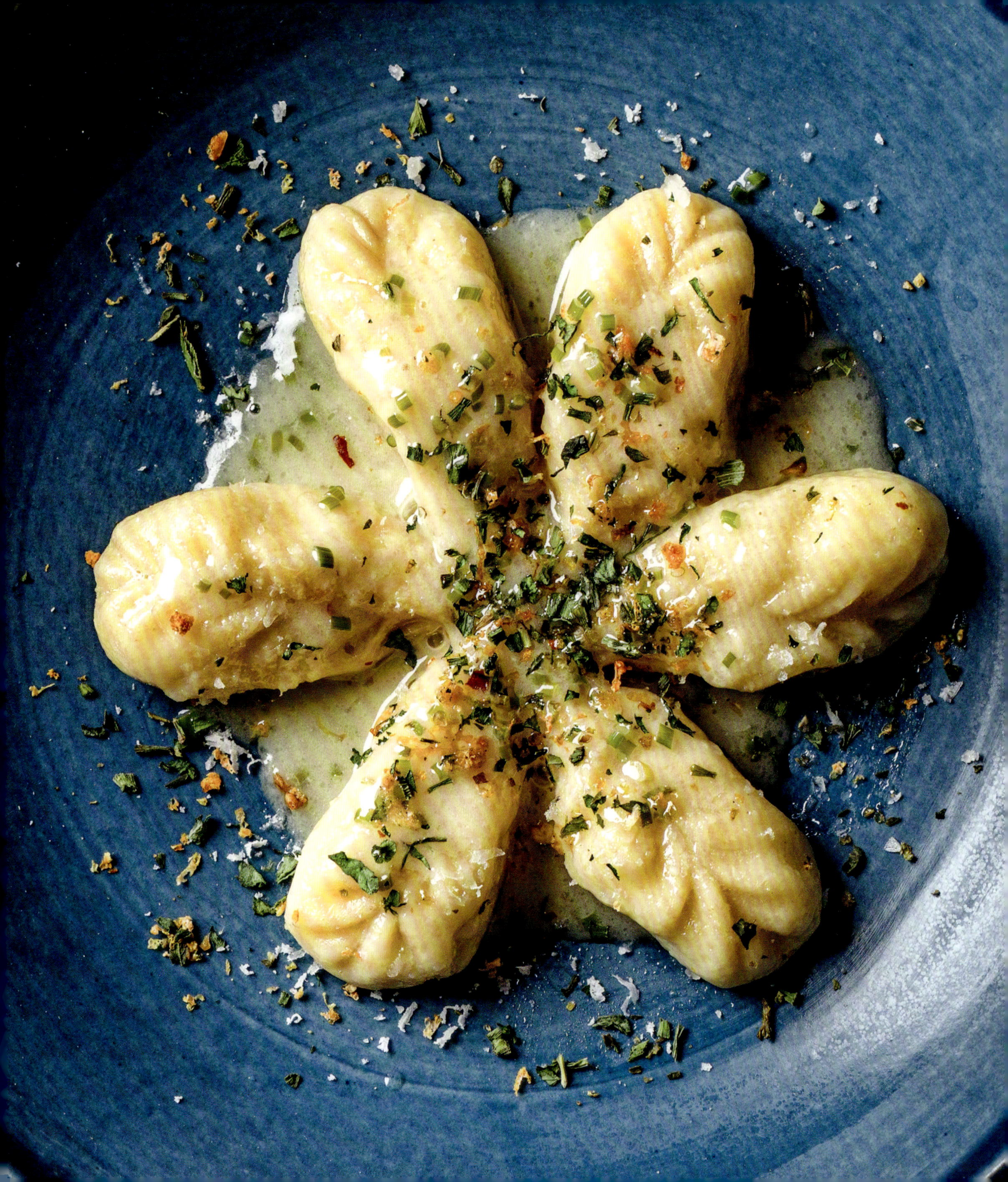

When finished, each filled pasta should have a teardrop shape that is plump and round at the end you started with, pointed at the end you finished with, and the top should look braided. Repeat with the remaining pasta dough and filling. As the culurgiones are formed, transfer them in a single layer to floured sheet pans. You should have about 40 culurgiones.

Cover the culurgiones and use them within 1 hour. (Or refrigerate them for up to 4 hours. You can also freeze them in a single layer until frozen solid, transfer them to zipper-lock bags, and freeze them for up to 3 days. Take the pasta straight from the freezer to the pasta water, adding a minute to the cooking time.)

Cook the culurgiones: Bring a large pot of water to a boil and add salt until it tastes like well-seasoned broth. Working in batches to prevent crowding, drop in the culurgiones and cover the pot to return the water quickly to a low boil. Uncover or partially cover to maintain the boil and boil the culurgiones until they are tender but still a little chewy when bitten, 2 to 3 minutes.

When the pasta water has almost come to a boil, in a deep 12-inch sauté pan, melt the butter over high heat. Right after dropping the culurgiones, add ¾ cup of the hot pasta water or saved pasta water (see page 31) to the pan and simmer until the mixture thickens slightly, about 2 minutes.

When the pasta is ready, use a spider strainer or slotted spoon to scoop the cooked culurgiones from the water and transfer them straight to the pan. Add the lemon juice and shake and swirl the pan until the sauce begins to hug the pasta, about a minute (keep the pasta moving, adding a little more pasta water if necessary to create a lightly thickened sauce). Taste the sauce and season with salt, pepper, and lemon juice until it tastes good to you. Remove from the heat and toss gently until the pasta and sauce marry, leaving a little sauce in the pan.

Spoon some of the sauce on the bottom of warmed plates. Transfer the culurgiones to the plates, arranging them over the sauce in a star pattern. Garnish with Parmesan and a few pinches of the gremolata.

SIMPLIFY IT

Skip the smoking: You could opt to *not* smoke the potatoes and cream. It will still be good! Or if you want to cheat, add ¼ teaspoon liquid smoke to the potato filling along with the cream.

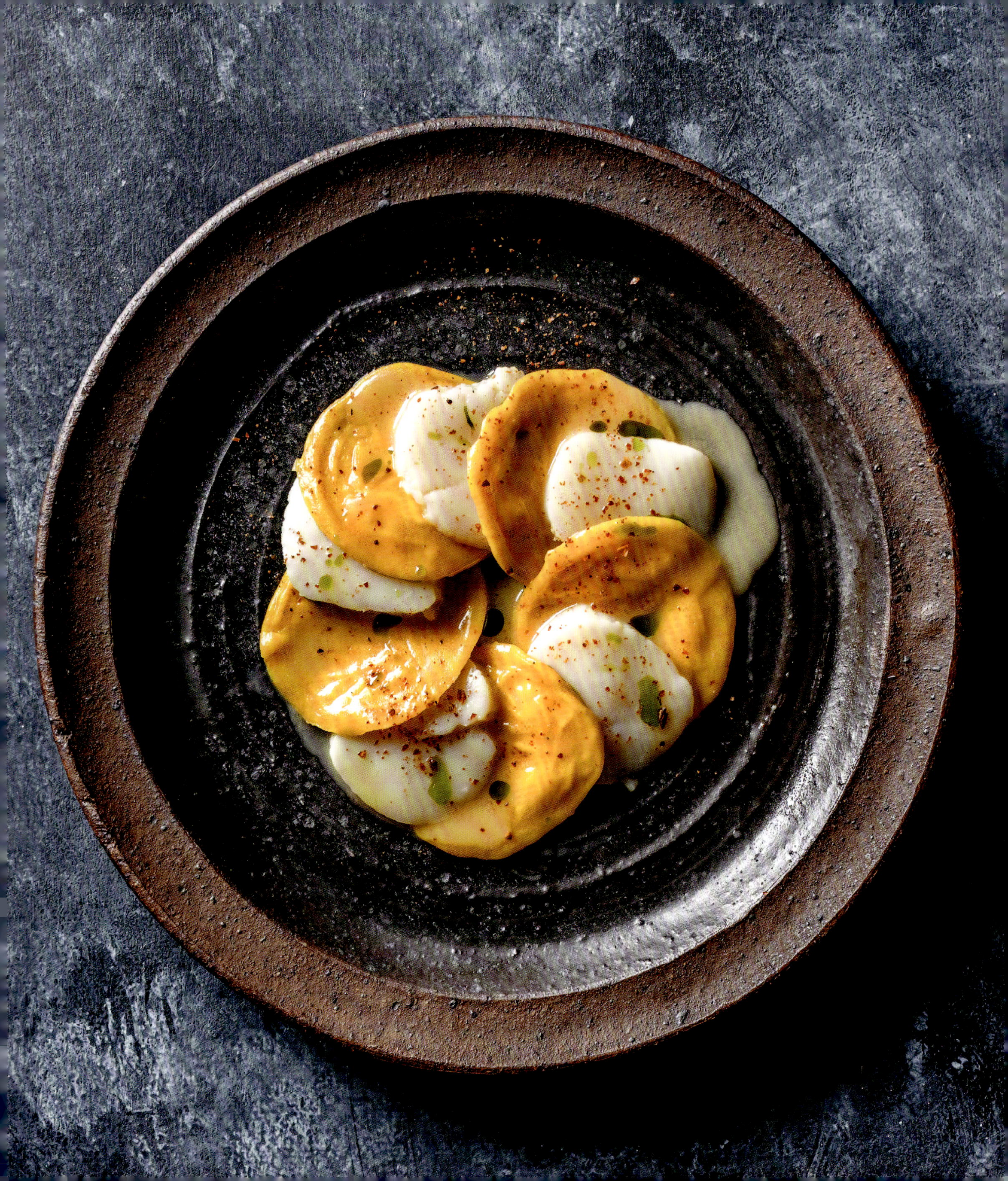

SCALLOP CORZETTI
WITH CLARIFIED POMODORO, TOMATO POWDER, AND BASIL OIL

In the summer of 2019, our pasta cook at Vetri Philly, Marco Gagliardi, was developing a clarified pomodoro sauce and he presented it with fettuccine and burrata. It was okay, but just okay. We kept workshopping the idea and pivoted from fettuccine to saffron corzetti, still with the burrata. That was a little better. Then Jacob Rozenberg said, "What about shingling the rounds of corzetti with thin coins of scallop all together with the pomodoro sauce and some basil oil?" That was the Hee Hee on the Ha Ha! **SERVES 4 TO 6**

Pomodoro and Tomato Powder

2½ pounds heirloom tomatoes, cored and coarsely chopped

½ medium yellow onion, sliced

¼ bunch fresh basil (about ½ cup loosely packed leaves)

2 teaspoons kosher salt

Basil Oil

3 ounces fresh basil leaves (about 5 cups loosely packed)

¾ cup canola oil

Scallops and Corzetti

12 super colossal sea scallops (U10 size; about 1½ pounds total), side muscles removed

½ cup extra-virgin olive oil

Juice of ½ lemon, plus more as needed

Kosher salt

1 pound fresh Saffron Corzetti (page 87)

5 tablespoons (2½ ounces) unsalted butter, cut into pieces

Make the pomodoro: In a large pot, combine the tomatoes, onion, basil, and salt and bring to a simmer over medium-high heat. Cut the heat to medium-low and gently simmer the tomatoes, stirring now and then, until they break down gradually to a saucy consistency, about 2 hours. Line a fine-mesh sieve with cheesecloth and set over a large bowl. Gently spoon the solids into the sieve and let drain in the refrigerator until a clear tomato liquid collects in the bowl, 8 to 12 hours. Keep the clarified pomodoro (tomato water) chilled until needed, up to 1 day. You should have about 1½ cups.

Make the tomato powder: Set your oven or a food dehydrator to 125° to 150°F. Gently lift the cheesecloth of pomodoro solids from the sieve and transfer it to a Silpat (silicone baking mat) set in a sheet pan or a dehydrator tray. Pick out and discard the basil and spread the remaining solids into a thin, even layer. Dehydrate until the solids are bone-dry and brittle, 12 to 15 hours.

Peel the dried "leather" off the baking mat, tear into small pieces, and grind to a powder in a clean coffee grinder, spice mill, or high-powered blender. Store in an airtight container at room temperature (preferably with a small desiccant pack, like the ones you find in vitamin bottles) until needed or up to 1 month. Use tomato powder anywhere you would use tomatoes.

Make the basil oil: Set up a medium bowl of ice water. Bring a medium pot of water to a boil. Plunge the basil leaves in the boiling water, keeping them submerged until bright green, about 30 seconds. Use a spider strainer to transfer the basil to the ice water, keeping it submerged to stop the cooking.

RECIPE CONTINUES

When cool, squeeze the basil over a sink to express excess moisture (squeeze it in your hands or through the spider strainer). Transfer to a blender or food processor along with the canola oil. Puree until super smooth, about 1 minute, scraping down the sides as necessary.

Heat a large sauté pan over high heat. When smoking-hot, add the basil oil and fry it until it turns bright green, about 1 minute. Line a fine-mesh sieve with cheesecloth and set it over a medium bowl. Set the bowl in a large bowl of ice to keep everything cold. Pour the oil into the cheesecloth to strain. The cold bowl will chill the oil rapidly to preserve the color. Cover and refrigerate until needed, up to 1 week. Use the basil oil anywhere you would use basil.

Marinate the scallops: Slice the scallops into coins so you get about 4 coins from each scallop (or fewer if you're working with smaller scallops). Transfer to a bowl, add the olive oil, lemon juice, and 1 teaspoon salt and shake gently to combine, using your fingers to make sure every coin gets evenly coated. Set aside.

Cook the corzetti: Bring a large pot of water to a boil and add salt until it tastes like well-seasoned broth. Drop in the corzetti, give it a stir, and cover the pot to quickly return the water to a boil. Uncover or partially cover to maintain the boil and boil the pasta, stirring occasionally, until it is tender but still a little chewy when bitten, 3 to 4 minutes.

While the pasta water is coming to a boil, in a deep 12-inch sauté pan, combine the butter and about 1½ cups of the clarified pomodoro sauce and bring to a boil. Simmer until the mixture thickens slightly, 2 to 3 minutes.

When the pasta is ready, use a spider strainer or a slotted spoon to scoop the cooked corzetti from the water and transfer the pasta straight to the pan. Shake and swirl the pan until the sauce begins to thicken and hug the pasta, 1 to 2 minutes (keep the pasta moving, adding a little pasta water if necessary to create a lightly thickened sauce). Add the scallop mixture and continue cooking and tossing gently until the scallops are nearly opaque, just a minute or two. Taste and add salt and lemon juice until it tastes good to you. Remove from the heat and toss until the pasta and sauce marry, leaving a little sauce in the pan.

Dish out the pasta onto warmed plates by shingling and alternating the corzetti and scallop coins in a circular pattern. Spoon some of the pan sauce over each serving and garnish with a drizzle of basil oil and a pinch of tomato powder.

Corn Anolini with Buttermilk Espuma and Caviar

During the pandemic, after what seemed like an eternity, indoor dining finally resumed in Philadelphia in September 2021. For that first indoor dinner, we wanted to make a menu that said "Boom! Vetri Cucina is back and fine dining is still here!" It was the height of sweet corn season, and we transformed a simple corn crema ravioli into something special by presenting it with platinum osetra caviar and foamed buttermilk. A beautiful celebration of a seasonal ingredient. For the espuma, you'll need a pressurized cream whipper. Or you could skip the espuma. I suppose you could skip the caviar, too. But then you're missing the point! To watch a video of making this pasta, scan the QR code on page 272. **SERVES 6**

Corn Filling

3 ears fresh sweet corn, shucked

4 tablespoons (2 ounces) unsalted butter, cut into pieces

¼ cup finely grated Parmesan cheese

Kosher salt

1 large egg yolk

Buttermilk Espuma

½ cup buttermilk

½ cup heavy cream

⅛ teaspoon (0.5g) xanthan gum

Make the corn filling: Cut the kernels from the corncobs and scrape the cobs with the blunt side of your knife to extract as much juice as possible. Cut the cobs into 1-inch-thick wheels, place in a medium saucepan, and add 8 cups water to make corncob stock. Bring to a boil over high heat. Cut the heat to low and simmer until the water tastes like corn, about 1 hour. Strain through a fine-mesh sieve and return the stock to the pot. Boil until reduced in volume to 1 cup, about 30 minutes.

When the stock is nearly ready, in a medium saucepan, melt the butter over medium-low heat. Add the corn kernels and sweat, tossing now and then, until the corn is tender but not browned, 10 to 12 minutes.

Pour in the cob stock and bring to a boil over high heat. Reduce the heat to medium-low and simmer until the liquid evaporates and the mixture is lightly thickened like porridge, 15 to 20 minutes. Puree in a blender or food processor with the Parmesan. Taste it and add salt until it tastes good to you (about 1 teaspoon should do it). Blend in the egg yolk. Spoon into a piping bag or zipper-lock bag, seal, and use immediately. (Or seal and refrigerate for up to 1 day.)

Make the buttermilk espuma: In the canister of a cream whipper (such as an iSi), combine the buttermilk, cream, and xanthan gum, swirling to combine the ingredients. Screw on the dispenser lid and charge with one N_2O cartridge. Shake to evenly distribute everything and use immediately. (Or refrigerate for up to 1 day. Bring to room temperature before using.)

RECIPE CONTINUES

Anolini

8 ounces Egg Yolk Dough (page 74), rolled into thin sheets about 1/32 inch (0.8mm) thick

All-purpose flour, for dusting

Kosher salt

6 tablespoons (3 ounces) unsalted butter, cut into pieces

6 tablespoons Prosecco

Freshly ground black pepper

½ cup finely grated Parmesan cheese

¼ cup caviar, preferably osetra or beluga

Make the anolini: Keep a spray bottle of water near your work area. Lay a sheet of pasta on a lightly floured surface. Fold the sheet over itself so it's half as long, then mark the center point with a small knife cut. Unfold the sheet to its full length again and mist the entire sheet lightly with water. Cut off the tip of the piping bag (or one corner if using a zipper-lock bag) to make a ½-inch-diameter hole. Pipe 1¼-inch balls of filling in rows along the length of the sheet stopping at the halfway point and leaving ½ inch of space around each ball. Refold the pasta sheet over the filling, draping it over the balls of filling until you reach the other end. Using your pinky finger, make an indent in the center of each ball of filling to create a dimple in the anolini.

Next, gently press the blunt side of a 1¼-inch cookie cutter or ring mold over each ball of filling to seal the pasta around the filling, without cutting through the pasta. Finally, press the sharp side of a 2-inch cookie cutter or ring mold, preferably fluted, around each ball of filling to cut round anolini that are 2 inches in diameter. Transfer to a lightly floured sheet pan and dust lightly with flour. Repeat with the remaining pasta and filling. You should have 40 to 45 anolini. Use them immediately. (Or cover and refrigerate for up to 2 hours. You can also freeze the anolini in a single layer and then transfer the frozen anolini to zipper-lock bags, seal the bags, and freeze them for up to 3 days. Take the pasta straight from the freezer to the pasta water.)

Cook the anolini: Bring a large pot of water to a boil and add salt until it tastes like well-seasoned broth. Drop in the anolini and cover the pot to quickly return the water to a boil. Uncover or partially cover to maintain the boil and boil the pasta, stirring occasionally, until it is tender but still a little chewy when bitten, about 2½ minutes.

When the pasta water has almost come to a boil, in a deep 12-inch sauté pan, melt the butter over high heat. Add the Prosecco and ½ cup of the hot pasta water or saved pasta water (see page 31). Boil the mixture until it thickens slightly, 3 to 4 minutes.

When the pasta is ready, use a spider strainer or slotted spoon to scoop the cooked anolini from the water and transfer them straight to the pan. Shake and swirl the pan until the sauce begins to hug the pasta, about a minute (keep the pasta moving, adding a little more pasta water if necessary to create a lightly thickened sauce). Taste the sauce and season with salt and pepper until it tastes good to you. Remove from the heat and toss gently until the pasta and sauce marry, leaving just a little sauce in the pan.

Dish out the anolini onto 6 small warmed plates (about 7 anolini per plate), placing the anolini around the perimeter of the plate and leaving a 2-inch-diameter empty space in the center. Sprinkle the Parmesan over the anolini, leaving the center empty. Spoon about ¼ teaspoon caviar into the dimple of each anolini. Just before serving, invert the whipped cream canister and squirt a 2-inch round of buttermilk espuma in the center of each plate.

Scan this code to watch a video of making Corn Anolini.

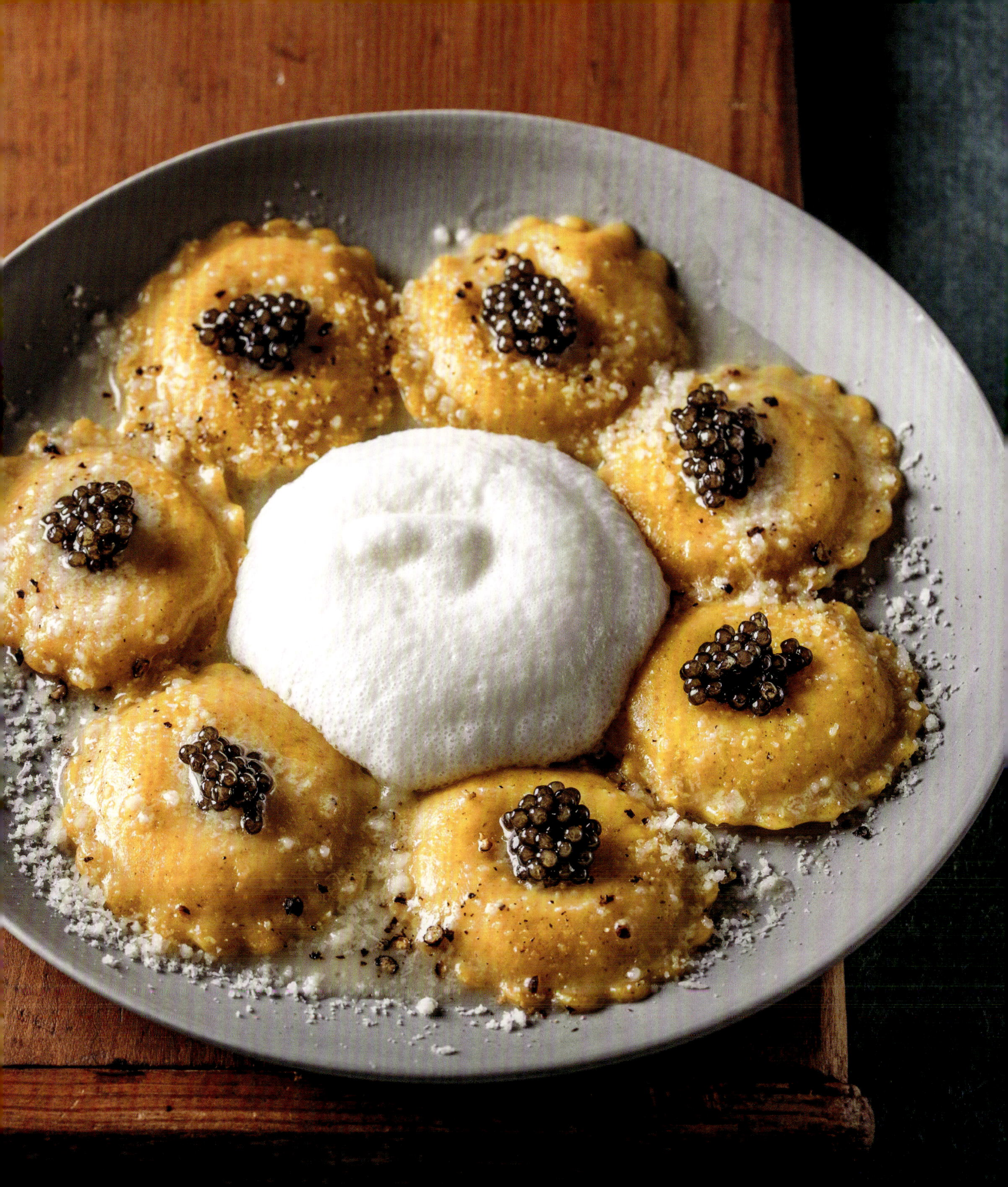

CHESTNUT

This is the first dish that Jacob Rozenberg ever put on a restaurant menu. He was on the pasta station at Osteria Philly and got completely inspired by chestnuts. He doubled down by putting chestnut puree in the filling and chestnut flour in the pasta dough. It's a great feeling when you see one of your inspirations through to completion and it goes on a menu for all the guests to enjoy. That's something we encourage with all our cooks to this day. Oh—and to get the most complex flavor in the honey, let it ferment for at least a week. Two is better. Two months is better still!

SERVES 4 TO 6

Fermented Honey

½ cup raw honey

A generous 3 tablespoons hot tap water

½ teaspoon coriander seeds, toasted

½ × ½-inch piece fresh ginger, peeled and sliced (about ½ teaspoon)

½ teaspoon fresh rosemary leaves

¼ teaspoon whole black peppercorns

Chestnut Filling

¼ cup extra-virgin olive oil

½ medium yellow onion, diced

1 pound peeled steamed chestnuts

1½ cups Chicken Stock (page 294), plus more as needed

½ cup finely grated Parmesan cheese

1 large egg yolk

1½ teaspoons kosher salt

Make the fermented honey: In a sterilized ½-pint glass jar, combine the honey, water, toasted coriander, ginger, rosemary, and peppercorns. Cover securely with cheesecloth and let sit at room temperature for at least 1 week or up to 1 month, stirring every day or two as it sits. The honey will continue to ferment and develop flavor the longer you let it sit. Before using, strain out the solids.

Make the chestnut filling: In a medium saucepan, heat the oil over medium heat. Add the onion and sweat, stirring a few times, until translucent but not browned, 5 to 6 minutes. Add the chestnuts and pour in enough stock to just cover the chestnuts. Bring to a simmer over medium-high heat. Cut the heat so that the stock gently simmers, cover, and cook until the chestnuts are very tender, 25 to 30 minutes.

Puree the mixture with a stick blender or in an upright blender and blend in the Parmesan, egg yolk, and salt. Add a little water if necessary to get the mixture to blend. The filling should have a consistency similar to ricotta cheese. Spoon it into a piping bag or zipper-lock bag, seal, and use within 1 hour. (Or seal and refrigerate for up to 1 day.)

Make the triangoli: Keep a spray bottle of water near your work surface. Lay a pasta sheet on a lightly floured surface and cut the sheet into 2¾-inch squares, preferably with a fluted cutter. (Keep the remaining dough covered as you work.) Mist the dough with water to help keep it from drying out and help create a good seal on the pasta. Cut off the tip of the piping bag (or one corner if using a zipper-lock bag) to make a 1-inch-diameter hole. Pipe about a 1-inch ball of filling into each square.

TRIANGOLI with FERMENTED HONEY, RICOTTA, and BROWN BUTTER

Triangoli

8 ounces Chestnut Dough (page 74), rolled into sheets about 1/32 inch (0.8mm) thick

All-purpose flour, for dusting

Kosher salt

8 tablespoons (4 ounces) unsalted butter, cut into pieces

1 cup ricotta impastata (see page 93), whipped in a food processor

Finely grated Parmesan cheese, for garnish

To shape each triangoli, lift up one corner of the dough and fold it over the opposite corner to make a triangle shape. Gently pat the dough around the filling with your fingertips to press out any air and press a bit more firmly at the edges to seal them. Transfer to a lightly floured sheet pan and dust lightly with flour. Repeat with the remaining dough and filling. You should have about 50 triangoli. Use them within 1 hour. (Or cover and refrigerate them in a single layer on a lightly floured tray for up to 4 hours. You can also freeze them in a single layer, transfer them to a zipper-lock bag, and freeze them for up to 3 days. Take the pasta straight from the freezer to the boiling pasta water, adding about 30 seconds to the cooking time.)

Cook the triangoli: Bring a large pot of water to a boil and add salt until it tastes like well-seasoned broth. Drop in the triangoli, give them a stir, and cover the pot to quickly return the water to a boil. Uncover or partially cover to maintain the boil and boil the pasta, stirring occasionally, until it is tender but still a little chewy when bitten, 3 to 4 minutes.

While the pasta water comes to a boil, in a medium sauté pan, heat the butter over medium heat and brown it until it is the color of hazelnuts, 2 to 4 minutes, swirling the pan for even browning. Watch carefully so that it doesn't burn. Remove from the heat and keep warm.

When the pasta is nearly done, smear a swath of whipped ricotta onto warmed plates. Using a spider strainer or large spoon, drain the triangoli and transfer to the plates, building them into a low mound. Drizzle with a little fermented honey and scatter on some grated Parmesan. Spoon the brown butter over top.

NEXT LEVEL PASTA

Sweet Potato Cappelletti with Granola and Foie Gras Torchon

When fall rolls around, you see squash pasta everywhere. Why? The same reason you see pumpkin spice everywhere. It's a home run! We decided to make things more interesting by swapping squash for sweet potatoes. When we brainstormed other fall sweet-salty flavor combos, granola immediately came to mind. Pasta and granola? Can it be done? We thought so. To bring everything together and add some richness, we gave the finished pasta a shower of foie gras shavings. You can buy the foie gras torchon online from places like Hudson Valley Foie Gras and D'Artagnan. Or you could skip it. In that case, the dish is vegetarian! To watch a video of making this pasta, scan the QR code on page 278. **SERVES 6**

Granola

- ¾ cup rolled oats
- ¼ cup raw almonds, finely chopped
- 3 tablespoons raw hazelnuts, skins removed (if not already) and finely chopped
- 3 tablespoons pumpkin seeds, finely chopped
- ¼ teaspoon crushed red pepper flakes
- Kosher salt
- 1 teaspoon honey

Sweet Potato Cappelletti

- 4 tablespoons (2 ounces) unsalted butter, cut into pieces
- 2 tablespoons extra-virgin olive oil
- ½ medium yellow onion, diced
- 1 pound sweet potatoes, peeled and diced

Make the granola: Preheat the oven to 350°F. Line a sheet pan with parchment paper.

In a medium bowl, combine the oats, almonds, hazelnuts, pumpkin seeds, and pepper flakes. Scatter on a pinch of salt and then gradually and evenly drizzle the honey over everything. Stir to get everything evenly coated in honey. Spread the mixture on the parchment in an even layer.

Bake until light golden brown, 15 to 20 minutes, stirring halfway through the baking. Let the granola cool completely, about 1 hour (the granola will crisp up more as it cools). It probably won't clump, but if it does, break any clumps into smaller pieces and store in an airtight container at room temperature for up to 2 weeks.

Make the sweet potato filling: In a large sauté pan, melt the butter and olive oil over medium heat. Add the onion and sweat, stirring a few times, until translucent but not browned, 4 to 5 minutes. Add the sweet potato and sage and cook, stirring occasionally, until the sweet potato is very soft, 15 to 20 minutes, adjusting the heat if necessary to prevent browning.

Transfer everything to a blender or food processor and puree until smooth like thick mashed potatoes, 1 to 2 minutes, scraping down the sides once or twice. Blend in the Parmesan. Taste the mixture and add salt until it tastes good to you. Blend in the egg yolk. Spoon the mixture into a piping bag or zipper-lock bag, seal, and use within 1 hour. (Or refrigerate for up to 1 day.)

RECIPE CONTINUES

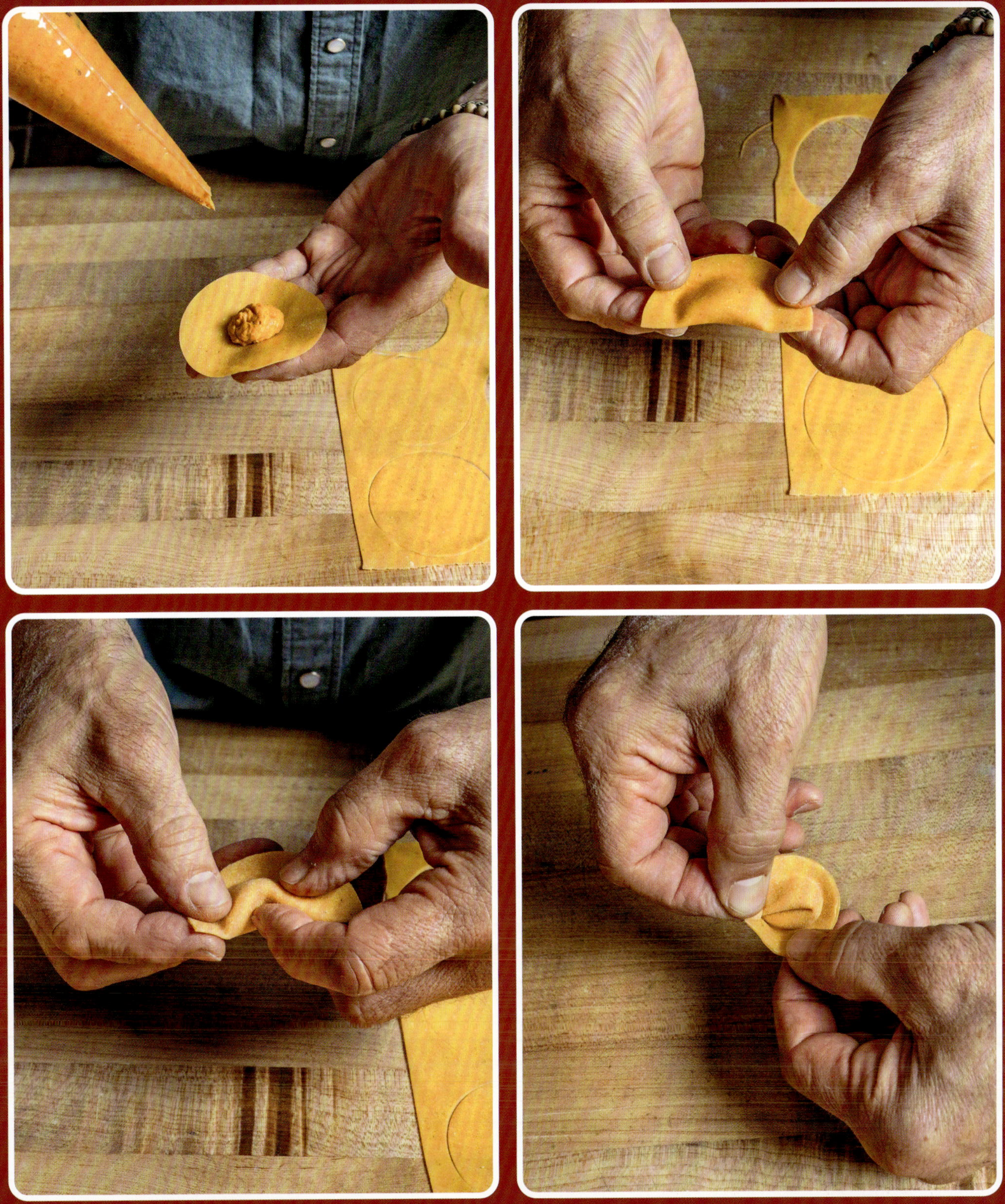

10 medium fresh sage leaves

¼ cup finely grated Parmesan cheese

Kosher salt

1 large egg yolk

Cappelletti and Assembly

1 pound Egg Yolk Dough (page 74), rolled into super-thin sheets about 1/32 inch (0.8mm) thick

All-purpose flour, for dusting

Kosher salt

8 tablespoons (4 ounces) unsalted butter, cut into pieces

Finely grated Parmesan cheese, for garnish

12 fresh sage leaves

4 ounces foie gras torchon, frozen

Scan this code to watch a video of making Sweet Potato Cappelletti.

Form the cappelletti: Keep a spray bottle of water near your work surface. Lay a pasta sheet on a lightly floured work surface and punch out 3-inch rounds with a ring mold or biscuit cutter. Mist the dough with water to help keep it from drying out and help create a good seal on the pasta. Cut off the tip of the piping bag (or one corner if using a zipper-lock bag) to make a ¾-inch-diameter hole. For each cappelletti, pipe a ¾-inch ball in the center of a round of dough. Fold the dough over the filling to make a half-moon shape. Use your fingers to pat the dough around the ball of filling to press out any air pockets.

To finish the shape, grab the two pointed ends of the half-moon, make a dimple in the filling on the straight side of the dough, then wrap the two dough points around the straight side of the filling and pinch them together to make a little hat shape. Transfer to a lightly floured tray and dust lightly with flour. Repeat with the remaining pasta and filling. You should have about 50 cappelletti. Use the cappelletti within 1 hour. (Or cover and refrigerate them in a single layer on a lightly floured tray for up to 4 hours. You can also freeze them in a single layer, transfer them to a zipper-lock bag, and freeze them for up to 3 days. Take the pasta straight from the freezer to the boiling pasta water, adding about 30 seconds to the cooking time.)

Cook the cappelletti: Bring a large pot of water to a boil and add salt until it tastes like well-seasoned broth. Drop in the cappelletti and cover the pot to return the water quickly to a boil. Uncover or partially cover to maintain the boil and boil the cappelletti until they are tender but still a little chewy when bitten, 3 to 4 minutes (about 30 seconds after they begin to float).

While the pasta water comes to a boil, in a medium sauté pan, melt the butter over medium heat. Add the sage and cook until the butter browns and the sage begins to get crispy, 4 to 6 minutes, swirling the pan for even browning. Remove from the heat and season with salt. Just before the pasta is ready, add the granola to the pan and swirl it around until coated in the brown butter.

When the pasta is ready, use a spider strainer or slotted spoon to scoop the cooked cappelletti from the water. Let them drain, then transfer to warmed plates, placing them upright. Grate some Parmesan over the pasta and spoon on the brown butter, distributing the sage and granola evenly among the plates. Partially unwrap the foie gras torchon and use a Microplane to grate some frozen foie over the top. Immediately rewrap and return the foie to the freezer. You'll have some foie left over; enjoy it on toast.

GNOCCHI DI SUSINE
WITH CINNAMON BREAD CRUMB BUTTER

Gnocchi di susine are plum dumplings from Trieste in northeast Italy, bordering on Slovenia. Even though the dough is made with potatoes, the gnocchi taste sort of like a cinnamon bun. They're usually served for dessert. One fall, we had just made some apple butter at Vetri Philly and didn't have any Damson plums, so we used the apple butter as a filling instead. It came out awesome! Kids love this one. To watch a video of making this pasta, scan the QR code on page 280. **SERVES 4**

- 2 pounds russet potatoes (about 4 medium), scrubbed
- Kosher salt
- 1 large egg, beaten
- 2 cups tipo "00" flour or all-purpose flour
- ⅔ cup stiff apple butter
- 16 tablespoons (8 ounces) unsalted butter, cut into pieces
- ½ cup plain dried bread crumbs
- ½ cup sugar
- 2 teaspoons ground cinnamon

Make the gnocchi: In a large saucepan, combine the unpeeled potatoes and cold water to cover by 1 inch. Add about 1 teaspoon salt, cover, and bring to a boil over high heat. Uncover and boil the potatoes until very tender, 20 to 25 minutes.

Remove the potatoes to a cutting board, let cool just enough to handle, and then remove the skins. Coarsely chop the potatoes and pass them through the fine holes of a food mill or potato ricer onto a clean work surface, discarding the skins. Season the potatoes lightly with about 1 teaspoon salt and then drizzle the beaten egg over the surface. Using a bench scraper, chop the potatoes, folding in the egg as you chop until it is evenly incorporated. Add 1 cup of the flour, chopping and folding until the flour is evenly incorporated. Repeat with remaining 1 cup flour. When fully mixed, everything should be evenly incorporated. Use your hands to gather all the stray bits together, kneading them into a cohesive dough. It should have a light and smooth consistency. Cover with plastic wrap and set aside for 30 minutes.

Bring a large pot of water to a boil and add salt until it tastes like well-seasoned broth. Pinch off a small piece of the gnocchi dough and drop it in the boiling water as a test. Cook until the piece of dough floats. Remove, taste, and add salt to the dough if you think it needs it.

Roll the gnocchi dough on a lightly floured surface to a round about ½ inch thick and about 18 inches in diameter. Cut 2½-inch-diameter rounds out of the dough and use your thumb to press a shallow dimple in the center of each round. You can also pinch off individual pieces of the dough and form

RECIPE CONTINUES

them by hand into 2½ × ½-inch thick rounds. For each gnoccho, put a dollop (about a teaspoon) of apple butter in the dimple on each round. Gently close the round of dough around the apple butter, pinching the edges closed and rolling gently between your palms to make an evenly stuffed round gnoccho. Repeat with the remaining dough and apple butter, transferring the gnocchi to a lightly floured sheet pan as they are done. You should have about 28 gnocchi. Use them within 1 hour. (Or cover and refrigerate them in a single layer on a lightly floured tray for up to 4 hours. You can also freeze them in a single layer, transfer them to a zipper-lock bag, and freeze them for up to 2 weeks. Take the pasta straight from the freezer to the boiling pasta water, adding about 30 seconds to the cooking time.)

Cook the gnocchi: While you're shaping the gnocchi, return the large pot of salted water to a boil. Add the gnocchi and cook until they float, 4 to 5 minutes (30 seconds after they start floating).

Just before the gnocchi are ready, in a large sauté pan, melt the butter over medium heat. Add the bread crumbs, sugar, and cinnamon and cook, shaking the pan for even melting, until the sugar melts, 1 to 2 minutes. You don't want this sauce to sit over the heat for too long or it will clump.

As soon as the gnocchi are ready, use a spider strainer to scoop them from the water and transfer them straight to the pan. Shake the pan to evenly bathe the gnocchi in the sauce.

Dish out the gnocchi onto warmed plates along with a generous spoonful of sauce.

Scan this code to watch a video of making Gnocchi di Susine.

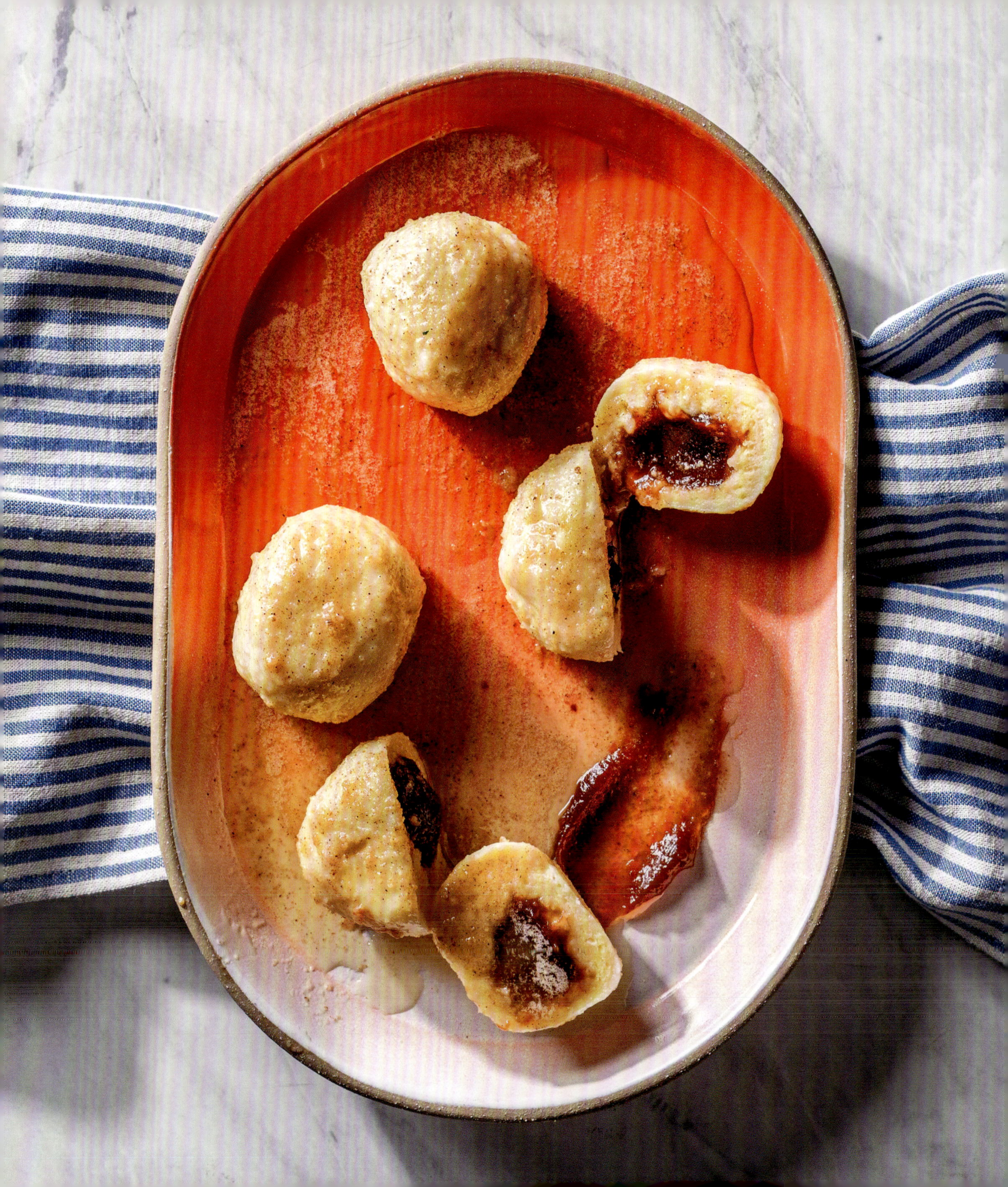

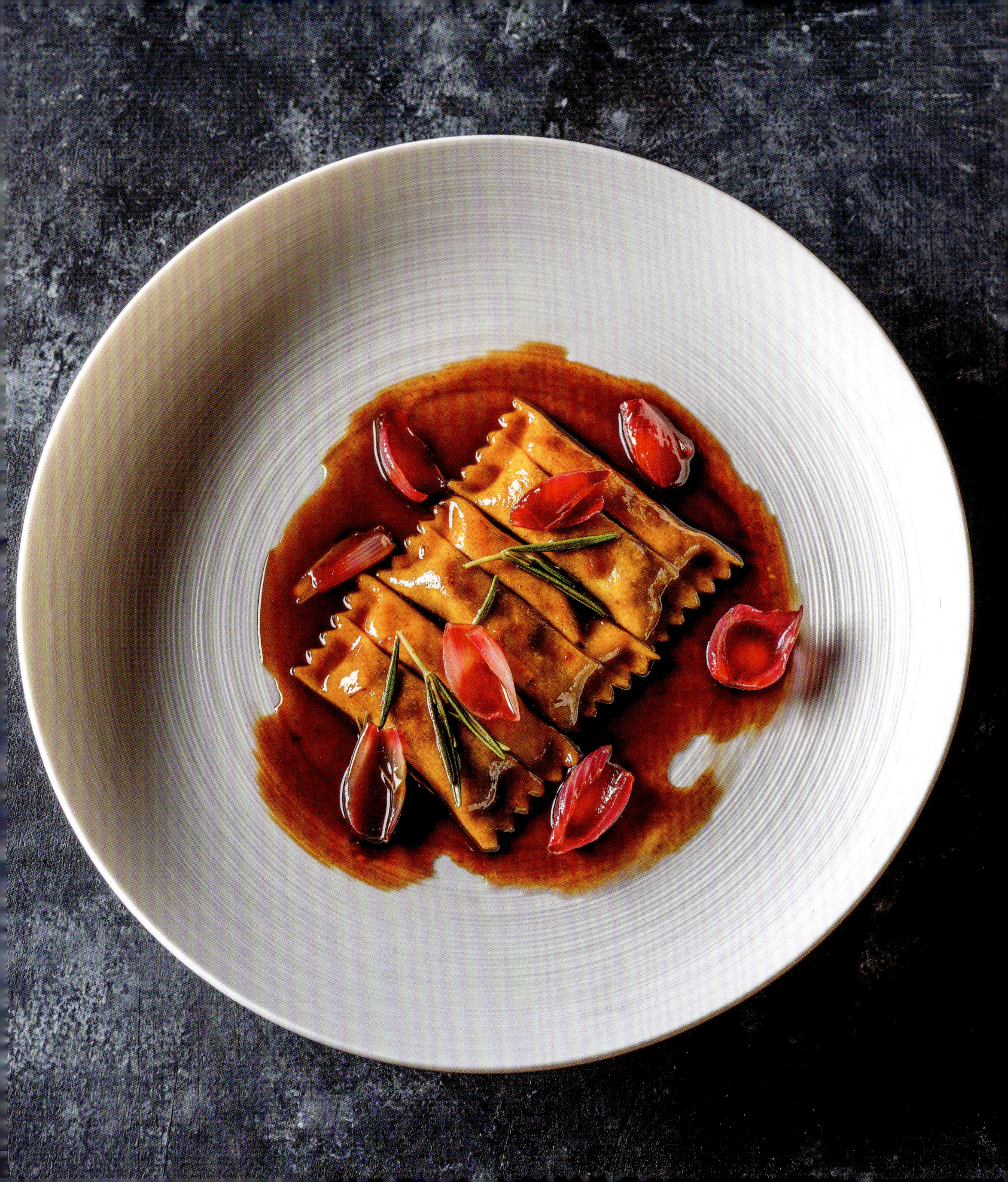

CARROT AND BRISKET DOPPIO RAVIOLI WITH BRISKET JUS AND RED PEARL ONION AGRODOLCE

Jacob Rozenberg and Casey Bayer head up the kitchen at Vetri Philly, and they both grew up in Jewish homes. Here, they take the deep, beefy flavors of Rosh Hashanah brisket braised in red wine with onions and carrots and deliver them in doppio ravioli. A bit of fig vin cotto (fig-vinegar syrup) deepens the flavors even more. One side of the pasta is filled with beefy brisket, the other with brown butter carrot puree. Take a bite of one side, or both—your choice! A simple onion agrodolce (sweet and sour) sauce makes both of the fillings pop in your mouth. You might want to start this one a day ahead and make the fillings in advance to break up the total time it takes. And you'll have some leftover filling. Serve it with polenta. Or, roll out another pound of dough, make more doppio ravioli, and freeze them for later. To watch a video of making this pasta, scan the QR code on page 287. **SERVES 6 TO 8**

Brisket Filling

- 1 (28-ounce) can peeled whole Italian plum tomatoes, preferably San Marzano, with their juice
- 1 small brisket (about 2½ pounds), fat trimmed to ⅛ inch thick
- Kosher salt and freshly ground black pepper
- Tipo "00" or all-purpose flour, for dusting
- 2 tablespoons canola oil
- 1 medium leek, white and light green parts only, cleaned and sliced (about 1 cup)
- 5 scallions, trimmed and chopped (about 1 cup)
- ½ medium fennel bulb, cored, trimmed, and chopped (about 1 cup)
- 4 ounces cremini (Baby Bella) mushrooms, chopped (about 1 cup)

Make the brisket filling: Add the canned tomatoes one by one to a small saucepan by holding a tomato over the pan, pinching and pulling out the core with your fingers (discard the core), and then crushing the tomato into the pan with your other hand. Pour in the tomato juice from the can. Set the pan over medium heat and simmer, stirring now and then to prevent burning, until the tomatoes thicken up a bit and reduce in volume by about one-third, 15 to 20 minutes.

Meanwhile, preheat the oven to 350°F.

Season the brisket all over with salt (about 1½ teaspoons) and dust all over with flour (a tablespoon or so). In a large Dutch oven or ovenproof heavy pan, heat the oil over medium-high heat. When hot, add the brisket and sear until browned all over, 5 to 6 minutes per side. Remove to a plate. Cut the heat to medium and add the leek, scallions, fennel, mushrooms, and garlic and cook until the vegetables are lightly browned, 4 to 6 minutes, scraping the pan bottom now and then to capture the browned bits. Add the cooked tomatoes and simmer until most of the liquid evaporates and the tomatoes darken a bit, 8 to 10 minutes. Add the wine and ¼ cup of the fig vin cotto, and simmer until most of the liquid evaporates, 12 to 15 minutes.

RECIPE CONTINUES

2 large garlic cloves, minced

½ (750ml) bottle dry red wine, such as Chianti (about 1⅔ cups)

½ cup fig vin cotto

3 sprigs fresh thyme

2 sprigs fresh rosemary

1 dried bay leaf

10 whole black peppercorns

1 large garlic clove, smashed

3 to 4 cups reduced Veal Stock (page 295) or store-bought demi-glace

½ cup finely grated Parmesan cheese

1 large egg

Carrot Filling

5 tablespoons (2½ ounces) unsalted butter, cut into pieces

1½ pounds carrots (10 to 12 medium), sliced into ½-inch-thick coins

3 tablespoons finely grated Parmesan cheese

Kosher salt and freshly ground black pepper

1 large egg yolk

Red Pearl Onion Agrodolce

4 ounces small red pearl onions (12 to 15), peeled and halved lengthwise

2 tablespoons Barolo vinegar

2 tablespoons (1 ounce) unsalted butter

1½ tablespoons sugar

¾ teaspoon kosher salt

1 sprig fresh thyme

Tie the thyme, rosemary, bay leaf, peppercorns, and garlic clove in cheesecloth (or a coffee filter) with kitchen twine to make a sachet. Return the brisket to the pan and add enough stock to barely cover the meat. Sink the sachet in the liquid, cover, and transfer to the oven.

Braise until the brisket is fork-tender, 3 to 4 hours. Check the brisket after 2 hours and again at the 3-hour mark, adding additional stock to keep the liquid level at least halfway up the meat. Let cool in the pan until warm.

Pour the pan contents into a medium-mesh sieve set over a bowl to capture the braising liquid. Save the liquid for the sauce. Discard the sachet and pass the meat and vegetables through the small die of a meat grinder (you can also shred the meat and then pulse the meat and vegetables several times in a food processor until very finely minced).

Transfer the ground mixture to the bowl of a stand mixer fitted with the paddle attachment. Add the Parmesan and remaining ¼ cup fig vin cotto. Whip everything on medium speed until blended and the consistency is similar to a thick pâté, about 2 minutes. If necessary, add a little of the braising liquid to reach that consistency. Taste it, adding salt and pepper until it tastes good to you, and then whip in the egg until thoroughly incorporated. Spoon the filling into a piping bag or zipper-lock bag, seal, and refrigerate until needed, up to 1 day.

Spoon off and discard the fat from the surface of the reserved braising liquid. Season the liquid with salt until it tastes good to you and then refrigerate in an airtight container until needed, up to 1 day.

Make the carrot filling: In large sauté pan, melt the butter over medium heat. Add the carrots and sauté, stirring now and then, until they are tender and the butter browns, 25 to 30 minutes.

Transfer the carrots and brown butter to a blender or food processor and add the Parmesan. Puree until smooth, 2 to 3 minutes, scraping down the sides as necessary. Taste the puree and add salt and pepper until it tastes good to you. Blend in the egg yolk. Spoon the filling into a piping bag or zipper-lock bag, seal, and refrigerate until needed, up to 1 day.

Make the agrodolce: In a small saucepan, combine the onions, ⅓ cup water, the vinegar, butter, sugar, salt, and thyme. Bring to a simmer over medium heat and simmer until the onions are tender and the liquid thickens to a thin syrup, 15 to 20 minutes. Remove from the heat and set aside.

Assemble the doppio ravioli: Keep a spray bottle of water near your work surface. Lay a pasta sheet on a lightly floured surface and trim the edges square. Cut the sheet into 4 × 3-inch rectangles and mist the dough with water to help keep it from drying out and help create a good seal on the pasta.

RECIPE CONTINUES

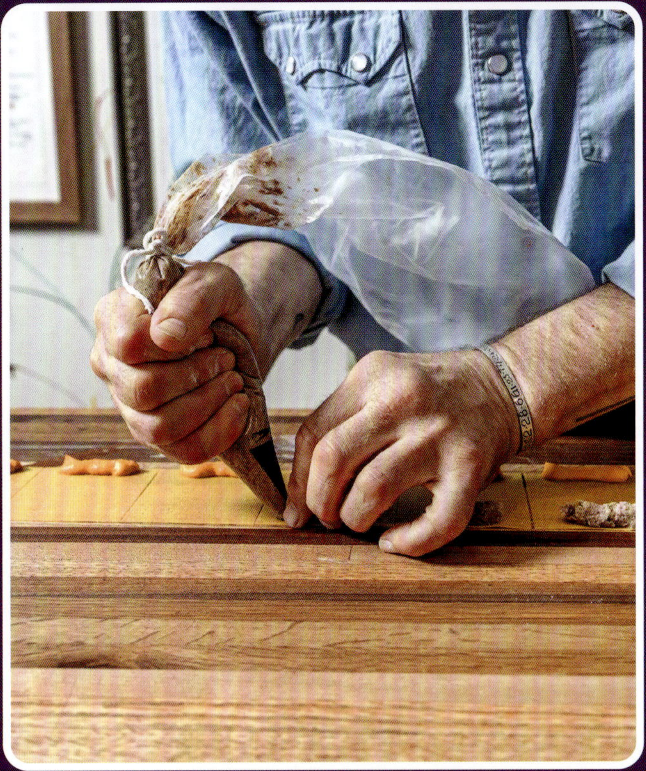
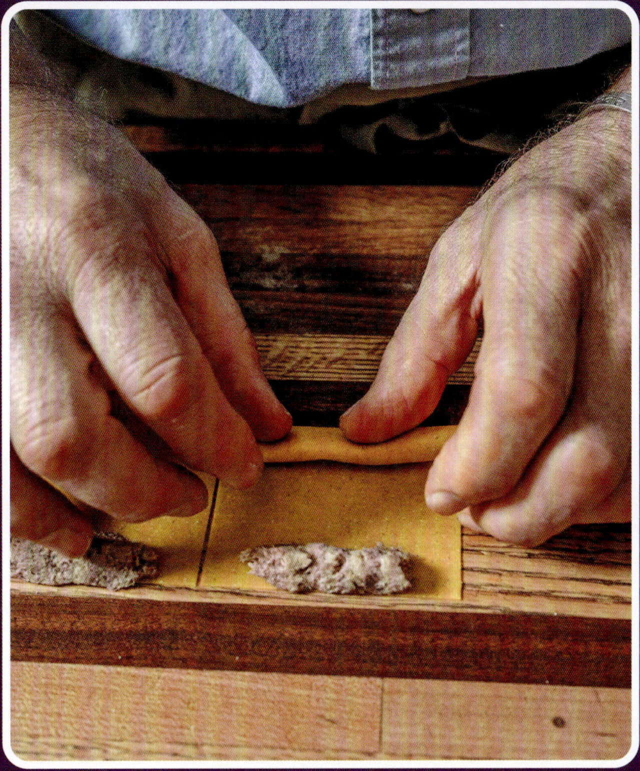
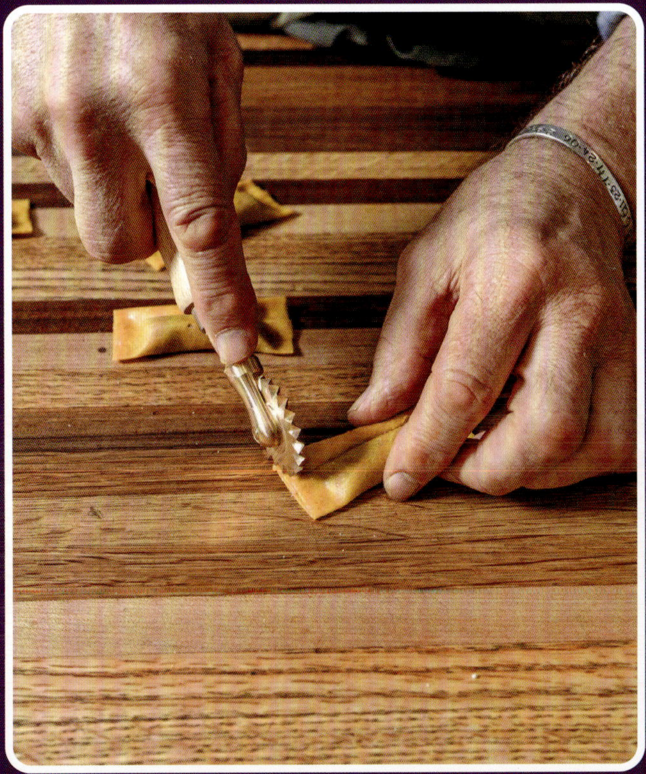
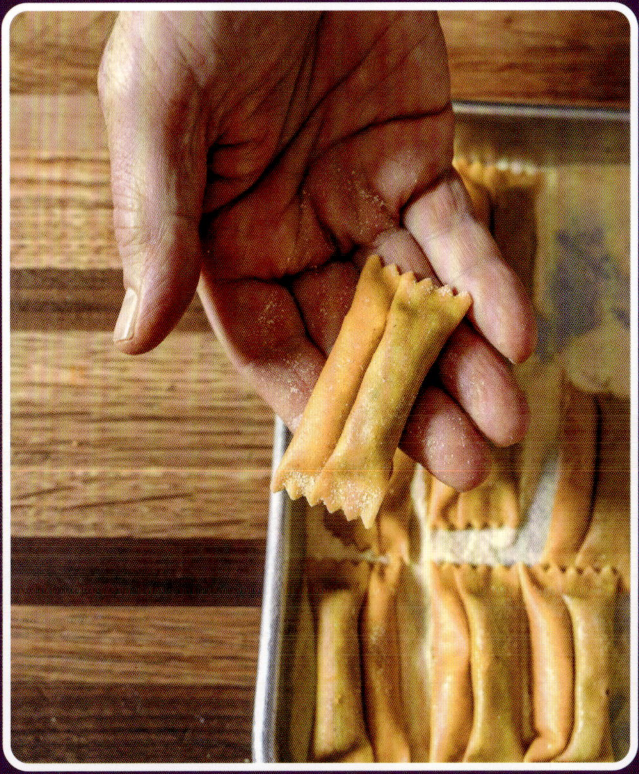

Doppio Ravioli

1 pound Egg Yolk Dough (page 74), rolled into thin sheets about 1/32-inch (0.8mm) thick

All-purpose flour, for dusting

Kosher salt

2 tablespoons bone marrow

1/4 teaspoon Barolo vinegar

Leaves picked from 2 sprigs fresh rosemary

1/4 teaspoon freshly ground black pepper, plus more for garnish

Extra-virgin olive oil, for drizzling

A chunk of Parmesan, for shaving

Cut off the tip of the piping bag (or one corner if using a zipper-lock bag) to make a ½-inch-diameter hole. On each rectangle, pipe each of the fillings along opposite short ends in a line about ½ inch wide by 2 inches long, leaving about ½ inch of space on either side of the fillings. Use a knife to lift one end of the pasta under one of the fillings and then roll and tuck that side of the pasta in tight toward the center, stopping at the center. Repeat with the other end of filling, rolling and tucking the pasta in tight so the pastas meet in the center.

You should be left with two fillings in about a 1 × 3-inch rectangular pasta. Gently pat the dough around the fillings with your fingertips to press out any air and press a bit more firmly at the edges to seal the edges. Trim the edges with a fluted pasta cutter. Transfer to a lightly floured tray and dust lightly with flour. Repeat with the remaining pasta and fillings. You should have 40 to 45 doppio ravioli. Use them within 1 hour. (Or cover and refrigerate them in a single layer on a lightly floured tray for up to 4 hours. You can also freeze them in a single layer, transfer them to a zipper-lock bag, and freeze them for up to 3 days. Take the pasta straight from the freezer to the boiling pasta water, adding about 30 seconds to the cooking time.)

Cook the doppio ravioli: Bring a large pot of water to a boil and add salt until it tastes like well-seasoned broth. Working in batches to avoid overcrowding, drop in the doppio ravioli, give them a gentle stir, and cover the pot to return the water quickly to a low boil. Uncover or partially cover to maintain the boil and boil the ravioli until they are tender but still a little chewy when bitten, 2 to 3 minutes.

While the pasta water comes to a boil, in a deep 12-inch sauté pan, melt the bone marrow over medium-high heat. When melted, add 1½ cups of the reserved braising liquid (if you have less than that, add enough veal stock to equal 1½ cups total volume). Add the Barolo vinegar, rosemary, and pepper and simmer the mixture until it reaches the texture of a medium-thin syrup that will lightly glaze the ravioli, 4 to 6 minutes.

When the pasta is ready, use a spider strainer or slotted spoon to scoop the cooked ravioli from the water and transfer them straight to the pan. Shake and swirl the pan until the sauce begins to glaze the pasta, about a minute (keep the pasta moving, adding a little pasta water if necessary to create a thin glaze on the pasta). Remove from the heat and toss gently until the pasta is nicely glazed, leaving a little sauce in the pan.

Spoon some of the sauce on the bottom of warmed plates. Transfer the doppio ravioli to the plates, arranging them right-side up. Spoon a few onion halves on each plate, drizzling some of the agrodolce liquid and rosemary leaves over the ravioli. Garnish with a drizzle of olive oil, a fresh crack of pepper, and a few shavings of Parmesan.

Scan this code to watch a video of making Carrot and Brisket Doppio Ravioli.

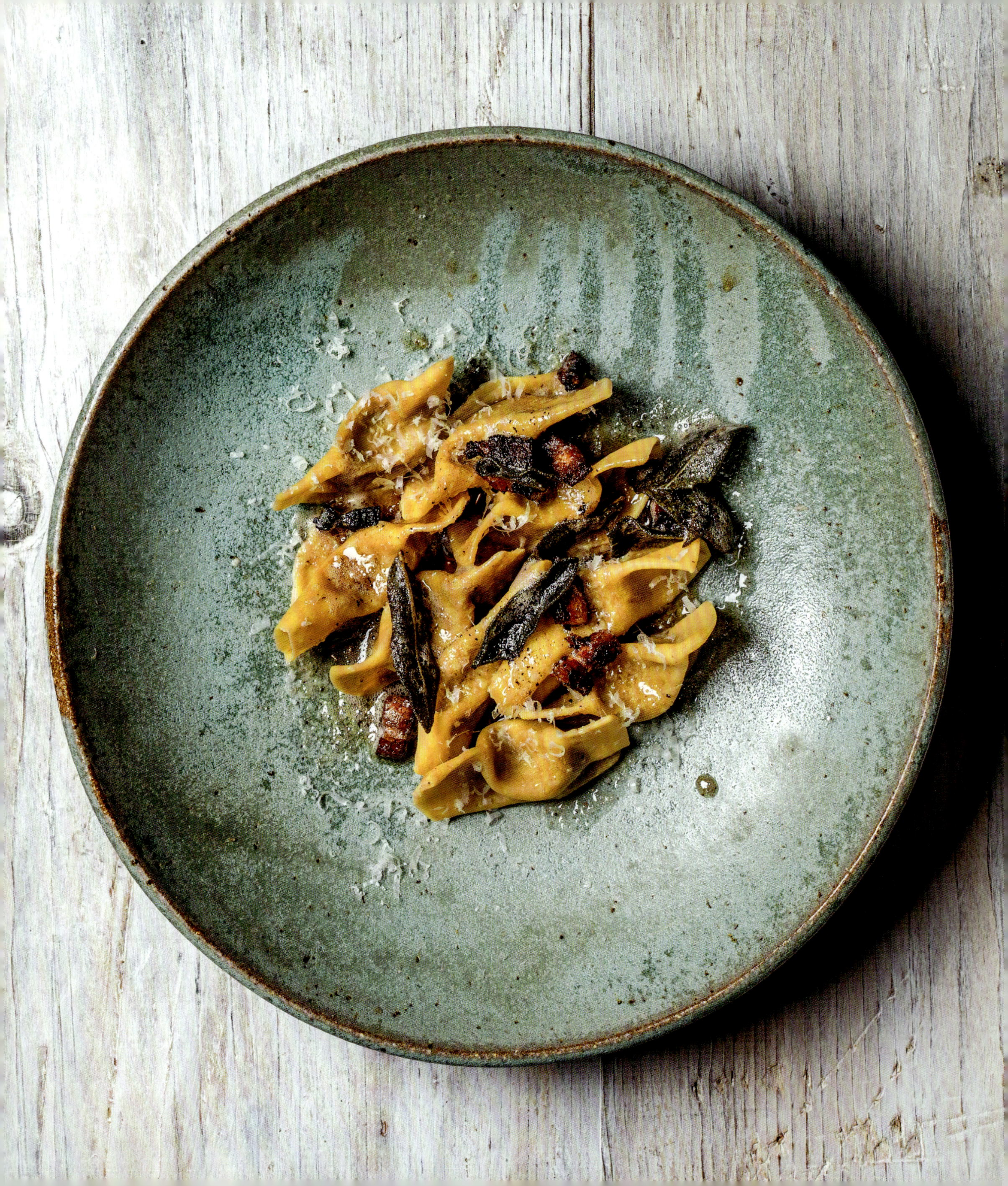

CASONCELLI WITH SAGE AND PANCETTA

This pasta has been the backbone of my restaurants for more than twenty-five years now. It was born in Bergamo out of the need to use every scrap of food in the house. Cooks would braise any and all bits of meat and poultry in red wine with herbs, and then grind it up with whatever cookies and dried fruit they had on hand to bulk it up into a pasta filling. This is the pasta that literally made me say, "I'm home—this is the food I need to learn and cook!" To watch a video of making this pasta, scan the QR code on page 290. **SERVES 4 TO 6**

Casoncelli Filling

- 2 tablespoons grapeseed oil or canola oil
- 10 ounces boneless pork shoulder, cubed or scraps
- 8 ounces boneless beef chuck, cubed or scraps
- 6 ounces boneless, skinless chicken thighs, cubed
- 2 ounces prosciutto, diced
- ½ medium yellow onion, diced (about ½ cup)
- ½ medium carrot, diced (about ⅓ cup)
- ⅛ small fennel bulb, diced (about 2 tablespoons)
- ½ cup dry white wine, such as pinot grigio
- 1 sprig fresh rosemary
- 1 sprig fresh thyme
- 1 garlic clove, smashed

Make the casoncelli filling: Preheat the oven to 325°F.

In a 5-quart Dutch oven, heat the oil over medium-high heat until it shimmers. Working in batches to avoid overcrowding, add the pork, beef, and chicken and sear, turning as needed for even browning, until deeply browned all over, 10 to 15 minutes total per batch. During the last 5 minutes of the last batch, add the chopped prosciutto. Once all the meat is browned, remove it to a bowl.

Cut the heat to medium and add the onion, carrot, and fennel and sweat until the vegetables are translucent and tender, but not too browned, 4 to 5 minutes, scraping the browned bits from the pan bottom. Return the meat and any accumulated juices to the pan and pour in the wine. Simmer until the pan goes dry, 4 to 6 minutes. Meanwhile, tie the rosemary, thyme, garlic, and bay leaf in cheesecloth (or a coffee filter) with kitchen twine to make a sachet.

Add enough stock to the pot to barely cover the meat. Sink the sachet in the liquid, cover the pot, and transfer to the oven.

Braise until the meat is very tender, 3 to 4 hours. Check the meat after 2 hours and again after 3 hours, adding stock as necessary to keep the pan from going dry. Let everything cool in the pan until warm.

Pour the pan contents into a medium-mesh sieve set over a bowl to capture the braising liquid. Save the liquid. Discard the sachet and pass the meat and vegetables through the small die of a meat grinder (you can also pulse the meat and vegetables several times in a food processor until very finely minced). Transfer to a medium bowl and add enough of the braising liquid and/or stock

RECIPE CONTINUES

1 dried bay leaf

2½ to 3 cups Veal Stock (page 295)

½ cup finely grated Parmesan cheese

3 tablespoons finely crushed amaretti cookies (2 to 3 cookies)

2 tablespoons minced golden raisins

Kosher salt and freshly ground black pepper

1 large egg

Casoncelli and Assembly

1 pound Egg Yolk Dough (page 74), rolled into sheets about $\frac{1}{32}$ inch (0.8mm) thick

All-purpose flour, for dusting

Kosher salt

8 tablespoons (4 ounces) unsalted butter, cut into pieces

4 ounces pancetta, cut into short ¼- to ½-inch-thick lardons

18 small fresh sage leaves

Finely grated Parmesan cheese, for garnish

Scan this code to watch a video of making Casoncelli.

to create a consistency similar to a creamy pâté. Stir in the Parmesan, crushed amaretti, and minced raisins until thoroughly incorporated. Taste the filling, adding salt and pepper until it tastes good to you. Then stir in the egg. Spoon the filling into a piping bag or a zipper-lock bag, seal, and refrigerate until needed, up to 1 day.

Assemble the casoncelli: Keep a spray bottle of water near your work surface. Lay a pasta sheet on a lightly floured work surface and trim the edges square. Mist the dough with water to help keep it from drying out and help create a good seal on the pasta. Cut off the tip of the piping bag (or one corner if using a zipper-lock bag) to make a ¾-inch-diameter hole. Pipe ¾-inch balls of filling down the center of both sheets, leaving 1½ to 2 inches of space between the balls. Lift the long edge of a pasta sheet—starting at one end and moving to the other—and fold it over the filling to meet the long edge on the other side. Pat the dough around each ball of filling to press out any air pockets. Using a 2- to 2½-inch round cutter, cut out half-moons by positioning only about half of the cutter over the pasta.

To finish the shape, gently roll the filled pasta from the flat edge onto the round edge of the half-moon. Use your finger to flatten each center slightly, creating a little dimple in the filling, so that the half-moon will stand up on the curved edge. Slightly pinch the pasta on either side of the filling to even out the shape. Transfer to a lightly floured tray and dust lightly with flour. Repeat with the remaining pasta and filling. You should have 50 to 60 casoncelli. Use the casoncelli within 1 hour. (Or cover and refrigerate them in a single layer on a lightly floured tray for up to 4 hours. You can also freeze them in a single layer, transfer them to a zipper-lock bag, and freeze them for up to 3 days. Take the pasta straight from the freezer to the boiling pasta water, adding about 30 seconds to the cooking time.)

Cook the casoncelli: Bring a large pot of water to a boil and add salt until it tastes like well-seasoned broth. Drop in the casoncelli, give them a stir, and cover the pot to return the water quickly to a boil. Uncover or partially cover to maintain the boil and boil the casoncelli until they are tender but still a little chewy when bitten, 3 to 4 minutes (about 30 seconds after they begin to float).

While the pasta water comes to a boil, in a medium sauté pan, melt the butter over medium heat. Add the pancetta and sage and cook, swirling the pan for even browning, until the butter browns and the pancetta and sage begin to get crispy, about 10 minutes, adjusting the heat to prevent burning. Remove from the heat.

When the pasta is ready, use a spider strainer or slotted spoon to scoop the cooked casoncelli from the water. Let them drain, then transfer to warmed plates, placing them upright. Grate some Parmesan over the pasta and spoon on the brown butter, distributing the pancetta and sage evenly among the plates.

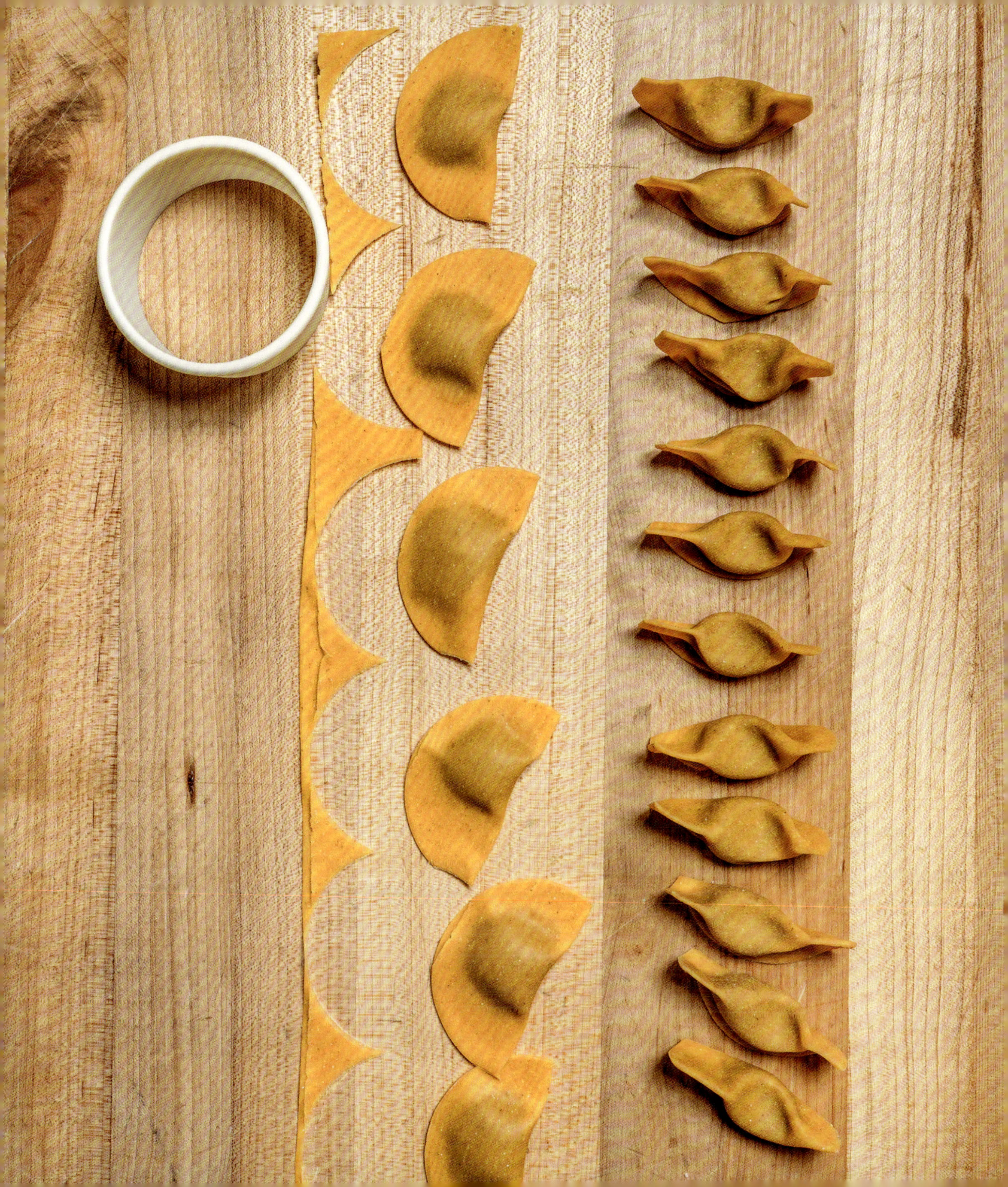

CIALZONS

Here's one of Friuli's older stuffed pastas, originating in the mountains of Carnia. The filling always includes both sweet and savory elements like dried fruit and ricotta, which is traditionally smoked in that region. Cialzons (or cjalsons) are typically served on Christmas Eve or with the Easter meal, and every family has their own recipe. I serve them with a foie gras sauce to amplify the savory element and add richness. Try this one when you want a taste of the Old World. To watch a video of making this pasta, scan the QR code on page 293. **SERVES 4 TO 6**

Ricotta and Fruit Filling

⅔ cup ricotta impastata (see page 93)

3 tablespoons minced dried apricots

3 tablespoons minced dried cranberries

3 tablespoons honey

3 tablespoons grappa

1 teaspoon ground cinnamon

Make the filling: In a small bowl, stir together the ricotta, apricots, cranberries, honey, grappa, and cinnamon until thoroughly combined. Spoon into a piping bag or zipper-lock bag, seal, and use within 1 hour. (Or seal and refrigerate for up to 1 day.)

Assemble the cialzons: Keep a spray bottle of water near your work surface. Lay a pasta sheet on a lightly floured work surface and punch out 3-inch rounds with a ring mold or biscuit cutter. Mist the dough with water to help keep it from drying out and help create a good seal on the pasta. Cut off the tip of the piping bag (or one corner if using a zipper-lock bag) to make a ¾- to 1-inch-diameter hole. For each cialzon, pipe a ¾- to 1-inch ball in the center of a round of dough. Fold the dough over the filling to make a half-moon shape. Use your fingers to pat the dough around the ball of filling to press out any air pockets.

To finish the shape, use your finger to push a dimple into the top side of each cialzon, making it look sort of like a dimpled pierogi. Transfer to a lightly floured tray and dust lightly with flour. Repeat with the remaining pasta and filling. You should have about 40 cialzons. Use the cialzons within 1 hour. (Or cover and refrigerate them in a single layer on a lightly floured tray for up to 4 hours. You can also freeze them in a single layer, transfer them to a zipper-lock bag, and freeze them for up to 3 days. Take the pasta straight from the freezer to the boiling pasta water, adding about 30 seconds to the cooking time.)

with Ricotta, Dried Fruit, and Foie Gras Sauce

Cialzons and Assembly

1 pound Cialzons Dough (page 89), rolled into thin sheets about 1/16 inch (1.5mm) thick

All-purpose flour, for dusting

6 ounces fresh foie gras, cleaned of all veins and finely chopped

4 tablespoons (2 ounces) unsalted butter, at room temperature

Kosher salt

Freshly ground black pepper

½ teaspoon unsweetened cocoa powder, preferably Dutch-process

Start the foie gras sauce: Pass the cleaned and chopped foie gras and the butter through the small holes of a food mill fitted with the fine disk. Transfer the mixture to a medium sauté pan and set aside.

Cook the cialzons: Bring a large pot of water to a boil and add salt until it tastes like well-seasoned broth. Drop in the cialzons, give them a stir, and cover the pot to return the water quickly to a boil. Uncover or partially cover to maintain the boil and boil the cialzons until they are tender but still a little chewy when bitten, 3 to 4 minutes.

As soon as you drop the pasta, remove ¾ cup of the hot pasta water or saved pasta water (see page 31) and let it cool a minute. While whisking constantly but gently, gradually add the pasta water to the sauté pan holding the foie gras and butter. Bring to a bare simmer over low heat, whisking constantly, and whisk until the liquid thickens slightly and becomes creamy, 3 to 4 minutes. The foie gras is temperature-sensitive, so take care to whisk constantly over low heat to keep the sauce from breaking (if it breaks, the fat will separate out). You want a smooth, creamy sauce. Season lightly with salt and pepper until it tastes good to you.

Spoon the foie gras sauce onto warmed plates. When the pasta is ready, use a spider strainer or slotted spoon to scoop the cooked cialzons from the water. Let them drain, then transfer to warmed plates, placing them upright on the sauce. Dust with the cocoa powder through a fine-mesh sieve.

Scan this code to watch a video of making Cialzons.

Chicken Stock with Variations

Never underestimate the power of great stock in your cooking. As a general rule of thumb, for a light stock, or if the bones you're using are on the small side, roast them only until they are lightly browned. For a dark stock or for big bones, roast until the bones are dark brown. And if your end goal is reduced stock (demi-glace), double this stock recipe or check the total yield so it reduces and cooks down to the total volume you're aiming for. Ask your butcher for animal bones, or buy bone-in cuts when you shop and remove the bones at home, saving them up in the freezer to make stock. **MAKES ABOUT 2½ QUARTS**

5 pounds chicken bones

2 tablespoons extra-virgin olive oil

1 medium yellow onion, diced (about 1½ cups)

2 large carrots, diced (about 1½ cups)

3 medium celery stalks, diced (about 1½ cups)

5 sprigs fresh flat-leaf parsley

2 large sprigs fresh rosemary

10 whole black peppercorns

1 garlic clove, peeled

1 dried bay leaf

Preheat the oven to 400°F.

Lay the bones in a single layer in a roasting pan and roast them until they are deeply browned, about 1 hour.

Transfer the browned bones to a stockpot and set the roasting pan over medium heat. Add about 1 cup water to deglaze the pan, scraping up any browned bits on the pan bottom. Scrape the pan contents into the stockpot and add another 4 quarts cold water.

Place the stockpot over medium heat and bring the liquid to just under a simmer. Do not let it boil. If it boils, your stock will be cloudy. Adjust the heat so that a few bubbles occasionally and lazily come to the surface, low to medium-low heat. Cook the stock uncovered for 1 hour, skimming any impurities from the surface now and then.

Meanwhile, in a large sauté pan, heat the oil over medium heat. Add the onion, carrots, and celery and sauté the vegetables, stirring now and then, until they are deeply browned, 8 to 10 minutes.

After the stock has cooked for 1 hour, add the sautéed vegetables. Cook the stock gently for another 6 hours, skimming the surface now and then.

Tie the parsley, rosemary, peppercorns, garlic, and bay leaf in cheesecloth (or a coffee filter) with kitchen twine to make a sachet. Sink the sachet in the stock and cook for another 2 hours, skimming the surface as before. The total cooking time should be about 8 hours.

Remove the pot from the heat. Using tongs, remove the bones, any large vegetable pieces, and the sachet and discard them. Let the stock cool until warm. Line a medium-mesh sieve with cheesecloth and strain the stock through the cheesecloth into 1-quart containers. Label, date, and refrigerate the stock for up to 1 week or freeze it for up to 3 months. Remove the fat from the surface before using.

SIMPLIFY IT

Use store-bought stock with a plus-up: Some of the bouillon concentrates like Better Than Bouillon aren't bad. But store-bought stock is often missing the velvety mouthfeel you get from using animal bones. To get that texture, add gelatin. Stir about ¼ teaspoon unflavored gelatin powder into every 1 cup cold stock. That'll help create a rich, gelatinous texture in your ragùs and other sauces. And if you can't find store-bought versions of the meat stocks called for in the pasta recipes in this book, you can always use chicken stock instead of duck or guinea hen stock and beef stock instead of veal or lamb stock.

LEVEL UP

Reduced Stock: After straining the stock, simmer it over medium heat until it reduces by half. Keep in mind that you may need to double or triple the recipe to get the volume of reduced stock you're aiming for.

Duck Stock: Use duck bones instead of chicken bones. Proceed as directed.

Guinea Hen Stock: Use guinea hen bones in place of chicken bones. Proceed as directed.

Beef Stock: Use beef bones instead of chicken bones and roast them for 1½ to 2 hours. Proceed as directed.

Veal Stock: Use veal bones instead of chicken bones and roast them for 1½ to 2 hours. Proceed as directed.

Lamb Stock: Use lamb bones instead of chicken bones and roast them for 1½ to 2 hours. Proceed as directed.

Pork Stock: Use pork bones instead of chicken bones and roast them for 1½ to 2 hours. Proceed as directed.

ACKNOWLEDGE

...MENTS

FROM MARC VETRI

First and foremost, I must thank my partner in crime David Joachim. I think you know my voice better than I know my own voice. What a viaggio it's been from the very first *Viaggio* book, to *Mastering Pasta*, to this latest book—our sixth! I really believe the world makes better pasta because of us!

Speaking of journeys, Jacob Rozenberg and Matt Rodrigue have been on one with me for many years. Your input and experience gave the narrative on these pages so much more depth and understanding. Seeing the technique through both of your eyes is the Hee Hee on the Ha Ha for this book!

Everyone needs a mama bear, and boy, do we have one in Carolyn Satlow. She pushed, guided, and focused us on the task at hand, as she does every day of my life.

My other partner in crime is Jeff Benjamin. You still do all the shit I don't like to do . . . so I can do all the shit I love . . . like write books about pasta. And I thank you!

Ed Anderson, I wouldn't want to do a cookbook shoot without you, not only because of your great photographs but also because you have that fifth and sixth gear that allows you to just go go go with a smile!

Chris Peterson, these videos are making this book next level . . . or shall I say . . . leveled up! Thanks for the patience and creativity!

The entire Clarkson Potter team has welcomed us with open arms, from the initial meetings with Raquel Pelzel to the baton handoff to Susan Roxborough and Elaine Hennig, to the open lines of communication with Aaron Wehner and Francis Lam. Thanks for being patient with us and pushing us to the finish line!

Big thanks to all of my squads at Vetri Cucina and Fiorella in Philly and Las Vegas for letting us crash the party and get in the way! Especially Michal Shelkowitz and the upstairs pastry team in Philly and Maddy Booth and the Community Kitchen at Vetri Community Partnership.

Last, and most important, to my family, Megan, Maurice, Catherine, and Mario . . . you guys allow me to do what I love to do . . . even though it pains you to keep hearing me talk about pasta! I love you guys more than words!

FROM DAVID JOACHIM

Marc, here's to book #6! You always amaze me with your boundless curiosity, creativity, and skill. Thank you for opening my eyes—yet again—to the infinite beauty of noodles. Huge thanks to the Vetri Family chefs Jacob Rozenberg, Matt Rodrigue, Casey Bayer, and Max Kaklins for your work on the recipes, for technique insights, and for cooking during the photo and video shoots.

While making this book, we got some incredible lessons on rare Sardinian pastas like su filindeu and andarinos di usini from Singaporean noodle savants Yum Hwa Lee and Denise Tsi: Thank you both for showing us what can be achieved with patience and practice. To Maddy Booth, I'm so glad you let us invade the Vetri Community Partnership kitchen for the book photos and videos—and that you're generally a badass. Props to professional cat-herder Carolyn Satlow for keeping the whole Vetri team organized and on schedule as we turned this germ of an idea into a living, breathing cookbook.

Liz Tarpy cross-tested all the recipes here, and they are better for it. Thanks, Liz, for your attention to detail.

If you missed the photo credit, Ed Anderson created the gorgeous photographs gracing these pages. Ed, you are the most humble image wizard I've ever known. You make tricky food photography look like child's play. You're a great whiskey-drinking partner to boot.

Thank you, Chris Petersen, for shooting the technique videos that accompany this book online. It's no small feat capturing the hand motions of intricate pasta shapes on film.

Sally Ekus, you and Lisa have been steadfast partners in this cookbook-making journey for more than twenty-five years. I am indebted to you both for your unwavering guidance, friendship, and pursuit of excellence.

This is the second book I've worked on with Clarkson Potter, and now I know how this publisher turns out such beautiful, engaging cookbooks every year: an amazing team. Thank you to Raquel Pelzel for lighting the torch on this book, Susan Roxborough and Elaine Hennig for carrying it, and Francis Lam and Aaron Wehner for lending a hand when the torch got a little hot. A hat tip to Ian Dingman and Yasmeen Bandoo for lighting up the pages with a bold design.

To my family, Christine, August, and Maddox, you are my everything. Every noodle, every sauce, every word, every thought would be impossible without you.

INDEX

Note: Page references in *italics* indicate recipe photographs.

A

Agnolotti
    Brandade, with Chives, 174–75
    Spring Pea, with Mint and Butter, *134*, 135–37
Almond(s)
    Basil Pesto, 103
    Tortellini with Truffle and Parmesan, *130*, 131–33
Anchovy, Broccoli di Ciccio, and Spring Onion Pesto, Mafaldine with, 145–46, *147*
Andarinos di Usini with Capon Ragù, Pistachios, and Apricots, 190–91
    rolling and shaping, *64*, 64
Anolini, Corn, with Buttermilk Espuma and Caviar, 271–72, *273*
Apples and Sage, Chicken Liver Caramelle with, *192*, 193–96
Apricots
    Capon Ragù, and Pistachios, Andarinos di Usini with, 190–91
    Cialzons with Ricotta, Dried Fruit, and Foie Gras Sauce, 292–93
Arrabbiata, Raschiatelli, with Provolone, *106*, 106–7
Artichokes, Pistachio, and Orange Zest, Trofie with, 100, *101*

B

Basil
    Calamari, and Meyer Lemon, Lorighittas with, *148*, 148–49
    Oil, Clarified Pomodoro, and Tomato Powder, Scallop Corzetti with, *268*, 269–70
    Pesto, 103
    Poppy Seed, and Prosciutto, Spaghetti alla Chitarra with, *214*, 215
Beans
    Mint Fazzoletti with Lamb al Latte Ragù, 231–32, *233*
Béchamel, 247
Beef
    Cannelloni with Oxtail and Cipollini, 244–47
    Carrot and Brisket Doppio Ravioli with Brisket Jus and Red Pearl Onion Agrodolce, *282*, 283–87
    Casoncelli with Sage and Pancetta, *288*, 289–90
    Francobolli with Short Ribs and Celery Root, *248*, 249–51
    Heart Bolognese, Ferricelli with, 234–35
    Shank and Peaches, Busiati Grano Arso with, *236*, 236–38
    Spaghetti alla Chitarra Frutti di Mare with Bone Marrow Sofrito, *158*, 158–60
    Stock, 295
Black peppercorns
    Our Cacio e Pepe, 36, *37*
Bone Marrow Sofrito, Spaghetti alla Chitarra Frutti di Mare with, *158*, 158–60
Brandade Agnolotti with Chives, 174–75
Bread flour
    about, 41–42
    Pici Dough, 82–85, *85*
Broccoli di Ciccio, Anchovy and Spring Onion Pesto, Mafaldine with, 145–46, *147*
Buckwheat Dough, 74
Buckwheat Maltagliati
    with Duck and Espresso Ragù, 184–86, *185*
    rolling and cutting, 81, *81*
Busiati
    Grano Arso with Beef Shank and Peaches, *236*, 236–38
    rolling and shaping, *65*, 65
Buttermilk Espuma and Caviar, Corn Anolini with, 271–72, *273*

C

Cabbage
    Pumpernickel Pappardelle with Duck Ragù, 182–83
Cacio e Pepe, Our, 36, *37*
Calamari
    Meyer Lemon, and Basil, Lorighittas with, *148*, 148–49
    Spaghetti alla Chitarra Frutti di Mare with Bone Marrow Sofrito, *158*, 158–60
Cannelloni
    Crab, with Saffron, *166*, 167–69
    with Oxtail and Cipollini, 244–47
    Capon Ragù, Pistachios, and Apricots, Andarinos di Usini with, 190–91
Cappelletti, Sweet Potato, with Granola and Foie Gras Torchon, 276–78
Caramelle, Chicken Liver, with Apples and Sage, *192*, 193–96
Carrot and Brisket Doppio Ravioli with Brisket Jus and Red Pearl Onion Agrodolce, *282*, 283–87
Casoncelli with Sage and Pancetta, *288*, 289–90
Castelrosso Fonduta and Escargots, Potato Ravioli with, 197–200, *201*
Cauliflower, Clams, and Speck Bread Crumbs, Fusilli with, *256*, 257–58

298

Cavatelli
  Pomodoro, Squash, 129
  Ricotta, with Veal Shank Ragù, 242–43
Cavatelli Dough
  Ricotta, 92–93, *93*
  Squash, 92
Caviar and Buttermilk Espuma, Corn Anolini with, 271–72, *273*
Celery Root and Short Ribs, Francobolli with, *248*, 249–51
Champagne, Scallop Raviolo with, *170*, 171–73
Cheese. *See also* Ricotta
  Almond Tortellini with Truffle and Parmesan, *130*, 131–33
  Eggplant Lasagnetta, *110*, 110–13
  Mushroom Rotolo with Taleggio Fonduta, *114*, 115–17
  Orecchiette with Lamb Merguez and Fiore Sardo, *228*, 229–30
  Our Cacio e Pepe, 36, *37*
  Raschiatelli Arrabbiata with Provolone, *106*, 106–7
  Spinach Gnocchi with Brown Butter and Shaved Ricotta Salata, *122*, 123–25
  Strozzapreti with Radicchio, Walnuts, and Gorgonzola, *98*, 99
Chestnut Dough, 74
Chestnut Fettuccine
  rolling and cutting, 80
  with Wild Boar Ragù, 211–12, *213*
Chestnut Triangoli with Fermented Honey, Ricotta, and Brown Butter, 274–75
Chicken
  Casoncelli with Sage and Pancetta, *288*, 289–90
  Skin Gremolata and Lemon Butter, Smoked Potato, Culurgiones with, 263–67, *266*
  Stock with Variations, 294–95
Chicken Liver
  Caramelle with Apples and Sage, *192*, 193–96
  Ragù, Straw and Hay Tagliolini with, *180*, *180*
  Ragù, Tagliolini with, *180*, 180–81
  Chili Crisp, Ginger, and Shrimp, Troccoli with, 161
Chitarra Dough, 66, 67–69
Chives, Brandade Agnolotti with, 174–75
Cialzons
  Dough, 89, *89*
  with Ricotta, Dried Fruit, and Foie Gras Sauce, 292–93

Cinnamon Bread Crumb Butter, Gnocchi di Susine with, 279–80, *281*
Clams
  Cauliflower, and Speck Bread Crumbs, Fusilli with, *256*, 257–58
  and Charred Lemon Brodo, Paccheri with, *142*, 143–44
  and Tarragon, Pistachio Corzetti with, 164–65
Conchiglie, Lobster, with Sauce Américaine, 261–62, *262*
Corn
  Anolini with Buttermilk Espuma and Caviar, 271–72, *273*
  Lobster, and Yuzu Kosho, Gnocchi Sardi with, 259, *260*
  and Scallions, Garganelli with, *108*, 108–9
Corzetti
  Dough, 86, 87–88
  Dough, Saffron, 87
  Pistachio, with Clams and Tarragon, 164–65
Crab Cannelloni with Saffron, *166*, 167–69
Cranberries
  Cannelloni with Oxtail and Cipollini, 244–47
  Cialzons with Ricotta, Dried Fruit, and Foie Gras Sauce, 292–93
Culurgione(s)
  Dough, 54
  Smoked Potato, with Lemon Butter and Chicken Skin Gremolata, 263–67, *266*

D

Doppio Ravioli, 286–87
Duck
  and Espresso Ragù, Buckwheat Maltagliati, 184–86, *185*
  Ragù, Pumpernickel Pappardelle with, 182–83
  Stock, 295

E

Eggplant Lasagnetta, *110*, 110–13
Egg(s)
  Dough, Half-and-Half, 70–81, *73*

Spaghetti alla Carbonara, 206, 206–7
  Yolk Dough, 74
Escargots and Castelrosso Fonduta, Potato Ravioli with, 197–200, *201*
Espresso and Duck Ragù, Buckwheat Maltagliati, 184–86, *185*

F

Farfalle
  with Guanciale, Peas, and Tarragon, *218*, 218–19
  rolling and cutting, 77, *77*
Fazzoletti, Mint
  with Lamb al Latte Ragù, 231–32, *233*
  rolling and cutting, 79
Ferricelli
  with Beef Heart Bolognese, 234–35
  Masa, with Pork Shank Ragù, 222–23
  rolling and shaping, 60, *60*
Fettuccine, Chestnut
  rolling and cutting, 80
  with Wild Boar Ragù, 211–12, *213*
Flours, 41–42
Foie Gras
  Sauce, Ricotta, and Dried Fruit, Cialzons with, 292–93
  Torchon and Granola, Sweet Potato Cappelletti with, 276–78
Francobolli with Short Ribs and Celery Root, *248*, 249–51
Fusilli with Clams, Cauliflower, and Speck Bread Crumbs, *256*, 257–58

G

Garganelli
  with Corn and Scallions, *108*, 108–9
  rolling and cutting, 78, *78*
Garlic
  Gnocchi Sardi with Monkfish Puttanesca, 162–63
  Roasted, 107
Ginger Chili Crisp and Shrimp, Troccoli with, 161

INDEX 299

Gnocchi
    Fennel Sausage Ricotta, with Zucchini Crema, *220*, 220–21
    Ricotta, with Brown Butter and Fried Leeks, 126–28
    Spinach, with Brown Butter and Shaved Ricotta Salata, *122*, 123–25
    Gnocchi di Susine with Cinnamon Bread Crumb Butter, 279–80, *281*
Gnocchi Sardi
    with Lobster, Corn, and Yuzu Kosho, 259, *260*
    with Monkfish Puttanesca, 162–63
    rolling and shaping, 62, *62*
Grano Arso
    Busiati, with Beef Shank and Peaches, *236*, 236–38
    Dough, 90
Granola and Foie Gras Torchon, Sweet Potato Cappelletti with, 276–78
Guanciale
    Peas, and Tarragon, Farfalle with, *218*, 218–19
    Spaghetti alla Carbonara, *206*, 206–7
Guinea Hen
    Bolognese, Raschiatelli with, *188*, 188–89
    Stock, 295

H

Half-and-Half Egg Dough, 70–81, *73*
Hand-Rolled Dough, 55–65
Hay Dough, 67
Herbs. *See specific herbs*
Honey, Fermented, Ricotta, and Brown Butter, Chestnut Triangoli with, 274–75

L

Lamb
    al Latte Ragù, Mint Fazzoletti with, 231–32, *233*
    Stock, 295
    Tortellini in Brodo, 239–40, *241*

Lamb Merguez and Fiore Sardo, Orecchiette with, *228*, 229–30
Lasagnetta, Eggplant, *110*, 110–13
Leeks, Fried, and Brown Butter, Ricotta Gnocchi with, 126–28
Lemon
    Charred, Brodo and Clams, Paccheri with, *142*, 143–44
    Meyer, Calamari, and Basil, Lorighittas with, *148*, 148–49
Liver
    Chicken, Caramelle with Apples and Sage, *192*, 193–96
    Chicken, Ragù, Straw and Hay Tagliolini with, *180*, 180
    Chicken, Ragù, Tagliolini with, *180*, 180–81
    Fiorella, and Orange Sausage Ragù, Ziti with, 216–17
Lobster
    Conchiglie with Sauce Américaine, 261–62, *262*
    Corn, and Yuzu Kosho, Gnocchi Sardi with, 259, *260*
    Spaghetti alla Chitarra Frutti di Mare with Bone Marrow Sofrito, *158*, 158–60
    Tagliolini with 'Nduja Bread Crumbs, *150*, 150–53
Lorighittas
    with Calamari, Meyer Lemon, and Basil, *148*, 148–49
    rolling and shaping, 63, *63*

M

Mafaldine with Broccoli di Ciccio, Anchovy and Spring Onion Pesto, 145–46, *147*
Maltagliati, Buckwheat
    with Duck and Espresso Ragù, 184–86, *185*
    rolling and cutting, 81, *81*
Mandilli
    with Perfect Basil Pesto, *102*, 103
    rolling and cutting, 75
Mantecare, 32, 257
Masa Dough, 91
Masa Ferricelli with Pork Shank Ragù, 222–23
Mint
    and Butter, Spring Pea Agnolotti with, *134*, 135–37
    Dough, 74

Fazzoletti, rolling and cutting, 79
Fazzoletti with Lamb al Latte Ragù, 231–32, *233*
Monkfish Puttanesca, Gnocchi Sardi with Monkfish, 162–63
Mushroom(s). *See also* Truffle
    Rotolo with Taleggio Fonduta, *114*, 115–17
    Tagliolini with Chicken Liver Ragù, *180*, 180–81
Mussels
    Pimentón Sorpresine with, 154–57, *155*
    Spaghetti alla Chitarra Frutti di Mare with Bone Marrow Sofrito, *158*, 158–60

N

'Nduja Bread Crumbs, Lobster Tagliolini with, *150*, 150–53
Nuts. *See specific nuts*

O

Oats
    Sweet Potato Cappelletti with Granola and Foie Gras Torchon, 276–78
Olives
    Gnocchi Sardi with Monkfish Puttanesca, 162–63
Onion(s)
    Cannelloni with Oxtail and Cipollini, 244–47
    Red Pearl, Agrodolce and Brisket Jus, Carrot and Brisket Doppio Ravioli with, *282*, 283–87
    Spring, Pesto, Broccoli di Ciccio, and Anchovy, Mafaldine with, 145–46, *147*
Orange
    Sausage and Fiorella Liver Ragù, Ziti with, 216–17
    Zest, Pistachio, and Artichokes, Trofie with, 100, *101*
Orecchiette
    with Lamb Merguez and Fiore Sardo, *228*, 229–30
    rolling and shaping, 57, *57*

P

Paccheri with Clams and Charred Lemon Brodo, 142, 143–44
Paglia e fieno (Straw and Hay Tagliolini with Chicken Liver Ragù), 68, 180, 181
Pancetta and Sage, Casoncelli with, 288, 289–90
Pappardelle
    Pumpernickel, rolling and cutting, 80, 80
    Pumpernickel, with Duck Ragù, 182–83
    Zucchini-Stuffed, with Squash Blossoms and Basil, 118, 119–21
Pasta. See also Pasta (fresh); specific pasta names
    cooking instructions, 29–31
    cooking water, saving, 31
    dried, buying, 32–34
    flavor combinations, 18
    garnishing and serving, 35
    mantecare, 32
    marrying with sauce, 32–33
    pairing shapes with sauces, 21–23
    ten commandments of, 19
Pasta (fresh), 40–53
    buying, 28
    Chitarra Dough, 66, 67–69
    Cialzons Dough, 89, 89
    Corzetti Dough, 86, 87–88
    Doppio Ravioli, 286–87
    flour for, 41–42
    Grano Arso Dough, 90
    Half-and-Half Egg Dough, 70–81, 73
    Hand-Rolled Dough, 55–65
    Masa Dough, 91
    mixing the dough, 42–45
    Pici Dough, 82–85, 85
    preparing, tips for, 27–28
    resting the dough, 45
    Ricotta Cavatelli Dough, 92–93, 93
    rolling and shaping, 47–53
    rolling with a machine, 50
    shaped, storing, 53
    substituting dried pasta for, 28
    thickness guidelines, 52–53
Pasta tools, 46
Peaches and Beef Shank, Busiati Grano Arso with, 236, 236–38
Pea(s)
    Guanciale, and Tarragon, Farfalle with, 218, 218–19
    Spring, Agnolotti with Mint and Butter, 134, 135–37
Peppers
    Lobster Tagliolini with 'Nduja Bread Crumbs, 150, 150–53
    Raschiatelli Arrabbiata with Provolone, 106, 106–7
Pesto, Basil, 103
Pici
    Dough, 82–85, 85
    Pomodoro, 104, 104–5
    rolling and shaping, 84
Pimentón Dough, 74
Pimentón Sorpresine
    with Mussels, 154–57, 155
    rolling and cutting, 79, 79
Pistachio(s)
    Artichokes, and Orange Zest, Trofie with, 100, 101
    Capon Ragù, and Apricots, Andarinos di Usini with, 190–91
    Corzetti with Clams and Tarragon, 164–65
Poppy Seed, Basil, and Prosciutto, Spaghetti alla Chitarra with, 214, 215
Pork. See also Guanciale; Sausage
    Casoncelli with Sage and Pancetta, 288, 289–90
    Fusilli with Clams, Cauliflower, and Speck Bread Crumbs, 256, 257–58
    Raschiatelli with Guinea Hen Bolognese, 188, 188–89
    Shank Ragù, Masa Ferricelli with, 222–23
    Spaghetti alla Chitarra with Basil, Poppy Seed, and Prosciutto, 214, 215
    Stock, 295
Potato(es)
    Brandade Agnolotti with Chives, 174–75
    Cialzons Dough, 89, 89
    Gnocchi di Susine with Cinnamon Bread Crumb Butter, 279–80, 281
    Ravioli with Escargots and Castelrosso Fonduta, 197–200, 201
    Smoked, Culurgiones with Lemon Butter and Chicken Skin Gremolata, 263–67, 266
    Sweet, Cappelletti with Granola and Foie Gras Torchon, 276–78
Prosciutto, Basil, and Poppy Seed, Spaghetti alla Chitarra with, 214, 215
Pumpernickel Pappardelle
    with Duck Ragù, 182–83
    rolling and cutting, 80, 80

R

Rabbit Bolognese, Tajarin with, 187
Radicchio, Walnuts, and Gorgonzola, Strozzapreti with, 98, 99
Raschiatelli
    Arrabbiata with Provolone, 106, 106–7
    with Guinea Hen Bolognese, 188, 188–89
    rolling and shaping, 61, 61
Ravioli
    Doppio, 286–87
    Potato, with Escargots and Castelrosso Fonduta, 197–200, 201
Raviolo, Scallop, with Champagne, 170, 171–73
Reduced Stock, 295
Rice
    Almond Tortellini with Truffle and Parmesan, 130, 131–33
Ricotta
    Cavatelli Dough, 92–93, 93
    Cavatelli with Veal Shank Ragù, 242–43
    Dried Fruit, and Foie Gras Sauce, Cialzons with, 292–93
    Eggplant Lasagnetta, 110, 110–13
    Fennel Sausage Gnocchi with Zucchini Crema, 220, 220–21
    Fermented Honey, and Brown Butter, Chestnut Triangoli with, 274–75
    Gnocchi with Brown Butter and Fried Leeks, 126–28
    impastata, about, 93
Rigatoni with Fiorella Sausage Ragù, 208–10, 209
Rotolo, Mushroom, with Taleggio Fonduta, 114, 115–17
Rye Dough, 74

S

Saffron
    Corzetti Dough, 87
    Crab Cannelloni with, 166, 167–69
    Dough, 74
Sage
    and Apples, Chicken Liver Caramelle with, 192, 193–96
    and Pancetta, Casoncelli with, 288, 289–90

Salt cod
  Brandade Agnolotti with Chives, 174–75
Sausage
  Fennel, Ricotta Gnocchi with Zucchini Crema, 220, 220–21
  Lobster Tagliolini with 'Nduja Bread Crumbs, 150, 150–53
  Orange, and Fiorella Liver Ragù, Ziti with, 216–17
  Ragù, Fiorella, Rigatoni with, 208–10, 209
Sausage, lamb. See Lamb Merguez
Scallions and Corn, Garganelli with, 108, 108–9
Scallop(s)
  Corzetti with Clarified Pomodoro, Tomato Powder, and Basil Oil, 268, 269–70
  Raviolo with Champagne, 170, 171–73
  Spaghetti alla Chitarra Frutti di Mare with Bone Marrow Sofrito, 158, 158–60
Seafood
  Brandade Agnolotti with Chives, 174–75
  Crab Cannelloni with Saffron, 166, 167–69
  Fusilli with Clams, Cauliflower, and Speck Bread Crumbs, 256, 257–58
  Gnocchi Sardi with Lobster, Corn, and Yuzu Kosho, 259, 260
  Gnocchi Sardi with Monkfish Puttanesca, 162–63
  Lobster Conchiglie with Sauce Américaine, 261–62, 262
  Lobster Tagliolini with 'Nduja Bread Crumbs, 150, 150–53
  Lorighittas with Calamari, Meyer Lemon, and Basil, 148, 148–49
  Mafaldine with Broccoli di Ciccio, Anchovy and Spring Onion Pesto, 145–46, 147
  Paccheri with Clams and Charred Lemon Brodo, 142, 143–44
  Pimentón Sorpresine with Mussels, 154–57, 155
  Pistachio Corzetti with Clams and Tarragon, 164–65
  Potato Ravioli with Escargots and Castelrosso Fonduta, 197–200, 201
  Scallop Corzetti with Clarified Pomodoro, Tomato Powder, and Basil Oil, 268, 269–70
  Scallop Raviolo with Champagne, 170, 171–73
  Spaghetti alla Chitarra Frutti di Mare with Bone Marrow Sofrito, 158, 158–60

Troccoli with Shrimp and Ginger Chili Crisp, 161
Semolina flour
  about, 42
  Chitarra Dough, 66, 67–69
  Grano Arso Dough, 90
  Half-and-Half Egg Dough, 70–81, 73
  Hand-Rolled Dough, 55–65
  Masa Dough, 91
Shrimp
  and Ginger Chili Crisp, Troccoli with, 161
  Lobster Conchiglie with Sauce Américaine, 261–62, 262
Sorpresine, Pimentón
  with Mussels, 154–57, 155
  rolling and cutting, 79, 79
Spaghetti
  alla Carbonara, 206, 206–7
  Our Cacio e Pepe, 36, 37
Spaghetti alla Chitarra
  with Basil, Poppy Seed, and Prosciutto, 214, 215
  Frutti di Mare with Bone Marrow Sofrito, 158, 158–60
  rolling and cutting, 69, 69
Speck Bread Crumbs, Clams, and Cauliflower, Fusilli with, 256, 257–58
Spinach
  Gnocchi with Brown Butter and Shaved Ricotta Salata, 122, 123–25
  Hay Dough, 67
Spring Onion Pesto, Broccoli di Ciccio, and Anchovy, Mafaldine with, 145–46, 147
Squash
  Blossoms and Basil, Zucchini-Stuffed Pappardelle with, 118, 119–21
  Cavatelli Dough, 92
  Cavatelli Pomodoro, 129
  Fennel Sausage Ricotta Gnocchi with Zucchini Crema, 220, 220–21
Stock, Chicken, with Variations, 294–95
Straw and Hay Tagliolini or Chitarra
  with Chicken Liver Ragù, 180, 180
  rolling and cutting, 68
Strozzapreti with Radicchio, Walnuts, and Gorgonzola, 98, 99
Sweet Potato Cappelletti with Granola and Foie Gras Torchon, 276–78

T

Tagliatelle, rolling and cutting, 76, 76
Tagliolini
  with Chicken Liver Ragù, 180, 180–81
  Chitarra Dough, rolling and cutting, 68
  Lobster, with 'Nduja Bread Crumbs, 150, 150–53
  or Chitarra, Straw and Hay, rolling and cutting, 68
  rolling and cutting, 75
  Straw and Hay, with Chicken Liver Ragù, 180, 180
Tajarin
  with Rabbit Bolognese, 187
  rolling and cutting, 76, 76
Tarragon
  and Clams, Pistachio Corzetti with, 164–65
  Guanciale, and Peas, Farfalle with, 218, 218–19
Tipo "00" flour
  about, 41
  Cialzons Dough, 89, 89
  Corzetti Dough, 86, 87–88
  Grano Arso Dough, 90
  Half-and-Half Egg Dough, 70–81, 73
  Ricotta Cavatelli Dough, 92–93, 93
Tomato(es)
  Eggplant Lasagnetta, 110, 110–13
  Ferricelli with Beef Heart Bolognese, 234–35
  Gnocchi Sardi with Monkfish Puttanesca, 162–63
  Orecchiette with Lamb Merguez and Fiore Sardo, 228, 229–30
  Pici Pomodoro, 104, 104–5
  Powder, Clarified Pomodoro, and Basil Oil, Scallop Corzetti with, 268, 269–70
  Rigatoni with Fiorella Sausage Ragù, 208–10, 209
  Squash Cavatelli Pomodoro, 129
Tools, 46
Tortellini
  Almond, with Truffle and Parmesan, 130, 131–33
  Lamb, in Brodo, 239–40, 241
Triangoli, Chestnut, with Fermented Honey, Ricotta, and Brown Butter, 274–75

Troccoli
  rolling and shaping, 58, *58*
  with Shrimp and Ginger Chili Crisp, 161
Trofie
  with Pistachio, Artichokes, and Orange Zest, 100, *101*
  rolling and shaping, 59, *59*
Truffle and Parmesan, Almond Tortellini with, *130*, 131–33

V

Veal
  Shank Ragù, Ricotta Cavatelli with, 242–43
  Stock, 295
Vegetables. *See specific vegetables*

W

Walnuts, Radicchio, and Gorgonzola, Strozzapreti with, *98*, 99
Wild Boar Ragù, Chestnut Fettuccine with, 211–12, *213*

Y

Yuzu Kosho, Lobster, and Corn, Gnocchi Sardi with, 259, *260*

Z

Ziti with Fiorella Liver and Orange Sausage Ragù, 216–17
Zucchini
  Crema, Fennel Sausage Ricotta Gnocchi with, *220*, 220–21
  -Stuffed Pappardelle with Squash Blossoms and Basil, *118*, 119–21

CLARKSON POTTER/PUBLISHERS
An imprint of the Crown Publishing Group
A division of Penguin Random House LLC
1745 Broadway
New York, NY 10019
clarksonpotter.com
penguinrandomhouse.com

Copyright © 2025 by Marc Vetri
Photographs copyright © 2025 by Ed Anderson

Penguin Random House values and supports copyright. Copyright fuels creativity, encourages diverse voices, promotes free speech, and creates a vibrant culture. Thank you for buying an authorized edition of this book and for complying with copyright laws by not reproducing, scanning, or distributing any part of it in any form without permission. You are supporting writers and allowing Penguin Random House to continue to publish books for every reader. Please note that no part of this book may be used or reproduced in any manner for the purpose of training artificial intelligence technologies or systems.

CLARKSON POTTER is a trademark and **POTTER** with colophon is a registered trademark of Penguin Random House LLC.

Library of Congress Cataloging-in-Publication Data
Names: Vetri, Marc, author. | Joachim, David, author. | Anderson, Ed (Edward Charles), photographer.
Title: The pasta book : recipes, techniques, inspiration / Marc Vetri and David Joachim ; photographs by Ed Anderson.
Identifiers: LCCN 2024060032 (print) | LCCN 2024060033 (ebook) | ISBN 9780593799475 (hardcover) | ISBN 9780593799482 (ebook)
Subjects: LCSH: Cooking (Pasta) | LCGFT: Cookbooks.
Classification: LCC TX809.M17 V465 2025 (print) | LCC TX809.M17 (ebook) | DDC 641.82/2—dc23/eng/20250208
LC record available at https://lccn.loc.gov/2024060032
LC ebook record available at https://lccn.loc.gov/2024060033

ISBN 978-0-593-79947-5
Ebook ISBN 978-0-593-79948-2

Editor: Susan Roxborough | Editorial assistant: Elaine Hennig
Designer: Yasmeen Bandoo | Design manager: Ian Dingman
Production designer: Christina Self
Production editor: Joyce Wong
Production: Kelli Tokos
Compositors: Merri Ann Morrell and Hannah Hunt
Food stylist: Marc Vetri
Prop stylist: Maeve Sheridan
Copyeditor: Kate Slate | Proofreaders: Ivy McFadden, Andrea Peabbles, Erica Rose
Indexer: Elizabeth Parson
Publicist: Kristin Casemore
Marketer: Allison Renzulli

Manufactured in China

10 9 8 7 6 5 4 3 2 1

First Edition

The authorized representative in the EU for product safety and compliance is Penguin Random House Ireland, Morrison Chambers, 32 Nassau Street, Dublin D02 YH68, Ireland, https://eu-contact.penguin.ie.